Mike McGrath

HTML, CSS & JavaScript

in easy steps

special edition

In easy steps is an imprint of In Easy Steps Limited
16 Hamilton Terrace · Holly Walk · Leamington Spa
Warwickshire · United Kingdom · CV32 4LY
www.ineasysteps.com

Notice of Liability
Every effort has been made to ensure that this book contains accurate
and current information. However, In Easy Steps Limited and the
author shall not be liable for any loss or damage suffered by readers
as a result of any information contained herein.

Trademarks
All trademarks are acknowledged as belonging to their respective
companies.

In Easy Steps Limited supports The Forest Stewardship Council (FSC),
the leading international forest certification organization. All our titles
that are printed on Greenpeace approved FSC certified paper carry the
FSC logo.

MIX
Paper from
responsible sources
FSC www.fsc.org   FSC® C020837

Printed and bound in the United Kingdom

ISBN 978-1-84078-878-5

Contents

How to Use This Book

The examples in this book demonstrate HTML, CSS, and JavaScript features that are supported by leading web browsers, and screenshots illustrate the actual results produced by the listed code examples. Colorization conventions are used to clarify the code listed in the steps...

HTML tags and punctuation are **Blue**, attribute values are **Orange**, and literal text is **Black**:

`<p class="frame">HTML, CSS & JavaScript in easy steps</p>`

CSS selectors, properties, and punctuation are **Blue**, attributes are **Orange**, specified values are **Red**:

`p.frame { color : White ; background : Green ; }`

JavaScript keywords and punctuation are **Blue**, specified names are **Red**, and literal values are **Black:**

`let greeting = 'Hello World!' ;`

All comments are colored green: `<!-- HTML Comments -->` `/* CSS & JS Comments */`

Additionally, in order to identify each source code file described in the steps, a file icon and file name appears in the margin alongside the steps:

| page.html | style.css | function.js | image.png | cursor.cur | data.xml | server.py |

The source code of HTML documents used in the book's examples is not listed in full to avoid unnecessary repetition – only the relevant code is listed for each example. You can download a single ZIP archive file containing all the example files by following these easy steps:

1. Browse to **www.ineasysteps.com** then navigate to Free Resources and choose the Downloads section

2. Next, find HTML, CSS, & JavaScript in easy steps in the list, then click on the hyperlink entitled All Code Examples to download the ZIP archive file

3. Now, extract the archive contents to any convenient location on your computer

If you don't achieve the result illustrated in any example, simply compare your code to that in the original example files you have downloaded to discover where you went wrong.

1 Get Started in HTML

This chapter is an introduction to the exciting world of HTML. It demonstrates how to create a valid HTML document and how to include style rules, script code, and linked resources.

Meet HTML

Historically, the desire to have text printed in specific formats meant that original manuscripts were "marked up" with annotation to indicate to the book printer how the author would like sections of text laid out. This annotation had to be concise and needed to be easily understood both by the printer and the author. A series of commonly-recognized abbreviations therefore formed the basis of a standard markup language.

HyperText Markup Language (HTML) is a modern standard markup language that uses common abbreviations called "tags" to indicate to the web browser how the author would like to have sections of a web page laid out. It was first devised in 1989 by British physicist Tim Berners-Lee at CERN in Switzerland (the European organization for nuclear research) to share all computer-stored information between the CERN physicists. Berners-Lee created a text browser to transfer information over the internet using hypertext to provide point-and-click navigation. In May 1990 this system was named the World Wide Web and was enhanced in 1993 when college student Marc Andreessen added an image tag. Now that HTML could display both text and images, the World Wide Web quickly became hugely popular.

As various web browsers were developed, their makers began to add individual proprietary tags – effectively creating their own versions of HTML! The World Wide Web Consortium (W3C) standards organization recognized the danger that HTML could become fragmented, so they created a standard specification to which all web browsers should adhere. This successfully encouraged the browser makers to support the standard tags. The final W3C standard specification of HTML5 is now continued by the Web Hypertext Application Technology Working Group (WHATWG) as the "HTML Living Standard".

The World Wide Web comprises a series of large-capacity computers, known as "web servers", which are connected to the internet via telephone lines and satellites. The web servers each use the HyperText Transfer Protocol (HTTP) as a common communication standard to allow any computer connected to any web server to access files across the web.

HTML web pages are merely plain text files that have been saved with a ".htm" or ".html" file extension, such as **index.html**

Hot tip

You can find the HTML Living Standard specification, and other related specifications, online at **whatwg.org**

In order to access an HTML file across the internet, its web address must be entered into the address field of the web browser. The web address is formally known as its "Uniform Resource Locator" (URL), and typically has three parts:

- **Protocol** – any URL using the HTTP protocol begins by specifying the protocol as **http://** or secure **https://**

- **Domain** – the host name of the computer from which the file can be downloaded. For instance: **www.example.com**

- **Path** – the file name prefixed by any parent directory names where applicable. For instance: **/htdocs/index.html**

A URL describing the location of a file by protocol, domain, and path is stating its full "absolute address". Files resident within the same domain can be referenced more simply by their "relative address", which means that files located in the same directory can be referenced just by their file name. Additionally, a relative address can reference a file in its parent directory by prefixing its name with "../". For instance, a file named "higher.html" in the parent directory can be referenced as **../higher.html**

How do web servers work?

When you enter a URL into the browser address field, the browser first examines the protocol. Where the protocol is specified as HTTP, or assumed to be HTTP if unspecified, the browser recognizes that a file is being sought from a web server. It then contacts a Domain Name Server (DNS) to look up the numerical Internet Protocol (IP) address of the specified domain name. Next, a connection is established with the web server at that IP address to request the file at the specified path. When the file is successfully located, it is copied back to the browser, otherwise the web server sends an error code, such as "404 – Page Not Found".

A successful response sends HTTP headers to the web browser, describing the nature of the response, along with a copy of the requested file. The HTTP headers are not normally visible but can be examined using various development tools, such as the F12 Developer Tools feature in the Google Chrome web browser.

Understand Structure

The skeletal structure of an HTML document has three parts:

- **Document type declaration** – declaring precisely which version of HTML is used to mark up the document.

- **Head section** – providing descriptive data about the document itself, such as the document's title and the character set used.

- **Body section** – containing the content that is to appear when the document gets loaded into a web browser.

Document type declaration

The document type declaration must appear at the start of the first line of every HTML document to ensure the web browser will "render" (display) the document in "Standards Mode" – following the HTML specifications. The document type declaration tag for all HTML documents looks like this:

```
<!DOCTYPE HTML>
```

It is important to note that HTML is not a case-sensitive language – so the document type declaration tag, and all other tags, may alternatively be written in any combination of uppercase and lowercase characters. For example, the following are all valid:

```
<!DOCTYPE html>
```

```
<!Doctype Html>
```

```
<!doctype html>
```

The choice of capitalization is yours, but it is recommended you adhere consistently to whichever style you choose. The document type declaration tag capitalization style favored throughout this book uses all uppercase to emphasize its prominence as the very first tag on each page – but all other tags are in all lowercase.

Those familiar with earlier versions of HTML may be surprised at the simplicity of the HTML document type declaration. In fact, the document type declaration in earlier versions was not actually part of the HTML language – so required lengthy references to schema documents. By contrast, the modern HTML document type declaration is an intrinsic part of HTML itself.

Hot tip

The document type declaration in earlier versions of HTML was part of the Standard Generalized Markup Language (SGML) from which HTML is derived.

The entire document head section and body section can be enclosed within a pair of **<html> </html>** tags to contain the rest of the document. The HTML specification actually states that these are optional, but it is logical to provide a single "root" element. Most HTML tags are used in pairs like this to act as "containers" with the syntax **< *tagname* > *data* </ *tagname* >**

Head section

The document's head section begins with an HTML opening **<head>** tag and ends with a corresponding closing **</head>** tag. Data describing the document can be added later between these two tags to complete the HTML document's head section.

Body section

The document's body section begins with an HTML opening **<body>** tag and ends with a corresponding closing **</body>** tag. Data content to appear in the browser can be added later between these two tags to complete the HTML document's body section.

Code comments

Comments can be added at any point within both the head and body sections between a pair of **<!--** and **-->** tags. Anything that appears between the comment tags is ignored by the browser.

Fundamental structure

So, the markup tags that create the fundamental structure of every HTML document look like this:

```
<!DOCTYPE HTML>

<html>
 <head>
  <!-- Data describing the document to be added here. -->
 </head>

 <body>
  <!-- Content to appear in the browser to be added here. -->
 </body>

</html>
```

An HTML "element" is any matching pair of opening and closing tags, or any single tag not requiring a closing tag – as described in the HTML element tags list on the inside front cover of this book.

The "invisible" characters that represent tabs, newlines, carriage returns, and spaces are collectively known as "whitespace". They may optionally be used to inset the tags for clarity.

Create Documents

The fundamental HTML document structure described on page 14, can be used to create a simple HTML document in any plain text editor – such as Windows' Notepad application. In order to create a valid "barebones" HTML document, information must first be added defining the document's primary written language, its character encoding format, and its title.

The document's primary language is defined by assigning a standard language code to a **lang** "attribute" within the opening **<html>** root tag. For the English language the code is **en**, so the complete opening root element looks like this: **<html lang="en">**

The document's character encoding format is defined by assigning a standard character-set code to a **charset** attribute within a **<meta>** tag placed in the document's head section. The recommended encoding is the popular 8-bit Unicode Transformation Format for which the code is **UTF-8**, so the complete element looks like this: **<meta charset="UTF-8">**

Finally, the document's title is defined by text between a pair of **<title> </title>** tags placed in the document's head section.

Follow these steps to create a valid barebones HTML document:

1. Launch your favorite plain text editor then start a new document with the HTML document type declaration **<!DOCTYPE HTML>**

2. Below the document type declaration, add a root element that defines the document's primary language as English
   ```
   <html lang="en">
     <!-- Head and Body sections to be added here. -->
   </html>
   ```

3. Within the root element, insert a document head section
   ```
   <head>
     <!-- Descriptive information to be added here. -->
   </head>
   ```

4. Within the head section, insert an element defining the document's encoding character set
   ```
   <meta charset="UTF-8">
   ```

Beware

HTML documents should not be created in word processors such as MS Word, as those apps include additional information in their file formats.

hello.html

Hot tip

The **<meta>** tag is a single tag – it does not have a matching closing tag. See the element tags list on the inside front cover of this book to find other single tags.

...cont'd

5 Next, within the head section, insert an element defining the document's title
`<title>`**Get Started in HTML**`</title>`

6 After the head section, insert a document body section
`<body>`
  `<!-- `**Actual document content to be added here.** ` -->`
`</body>`

7 Within the body section, insert a size-one large heading
`<h1>`**Hello World!**`</h1>`

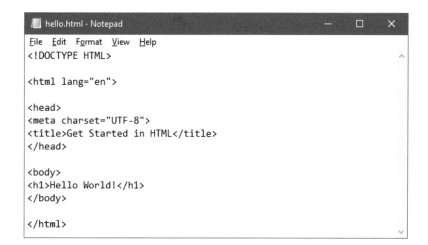

The quotation marks around an attribute value are usually optional but are required for multiple values. For consistency, attribute values in the examples throughout this book are all surrounded by quotation marks.

17

8 Set the file's encoding to the UTF-8 format, then save the document as "hello.html"

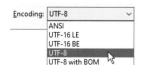

9 Now, open the HTML document in a modern web browser to see the title displayed on the title bar or tab, and the document content displayed as a large heading

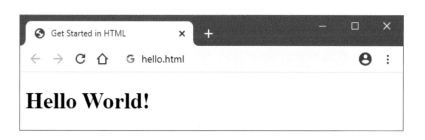

You will discover more about headings on pages 34-35.

Validate Documents

Just as text documents may contain spelling and grammar errors, HTML documents may contain various errors that prevent them from conforming to the specification rules. In order to verify that an HTML document does indeed conform to the rules of its specified document type declaration, it can be tested by a validator tool. Only HTML documents that pass the validation test successfully are sure to be valid documents.

Web browsers make no attempt at validation so it is well worth verifying every HTML document with a validator tool before it is published, even when the content looks fine in your web browser. When the browser encounters HTML errors it will make a guess at what is intended – but different browsers can make different interpretations so may display the document incorrectly. Conversely, valid HTML documents should always appear correctly in any standards-compliant browser.

The World Wide Web Consortium (W3C) provides a free online validator tool at **validator.w3.org** that you can use to check the syntax of your web documents:

1 With an internet connection, open your web browser and navigate to the W3C Validator Tool at **validator.w3.org** then click on the **Validate by File Upload** tab

Hot tip

Other tabs in the validator allow you to enter the web address of an HTML document located on a web server to "Validate by URI" or copy and paste all code from a document to "Validate by Direct Input".

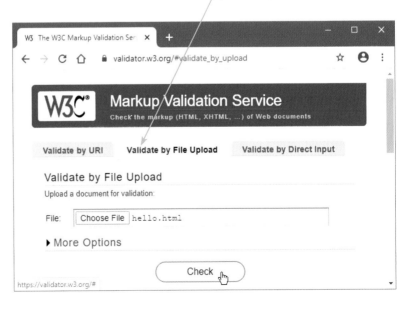

...cont'd

2 Click the **Browse** button then navigate to the HTML document you wish to validate – once selected, its local path appears in the validator's "File" field

3 Next, click the validator's **Check** button to upload a copy of the HTML document and run the validation test – the results will then be displayed

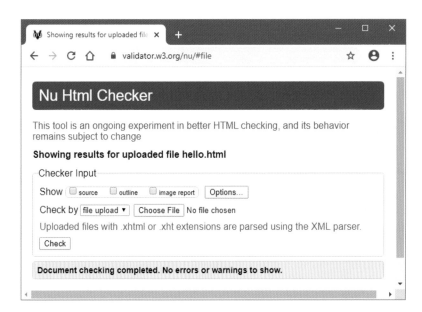

The validator automatically detects the document's character set and HTML version.

If validation fails, the errors are listed so you may easily correct them. When validation succeeds, you may choose to include a suitable logo at the end of the document to prove validation:

The validation logo can be customized to describe the technology classes used by the web page. Discover the logo Badge Builder online at **w3.org/html/logo** where you can generate the code to paste into your HTML document and so display a suitable logo.

Bestow Titles

The specifications require every HTML document to have a title, but its importance is often overlooked. The document title should be carefully considered, however, as it is used extensively:

- **Bookmarks** – save the document title to link back to its URL.

- **Title Bar** – a web browser window may display the title.

- **Navigation Tab** – a web browser tab may display the title.

- **History** – saves the document title to link back to its URL.

- **Search Engines** – read the document title and typically display it in search results to link back to its URL.

Document titles should ideally be short and meaningful – each tab on a modern tabbed browser may display only 10 characters.

Document titles throughout a website should follow a consistent naming convention and capitalize all major words. One popular naming convention provides a personal or company name and brief page description separated by a hyphen. For example, "Amazon - C Programming in easy steps". An alternative puts the description first, so it remains visible when the title is truncated. For example, "C Programming in easy steps - Amazon".

The specifications do not define a naming scheme for document titles but do encourage authors to consider accessibility issues in all aspects of their web page designs.

You can find a chart of all character entities at dev.w3.org/html5/html-author/charref

Document titles and document content may contain special characters that are known in HTML as "entities". Each entity reference begins with an ampersand and ends with a semicolon. For example, the entity **<** (less than) creates a "<" character and the entity **>** (greater than) creates a ">" character. These are often needed to avoid confusion with the angled brackets that surround each HTML tag. Other frequently used entities include ** ** (a single non-breaking space), **•** (bullet point), **©** (©), **®** (®), **™** (™), and **"** (quotation mark). These are best avoided in document titles, however, as the vocal narrator used by visually impaired viewers may read each entity character as a word.

1 Start a new HTML document with a type declaration
```
<!DOCTYPE HTML>
```

title.html

2 Add a root element containing head and body sections
```
<html lang="en">

<head>
<!-- Data describing the document to be added here. -->
</head>

<body>
<!-- Content to appear in the browser to be added here. -->
</body>

</html>
```

3 Within the head section, insert a meta element specifying the character set and an empty title element
```
<meta charset="UTF-8">
<title> </title>
```

The character set can be defined in uppercase, as shown here, or in lowercase as "utf-8".

4 Within the title element insert a title including entities
```
&lt;HTML in easy steps&gt;
```

5 Save the document then open it in your web browser

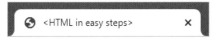

6 Start a vocal narrator to hear that the title may be read out as "Less-than-HTML-in-easy-steps-greater-than"

7 Edit the document title to make it more user-friendly
```
&quot;HTML in easy steps&quot;
```

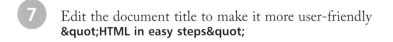

8 Save the document once more then open it in your web browser to hear the narrator now read the document title as "HTML in easy steps"

In Windows 10, press **WinKey + Ctrl + Enter** to launch the narrator, then click the tab to hear the title. Title text that is not visible on the tab will still be read by the narrator. Windows 10 ignores angled brackets in a title, but they are read literally by the narrator in earlier versions of Windows.

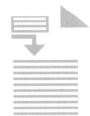

Supply Metadata

Meta information is simply data that describes other data. In the context of HTML, document metadata describes the document itself – rather than the document's contents.

HTML metadata is defined in the head section of the HTML document using the **<meta>** tag. The **<meta>** tag is an "empty" tag that needs no matching closing tag to create an HTML element – it is only used to specify information with its tag attributes. Previous examples have used this tag to specify the document's character-set. Further **<meta>** tags can be added to describe other aspects of the document.

Given the number of handheld devices that may view a web page, it is useful to optimize the page for smaller screens by including this **<meta>** tag in all your HTML documents' head sections:

```
<meta  name="viewport"
         content="width=device-width, initial-scale=1">
```

This will ensure your document will fill the device screen width and sets the initial zoom level so the content is not zoomed.

A **<meta>** tag can also assign a document HTTP header property to an **http-equiv** attribute and can specify that property's value to a **content** attribute. You can assign the HTTP "refresh" property to an **http-equiv** attribute to reload the page after a number of seconds specified to its **content** attribute – for example, to reload the page after five seconds, like this:

```
<meta http-equiv="refresh" content= "5">
```

This technique is often used on websites to dynamically update news or status items, as it does not depend on JavaScript support.

Another popular use redirects the browser to a new web page after a specified number of seconds, like this:

```
<meta http-equiv="refresh" content= "5 ; url='new-page.html' ">
```

In this case, the **<meta>** tag's **content** attribute specifies both the number of seconds to delay and the new URL to load.

Hot tip

Setting the **width** to the **device-width** typically sets the **initial-scale** to **1** automatically, but it doesn't hurt to set it explicitly as meta data.

1 Create a barebones HTML document

```
<!DOCTYPE HTML>
<html lang="en">
<head>
<meta charset="UTF-8">
<!-- More metadata to be inserted here. -->
<title>Meta Refresh</title>
</head>
<body>
<h1>Moving in 5 Seconds...</h1>
</body>
</html>
```

refresh.html

2 Insert two more elements of metadata

```
<meta  name="viewport"
        content="width=device-width, initial-scale=1">
<meta http-equiv="refresh"
        content= "5 ; url='https://ineasysteps.com' ">
```

3 Save the document then open it in your web browser and wait five seconds to see the browser redirect

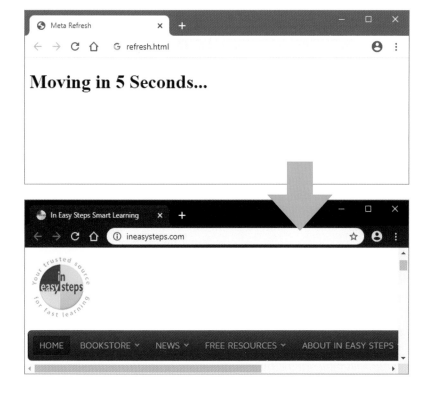

Hot tip

When you only specify the domain to the **url** attribute, as in this case, the browser will automatically load the **index.htm**l page at that domain location.

23

Describe Contents

In addition to specifying the document's character-set and expiry date, **<meta>** tags can be used to provide information that may be used by search engines. This offers no guarantee of high ranking, however, as search engines also use other page information for that purpose – especially the document title. Typically, a Search Engine Results Page (SERP) will show the meta description in search results below the page title.

Search Engine Optimization (SEO) is highly prized to ensure a web page will appear at the top of a SERP to increase traffic to a website. Unfortunately, there is no sure-fire technique to achieve this as the search engines constantly change the algorithm by which pages are ranked. It is, however, useful to provide metadata that describes the page content.

Descriptive **<meta>** tags have a **name** attribute that is assigned a "description" value, and a **content** attribute that is assigned a description of the page contents.

The description should be between 50-160 characters long, as lengthy descriptions may be truncated. The description should include keywords relative to the text content. For example, a search for "italian ceramics" could return all web pages with "italian" and "ceramics" in their description.

The description serves as advertising copy so a readable, compelling description using important keywords will encourage visits to the page from a SERP. You should not repeat keywords in the description, but do try to use the plural form for keywords – to match searches made with both the single and plural form of that word. Additionally, you should not include double quotation marks in the description as Google may truncate the description at a double quotation mark.

If a website contains pages of identical or very similar content, you can specify which page is to be indexed by including a "canonical link" in your HTML code to indicate the preferred source. This uses a **<link>** tag containing a **rel** (relationship) attribute to specify a "canonical" value, and an **href** (hypertext reference) attribute to specify the URL address of the preferred page.

All search engines find pages to add to their index – even if the page has never been submitted to them.

Always include the three most important keywords in the description.

1 Create a barebones HTML document

```
<!DOCTYPE HTML>
<html lang="en">
<head>
<meta charset="UTF-8">
<!-- More metadata to be inserted here. -->
<title>Tuscan Home Decor</title>
</head>
<body> <h1>Beautiful Tuscan Ceramics</h1> </body>
</html>
```

keywords.html

2 Insert a metadata description of the web page

```
<meta name="description" content="Explore our
extensive range of high quality italian ceramics including
tuscan majolica, dinnerwares, vases, plates, and bowls">
```

3 Next, in the head section, add an element to specify that this page is the preferred page for indexing purposes

```
<link rel="canonical"
        href="https://www.example.com/keywords.html" >
```

4 Save the document then visit the Chrome Web Store at **chrome.google.com/webstore/category/extensions** and search for "seo" to add a search engine analysis extension

5 Open the HTML document in the Google Chrome web browser then use the analysis tool to see the meta data

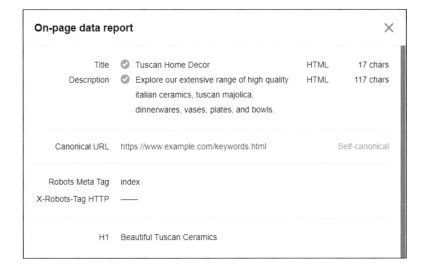

On-page data report ✕

Title	✅ Tuscan Home Decor	HTML	17 chars
Description	✅ Explore our extensive range of high quality italian ceramics, tuscan majolica, dinnerwares, vases, plates, and bowls.	HTML	117 chars
Canonical URL	https://www.example.com/keywords.html		Self-canonical
Robots Meta Tag	index		
X-Robots-Tag HTTP	——		
H1	Beautiful Tuscan Ceramics		

Hot tip

There are a number of free meta tag generators available online – enter "free meta tag generator" into a search engine.

Add Styles

Cascading Style Sheets (CSS) rules can be incorporated within HTML documents to control the presentational aspects of each element on the page. The use of style sheets has replaced all features of HTML that formerly related to presentation. For example, the **<font>** tag has become obsolete, as font family, weight, style, and size are now specified by a style sheet rule.

Style sheets embedded with **<style> </style>** tags can be added within the head section of an HTML document to enclose rules governing how the content will appear. For example, a simple style sheet containing rules to determine the appearance of all size-one headings could look like this:

<style>

h1 { color : red ; background : yellow ; }

</style>

This is acceptable and will validate but, in line with the aim of HTML to separate content from presentation, style sheets may be contained within a separate file. The great advantage of placing style sheets in separate files is that they can be applied to multiple HTML documents – thus making website maintenance much easier. Editing a shared style sheet instantly affects each HTML document that shares that file.

An external style sheet is incorporated within an HTML document by adding a **<link>** tag in the document's head section. This must contain a **rel** (relationship) attribute assigned a "stylesheet" value, and the URL of the style sheet must be assigned to its **href** (hypertext reference) attribute – for example, add an adjacent style sheet file named "style.css", like this:

<link rel="stylesheet" href="style.css">

You can also specify style rules "in-line" to a style attribute of presentational HTML tags, like this:

<h1 style="color:red">

In-line style rules are useful in some circumstances but can make page maintenance more difficult.

Beware

When multiple rules select the same property of an element for styling, the rule read last by the browser will generally be applied, but in-line rules take precedence over embedded rules and external rules. Embedded rules take precedence over external rules.

1 Create a barebones HTML document

```
<!DOCTYPE HTML>
<html lang="en">
<head>
<meta charset="UTF-8">
<title>Style Sheet Example</title>
</head>
<body>
<h1>Styled Heading</h1>
</body>
</html>
```

style.html

2 Next, in the head section, add an embedded style sheet

```
<style>
h1 { color : Red ; background : Yellow ; }
</style>
```

3 Now, in the head section, insert a link to an adjacent external style sheet file

```
<link rel="stylesheet" href="style.css">
```

style.css

4 Save the HTML document then open a new text editor window and precisely copy this style sheet

```
h1
{
        border : 10px dashed Blue ;
        padding : 5px ;
        width : 500px ;
}
```

5 Save the Cascading Style Sheets file in the same directory as the HTML document, then open the web page in your browser to see the style rules applied

Some HTML elements, such as **<div>** and **<span>** (see page 46), exist purely for styling. CSS is a separate topic but many examples in this book include embedded CSS style sheet rules to provide standalone example files that demonstrate the use of HTML elements. Some examples include unlisted CSS rules to illustrate the size and position of HTML elements and their content in screenshots.

Include Scripts

Scripts can be incorporated within HTML documents to interact with the user and to provide dynamic effects. This ability has become increasingly important with the development of pages in which sections of the page can be dynamically updated. Previously, the browser would typically request an entire new page from the web server, which was less efficient and more cumbersome.

JavaScript code enclosed by **<script> </script>** tags can be embedded within an HTML document. These are best placed in the body section of the document, just before the **</body>** closing tag, so the browser can process the content of the document before reading the script.

Remember that the **<script>** tag always needs to have a matching closing tag.

In line with the aim of HTML to separate content from presentation, scripts may also be contained in a separate file. In this case, the URL address of the script file must be assigned to a **src** attribute within the **<script>** tag. The **</script>** closing tag is also required. These, too, can be placed at the end of the body section of the HTML document, as the browser will treat the external script as if it was embedded there – for example, to add an adjacent external script file named "script.js", like this:

```
<script src="script.js"></script>
```

You can also specify script "in-line" to on-event attributes of HTML tags. For example, to recognize a mouse click event:

```
<h1 onclick="alert('Clicked!')">
```

In-line script is useful in some circumstances but can make page maintenance more difficult. Alternative fallback content can be provided in the document's body section between **<noscript> </noscript>** tags, which will only be displayed when script functionality is absent or disabled.

script.html

1 Create a barebones HTML document

```
<!DOCTYPE HTML>
<html lang="en">
<head>
<meta charset="UTF-8">
<title>JavaScript Example</title>
</head>
<body>
</body>
</html>
```

28

2 In the body section, insert a fallback message and heading
```
<noscript>JavaScript Is Not Enabled!</noscript>
<h1 onclick="this.innerText='Mouse Clicked!';
        this.style.color='Red'">Active Heading</h1>
```

3 At the end of the body section, add an embedded script and nominate an external script
```
<script>
document.getElementsByTagName('h1')[0].onmouseover =
function ( ) {
this.innerText= 'Mouse Is Over' ; this.style.color='Blue' }
</script>
<script src="script.js"></script>
```

4 Save the HTML document then open a new text editor window and create the external script
```
document.getElementsByTagName('h1')[0].onmouseout =
function ( ) {
this.innerText= 'Active Heading' ; this.style.color = 'Black' }
```

script.js

5 Save the JavaScript file as "script.js" in the same directory as the HTML document, then open the web page in your browser and click on the heading

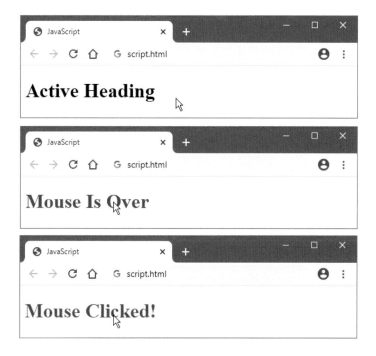

Don't forget

Some HTML elements, such as **<template>** and **<slot>** (see page 120), exist purely for scripting. JavaScript is a separate topic but many examples in this book include embedded JavaScript code to provide standalone example files that demonstrate the use of HTML elements.

Link Resources

The **<link>** tag that was used in an earlier example to incorporate a style sheet in an HTML document can also be used to incorporate other resources into a document.

This tag may only appear in the head section of a document, but the head section can contain many **<link>** tags. Each **<link>** tag must contain **rel** and **href** attributes, stating the relationship and location of the link resource. It may also include a **type** attribute where appropriate, to hint at the MIME type of the link resource.

Permitted rel (relationship) values				
alternate	author	bookmark	help	icon
license	next	nofollow	noreferrer	prev
search	stylesheet	tag	shortcut icon	

Hot tip

MIME (Multipart Internet Mail Extension) types describe file types – such as **text/html** for HTML files. You can find the list of official MIME types at **https://www.iana.org/assignments/media-types/media-types.xhtml**

Many of the link types above are intended to help search engines locate resources associated with that HTML document, and the **<link>** tag may also include a **title** attribute to further describe the resource – for example, a version of the page in another language:

```
<link rel="alternate" type="text/html" href="esp.html"
        title="Esta página en Español - This page in Spanish" >
```

In this case, the location of the resource is specified using a relative address that, by default, the browser will seek in the directory in which the HTML document is located. The browser can, however, be made to seek a relative address in a different directory by inserting a **<base>** tag at the start of the document's head section. Its **href** attribute can then specify the absolute directory address – for example, to specify a separate "resources" directory, like this:

```
<base href= "http://localhost/resources/">
```

Beware

When using a **<base>** element it must be placed in the head section before any **<link>** elements.

It is popular to link an icon resource to display in the web browser. This is named exactly as "favicon.ico" and can be placed in the same directory as the HTML document, or in a directory specified by the **<base>** tag. All browsers recognize any other resources in the directory specified by the **<base>** tag.

...cont'd

1 Create a new HTML document that includes metadata, a linked resource, and areas for style rules and script code

```
<!DOCTYPE HTML>
<html lang="en">
<head>
<meta charset="UTF-8">
<meta name="viewport"
        content="width=device-width, initial-scale=1">
<link rel="shortcut icon" href="favicon.ico">
<title>Document Title</title>
<style>

</style>
</head>
<body>


<script>

</script>
</body>
</html>
```

This template is the basic HTML document that is used in all ensuing examples to create a new HTML document – only the title changes to suit each example.

2 At the beginning of the head section, insert an element to specify a base "resources" directory
`<base href="http://localhost/resources/">`

favicon.html

3 Change the document title to "Favicon", then save the HTML document

4 Open an icon editor and create an icon sized 32 x 32 pixels and save your icon alongside the HTML document, or in the "resources" directory, named as "favicon.ico"

favicon.ico 32px x 32px

5 Open the HTML document in your web browser via a web server to see the icon resource appear in the browser

You can force your browser to refresh the favicon by assigning **favicon.ico?v=2** to the link's **href** attribute.

Summary

- The Web Hypertext Application Technology Working Group (WHATWG) oversees the HTML Living Standard.

- HyperText Transfer Protocol (HTTP) is the common communication standard used by web servers.

- A Uniform Resource Locator (URL) is an absolute web address comprising protocol, domain, and path components.

- A relative address can reference an adjacent file by its name, and may use the ../ syntax to reference a parent directory.

- Web servers send response headers back to the requesting computer and a copy of the requested file, or an error code.

- Each HTML document should have a document type declaration, a head section, and a body section.

- Information about the document itself is contained in the head section, and content is contained in the body section.

- The document's written language is specified to a **lang** attribute in the opening **<html>** root element.

- The document's character-set encoding is specified to a **charset** attribute in a **<meta>** tag within the head section.

- The document's title is specified between **<title> </title>** tags within the head section.

- The free online W3C validator tool can be used to verify that an HTML document is free of errors.

- Metadata describes the document, and a content description can be used by search engines to index the web page.

- The **<style> </style>** tags can be used to embed style sheets within an HTML document.

- The **<script> </script>** tags can be used to include internal and external JavaScript code in an HTML document.

- The **<link>** tag can be used to embed external style sheets and other resources within an HTML document.

2 Structure Web Pages

This chapter demonstrates how to position page content into groups and sections.

Proclaim Headings

HTML heading elements are created using **<h1>**, **<h2>**, **<h3>**, **<h4>**, **<h5>**, and **<h6>** tags. These are ranked in importance by their numeric value – where **<h1>** has the greatest importance, and **<h6>** has the least importance. Each heading requires a matching closing tag and should only contain heading text. Typically, the heading's font size and weight will reflect its importance, but headings also serve other purposes.

Heading elements should be used to implicitly convey the document structure by correctly sequencing them – so **<h2>** elements below an **<h1>** element, **<h3>** elements below an **<h2>** element, and so on. This structure helps readers quickly skim through a document by navigating its headings. Search engine spiders may promote documents that have correctly sequenced headings as they can use the headings in their index. They assume headings are likely to describe their content so it is especially useful to include meta keywords from the document's head section in the document's headings.

The **<h1>** element is by far the most important heading, and should ideally appear only once to proclaim the document heading. Often, this can be a succinct version of the document title. Below that, a number of **<h2>** headings can proclaim topical headings for long documents. Each topic might contain individual article headings within **<h3>** elements, followed by paragraph **<p>** elements containing the actual article content.

Beware

Never use heading elements for their font properties as these can be overridden by style sheet rules – always consider headings to represent structure.

heading.html

1 Create an HTML document (as the template on page 31)

2 Within the body section, insert a main document heading
<h1>Document Heading</h1>

3 Next, within the body section, insert a topic heading
<h2>Topic Heading</h2>

4 Now, within the body section, insert some article headings followed by paragraphs containing the article content
<h3>Article Heading</h3>
<p>Article content...</p>

<h3>Article Heading</h3>
<p>Article content...</p>

...cont'd

5 Finally, add another topic with two more articles
`<h2>Topic Heading</h2>`

`<h3>Article Heading</h3>`
`<p>Article content...</p>`

`<h3>Article Heading</h3>`
`<p>Article content...</p>`

6 Save the HTML document then open it in your web browser to see the headings and document structure

You will discover more about the `<p>` paragraph element on page 50.

All screenshots throughout this chapter have added (unlisted) style rules to more clearly illustrate the elements described.

35

Structural outline
Document Heading
Topic Heading
Article Heading
Article Heading
Topic Heading
Article Heading
Article Heading

The document structure created by the sequenced headings is known as the document "outline". Properly constructed outlines allow a part of the page, such as a single article, to be easily syndicated into another site. The outline for the document above is illustrated alongside the screenshot above.

Group Headings

Headings sometimes have a sub-heading or tagline. For example, a document heading could be marked up like this:

```
<h1>American Airlines</h1>
<h2>Doing What We Do Best</h2>
```

Unfortunately, this would strictly require all subsequent headings to be **<h3>** down to **<h6>** – to maintain a correctly sequenced outline. Fortunately, HTML provides a grouping solution with the **<hgroup> </hgroup>** element. This can be used to enclose both the heading and sub-heading, like this:

```
<hgroup>
<h1>American Airlines</h1>
<h2>Doing What We Do Best</h2>
</hgroup>
```

A document may contain multiple **<hgroup>** elements, and each **<hgroup>** element may contain headings **<h1>** down to **<h6>**.

Complete headers may be enclosed in **<header> </header>** tags to include a heading element, or **<hgroup>** element, along with other introductory items – such as a banner, logo, or a table of contents.

Beware

You cannot nest **<header>** elements one within another.

36

header.html

1 Create an HTML document (as the template on page 31)

2 Within the body section, insert a main document heading that includes a banner image
```
<header>

<img src="header-banner.png" width="500"
        height="72" alt="Banner">

<hgroup>
<h1>HTML</h1>
<h2>Building better websites</h2>
</hgroup>

</header>
```

Hot tip

You will discover more about the **<img>** image element on page 98.

3 Next, within the body section, insert a topic and article
```
<hgroup>
<h2>Topic Heading</h2>
<h3>Article Heading</h3>
</hgroup>

<p> Article Content...</p>
```

4 Now, within the body section, insert a second topic with a single article

```
<hgroup>
<h1>CSS</h1>
<h2>Cascading Style Sheets</h2>
<h3>Article Heading</h3>
</hgroup>

<p>Article content...</p>
```

5 Save the HTML document then open it in your web browser to see the grouped headings and document header

The **<hgroup>** element only groups headings **<h1>** to **<h6>**, but the **<header>** element groups headings and additional items.

Structural outline

HTML: Building better websites
 Topic Heading: Article Heading

CSS: Cascading Style Sheets: Article Heading

Include Navigation

Groups of hyperlinks on a web page, which enable the user to navigate around the page or website, should be enclosed between **<nav> </nav>** tags, or **<menu> </menu>** tags for other links.

This group of links may typically be a horizontal menu in the document header – often called a navigation bar ("nav bar") – or may be a vertical menu down the edge of the page. Note that the **<nav>** element is simply a wrapper around the menu – it does not replace any structural elements.

1 Create an HTML document (as the template on page 31)

nav.html

2 Within the body, insert a header containing a logo, document heading, and horizontal page navigation bar

```
<header>

<img id="logo" src="nav-logo.png" alt="Logo">

<h1>Building better websites</h1>

<nav id="horizontal">
<h2>Site Links</h2> <p>
<a href="#html">Markup</a> |
<a href="#js">Scripting</a> |
<a href="#css">Style Sheets</a> </p>
</nav>

</header>
```

Hot tip

You will discover more about the **<a>** anchor element on page 72 and find details about the **
** line break element on page 50.

3 Next, in the body, insert a vertical site navigation menu

```
<nav id="vertical" >
<h2>Page Links</h2>
<p>Further Reading
<br><br> <a href="nav-js.html">JavaScript</a>
<br><br> <a href="nav-css.html">CSS</a> </p>
</nav>
```

Beware

Not every group of hyperlinks is eligible to be contained in a **<nav>** element – only those that provide page-wide or site-wide navigation.

4 Now, add topic headings and content

```
<h2 id="html">HTML</h2>
<p>All about markup...</p>

<h2 id="js">JavaScript</h2
<p>All about scripting...</p>

<h2 id="css" >CSS</h2>
<p>All about style sheets...</p>
```

5 Add a style sheet to position the logo image, horizontal navigation bar, and vertical navigation menu

```
<style>
#logo   { float : left ; }
#horizontal      { padding-left : 100px ; display : block ; }
#vertical { float : left ; padding : 0px 30px 30px 30px ; }
</style>
```

6 Save the HTML document, then open the web page in your browser and try out the navigation links

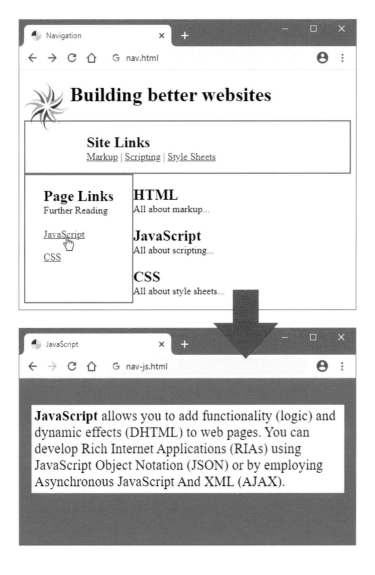

Structural outline
  └ Building better websites
      ├ Site Links
      ├ Page Links
      ├ HTML
      ├ JavaScript
      └ CSS

Hot tip

It is popular to create vertical navigation menus as unordered lists – see page 82.

Complete Framework

Just as a typical HTML document may contain a document heading or header group it may also contain a footer, or footer group, at the bottom of the page. The content of each footer is contained between **<footer>** **</footer>** tags and provides information about that part of the document.

Typically, a **<footer>** element might contain the author's name, the author's contact details within an **<address>** element, or copyright and legal disclaimers within a **<small>** element. Like a **<header>** element, a **<footer>** element can also contain hyperlinks for page and site navigation within a nested **<nav>** element.

The document heading and footer can sensibly be separated by a **<main>** **</main>** element that will contain the page content.

framework.html

1 Create an HTML document (as the template on page 31)

2 Within the body, insert a document heading
<h1 id="top">Interesting Articles</h1>

3 Next, add a main content container
<main>

<!-- Page content to be inserted here. -->

</main>

4 In the main content container, insert two articles that are the main page content
<article>

<h2 id="art-1">Sally's Article</h2>
<p>Article content...</p>

</article>

<article>

<h2 id="art-2">Terry's Article</h2>
<p>Article content...</p>

</article>

Don't forget

The HTML **<article>** elements might also each contain a **<footer>** element providing contact details for the article's author.

5 Finally, within the body, insert a document footer containing page navigation hyperlinks, copyright details, and a URL address

```
<footer>

<nav>
<h3>Information</h3>
<a href="#art-1">Sally's Article</a> -
<a href="#art-2">Terry's Article</a> -
<a href="#top">Top of Page</a>
</nav>

<small>Copyright &copy;  Example Corporation</small>
<address>www.example.com</address>

</footer>
```

6 Save the HTML document, then open the web page in your browser to see that the document structure comprises a heading, page content, and footer area

Structural outline
└ Interesting Articles
  ├ Sally's Article
  ├ Terry's Article
  └ Information

Create Sections

In HTML all content within the **<body>** element is considered to be part of a "section". Section limits are defined implicitly by correctly sequenced headings in the document outline. Section limits are defined explicitly by placing content within the **<header>**, **<main>**, and **<footer>** framework elements demonstrated on pages 40-41.

Page content within the document body or **<main>** element can also be arranged in sections between **<section> </section>** tags. Each section might typically begin with its own heading followed by articles. Similarly, each article might typically begin with its own heading followed by one or more paragraphs.

In understanding the **<section>** and **<article>** elements it helps to consider the way a newspaper contains various sections – news, sport, real estate, and so on. Each section contains various articles.

section.html

1 Create an HTML document (as the template on page 31)

2 Within the body, insert a document heading
```
<h1>Newspaper</h1>
```

3 Next, add a main content container
```
<main>

<!-- Page content to be inserted here. -->

</main>
```

Hot tip

<section> elements are not required in short documents like this one – unless you particularly want to add section headings and footers.

4 Now, in the main content container, insert a section containing two articles
```
<section>
<h2>News Section</h2>

<article>
<h3>Article #1</h3>
<p>Article content...</p>
</article>

<article>
<h3>Article #2</h3>
<p>Article content...</p>
</article>

</section>
```

...cont'd

5 Next in the main content container, insert another section containing a single article

```
<section>
<h2>Sport Section</h2>

<article>
<h3>Article #1</h3>
<p>Article content...</p>
</article>

</section>
```

Hot tip

A **<section>** is just a grouping element but an **<article>** contains a stand-alone composition.

6 After the main content container, add a page footer

```
<footer>
<small>Copyright &copy;  Example Corporation</small>
</footer>
```

7 Save the HTML document then open it in your browser to see the article content displayed in sections

Don't forget

The document, section, and article headings appear correctly nested in the document outline.

Structural outline
```
└ Newspaper
       ├ News Section
                ├ Article #1
                └ Article #2
       └ Sport Section
                └ Article #1
```

Provide Asides

HTML usefully provides **<aside> </aside>** tags that can be nested within an **<article>** element in order to incorporate content that is somewhat related to the main content of that article. These allow for supplemental yet separate content to be included – typically displayed as a sidebar or footnote.

Content within an **<aside>** element should be stand-alone information that is related to the article, such as pull-quotes extracted from an affiliated article, a glossary of terms used within the article, or even hyperlinks to pages providing further reading associated with the article.

Alternatively, the **<aside>** element can be used alone, without an **<article>** element, to contain secondary content that is related to the entire page, such as related advertising or a web blog.

aside.html

1 Create an HTML document (as the template on page 31)

2 Within the body, insert a document heading
<h1>Famous Quotes</h1>

3 Next, add a main content container
<main>

<!-- Page content to be inserted here. -->

</main>

4 Now, in the main content container, insert an article containing a heading, a paragraph, and an aside element
<article>
<h2>Happiness</h2>

**<p><q>The secret of happiness is not in doing what one likes, but in liking what one has to do.</q>
**
<cite>James M. Barrie</cite></p>

<aside>James M. Barrie (1860 - 1937) was a Scottish author and playwright.</aside>

</article>

Don't forget

The HTML **<aside>** and **<nav>** elements may also each contain a **<footer>** element.

44

5 In the main content container, insert a second, similar article – containing a **class** attribute for sidebar styling

```
<article class="sidebar">
<h2>Cynicism</h2>

<p> <q>A cynic is a man who knows the price of
everything<br>but the value of nothing.</q> <br>
<cite>Oscar Wilde</cite></p>

<aside>Oscar Wilde (1854 – 1900)<br>
was an Irish writer and poet.</aside>

</article>
```

Avoid using the **<aside>** element to contain unrelated advertising.

6 Add a page footer after the main content container, then add a style sheet to control the position of the aside

```
<footer>
<small>Copyright &copy; Example Corporation</small>
</footer>

<style>
article.sidebar > p,aside
{ display : table-cell ; padding-right : 20px ; }
</style>
```

Do not use the **<aside>** element to contain navigation hyperlinks – those should always be contained inside a **<nav>** element.

7 Save the HTML document and the style sheet, then open the web page in your browser to see how the asides appear

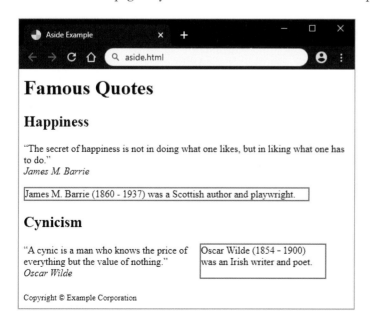

45

Revise Divisions

The **<div> </div>** division tags, which were used widely in earlier versions of HTML, continue to be supported for backward-compatibility – but the **<div>** element provides no semantic meaning so is best avoided in favor of more meaningful tags.

Unlike other meaningful elements such as **<header>**, **<main>**, **<section>**, **<article>**, **<nav>**, and **<footer>**, the meaningless **<div>** element is anonymous. For example, a smart browser might have a shortcut key to jump to the page's navigation section. This section is easily identifiable when contained in a meaningful **<nav>** element, but not so obvious when contained in a meaningless **<div>** element.

Only use the **<div>** element for styling – always look for a meaningful element to use instead.

The **<div>** element remains useful for styling purposes, as do the similarly anonymous **<span> </span>** tags. Although the **<div>** and **<span>** elements are meaningless alone, they can include an identifying **id**, **class**, or **style** attribute for application of style rules.

Documents that use the **<div>** element for structural rather than stylistic purposes should be revised to use meaningful elements instead – for example, given the document elements below:

46

![HTML]

divided.html

```
<body>

<div class="header">
<h1>Web Languages</h1>
</div>

<div class="nav">
<h2>Menu</h2>
<p><a href="nav-js.html">JavaScript</a></p>
<p><a href="nav-css.html">Cascading Style Sheets</a></p>
</div>

<div class="main">
<h2> <span style="font-style:italic" > HyperText</span>
Markup Language</h2>
<p>All about HTML...</p>

<h2><span style="font-style:italic" >eXtensible </span>
Markup Language</h2>
<p>All about XML...</p>
</div>

<div class="footer">
<p><small>Copyright &copy; Example Corporation</small></p>
</div>

</body>
```

Structural outline
  Web Languages
    Menu
    HyperText Markup Language
    eXtensible Markup Language

...cont'd

1 Replace the "header" class **<div>** with a **<header>** element

2 Replace the "nav" class **<div>** with a **<nav>** element

3 Replace the "main" class **<div>** with a **<main>** element

revised.html

4 Add **<article>** elements around heading and paragraphs, then replace the **<span>** elements with **<em>** elements – for automatic emphasis

```
<article>

<h2><em> HyperText</em> Markup Language</h2>
<p>All about HTML...</p>

</article>

<article>

<h2><em>eXtensible</em>Markup Language</h2>
<p>All about XML...</p>

</article>
```

You will discover more about the **<em>** emphasis element on page 54.

5 Replace the "footer" class **<div>** with a **<footer>** element

6 Save the edited document, then open both documents in your browser to see they look identical – the structure is the same but the revision gives semantic meaning

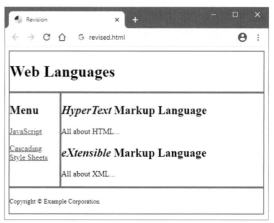

Also amend any associated style sheets to select the new elements.

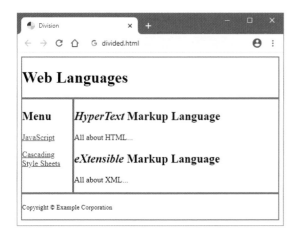

Summary

- Heading elements `<h1>`, `<h2>`, `<h3>`, `<h4>`, `<h5>`, and `<h6>` are ranked in order of importance from `<h1>` down to `<h6>`.

- Correctly sequenced heading elements implicitly convey the document structure – to create the document outline.

- The `<hgroup>` element can be used to enclose both a heading and sub-headings – from `<h1>` down to `<h6>`.

- Complete headers, including a logo, banner, and headings `<h1>` to `<h6>` can be enclosed in a `<header>` element.

- Groups of hyperlinks providing page or site navigation should be enclosed within a `<nav>` element.

- A `<nav>` element is just a wrapper around a menu, typically displayed horizontally in the header or vertically in a sidebar.

- A web page body section framework may comprise `<header>`, `<main>`, and `<footer>` elements.

- Typically, a `<footer>` element might contain contact details in an `<address>` element or legal details in a `<small>` element.

- Each document `<section>` element will typically begin with a section heading, followed by one or more articles.

- Each document `<article>` element will typically begin with an article heading, followed by one or more paragraphs.

- Stand-alone information related to an article can be enclosed within an `<aside>` element nested in an `<article>` element.

- The `<div>` and `<span>` elements are meaningless but are useful for styling purposes.

3 Manage Text Content

Insert Paragraphs

All text content is traditionally separated into sentences and paragraphs to be more easily read and more readily understood. This is also true for text content in HTML documents, and their paragraphs are contained within **\<p\> \</p\>** tags. Each paragraph element is visually separated from the next one by the browser – typically leaving two empty lines between them.

Text within a paragraph will normally automatically wrap to the next line when it meets the element's edge, but it can be forced to wrap sooner by inserting a line break **\<br\>** tag.

For emphasis, a horizontal rule **\<hr\>** tag can be inserted between paragraphs to draw a line separating them. The **\<hr\>** tag cannot, however, be inserted inside a paragraph to separate sentences. You may be surprised to find the **\<hr\>** tag in HTML as it would seem to perform a purely presentational function. It is, however, described in the specifications as representing a "paragraph-level thematic break", such as a scene change in a story.

The **\<br\>** tag and **\<hr\>** tag are both single tags that need no matching closing tag.

para.html

1 Create an HTML document

2 Insert a large heading within the body section
<h1>**The Statue of Liberty**</h1>

3 Next, add a paragraph within the body section
<p>**The Statue of Liberty was built over nine years by French sculptor Auguste Bartholdi. Upon its completion in 1884 all 350 individual pieces of the statue were packed into 214 crates for the long boat ride from France to New York.**</p>

4 After the paragraph, add a horizontal ruled line
<hr>

5 After the horizontal ruled line, add a second paragraph
<p>**The statue arrived in America several months later and was reconstructed on Liberty Island. Auguste Bartholdi thought that the New York harbor was the perfect setting for his masterpiece because it was where immigrants got their first view of the New World.**</p>

6 Now, insert breaks into the paragraphs to control the length of their lines

```
<p>The Statue of Liberty was built over nine years
<br>by French sculptor Auguste Bartholdi.
<br>Upon its completion in 1884 all 350 individual pieces
of the statue were packed into 214 crates for the long
boat ride from France to New York.</p>

<p>The statue arrived in America several months later
<br>and was reconstructed on Liberty Island.
<br>Auguste Bartholdi thought that the New York harbor
was the perfect setting for his masterpiece because it was
where immigrants got their first view of the New World.
</p>
```

7 Save the HTML document then open it in your web browser to see the heading, paragraphs, forced line breaks, and horizontal ruled line

Hot tip

The **<hr>** element can be considered to be the HTML equivalent of the *** section separator often found in stories and essays.

The Statue of Liberty

The Statue of Liberty was built over nine years
by French sculptor Auguste Bartholdi.
Upon its completion in 1884 all 350 individual pieces of the statue were packed into 214 crates for the long boat ride from France to New York.

The statue arrived in America several months later
and was reconstructed on Liberty Island.
Auguste Bartholdi thought that the New York harbor was the perfect setting for his masterpiece because it was where immigrants got their first view of the New World.

Include Quotations

It is important to recognize that some HTML elements produce a rectangular block area on the page in which to display content, while others merely produce a small block on a line within an outer containing block. These are referred to as "flow" and "phrasing" elements. Phrasing elements, which produce a small block on a line, must always be enclosed by a flow element, which produces the larger containing block, such as **<p> </p>**. The difference between flow elements and phrasing elements can be seen by contrasting how web browsers display the two HTML elements that are used to include quotations in documents.

The **<blockquote> </blockquote>** tags are intended to surround long quotations from another source, which can be specified by its **cite** attribute. For this element, the browser typically produces a rectangular block area to contain the quotation, starting on a new line and indented from surrounding content – so **<blockquote>** is a flow element.

The **<q> </q>** tags, on the other hand, are intended to surround short quotations from another source, which can be specified by its **cite** attribute. For this element, the browser typically produces a small block area on the current line to contain the quotation – so **<q>** is a phrasing element.

Unlike the **<blockquote>** flow element, the **<q>** phrasing element causes the browser to automatically add quotation marks around the element's content when it gets displayed on the page. Ideally, these should be double quotation marks surrounding the entire element content, and single quotation marks around any inner nested quotations, but its implementation may vary.

quote.html

1 Create an HTML document

2 Insert a paragraph within the body section
<p>A Paragraph Flow Block!</p>

3 Within the body section, insert a blockquote containing two small nested quotations
<blockquote cite="http://www.example.com/origin.html">
**A Blockquote Flow Block!
Paul said, <q>I saw Emma at lunch, she told me <q>Susan wants you to get some ice cream on your way home.</q> I think I will get some at Ben and Jerry's on Main Street.</q> </blockquote>**

④ Save the HTML document then open it to compare the double quote marks, single quote marks, and apostrophe

⑤ Insert this style sheet into the head section of the document, then reload the page to reveal the blocks

```
<style>
p, blockquote { border : 2px solid Green ; }
q { background : LawnGreen ; }
</style>
```

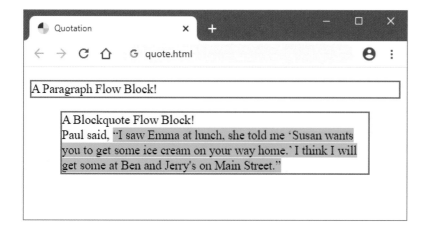

Add Emphasis

HTML provides four phrasing elements that can be used to emphasize text within the body of a document:

- Text enclosed between **<b>** **</b>** tags is enhanced without conveying extra importance, such as keywords in a paragraph – typically displayed in a bold font.

- Text enclosed between **<i>** **</i>** tags is enhanced without conveying extra importance, such as technical terms in a paragraph – typically displayed in an italic font.

- Text enclosed between **<strong>** **</strong>** tags gains increased importance, without changing the meaning of the sentence – typically displayed in a bold font.

- Text enclosed between **<em>** **</em>** tags should be stressed to deliberately affect the meaning of the sentence – typically displayed in an italic font.

It is perhaps surprising that the **<b>** and **<i>** tags remain in HTML, as they outwardly suggest that content should be presented in a bold or italic font – contradicting the aim of HTML to separate structure from presentation. According to the specifications, their meaning has been redefined, however, so content within a **<b>** element should be "stylistically offset" and that within an **<i>** element should be seen as in an "alternate voice". In real terms, these are nonetheless represented by bold and italic fonts, but should only be used as a last resort as they do not convey meaning – use **<strong>** and **<em>** tags instead.

The advantage of the **<strong>** and **<em>** tags is that they describe the importance of their content relative to surrounding text and let the browser choose how it should be presented. Additionally, these tags are more relevant to suggest how narrators should convey their content vocally.

As with many HTML tags, the **<strong>** and **<em>** tags can be nested but care must be taken to close nested elements correctly. For example, **<strong><em>...</em></strong>** is the correct order, whereas **<strong><em>...</strong></em>** is incorrect and will not validate.

Don't forget

The specifications encourage web page authors to consider accessibility issues in all aspects of their web page designs.

1 Create an HTML document

emphasis.html

2 Within the body section, add a paragraph that emphasizes some text without affecting the meaning of the sentence

```
<p>
<strong>Warning.</strong>
This dungeon is dangerous.
<strong>Avoid the ducks.</strong>
Take any gold you find.
<strong>Do not take any of the diamonds, they are
explosive.</strong> You have been warned.
</p>
```

3 Next, within the body section, add paragraphs that emphasize some text to affect the meaning of the sentence

```
<p><em>Puppy dogs</em> are cute.</p>

<p>Puppy dogs <em>are</em> cute.</p>

<p>Puppy dogs are <em>cute.</em></p>
```

Hot tip

The **<b>** tag should be avoided wherever possible, but one legitimate use is to mark up the lead sentence of an article.

4 Insert this style sheet into the head section of the document to highlight the emphasized text

```
<style>
strong, em { background : LawnGreen ; }
</style>
```

5 Save the HTML document then open it in your web browser to see how the text has been emphasized

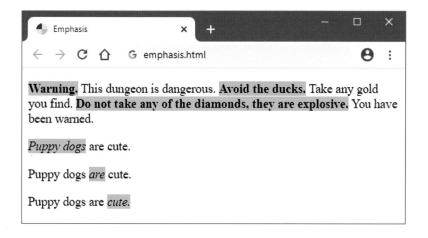

Add Modifications

HTML provides three elements that can be used to format text within the body of a document:

- Text enclosed between **<small> </small>** tags is regarded as a side comment to surrounding text, such as copyright information – typically displayed in a smaller font.

- Text enclosed within **<del> </del>** tags is regarded as having been removed from the document, such as a completed item in a to-do list – typically displayed with a strike-through line.

- Text enclosed within **<ins> </ins>** tags is regarded as having been added to the document, such as a new additional item in a "to do" list – typically displayed with an underline.

The **<small>** tag is only meant to contain short comments that supplement surrounding content. It is not intended for use with large sections of text, such as multiple paragraphs, as that would be considerably more than a side comment.

In displaying content contained within a **<small>** element, the web browser considers the size of the font used to display the surrounding content, then applies an appropriate reduction. Therefore, where the surrounding content is displayed with a font of 12-point size, content contained within a **<small>** element might be displayed with a font of 10-point size – the precise size is determined by the browser.

Both **<del>** and **<ins>** elements can be used within a section of content, to markup snippets of changed text, and to enclose entire sections of changed content, such as replaced paragraphs.

Hot tip

The **<del>** and **<ins>** tags may optionally include a **cite** attribute to specify the URL of a document explaining the changes made.

format.html

1. Create an HTML document

2. Within the body section, insert a paragraph containing a side comment for legal purposes

```
<p>Example Corp today announced record profits for
the second quarter <small>(Full Disclosure: EG News
is a subsidiary of Example Corp)</small>, leading to
speculation about a merger with Demo Group.</p>
```

...cont'd

3 Next, insert a large heading and a regular paragraph
```
<h1>To Do List</h1>
<p>Empty the dishwasher</p>
```

4 Now, insert a paragraph that has been deleted
```
<del><p>Take out the trash</p></del>
```

5 Then, insert a paragraph that has been added
```
<ins><p>Sweep the yard</p></ins>
```

6 Finally, insert a paragraph that has been added, which contains a text snippet that has been changed
```
<ins>
<p>Feed the <del>dog</del><ins> cat</ins></p>
</ins>
```

7 Save the HTML document then open it in your web browser to see how the text has been formatted

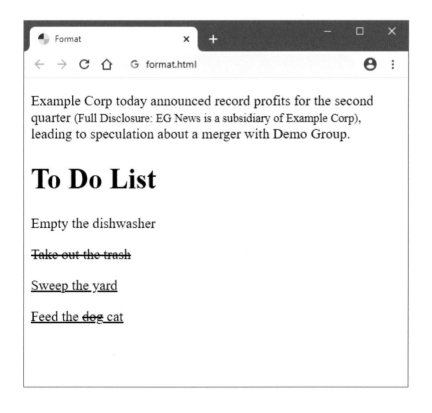

57

The **<small>** tag does not denote content of lesser importance, only that it is a side comment to surrounding text.

Add Phrasing

HTML provides four phrasing elements that can be used to mark text for special treatment within the body of a document:

- Text enclosed between **<s> </s>** tags is marked as being superseded by more accurate or relevant up-to-date content – typically displayed with a strike-through line.

- Text enclosed between **<u> </u>** tags is marked as being different in some way to normal text content – typically displayed with an underscore line to underline the text.

- Text enclosed between **<mark> </mark>** is marked as being of special significance for reference – typically displayed in a colored background block to highlight the text.

- Text broken by a **<wbr>** tag is invisibly marked as being a suitable point at which to break a line of text – representing a word-break opportunity.

It is important to note that specifications state that the **<s>** tag should not be used to indicate edited content within a document. The **<del>** tag should be used instead to indicate document edits.

Similarly, the **<mark>** tag should not be used to emphasize the importance of text content, but should only be used to highlight the relevance of text within a document. The **<strong>** and **<em>** tags should be used instead to indicate emphasis.

The **<u>** tag was deprecated in the HTML5.0 specification, as underlined text within a document traditionally indicates hyperlinks. The **<u>** tag has, however, been reinstated for the purposes of labeling misspelled words or proper names in Chinese. Authors are nonetheless strongly discouraged from using the **<u>** tag for emphasis, to avoid confusion with hyperlinks. Once again, the **<strong>** and **<em>** tags should be used instead to indicate emphasis.

Where the document contains lengthy content that may exceed the width of the browser, you may wish to use the **<wbr>** tag to indicate appropriate points at which a line-break can be inserted.

Beware

Use style sheet rules for presentation purposes rather than the **<u>** tag for underlines.

1. Create an HTML document

mark.html

2. Within the body section, add a paragraph that marks a word-break opportunity
```
<p>Microsoft Surface Pro 7
<wbr>- 256GB / Intel Core i7</p>
```

3. Next, within the body section, add a paragraph that marks a superseded price and provides a current price
```
<p><s>$1,499</s> $1,299</p>
```

4. Now, within the body section, add paragraphs that mark text for reference and mark a misspelled word
```
<p>Memory: <mark>16GB</mark>
<br>Screen: <mark>12.3-inch</mark></p>
<p>Surface <u>Penn</u> Included</p>
```

5. Save the HTML document then open it in your web browser to see how the text has been marked

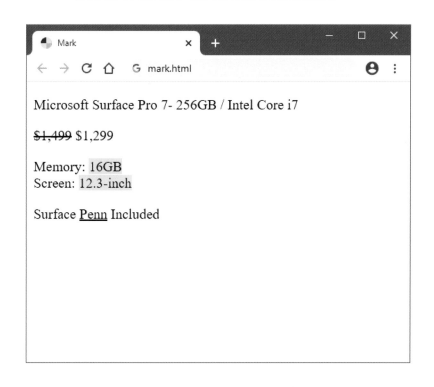

Suggesting word-break opportunities with **<wbr>** is particularly suitable for small devices, but implementation is dependent upon support for this feature in the browser.

Retain Formatting

Where it is desirable to have the browser render text content that has been "preformatted", the web page author can enclose that content between **<pre> </pre>** flow element tags. These advise the browser that the following instructions should be applied:

● Preserve white space.

● Render all text with a fixed-width font.

● Disable automatic word-wrapping.

● Do not disable bi-directional processing.

Preserving the white space retains all spaces, tabs, and line breaks. This is great to display lengthy poems in which every second line is indented – for example, with this verse:

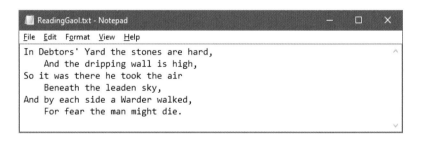

```
In Debtors' Yard the stones are hard,
    And the dripping wall is high,
So it was there he took the air
    Beneath the leaden sky,
And by each side a Warder walked,
    For fear the man might die.
```

Beware

Use spaces rather than tabs when preparing preformatted text.

In this case, each second line is indented by four-character widths – created by hitting the space bar four times to insert four invisible space characters. These indents will be exactly preserved by the **<pre>** element as four-character widths.

Tab characters, on the other hand, can present some surprises as they are usually interpreted by a browser as eight-character widths. This agrees with the tab size in Windows' Notepad application but other text editors can vary. This means that preformatted text containing tab characters may appear to be misaligned by the **<pre>** element. It is for this reason that the specifications discourage the use of tab characters when creating preformatted text content.

The **<pre> </pre>** tags can also be useful to ensure "Text-Art" (sometimes used as web forum signatures) will appear as intended.

…cont'd

1 Create an HTML document

2 Within the body section, insert a document heading
`<h1>Text-Art Signature</h1>`

3 Ensure that the font in your text editor is set to a fixed width font, such as Lucida Console for Notepad

preformat.html

4 Next, in the body section, insert a **`<pre>`** element containing preformatted content in a fixed width font – and produced without any tab characters
`<pre>`

`</pre>`

Notice that **`<pre>`** is a flow element so it does not need to be enclosed within a paragraph – it creates its own block.

5 Save the HTML document then open it in your web browser to ensure the content retains preformatting

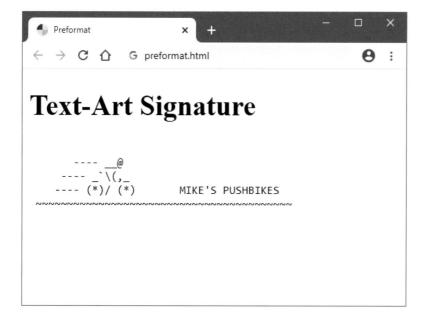

You can use any character within a fixed width font to create your Text-Art – Windows users can use the Character Map program in System Tools to select special characters from the Lucida Console font.

Use Superscript

Regular text in a paragraph area of a web page is displayed in invisible inline phrasing boxes that comprise an outer logical box, and an inner font box containing a baseline:

An inline phrasing box.

Logical box
Baseline
Font box

The vertical line spacing is determined by the font height to allow space between characters that extend below the baseline, such as "p", and tall characters that extend upwards, such as "b", plus a vertical margin area.

> Text in a paragraph written in an inline phrasing box.
> Lines are spaced so characters do not collide. ™

You can find a chart of all character entities at dev.w3.org/html5/html-author/charref

Additionally, the font box will accommodate "superscript", such as the trademark symbol ™ produced by the **™** character entity. Superscript is any text, number, or symbol that appears smaller than regular text and is set above the baseline. Mathematical formulae can use superscript to indicate numeric powers with the character entities **²** for ^{2} and **³** for ^{3}. The font box will also accommodate "subscript" – that appears smaller than regular text and is set below the baseline.

The height available for superscript and subscript with the standard vertical line spacing is limited so the character size is restricted. Rather than use character entities for this purpose it is often better to use the HTML **** tags for superscript and **** tags for subscript. These elements increase the vertical line spacing to allow more prominent superscript and subscript characters. For example, **²** is larger than **²**. Additionally, any content can be included within these elements so you are not restricted to available character entity references.

> Lines are spaced so characters do not collide with the superscript below.
> Text line in a paragraph containing ^{superscript} and $_{subscript}$
> Lines are spaced so characters do not collide with the subscript above.

1 Create an HTML document

HTML

modify.html

2 Within the body section, insert a paragraph containing superscript produced by character entities

```
<p>
Square of four: 4&sup2; = 16 <br>
Cube of four: 4&sup3; = 64
</p>
```

3 Now, in the body section, insert a similar paragraph containing superscript produced by HTML elements

```
<p>
Square of four: 4<sup>2</sup> = 16 <br>
Cube of four: 4<sup>3</sup> = 64
</p>
```

4 Finally, in the body section, insert a paragraph containing subscript produced by HTML elements

```
<p>
Water: H<sub>2</sub>O <br>
Oil of Vitriol: H<sub>2</sub>SO<sub>4</sub>
</p>
```

5 Save the document then open it in your browser to compare the superscript and to see the subscript text

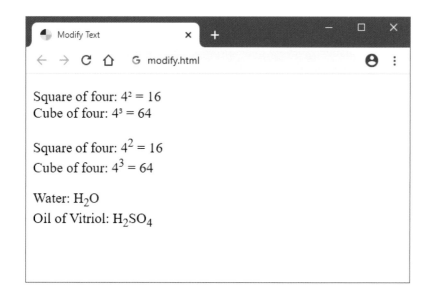

Square of four: 4^2 = 16
Cube of four: 4^3 = 64

Square of four: 4^2 = 16
Cube of four: 4^3 = 64

Water: H_2O
Oil of Vitriol: H_2SO_4

Hot tip

When using superscript ^{2} in paragraphs to denote area, such as 10 feet^2, you may prefer to use the entity **²** rather than **²** to keep line spacings equal.

63

Display Code

HTML provides five phrasing elements specifically to include computer program code within the body of a document:

- Complete program code, or snippets, can be enclosed between **<code> </code>** tags for display in a suitable font.

- Program variable instances can be enclosed between **<var> </var>** tags to differentiate them from regular text.

- Sample program input and output can be enclosed between **<samp> </samp>** tags to differentiate them from regular text.

- Content that also has associated machine-readable code can be enclosed between **<data> </data>** tags and the code specified to its required **value** attribute.

- Dates and times can be enclosed in **<time> </time>** tags and a machine-readable version specified to its **datetime** attribute.

The **<data>** element could, for example, describe a book title and its machine-readable ISBN, then the **<time>** element could describe that book's publication date:

HTML

code.html

1 Create an HTML document

2 In the body section, insert a program description containing variables, sample input, and sample output

```
<p>
This program assigns an input value to
<var>degF</var>
then performs a conversion on that value, assigning the
result to
<var>degC</var>
for output. For example, input of
<samp>98.6</samp>
will output
<samp>37C</samp>.
</p>
```

3 Now, in the body section, state the program code source

```
<data value="978-1-84078-719-1">
C++ Programming in easy steps, 5th Edition</data>
<time datetime="2023-12-15">
(December 25th, 2023)</time>
```

Hot tip

The datetime value of a **<time>** element must be in a valid format – for example, as full datetime with **2023-12-25 14:30** or month as **2023-12** or date as **2023-12-25** or day with **12-25** or time only as **14:30**.

...cont'd

4 Next, in the body section, insert the preformatted program code

```
<pre>
<code>
#include &lt;iostream&gt;
using namespace std;

int main()
{
  float degF, degC;
  cout &lt;&lt; "Enter Fahrenheit Temperature: ";
  cin &gt;&gt; degF;
  degC = ((degF - 32.0 ) * (5.0 / 9.0));
  cout &lt;&lt; degF &lt;&lt; "F is " &lt;&lt; degC &lt;&lt; "C";
  cout &lt;&lt; endl;
  return 0;
}
</code>
</pre>
```

Beware

Note that all angled bracket characters in the program code have been replaced by character entities to avoid conflict with the HTML tags.

5 Save the HTML document then open it in your web browser to see how the program description, source details, and program code is displayed

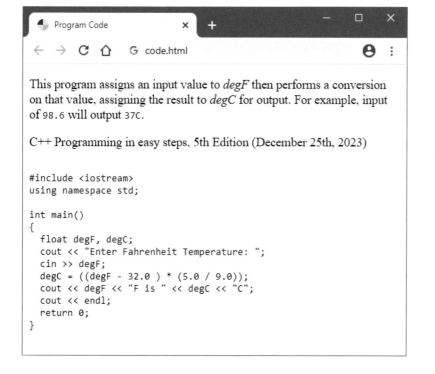

This program assigns an input value to *degF* then performs a conversion on that value, assigning the result to *degC* for output. For example, input of 98.6 will output 37C.

C++ Programming in easy steps, 5th Edition (December 25th, 2023)

```
#include <iostream>
using namespace std;

int main()
{
  float degF, degC;
  cout << "Enter Fahrenheit Temperature: ";
  cin >> degF;
  degC = ((degF - 32.0 ) * (5.0 / 9.0));
  cout << degF << "F is " << degC << "C";
  cout << endl;
  return 0;
}
```

Don't forget

Remember to insert the phrasing **<code>** element within a **<pre>** flow element to preserve the program code layout in an HTML document.

Give Advice

HTML provides four phrasing elements that can be used to designate advisory phrases within the body of a document:

- Text can be enclosed between **<abbr> </abbr>** tags to indicate it is an abbreviation.

- Text can be enclosed between **<cite> </cite>** tags to indicate it is a citation or reference from another source.

- Text can be enclosed between **<dfn> </dfn>** tags to indicate it is the definitive instance of that term.

- Text can be enclosed between **<kbd> </kbd>** tags to indicate input to be entered by the user from the keyboard.

Every HTML element that can legally appear within the body of a document may optionally include a **title** attribute. Values specified to a **title** attribute are typically displayed as a tooltip that pops up when the user places the cursor over the element. This means that each of the phrasing elements listed above can include a **title** attribute to expand on the meaning of its content.

advice.html

1. Create an HTML document

2. In the body section, insert a paragraph containing an abbreviation with tooltip advice
```
<p>
<abbr title="HyperText Markup Language">
HTML
</abbr> in easy steps</p>
```

3. Next, insert a citation reference with tooltip advice
```
<p>
<cite title="Inventor of the HyperText Markup
Language">Sir Tim Berners-Lee</cite></p>
```

4. Now, insert a definitive term with tooltip advice
```
<p>
<dfn title="The popular language of the World Wide Web.
Commonly abbreviated to 'HTML'">
HyperText Markup Language</dfn></p>
```

Don't forget

Remember to use single quote marks for nested quotes – as with 'HTML' in Step 4.

5 Then, insert a keyboard instruction with tooltip advice

```
<p>
<kbd title="Press the Y key on your keyboard to execute
a script. This requires JavaScript to be enabled in your
browser">Hit Y to Continue.</kbd></p>
```

6 Finally, add a script that will respond to the keyboard instruction

```
<script>

function showkey( e ) {

  if( e.keyCode === 89 || e.keyCode === 121 )
  {
    alert( 'Y pressed. Thank You.' )
  }
}

document.onkeydown = showkey

</script>
```

Hot tip

The script looks at the keycode when the key gets pressed and will respond to lowercase "y" and uppercase "Y".

7 Save the HTML document, then open it in your browser and place the cursor over the elements to see the tooltips

8 With JavaScript enabled in your browser, hit the Y key to see the script response

This page says

Y pressed. Thank You.

OK

Gauge Quantity

The value within a range can be represented visually on a web page using an HTML **<meter>** element to display a gauge.

The **<meter>** element must include a **value** attribute that defines a fractional measurement. Optionally, the **<meter>** tag may also include **min** and **max** attributes to specify minimum and maximum range boundaries. If these are omitted, the default range 0-1 is assumed.

The **<meter>** tag may also include **low** and **high** attributes to specify low and high positions within a range, and an **optimum** attribute can specify an ideal preferred position within a range.

The **low** and **high** attributes can specify a sub-optimal range within the overall range specified by the **min** and **max** attributes. This can, in effect, separate the gauge into three parts – low, medium, and high. Although not included in the HTML standard specifications, these three parts can be denoted by the web browser using different colors. For example, the Google Chrome browser sensibly uses red for the low part, yellow for the medium part, and green for the high part.

It is recommended that the **<meter>** element should include text describing the state of the gauge that will be displayed only in browsers that do not display this element visually.

Interactive **<details>** and **<summary>** elements can respond to user actions without scripting to disclose additional information. Typically, the **<details>** element provides a "disclosure widget" on the web page represented by a triangular arrow. A nested **<summary>** element displays a caption describing information hidden within the widget. The additional information is contained within elements nested within the **<details>** element, after the **<summary>** element.

When the user clicks the **<summary>** element, the widget state changes from "closed" to "open" and the hidden information is revealed. Clicking the **<summary>** element once more will close the widget and hide the information again.

Hot tip

The triangular arrow twists around to represent the open and closed state of the widget – consequently, these widgets are sometimes called "twisties".

...cont'd

meter.html

1 Create an HTML document

2 In the body section, insert an article containing a meter with a range 0-100, a sub-optimal range 15-50, an optimum value of 100, and a current value of 80%

```
<article><h2>Gauge</h2>Fuel Level:
<meter min="0" low="15" high="50" max="100"
optimum="100" value="80" >80%</meter>
<!-- Details to be inserted here. -->
</article>
```

3 Insert details describing the current status of the gauge

```
<details>
<summary>Status</summary>
OK to Continue...
</details>
```

4 Repeat Steps 2 and 3 twice, to create two more gauges, then edit their current values to 40 and 10 respectively, and supply appropriate descriptions

5 Save the HTML document then open it in your browser and click each **<summary>** element to see its description

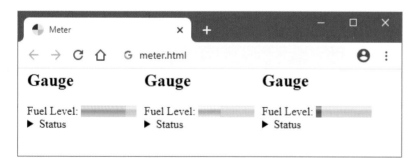

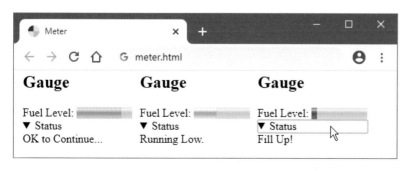

Beware

The **<meter>** element should only be used to indicate a fractional measurement within a specified range, not to indicate progress – use the **<progress>** element for that (see page 116).

Without the bi-direction override, these character entities get displayed in their logical order as לארשי – which is back-to-front for the right-to-left Hebrew language.

Direct Language

The recommended UTF-8 document encoding format provides support for bi-directional text, so that characters from languages written right-to-left, such as Hebrew, are automatically written in that direction and may appear alongside left-to-right text such as English. Content to be read in right-to-left direction should be enclosed within **<bdi>** **</bdi>** bi-directional isolation tags so as not to confuse the browser, as it expects to read left-to-right. Additionally, HTML provides a **<bdo>** bi-direction override element to which a text direction can be explicitly specified as either "ltr" or "rtl" by its **dir** attribute. The bi-direction override allows characters from right-to-left languages to be written as character entities in an HTML document in "logical" left-to-right order, but to be displayed in "visual" right-to-left order. For example, the **<bdo>** element below encloses five-character entities from left-to-right, in the order they may have been entered, but displays them right-to-left:

<bdo dir="rtl">ישראל</bdo>

.... appears as ישראל (Yiśrā'ēl in the Latin alphabet).

Ruby annotation

For Eastern languages, HTML supports "Ruby annotation" that usefully provides pronunciation alongside text. In Japanese, for example, there is more than one alphabet. Text written in the semantic "Kanji" alphabet, which has thousands of characters, is often annotated with its equivalent in the phonetic "Hiragana" language, which has around 50 characters, to aid pronunciation. This is called "Furigana" in Japanese and "Ruby" in English – named after the small font used to indicate the pronunciation. For the benefit of Westerners, the Japanese Kanji text can be annotated with "Romaji" – its Latin alphabet equivalent. Similarly in Chinese, text written in the "Mandarin" alphabet can be annotated with "Pinyin" – its Latin alphabet equivalent.

HTML Ruby annotation is entirely enclosed between root **<ruby>** **</ruby>** tags. This element may then enclose the Eastern text within **<rb>** **</rb>** tags (Ruby base) and the pronunciation between **<rt>** **</rt>** (Ruby text) tags. Optionally, an English language equivalent may be provided within **<rtc>** **</rtc>** tags.

…cont'd

ruby.html

1 Create an HTML document type

2 In the body section, insert an element for Japanese text
with its appropriate pronunciation annotation
<ruby>

```
<!-- Japanese Kanji text. -->
<rb>東 京</rb>
<!-- Romaji annotation. -->
<rt>tō kyō</rt>
<!-- English equivalent text. -->
<rtc>Tokyo</rtc>

</ruby>
```

3 Next, insert an element for Chinese text
with its appropriate pronunciation annotation
<ruby>

```
<!-- Chinese Mandarin text. -->
<rb>北 京</rb>
<!-- Pinyin annotation. -->
<rt>běi jīng</rt>
<!-- English equivalent text. -->
<rtc>Beijing</rtc>

</ruby>
```

4 Save the HTML document then open it in your browser
to see the text and ruby annotations

Don't confuse Ruby
annotation with the
unconnected Ruby
programming language.

Create Hyperlinks

When the internet carried only text content, "hypertext" provided the ability to easily access related documents and was fundamental to the creation of the World Wide Web. Today, images can also be used for this purpose so any navigational element of a web page is now referred to as a "hyperlink" (or simply as a "link").

Hyperlinks are enclosed between **<a>** **</a>** anchor tags, which specify the target URL to an **href** (hypertext reference) attribute in the opening tag. Optionally, the **<a>** tag can also include a **title** attribute to specify text to display in a "tooltip" that will appear when the user places the cursor over the hyperlink.

The web browser will display a hyperlink in a manner that distinguishes it from regular text – typically, hypertext gains an underline and image-based hyperlinks gain a colored border.

Each web page hyperlink is sensitive to three interactive states:

- **Hover** – gaining focus, the cursor is placed over the hyperlink.

- **Active** – retrieving the linked resource, the user clicks the hyperlink.

- **Visited** – the linked resource has previously been retrieved.

Style rules can be used to emphasize each hyperlink state:

link.html

1 Create an HTML document

2 Next, add a link to a style sheet in the head section
```
<link rel="stylesheet" href="link.css">
```

3 Now, in the body section, insert a hyperlink to a target page – including tooltip advice
```
<a href="link-target.html"
title="A hyperlink to a target page">Visit Target</a>
```

link-target.html

4 Save the HTML document, then create a similar second document that links the same style sheet and contains a hyperlink targeting the first document
```
<a href="link.html"
title="A hyperlink to return">Return</a>
```

...cont'd

5 Save the second HTML document alongside the first, then create a style sheet to emphasize each hyperlink state
a:hover { background : Yellow ; }
a:active { background : Red ; color : White ; }
a:visited { background : Aqua ; }

link.css

6 Save the style sheet alongside the two HTML documents, then open the first page in your browser to see the hyperlink in its default state

7 Place the cursor over the hyperlink to see the hyperlink in its hover state

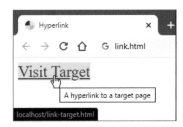

8 Hold down the left mouse button on the hyperlink to see the hyperlink in its active state

9 Release the mouse button to load the target page

10 Click the hyperlink in the target page to reload the first page

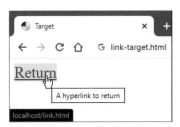

If you click the link to load the target page again, the browser recognizes it has been previously visited from the first page.

11 See that the hyperlink on the first page is now in its visited state

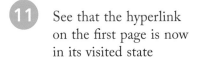
Don't forget

Access Keys

There are three ways to access the target of a hyperlink:

- **Pointer** – a mouse or similar device places a screen pointer over a hyperlink, then the user clicks to access its target.

- **Tab** – repeatedly hit the Tab key to successively focus on each hyperlink in turn, then hit Return to access the target of the currently selected hyperlink.

- **Access Key** – hit a designated character key to focus on a particular hyperlink, then hit Return to access its target.

A designated character key is specified for a hyperlink by the **accesskey** attribute of an **<a>** anchor tag. The method to utilize the designated key generally requires the user to press **Alt** + *accesskey* with most web browsers, such as Google Chrome, but it's **Alt** + **Shift** + *accesskey* with Firefox.

keys-home.html

1 Create an HTML document

2 Next, add a style sheet in the head section to remove default hyperlink styles
```
<style>
a        { text-decoration : none ; color : Black ; }
a:focus { background : Red ; color : White ; }
</style>
```

3 Now, in the body section, insert two hyperlinks that designate different numeric access key characters
```
<a href="keys-home.html" accesskey="1">
Home Page</a> |
<a href="keys-catalog.html" accesskey="2">
Catalog Page</a>
```

keys-catalog.html

4 Save the HTML document then create a similar second document containing the same two hyperlinks – but without the style sheet that removes default styles
```
<a href="keys-home.html" accesskey="1">
Home Page</a> |
<a href="keys-catalog.html" accesskey="2">
Catalog Page</a>
```

5 Save the second HTML document alongside the first, then open the first web page in your browser to see the hyperlinks without their default styles

Removing the default hyperlink styles means they are no longer easily recognizable as links – so it is best avoided unless some other indication makes the user aware they can be used for navigation purposes.

6 Hit the **Tab** key repeatedly until the second hyperlink receives focus, then hit **Return** to follow that link

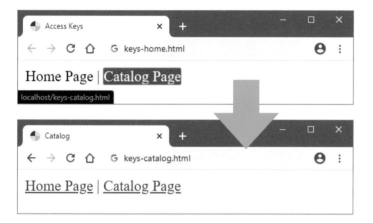

7 Press the access key combination and number 1 key (e.g. **Alt + 1**) then hit **Return** to follow the first hyperlink

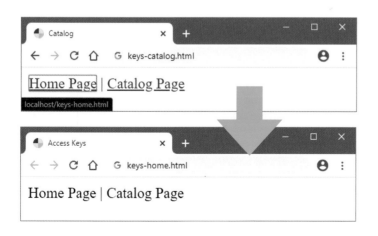

Mac users should press CMD + *accesskey* with their Safari browser.

Fragment Links

Hyperlinks can target a specific point in a document that has been created with a "fragment" identifier – an element with a unique identifying name assigned to an **id** attribute in its opening tag. Within the hyperlink, the fragment identifier is specified to an **href** attribute in the opening **<a>** tag prefixed by a # hash character. For example, the tag **<a href="#top">** targets an element within the same document that contains the unique fragment identifier name of "top".

A hyperlink can also target a specific point in a different document using the document's URL, followed by a # hash character, then the fragment identifier. For example, the tag **<a href="index.html#top">** targets an element within a document named "index.html" that contains the unique fragment identifier name of "top".

Following a hyperlink to a fragment identifier displays the document from the point where the fragment identifier appears:

1 Create an HTML document

2 Within the body section, insert two hyperlinks that contain fragment identifiers and also target different fragments
<a id="top" href="#btm">Skip to Page Foot</a> |
<a id="next-btm" href="frag-next.html#btm">
Skip to Next Page Foot</a>

frag.html

3 Next, in the body, insert a paragraph representing content, followed by a hyperlink containing a fragment identifier that targets the first hyperlink in the document
** **
<a id="btm" href="#top">Skip to Page Head</a>

4 Save the HTML document then create a second similar document with hyperlinks both above and below content
<a id="top" href="#btm">Skip to Page Foot</a>
<p style="height:700px;background:Red">Content...</p>

<a id="btm" href="#top">Skip to Page Head</a> |
<a id="prev-top" href="frag.html#top">
Skip to Previous Page Head</a>

frag-next.html

5 Save the second HTML document alongside the first, then open the first page in your browser and click the first hyperlink to go to the bottom of this page

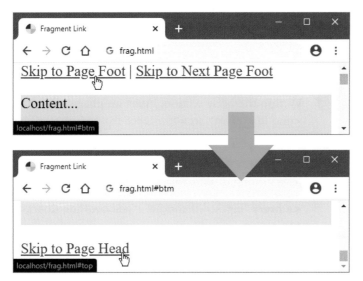

The # hash character is used in HTML to target fragments and to specify hexadecimal color values, and in CSS to select elements by their **id** attribute for styling. Hexadecimal color values specify Red, Green, Blue components that make up the color – for example, the color Red is hexadecimal **#FF0000**.

6 Next, click the hyperlink to return to the top of this page

7 Now, click the second hyperlink to go to the bottom of the next page

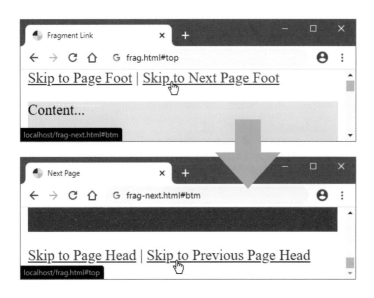

At the end of lengthy pages include a hyperlink to a fragment at the top of the page so the user need not scroll back up.

Protocol Links

The **href** attribute of a hyperlink will typically target a resource using the HyperText Transfer protocol (**http:** or secure **https:**) but it may also target resources using other protocols.

Script functions can be called with the **javascript:** protocol, and email clients can be invoked by the **mailto:** protocol:

protocol.html

1 Create an HTML document

2 Within the body section, insert an image of a chart
`<img id="chart" src="protocol-chart.png" alt="Chart">`

3 Next, insert a paragraph containing two hyperlinks that target different protocols
```
<p id="links">
<a href="javascript:toggle( )">Show/Hide Chart</a>
<br>
<a href="mailto:wendy@example.com">Email Wendy</a>
</p>
```

4 Now, add a style sheet with a rule to hide the image, and a rule to style the paragraph
```
<style>

img#chart { visibility : hidden ; height : 0px ; }
p#links { padding : 5px ; border : 1px solid ;
                    float : left ; width : 200px ; }
</style>
```

This script first examines the current visibility status of the image element, then reverses it.

5 Finally, add a script to alternately reveal and hide the image whenever the first hyperlink gets clicked
```
<script>

function toggle( ) {
  const chart = document.getElementById( 'chart' )
  let hid = ( chart.style.visibility !== 'visible' )
  chart.style.visibility = ( hid ) ? 'visible' : 'hidden'
  chart.style.height = ( hid ) ? 'auto' : '0px'
}

</script>
```

6 Save the HTML document, then open it in your browser and click on the first link to reveal the chart image

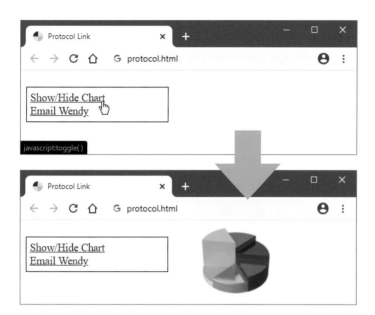

7 Click on the first hyperlink to hide the chart image again

8 Click on the second hyperlink to launch your default client email application – ready to send a message

The **mailto:** protocol automatically adds the email address of the recipient in the "To" field of the email client.

Summary

- Paragraph **<p>** elements can include **
** line break tags, and paragraphs can be separated by **<hr>** horizontal ruled lines.

- Long quotations may be enclosed within a **<blockquote>** flow element, and short quotations within a **<q>** phrasing element.

- The **<em>** and **<strong>** phrasing elements are preferred over the **<b>** and **<i>** phrasing elements to emphasize text.

- Side comments can be enclosed within a **<small>** element and the **<ins>** and **<del>** elements used to indicate replaced text.

- The **<s>** element denotes superseded content, and the **<mark>** element is used to highlight content for reference.

- The **<u>** element denotes different text, and the **<wbr>** element can be used to suggest an appropriate break point.

- To avoid misalignment, tab spacing should be avoided when creating preformatted text for inclusion within a **<pre>** element.

- Superscript and subscript can be included using character entities or using the **<sup>** and **<sub>** elements.

- Program code can be included in an HTML document using the **<code>**, **<var>**, and **<samp>** elements.

- Machine-readable code can be specified to a **value** attribute of the **<data>** tag and to a **datetime** attribute of the **<time>** tag.

- The **<abbr>**, **<cite>**, **<dfn>**, and **<kbd>** elements provide advice.

- Many elements can include a **title** attribute to provide tooltips.

- The **<bdi>** and **<bdo>** bi-directionals elements can be used to surround items of text written in a language read right-to-left.

- Ruby annotation uses **<ruby>**, **<rb>**, **<rt>**, **<rp>**, and **<rtc>** elements to provide pronunciation aid for Eastern languages.

- The **<a>** tag can create hyperlinks to other web pages, page fragments, or protocols such as **javascript:** and **mailto:**.

4

Write Lists and Tables

Unordered Lists

Unordered lists, where the sequence of list items is not important, typically place a bullet point before each item to differentiate list items from regular text.

In HTML, unordered lists are created with **<ul> </ul>** tags, which provide a container for list items. Each list item can be created using **<li> </li>** tags to enclose the item, or optionally just using **<li>** to precede the item – either form of **<li>** element validates as correct HTML. An unordered list **<ul>** element can contain numerous list item **<li>** elements.

The bullet point that differentiates unordered list items from regular text may be one of these three marker types:

- **Disc** – a filled circular bullet point (the default style).

- **Circle** – an unfilled circular bullet point.

- **Square** – a filled square bullet point.

A style rule can specify any one of the above values to the unordered list's **list-style-type** property, or a **none** value can be specified to that property to suppress bullet points.

Each HTML list also has a **list-style-image** property that can specify the URL of an image to be used as the list's bullet point. This will appear in place of any of the marker-type bullet points. Where the web browser cannot use the specified image, the marker specified to its **list-style-type** property will be used, or when no marker has been specified, the default will be used.

ulist.html

1 Create an HTML document

2 Within the body section, insert an unordered list that will display the default disc bullet points
```
<ul>

<li>HTML</li>
<li>Cascading Style Sheets</li>
<li>JavaScript</li>

</ul>
```

3 Next, insert an unordered list that will display the circle bullet points

```
<ul style="list-style-type:circle">
<li>C Programming</li>
<li>C++ Programming</li>
<li>C# Programming</li>
</ul>
```

4 Now, insert an unordered list that will display the square bullet points

```
<ul style="list-style-type:square" >
<li>Bash<li>PHP<li>Python</ul>
```

5 Finally, insert an unordered list that will display an image as bullet points

```
<ul style="list-style-image:url(ulist-go.png)" >
<li>Access</li>
<li>Excel VBA</li>
<li>Visual Basic</li>
</ul>
```

ulist-go.png
21px x 21px

6 Save the HTML document, then open it in your browser to see the unordered list bullet points

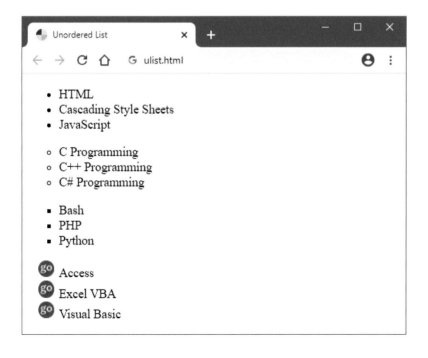

Note that in CSS terms, the lists are written in a content box with their bullet points drawn in its left padding area.

Ordered Lists

1
2
3

Ordered lists, where the sequence of list items is important, number each item to differentiate list items from regular text.

In HTML, ordered lists are created with **<ol>** **</ol>** tags, which provide a container for list items. As with unordered lists, each list item can be created using **<li>** **</li>** tags to enclose the item, or optionally just using **<li>** to precede the item – either form of **<li>** element validates as correct HTML. An ordered list **<ol>** element can contain numerous list item **<li>** elements.

The automatic numbering that differentiates ordered list items from regular text may be one of these six numbering types:

- **Decimal** – traditional numerals (the default style).

- **Roman** – classical numerals.

- **Latin** – traditional alphabetical lettering.

- **Greek** – classical alphabetical lettering.

- **Georgian** – traditional Georgian numbering.

- **Armenian** – traditional Armenian numbering.

A style rule can specify any of the above numbering types to the list's **list-style-type** property with the following values:

Type	Value
Decimal	**decimal** or **decimal-leading-zero**
Roman	**lower-roman** or **upper-roman**
Latin	**lower-latin** or **upper-latin** **lower-alpha** or **upper-alpha**
Greek	**lower-greek**
Georgian	**georgian**
Armenian	**armenian**

Additionally, a **none** value can be specified to suppress numbering. List item numbering will normally begin at one but a different start point can be specified to a **start** attribute in the **<ol>** tag.

Don't forget

When no numbering type has been specified, the default will be used.

...cont'd

1 Create an HTML document

olist.html

2 Within the body section, insert an ordered list that will display default numbering

```html
<ol>

<li>HTML</li>
<li>Cascading Style Sheets</li>
<li>JavaScript</li>

</ol>
```

3 Next, insert an ordered list that will display Roman numbering

```html
<ol style="list-style-type:upper-roman">
<li>C Programming</li>
<li>C++ Programming</li>
<li>C# Programming</li>
</ol>
```

4 Now, insert an ordered list that will begin numbering at one hundred (100)

```html
<ol start="100" >
<li>Bash<li>PHP<li>Python</ol>
```

5 Save the HTML document, then open it in your browser to see the ordered list numbering

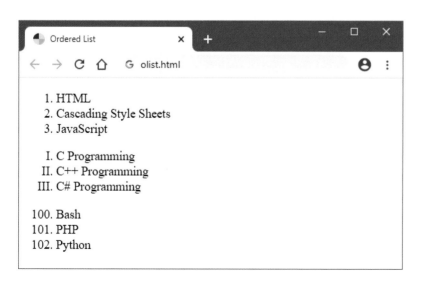

Hot tip

As with the markers in unordered lists, numbering is drawn in the left padding area of the list's content box.

Description Lists

A description list is a unique type of list in which each list item has two parts – the first part being a term, and the second part being a description of the term in the first part. This is referred to as a name/value pair. For example, a name/value pair for the term "sun" could be "sun/the star at the center of our solar system".

In HTML, description lists are created with **<dl> </dl>** tags, which provide a container for list items. Each list item term is contained between **<dt> </dt>** definition term tags, and each list item description is contained between **<dd> </dd>** definition description tags. Optionally, the **</dt>** and **</dd>** closing tags may be omitted – either form of **<dt>** and **<dd>** element is valid.

Each list item in a description list can contain multiple **<dt>** definition term elements and multiple **<dd>** definition description elements – to allow a single term to have multiple descriptions, or multiple terms to have a single description. Typically, browsers display the definition descriptions inset from their terms.

Description lists are also useful to contain a series of questions and related answers, or any other groups of name/value data.

dlist.html

1 Create an HTML document

2 Within the body section, insert a description list containing two question and answer name/value pairs
```
<dl>
  <dt>What is HTML?</dt>
  <dd>The HyperText Markup Language</dd>

  <dt>What is it used for?</dt>
  <dd>Web page structure.</dd>
</dl>
```

3 Next, in the body section, insert a description list describing the use, pronunciation, and meaning of a term
```
<dl>
<dt><dfn>Homonym</dfn></dt>
<dd class="grammar">noun</dd>
<dd class="spoken">[hom-uh-nim]</dd>
<dd>a word the same as another in sound and spelling
but different in meaning</dd>
</dl>
```

...cont'd

4 Now, insert a description list describing the use, pronunciation, and several meanings of a term

```
<dl>
<dt><dfn>Mouse</dfn></dt>
<dd class="grammar">noun</dd>
<dd class="spoken">[mous]</dd>
<dd>a small animal of various rodent families</dd>
<dd>a palm-sized button-operated device used to move a
computer cursor</dd> <dd>a quiet, timid person</dd>
</dl>
```

5 Add a style sheet to color the question and definition terms in the lists, and to color some specific descriptions

```
<style>
dt { color : Blue ; }
dfn { color : Red ; font-size : 20pt ; }
dd.grammar { color : Green ; }
dd.spoken { color : Purple ; }
</style>
```

6 Save the HTML document, then open it in your browser to see the name/value pairs

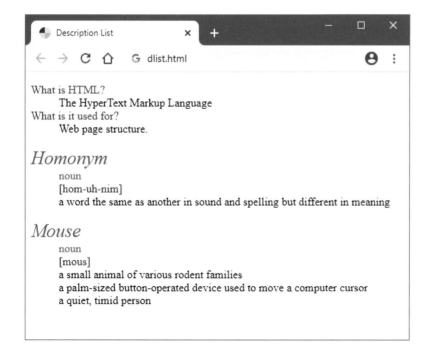

The **<dt>** element alone does not indicate its content is a term being defined – a nested **<dfn>** element must be used for that purpose.

Do not use a definition list to mark up dialog – use paragraphs to mark up each piece of dialog instead.

87

Basic Table

Data is often best presented in tabular form, arranged in rows and columns to logically group related items, so it is easily understood.

In HTML, tables are created with **<table>** **</table>** tags, which provide a container for table rows. Each table row is created with **<tr>** **</tr>** tags, which provide a container for a line of table data cells. Each table data cell is created with **<td>** **</td>** tags, which enclose the actual data to be presented. Optionally, the **</td>** and **</tr>** closing tags may be omitted – either form of **<td>** and **<tr>** element is valid.

A **<table>** element will typically contain numerous **<tr>** elements to create a table displaying multiple rows of data. Similarly, each **<tr>** element will typically contain numerous **<td>** elements to create a table of multiple columns of data. It is important to note, however, that each **<tr>** row in the table must contain the exact same number of **<td>** cells – so, for example, if the first **<tr>** row contains five **<td>** cells, all **<tr>** rows must contain five **<td>** cells.

table.html

Omit the closing **</td>** cell tags but include the closing **</tr>** tags to more clearly denote the end of each table row.

1 Create an HTML document

2 Within the body section, insert a table element
<table>
<!-- Table rows to go here. -->
</table>

3 Now, within the table element, insert three table rows – that each contain three table data cells
<tr> <td>Cell 1.1 <td>Cell 1.2 <td>Cell 1.3 </tr>
<tr> <td>Cell 2.1 <td>Cell 2.2 <td>Cell 2.3 </tr>
<tr> <td>Cell 3.1 <td>Cell 3.2 <td>Cell 3.3 </tr>

4 Add a style sheet to set the table width and border, cell borders, and borders of headings that will be added later
<style>
table { width : 500px ; border : 5px solid Black ; }
td,th { border : 1px solid Black ; }
</style>

5 Save the HTML document, then open it in your browser to see a basic table

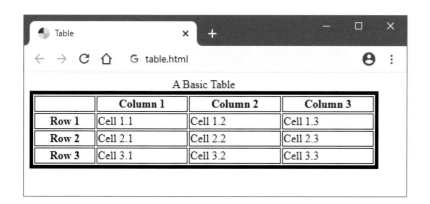

Cell 1.1	Cell 1.2	Cell 1.3
Cell 2.1	Cell 2.2	Cell 2.3
Cell 3.1	Cell 3.2	Cell 3.3

A table title can be specified with **<caption> </caption>** tags, and row and column headings can be added between **<th> </th>** tags.

6 Immediately following the opening table tag, insert a caption title
<caption>A Basic Table</caption>

7 Next, insert a new row of four column headings
<tr><th><th>Column 1<th>Column 2<th>Column 3</tr>

8 Now, insert a heading at the start of each following row
<tr><th>Row 1<td>Cell 1.1<td>Cell 1.2<td>Cell 1.3</tr>
<tr><th>Row 2<td>Cell 2.1<td>Cell 2.2<td>Cell 2.3</tr>
<tr><th>Row 3<td>Cell 3.1<td>Cell 3.2<td>Cell 3.3</tr>

9 Save the edited HTML document, then refresh your browser to view the additions

A Basic Table

	Column 1	Column 2	Column 3
Row 1	Cell 1.1	Cell 1.2	Cell 1.3
Row 2	Cell 2.1	Cell 2.2	Cell 2.3
Row 3	Cell 3.1	Cell 3.2	Cell 3.3

Beware

If a **<caption>** element is to be included it must immediately follow the opening **<table>** tag.

Beware

The closing **</th>** tag is optional but the number of opening **<th>** headings must exactly match the number of rows and columns.

Don't forget

Subsequent examples in this chapter build upon this simple table example as more table features are introduced.

Span Cells

An individual table cell can be combined with others vertically to span down over multiple rows of a table.

The number of rows to be spanned is specified to a **rowspan** attribute in the spanning cell's **<td>** tag. Cells in the rows being spanned must then be removed to maintain the table symmetry.

rowspan.html

1 Make a copy of the **table.html** document, created in the example on pages 88-89, and rename it "rowspan.html"

2 Change the document and table titles
<title>**Row Spanning Example**</title>

<caption>**A Table Spanning Rows**</caption>

3 In the table data element containing the text "Cell 1.1", insert an attribute in its opening tag and edit its content
<td rowspan="2">**Cell 1.1+2.1**</td>

4 Next, delete the table data element containing the text "Cell 2.1" – as this cell is now spanned

5 Now, add rules to the style sheet style to color the background of cells that span rows
td[rowspan="2"] { background : Pink ; }
td[rowspan="3"] { background : HotPink ; }

6 Save the HTML document, then open it in your browser to see the cell spanning two rows in Column 1

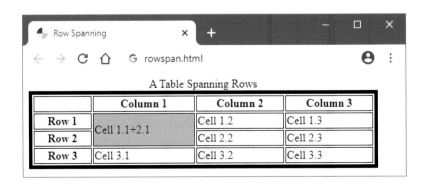

...cont'd

7 Next, insert an attribute into the table data element containing the text "Cell 2.2" and edit its content
`<td rowspan="2">Cell 2.2+3.2</td>`

8 Now, delete the table data element containing the text "Cell 3.2" – as this cell is now spanned

9 Save the edited HTML document, then refresh your browser to see the cell spanning two rows in Column 2

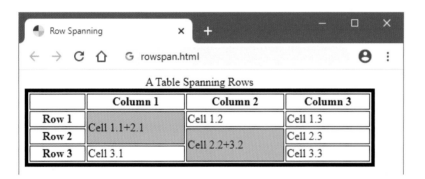

10 Next, insert an attribute into the table data element containing the text "Cell 1.3" and edit its content
`<td rowspan="3">Cell 1.3+2.3+3.3</td>`

11 Now, delete the table data elements containing the text "Cell 2.3" and "Cell 3.3" – as these cells are now spanned

12 Save the edited HTML document then refresh your browser to see the cell spanning three rows in Column 3

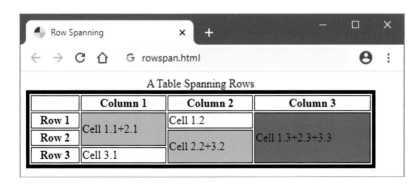

Don't forget

Notice that by default text in each cell is left-aligned and horizontally centered in merged cells.

Enhance Tables

Tables can be enhanced by the addition of special header and footer rows above and below the regular table content, which provide additional table information.

In HTML, table header information is contained between **\<thead\>** **\</thead\>** tags, and table footer information is contained between **\<tfoot\>** **\</tfoot\>** tags. When a table has a **\<thead\>** and/or a **\<tfoot\>** element, all regular table rows must be enclosed between **\<tbody\>** **\</tbody\>** tags.

In long tables, rows can be grouped into separate table body sections using multiple **\<tbody\>** elements. When these are printed, each paper page can repeat the table header and footer information.

It is important to note that a **\<thead\>** element must appear before the first **\<tbody\>** element within the **\<table\>** element, but after the **\<caption\>** element if one is present.

enhance.html

1 Make a copy of the **table.html** document, created on pages 88-89, and rename it "enhance.html"

2 Change the document and table titles
\<title\>**Enhanced Table Example**\</title\>

\<caption\>**An Enhanced Table**\</caption\>

3 Add rules to the style sheet to style a table header, a second table body heading, and a final table footer
thead { background : Pink ; }
th.next { background : DeepPink ; color : White ; }
tfoot { background : HotPink ; }

4 Immediately after the caption, insert a table header containing a single row that spans all four columns
\<thead\>
\<tr\>\<td colspan="4"\>**Header Information**\</tr\>
\</thead\>

5 After the header, add a table body element to enclose all the regular existing table rows
\<tbody\>
\<!-- Existing row elements go here. --\>
\</tbody\>

6 After the table body element, insert a second table body element containing four more table rows
```
<tbody>

<tr><th colspan="4" class="next">Next section</tr>
<tr>
<th>Row 4<td>Cell 4.1<td>Cell 4.2<td>Cell 4.3</tr>
<tr>
<th>Row 5<td>Cell 5.1<td>Cell 5.2<td>Cell 5.3</tr>
<tr>
<th>Row 6<td>Cell 6.1<td>Cell 6.2<td>Cell 6.3</tr>

</tbody>
```

7 After the second table body, insert a table footer containing a single row that spans all four columns
```
<tfoot>
<tr><td colspan="4">Footer Information</tr>
</tfoot>
```

8 Save the HTML document, then open it in your browser to see the enhanced table

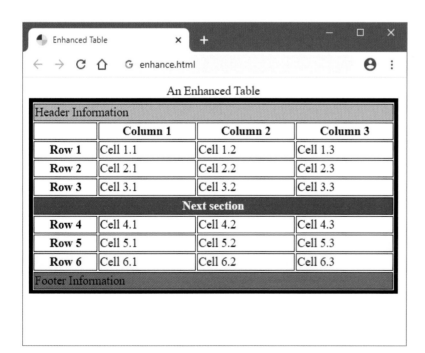

Don't forget

Table headers and footers should only contain information – all table data should appear in the table body.

Control Columns

Where a table simply has an overall width specified by a style rule, the browser will by default calculate the width of each column according to its content – columns with broad content will be wider than columns with slender content. Greater control over column width can be achieved using **<col>** tags to represent individual columns, so rules can specify their size and appearance.

A single **<col>** element can also represent multiple columns by including a **span** attribute to specify a number of columns. So, a style rule specifying a column width will be applied to all the columns that **<col>** element represents. Alternatively, the **<th>** or **<td>** tags can include a **colspan** attribute to specify a number of columns to span.

Optionally, **<col>** elements may be enclosed between **<colgroup>** **</colgroup>** tags to allow styling of both column groups and individual columns.

column.html

1 Create an HTML document

2 Within the body section, insert a table element that includes a caption
```
<table>
<caption>Breakfast Flights</caption>

<!-- Table content to go here. -->

</table>
```

The **<col>** tag is a single tag – it does not have a matching closing tag.

3 Next, in the table, insert a column group that includes a class name for styling and contains a single column
```
<colgroup class="sidebar">
<col>
</colgroup>
```

4 Now, insert two more column groups that include class names for both group styling and individual styling
```
<colgroup class="info">
<col class="stripe"> <col> <col class="stripe">
</colgroup>

<colgroup class="info">
<col> <col class="stripe">
</colgroup>
```

5 After the column groups, insert a table header, a table body, and a table footer – each with six columns
```
<thead><tr><th colspan="6"><!-- Header. --></thead>

<tbody><!-- Rows with six cells each. --></tbody>

<tfoot><tr><td colspan="6"><!-- Footer. --></tfoot>
```

6 Add a style sheet with rules to specify the appearance of the table, and its header, footer, and data cells
```
</style>
table { width : 500px ; border-collapse : collapse ; }
tbody th { background : DeepPink ; color : White ; }
tbody td { padding : 3px ; text-align : center ; }
tfoot { font-size : small ; }
</style>
```

7 Next, add rules to specify the width of each column
```
colgroup.sidebar col { width : 70px ; }
colgroup.info col { width : 80px ; }
```

8 Now, add rules to style groups and individual columns
```
colgroup.info { border-left : 2px solid White ; }
colgroup col.stripe { background : Pink ; }
```

9 Save the HTML document, then open it in your browser to see distinct column groups

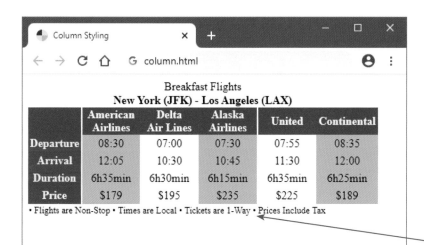

Breakfast Flights
New York (JFK) - Los Angeles (LAX)

	American Airlines	Delta Air Lines	Alaska Airlines	United	Continental
Departure	08:30	07:00	07:30	07:55	08:35
Arrival	12:05	10:30	10:45	11:30	12:00
Duration	6h35min	6h30min	6h15min	6h35min	6h25min
Price	$179	$195	$235	$225	$189

• Flights are Non-Stop • Times are Local • Tickets are 1-Way • Prices Include Tax

Hot tip

The • character entity is used in this table footer to create bullet points.

Summary

- The HTML **<ul>** element creates an unordered bullet point list that contains individual list items within **<li>** elements.

- A **list-style-type** property can specify that unordered list items should have a **disc, circle,** or **square** bullet point, or **none**.

- A **list-style-image** property can specify the URL of an image that should appear in place of list item bullet-points.

- The **<ol>** element creates an ordered numerical list that contains individual list items within **<li>** elements.

- A **list-style-type** property can specify how ordered list items should be numbered, such as **decimal, upper-latin,** or **none**.

- The **<dl>** element creates a definition list containing terms in **<dt>** elements, and their descriptions in **<dd>** elements.

- The HTML **<table>** element creates a table, and may optionally first enclose a **<caption>** element to title the table.

- Each table row is created with a **<tr>** element to contain numerous **<th>** heading elements and **<td>** data elements.

- Table cells can span down other cells using the **rowspan** attribute, and cells to the right using the **colspan** attribute.

- Adding **<thead>** and **<tfoot>** elements immediately after the **<caption>** element enhances a table with a header and footer.

- Tables that have a header and footer must also enclose all regular table rows within a **<tbody>** element.

- Table columns can be grouped using a **<colgroup>** element for styling.

- Each table column can be represented by a **<col>** element so it can be individually styled.

5

Incorporate Media Content

This chapter demonstrates how to include images and other media in page content.

Add Images

The ability to add images to HTML document content introduces lots of exciting possibilities. An image is easily added to the document using the **<img>** tag, which should preferably always include these attributes:

● A **src** attribute is required to specify the image location URL, by either its absolute or relative path.

● A **width** attribute is recommended to specify the pixel width of the area the image will occupy on the page.

● A **height** attribute is recommended to specify the pixel height of the area the image will occupy on the page.

● An **alt** attribute is recommended to specify text describing the image, for occasions when the image cannot be loaded.

The values assigned to the **width** and **height** attributes instruct the web browser to create a content area on the web page of that size. This need not be the actual dimensions of the image, as the web browser can render the image in another specified size. Care must be taken to avoid distortion by ensuring the dimensions are scaled in proportion to the actual image size. Additionally, images should only be scaled down, as scaling up often results in pixelation – where individual pixels are visible to the eye. It is inefficient, however, to rely upon the browser to scale images that are not to be displayed full size, as this requires downloading unnecessarily larger files. It is better to adjust the image size to the actual dimensions it will occupy on the web page using a graphics editor, such as Adobe Photoshop, so it will download and display faster.

Don't forget

Attributes in HTML tags can appear in any order.

Beware

Avoid the BMP bitmap file format for web graphics – saving the original image shown here as **fish.bmp** creates a file size of 790KB!

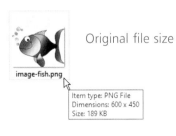

Original file size

Item type: PNG File
Dimensions: 600 x 450
Size: 189 KB

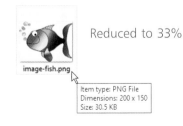

Reduced to 33%

Item type: PNG File
Dimensions: 200 x 150
Size: 30.5 KB

The optimum file type for web bitmap graphics is the popular non-proprietary Portable Network Graphics (PNG) format, which produces compact files and supports transparency.

1 Create an HTML document

image.html

2 Within the body section, insert three image elements – to display a graphic at full size plus two scaled versions
```
<img src="image-fish.png"
     width="200" height="150" alt="Fish">
<img src="image-fish.png"
     width="150" height="112" alt="Fish">
<img src="image-fish.png"
     width="100" height="75"  alt="Fish">
```

3 Save the HTML document then open it in your browser to see the full-size image and the two scaled versions

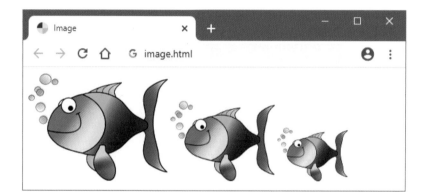

image-fish.png
200px x 150px

4 Now, insert this attribute into each image element
style="background:Aqua"

5 Refresh your browser to see the colored backgrounds

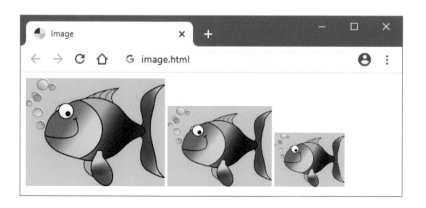

Image Maps

A single image can target multiple hyperlink resources if an image "map" is added to define "hot spot" areas for each hyperlink. To use an image map, the **<img>** tag must include a **usemap** attribute to specify a map name, prefixed by a **#** hash character. The image map itself is contained between **<map>** **</map>** tags, and its name is specified by a **name** attribute in the opening **<map>** tag.

Each area of the image that is to become a hyperlink hot spot is defined by four attributes of an **<area>** tag within the **<map>** element. The **shape** attribute specifies its shape as **rect** (rectangle), **circle**, or **poly** (polygon), and the **coords** attribute specifies a comma-separated list of its x-axis and y-axis coordinates:

Shape	Coordinates
rect	top-left x, top-left y, bottom-right x, bottom-right y
circle	center x, center y, radius
poly	x1, y1, x2, y2, x3, y3, etc. – one pair for each point. The first and final point must have identical coordinates to complete the shape

Additionally, each **<area>** tag must have an **href** attribute, to specify the hyperlink's URL target, and an **alt** attribute to specify alternative text to be displayed when images are not enabled.

1 Create an HTML document

map.html

2 Within the body section, insert an image and map element
```
<img src="map.png" alt="Search" usemap="#search">
<map name="search">

<!-- Areas to go here. -->

</map>
```

map.png
400px x 200px

3 Within the map element, define a rectangular hot spot covering the top-left quarter of the image – from a top-left point at xy:0,0 to a bottom-right point at xy:200,100
```
<area  shape="rect" coords="0,0,200,100"
       href="https://www.bing.com"
       alt="Bing Panel" title="Link to Bing">
```

...cont'd

4 Now, in the map element, define three hot spots of the same size covering the other three quarters of the image

```
<area   shape="rect" coords="200,0,400,100"
        href="https://www.ask.com"
        alt="Ask Panel" title="Link to Ask">

<area   shape="rect" coords="0,100,200,200"
        href="https://www.google.com"
        alt="Google Panel" title="Link to Google">

<area   shape="rect" coords="200,100,400,200"
        href="https://www.yahoo.com" alt="Yahoo Panel"
        title="Link to Yahoo">
```

5 Save the HTML document, then open it in your browser to see the tooltips describe each hot spot that you can click to open its associated target

Do not leave any spaces in the comma-separated list of coordinates.

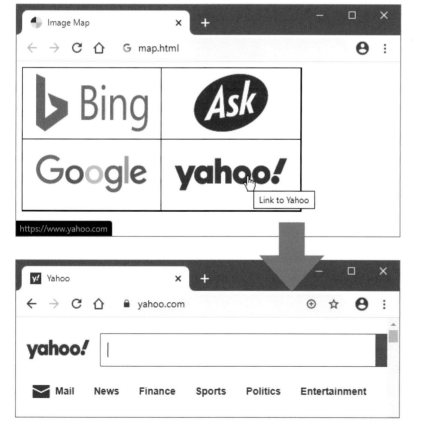

Validation will fail unless each **<area>** tag includes an **alt** attribute.

Reference Figures

With the latest HTML specifications, the web page author now has additional means by which to insert images into a web page. An **\<img\>** tag can be nested within a **\<figure\> \</figure\>** element to embed an image that is related to the main text content but whose removal would not disrupt the text's meaning.

As the nested image, in effect, is now self-contained as a "figure" it can be positioned away from the text if desired, and referenced by a caption within a nested **\<figcaption\> \</figcaption\>** element:

figure.html

1 Create an HTML document

2 Within the body section, insert a heading
```
<h1>Web Development Stacks</h1>
```

3 Next, insert a captioned figure
```
<figure id="front-stack" >

<img src="figure-front.png" alt="Front-end"
       width="160" height="145">
<figcaption class="reference">
Figure 1:Front-end Technologies
</figcaption>

</figure>
```

4 Now, insert text content that makes reference to the previous captioned figure
```
<p>Front-end development, also known as client-
side development, is the practice of producing HTML
documents, CSS style sheets, and JavaScript script code
<span class="reference" >(Figure 1)</span>
for a website or Web Application - so a user can see and
interact with them directly.</p>
```

5 Insert a second captioned figure
```
<figure id="back-stack" >

<img src="figure-back.png" alt="Back-end"
       width="160" height="128" >
<figcaption class="reference" >
Figure 2:Back-end Technologies
</figcaption>

</figure>
```

Hot tip

Always refer to figures only by their label – avoid using reference terms like "in the figure on the right" so the document layout can be easily changed without creating confusion.

6 Now, insert text content that makes reference to the second captioned figure

<p>Back-end development, also known as server-side development, is the practice of producing complex websites using programming languages such as SQL, Java, PHP, or .NET <span class="reference" >(Figure 2)</span> to provide features beyond front-end capabilities.</p>

7 Add a style sheet to position each captioned figure and to specify some font styles

<style>
figure#front-stack { float : left ; margin-top : 0px ; }
figure#back-stack { float : right ; margin-top : 0px ; }
.reference { color : Red ; font-weight: bold ; }
p:first-letter { font-size : xx-large ; }
</style>

8 Save the HTML document and style sheet then open the web page in your browser to see the captioned figures

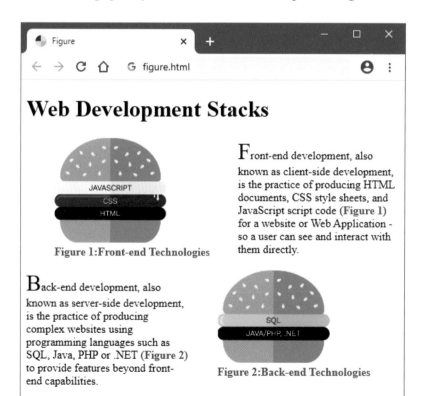

Don't forget

You can discover more about back-end technologies with the companion books in this series on SQL, Java, PHP, Python, and MySQL at www.ineasysteps.com

Select Pictures

As web content is increasingly being accessed on small handheld devices, the latest HTML specifications allow the web page author to specify alternative images to be displayed on the web page according to the size of the device screen.

A **<picture> </picture>** element is used to contain multiple image sources from which the browser can select the most appropriate size. Each image source is specified to the **srcset** attribute of a nested **<source>** element, and the minimum screen width suitable for that image is specified to its **media** attribute. The assignment requires an unusual syntax that states the size to a **min-width** property within **( )** parentheses – for example, to specify that an image is suitable for display only on devices whose screen width exceeds 500 pixels with **media="(min-width : 500px)"**

Usefully, the **<picture> </picture>** element can enclose a final regular **<img>** element to specify the image to be displayed on older web browsers that do not support this selection feature:

HTML

picture.html

1 Create an HTML document

2 Within the body section, insert a container element
<picture>

```
<!-- Image sources to be inserted here -->
```

</picture>

Don't forget

The **<source>** element does not require a closing tag. It is also used within the **<audio>** element (see page 112), and with the **<video>** element (see page 114).

3 Next, insert an image source for display only on devices whose screen width exceeds 500 pixels
<source media="(min-width : 500px)"
        srcset="picture-large.png" >

4 Now, insert an image source for display only on smaller devices whose screen width exceeds 200 pixels
<source media="(min-width : 200px)"
        srcset="picture-small.png" >

5 Finally, insert an image source for display only on older browsers that do not support the selection feature
<img   alt="Regular Guy"
        src="picture-medium.png"
        width="250" height="250">

6 Save the HTML document, then open it in various browsers to see an appropriately-sized image

The images in this example have these sizes:
large – 500px x 500px
medium – 250px x 250px
small – 125px x 125px

If you examine the browser cache you should see that it has only efficiently downloaded the appropriate image to be displayed, not all images.

Embed Objects

An external resource can be embedded into an HTML document using **<object> </object>** tags to define the resource. When the resource is an image it will be treated much like those specified by **<img>** elements, otherwise a plugin may be sought to process the resource. The **<object>** element can specify the resource's URL to its **data** attribute, and the resource type to its **type** attribute. The resource type must be a valid MIME type describing the resource.

This table lists some popular MIME types. Further details can be found on the W3C website at www.w3.org

MIME Type	Object File Format
image/png	PNG image resource
image/jpeg	JPG, JPEG, JPE image resource
image/gif	GIF image resource
image/svg+xml	SVG vector image resource
text/plain	TXT regular plain text resource
text/html	HTM, HTML markup text resource
application/pdf	PDF portable document resource
application/msword	DOC Word document resource
application/x-java-applet	CLASS Java applet resource
audio/x-wav	WAV sound resource
audio/mpeg	MP3 music resource
video/mp4	MP4 video resource
video/x-mpeg	MPEG, MPG, MPE video resource
video/x-msvideo	AVI video resource
video/x-msv-wmv	WMV Windows video resource
video/quicktime	MOV Quicktime video resource

Each **<object>** element can specify dimensions in which to display visual content using its **width** and **height** attributes. Where the resource is an image, the **<object>** element can also include a **usemap** attribute to specify the name of an image map, just like those produced for an **<img>** element.

Optionally, fallback text can be included between the **<object> </object>** tags that will only be displayed by the browser in the event that the resource cannot be embedded within the document – for example, when an appropriate plugin cannot be found.

All **<object>** elements must contain at least one **data** attribute or one **type** attribute.

1 Create an HTML document

2 Within the body section, insert a paragraph wrapper
**\<p>This is text in the main document that...\
**

\<!-- Resource object to be embedded here. -->

**\
...continues around an embedded resource.\</p>**

object.html

3 Within the paragraph, insert a PDF object to embed
**\<object data="object-chart.pdf" type="application/pdf"
        width="500" height="350">**
[PDF Document - May require the Adobe Reader plugin]
\</object>

object-chart.pdf
(external resource)

4 Save the HTML document alongside the specified resource file then open the web page in your browser to see the embedded object

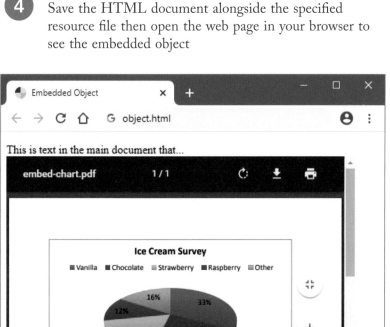

If you can disable PDF support then re-open this example you will see the fallback text appear in place of the embedded PDF document.

Embed Vectors

The HTML **<embed>** element allows you to integrate an external resource for interaction with the HTML document.

Web browsers that support modern HTML also support Scalable Vector Graphics (SVG). Unlike bitmap graphic formats such as PNG, which store their graphic information as the color of each pixel, vector graphics store the graphic information as a series of "paths". This is a highly efficient way to describe graphics.

Most importantly, vector graphics can be scaled without loss of fidelity. This means that they can be infinitely enlarged without suffering the pixelation experienced when enlarging bitmap images, such as those in PNG, JPG, or GIF file formats.

SVG Vector x 3   PNG Bitmap x 3

Hot tip

Static SVG images can alternatively be embedded using the **<img>** element – just like any other image.

SVG is not actually part of HTML but is a specification based on the eXtensible Markup Language (XML), so it describes vector images in text files. These can be created manually but it's far simpler to use a vector graphics editor such as Adobe Illustrator.

SVG images can be zoomed without loss of definition and can be printed in high quality without loss of resolution.

SVG files can also be scripted. Adding JavaScript functionality to a static vector image makes it possible to create interactive SVG objects. This means that every element and every attribute within an SVG file can be animated.

Both static SVG images and interactive SVG objects can be embedded in HTML by specifying the MIME type of "image/svg+xml" to the **<embed>** element's **type** attribute.

...cont'd

1 Create an HTML document

2 In the body section, insert an element to embed an interactive scalable vector graphic

```
<embed src="vector-picker.svg" type="image/svg+xml"
       width="280" height="200" >
```

vector.html

3 Save the HTML document alongside the SVG file, then open the web page in your browser to see the embedded interactive scalable vector graphic

vector-picker.svg
(external resource)

4 Pick a color by clicking any circled color sample in the image to interact with the vector graphic

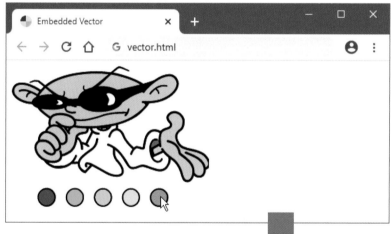

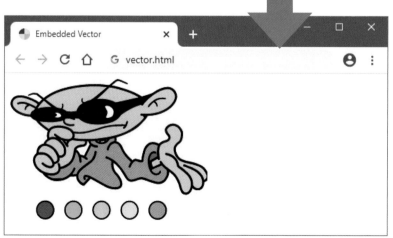

Don't forget

You can examine how JavaScript has been incorporated into this SVG document by downloading the examples archive from: www.ineasysteps. com/resource-centre/ downloads

109

Incorporate Media Content

Embed Frames

External resources can be embedded in an HTML document within an "inline frame" using **<iframe> </iframe>** tags. These create a fixed area on the page in which to display the embedded resource. The inline frame's dimensions must be specified to the **<iframe>** element's **width** and **height** attributes, and the URL of the external resource to its **src** attribute. Where the dimensions of the external resource exceed those of the inline frame, the browser automatically adds scroll bars so the user can view the entire content.

Each **<iframe>** element may also optionally contain a **name** attribute to specify a unique identifier for that frame. This allows hyperlinks to then load the URL specified to their **href** attribute into the inline frame (rather than replace the entire page) by assigning the frame name to a **target** attribute in the **<a>** element. For example, a hyperlink could target an inline frame named "topbox" with **<a href="some.html" target="topbox">**

Typically, inline frames are useful to provide supplemental content while maintaining a compact page format.

iframe.html

1 Create an HTML document

2 Within the body section, insert an article containing a heading and descriptive paragraph, and with a specified class name for positional styling purposes
<article class="left200">

<h3>Concept Cars</h3>
<p>Many of the creative and innovative concept cars premiered at the recent motor show left the audience in eager anticipation of their production.</p>

</article>

concept.html
(external resource)

3 Next, in the body, as an aside, insert an inline frame to load a document containing relevant text and illustrative photographs positioned horizontally side-by-side
<aside>

<iframe src="concept.html" width="300" height="220">

</iframe>

</aside>

...cont'd

4 Now, add a style sheet to size the article and position it to the left of the inline frame

```
<style>
article.left200 { width : 200px ; float : left ;
                  margin-right : 10px ; }
</style>
```

5 Save the HTML document alongside the external resource, then open it in your browser to see the article and the inline frame content

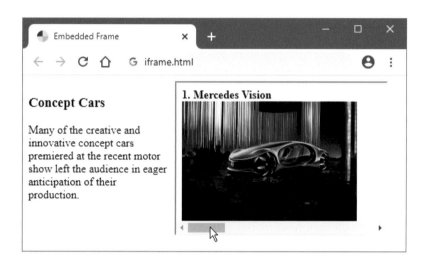

Don't forget

A fallback message can be provided between the **<iframe> </iframe>** tags to be displayed when inline frame support is disabled.

6 Drag the scrollbar to advance through the content

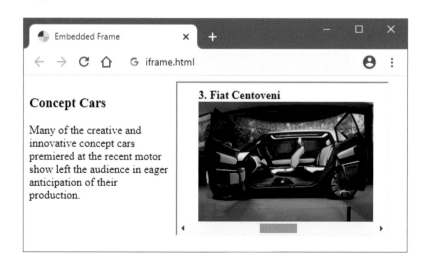

Hot tip

Embedding documents within inline frames is particularly favored on property websites to accompany property descriptions with photographs in a compact page format.

Add Audio

External audio resources such as MP3 music files can be embedded in an HTML document using **<audio> </audio>** tags.

The **<audio>** element can include a **src** attribute to specify the URL of the audio resource to embed, and may include additional attributes to determine how the audio resource will be used:

- **autoplay** – a boolean attribute that specifies the browser should immediately begin playing the audio resource.

- **loop** – a boolean attribute that specifies the browser should play the audio resource repeatedly.

- **controls** – a boolean attribute that specifies the browser should display user controls to start or stop the audio playing.

- **preload** – accepts values of "auto" or "none" to suggest the browser should load the audio resource so it is ready to play.

Boolean attributes, like the **autoplay**, **loop**, and **controls** attributes, need have no assigned value – their presence alone within the element is sufficient for the browser to understand their purpose.

Browsers rely upon an in-built "codec" (**co**der-**dec**oder) to decode audio resources so they can be played. Sadly, not all browsers incorporate the same audio codec:

- **Advanced Audio Coding (AAC)** – codec "mp4a.40.2" supported by modern browsers such as Google Chrome, Firefox, and Microsoft Edge for MP3 audio.

- **Ogg audio** – codec "vorbis" supported by other browsers for audio files in OGG format.

This inconsistency therefore requires audio resources to be encoded twice for playback across all browsers. Two **<source>** elements may be nested within an **<audio>** element for this purpose, rather than specifying a single resource URL to a **src** attribute in the **<audio>** tag. For each file format, the **<source>** elements can then specify their resource URL to a **src** attribute, and their MIME type to a **type** attribute. The browser will only load the supported audio resource for playback.

A boolean value can be only True or False. By default, attributes that represent boolean values are True unless they are assigned a value of False.

A fallback message can be included between the **<audio> </audio>** tags to be displayed when audio playback support is disabled.

1 Create an HTML document

audio.html

2 In the body section, insert an element to embed an audio resource in the MP3 format for automatic playback
```
<audio src="audio.mp3" autoplay >
[ Fallback Message ]
</audio>
```

3 Save the HTML document then open the web page to hear automatic audio playback in supported browsers

Beware

Avoid automatic audio playback on websites as many users detest the autoplay feature.

4 Next, replace both previous attributes with one to display user controls for audio playback
```
<audio controls>

<!-- Sources to be inserted here. -->

</audio>
```

5 Now, in the audio element, insert elements to specify audio resources to be embedded for all browsers
```
<source src="audio.mp3" type="audio/mpeg" >
<source src="audio.ogg" type="audio/ogg" >
```

audio.mp3   audio.ogg
(external resources)

113

6 Save the HTML document again, then open the web page in any browser and use the controls to hear playback

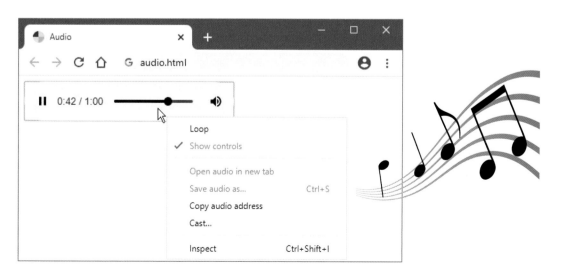

Add Video

External video resources such as MP4 video files can be embedded in an HTML document using **<video> </video>** tags.

To determine how the video resource will be used, the **<video>** element can include **src, autoplay, loop, controls**, and **preload** attributes, just like the **<audio>** element in the example on pages 112-113. Additionally, the dimensions of the area in which to display the video on the page can be specified to **width** and **height** attributes.

There are two main video compression standards:

- **Advanced Video Coding (AVC)** – a patented standard that is also known as H.264 or MPEG-4 (**.mp4** files).

- **WEBM video** – a royalty-free alternative to the patented H.264 and MPEG-4 standard (**.webm** files).

Video resources can be encoded in each format for playback across all browsers and embedded using **<source>** elements nested within a **<video>** element. For each file format, the **<source>** elements can then specify their resource URL to a **src** attribute, and the MIME type of each video file can be specified to the **type** attribute. The browser will only load the supported video resource for playback.

A **<track>** tag may be nested within a **<video>** element to specify the location of a Web Video Text Tracks (WebVTT) subtitles file to its **src** attribute. This may include a **kind** attribute to describe the track and **srclang** to describe the language. The tag must also include a boolean **default** attribute to use the specified file.

The subtitles file begins with **WEBVTT**. Start and end timing cues are added on new lines in the format HH:MM:SS.sss and separated by **-->** . The associated subtitle caption appears on a new line below each timing cue, like this:

WEBVTT

00:00:01.000 --> 00:00:04.000
Playing Guitar with "HTML in easy steps"

00:00:05.000 --> 00:00:06.000
Thanks for watching

You can discover more about the WebVTT subtitle format online at **www.w3.org/TR/webvtt1**

Note that the milliseconds are separated by a period (full stop) – not a colon.

video.vtt

...cont'd

1 Create an HTML document

video.html

2 In the body section, insert an element to display user controls for video playback
```
<video controls >
<!-- Sources to be inserted here. -->
[ Fallback Message ]
</video>
```

3 Next, in the video element, insert elements to embed a video resource and to specify a subtitle file
```
<source src="video.mp4" type="video/mp4" >
<source src="video.webm" type="video/webm" >
<track src="video.vtt"
        kind="subtitles" srclang="en" default>
```

video.mp4   video.webm
(external resources)

4 Save the HTML document then open the web page in any browser and use the controls to see video playback

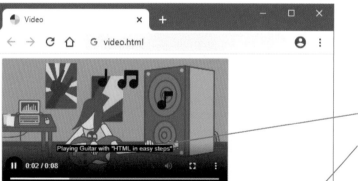

This short video displays a subtitle for 4 seconds then later displays a second subtitle.

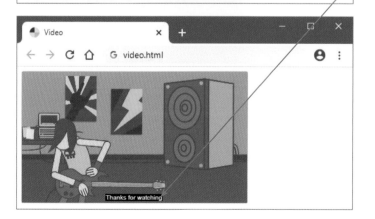

Indicate Progress

If you prefer not to provide the browser's standard controls for playback of audio or video, the **controls** attribute can be omitted from the **<audio>** and **<video>** tags. The JavaScript **play( )** and **pause( )** methods of an embedded media object can then be called to control playback from an **onclick** event-handler script function.

A visual indicator of media playback can be displayed using a **<progress> </progress>** element to present a "progress bar". Within the **<progress>** tag, a **value** attribute determines the extent of progress towards completion. This can be dynamically updated in synchronization with media playback from an **ontimeupdate** event-handler script function.

Embedded media objects have a **currentTime** property, which stores the elapsed time since playback began, and a **duration** property that stores total playback time. These can be used to calculate playback progress as a percentage:

progress.html

audio.mp3   audio.ogg
(external resources)

Hot tip

Include an **id** attribute in the **<audio>** tag to reference the media from script, and in all other tags the script needs to reference.

1 Create an HTML document

2 In the body section, insert elements to embed an audio resource for manual playback
```
<audio id="snd">

<source src="audio.mp3" type="audio/mpeg" >
<source src="audio.ogg" type="audio/ogg" >
[ Fallback Message ]

</audio>
```

3 Next, insert an image button to control payback
```
<img id="ctl" src="progress-button.png"
        width="32" height="32" alt="Control" >
```

4 Now, insert elements to present a visual indicator and calculated percentage as playback proceeds
```
<progress id="bar" value="0"></progress>

<span id="num">[Audio]</span>
```

5 Add a script with a function to initialize variables when the HTML document has loaded

```
<script>
( function ( ) {

  const snd = document.getElementById( 'snd' )
  const ctl = document.getElementById( 'ctl' )
  const bar = document.getElementById( 'bar' )
  const num = document.getElmentById( 'num' )
  let run = true

  /* Event-handler functions go here. */

} ) ( )
</script>
```

The control will play or pause playback according to the boolean value of the **run** variable.

6 Insert a function to control playback

```
ctl.onclick = function( ) {
  ( run ) ? snd.play( ) : snd.pause( )
  run = !run }
```

The **currentTime** and **duration** properties store time in seconds as floating-point values, so need to be rounded down with **Math.floor( )**

7 Insert a function to display playback progress

```
snd.ontimeupdate = function( ) {
  bar.value = ( snd.currentTime / snd.duration )
  num.innerHTML = Math.floor( 100 * bar.value) + '%' }
```

8 Save the HTML document, then open it in a browser and click the button to see playback progress

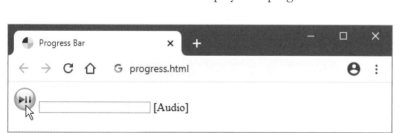

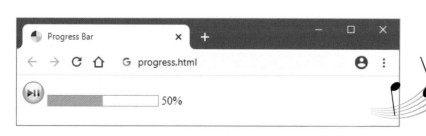

117

Use Templates

The HTML **<template> </template>** element allows you to include content that is not be displayed on the page immediately when the web page loads into the browser.

Content that is stored inside a **<template>** element can be loaded later using JavaScript to display the content on the web page. This is useful when you have content that may be added repeatedly.

Template content is a "DocumentFragment" object that the script can copy. The copy can then be appended as a "child" element of existing content. A script can also remove child elements from content.

template.html

star.png32px x 32px
(gray area is transparent).

1 Create an HTML document

2 Within the body section, add two paragraphs that will call script functions when clicked
```
<p id="hotel" style="cursor:pointer"
        onclick="addStar( this )">Hotel Mistrale</p>

<p id="clear" style="cursor:pointer"
        onclick="removeStars( )">Clear</p>
```

3 Next, add template content that will be appended to existing content by a script function
```
<template>

<img src="star.png" alt="Gold Star">

</template>
```

4 Now, add a script function to copy the template content and append it to the first paragraph when clicked
```
<script>

function addStar( hotel ) {
  const temp = document.getElementById( 'star' )
  const copy = temp.content.cloneNode( true )
  hotel.appendChild( copy )
}

// Second function to be inserted here.

</script>
```

5 Then, insert a function to remove all child elements from the first paragraph when the second paragraph is clicked

```
function removeStars( ) {
  const hotel = document.getElementById( 'hotel' )
  while ( hotel.ChildElementCount > 0 )
  {
    hotel.removeChild( hotel.lastChild )
  }
}
```

6 Save the HTML document alongside the star image, then open it in your browser and click to add/remove content

Hot tip

Before the **<template>** tag was introduced into HTML, the script would have to create the HTML child element content, but using a template is much more convenient.

119

Insert Slots

The **<template>** element, demonstrated in the example on pages 118-119, can only append the content defined within the template element. A template can be made more flexible, however, by including HTML **<slot> </slot>** elements within the **<template>** element, whose content can differ in each instance of the template.

The **<slot> </slot>** tags can, optionally, enclose default text, but the opening **<slot>** tag must include a **name** attribute that will identify that slot as a placeholder within the template.

The **<slot>** element placeholders are filled with content by including a **slot** attribute within an HTML element that nominates the matching **name** attribute value of the slot. JavaScript can then be used to append the combined template and slot content to the web page.

HTML

slot.html

1 Create an HTML document

2 Within the body section, add two divisions that each enclose three spans nominating the same three slots

```
<div class="homonym">
<span slot="word">Air</span>
<span slot="def-1">A lilting tune</span>
<span slot="def-2">What we breathe</span>
</div>

<div class="homonym">
<span slot="word">Current</span>
<span slot="def-1">A flow of water</span>
<span slot="def-2">Up to date</span>
</div>
```

Beware

The style sheet must be included in the template or its rules will not be applied to the template's elements.

3 Next, add a template of a description list whose terms and descriptions provide the nominated slots

```
<template id="list-template">
<dl>
<dt><slot name="word">Term</slot>
<dd><slot name="def-1">1st Definition</slot>
<dd><slot name="def-2">2nd Definition</slot>
</dl>
<style>
dl { width : 250px ; border : 1px solid ; }
dt { background : Orange ; color : White ; }
</style>
</template>
```

4 Now, add a script to combine the list template with the text content of the nominated slots when the page loads

```
<script>

( function ( ) {
  const homs =
          document.getElementsByClassName( 'homonym' )
  const temp = document.getElementById( 'list-template' )

  if( 'attachShadow' in homs[ 0 ] )
  {
    let i, copy, shadow

    for( i = 0 ; i < homs.length ; i++ )
    {
      copy = temp.content.cloneNode( true )
      shadow = homs[ i ].attachShadow( { mode: 'closed' } )
      shadow.appendChild( copy )
    }

  }

} ) ( )

</script>
```

Strictly speaking, this example creates a "Shadow Document Object Model" (ShadowDOM) that the script then appends to the original document. The **closed** mode simply prevents scripting access to the ShadowDOM via the **shadowRoot** property of the HTML element.

5 Save the HTML document, then open it in your browser to see the combined template and slot content

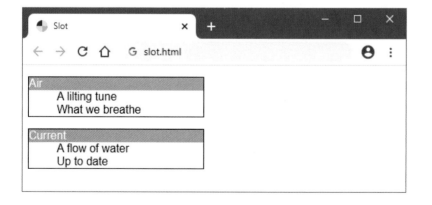

The **slot** attribute can only appear in these HTML tags:
<article>
<aside>
<blockquote>
<body>
<div>
<footer>
<h1-6>
<header>
<main>
<nav>
<p>
<section>
<span>

Employ Dialogs

You can create a "modal" dialog, to which the user must respond before regaining access to the web page, by enclosing the dialog's content between **<dialog>** **</dialog>** tags.

A modal dialog appears on a layer above all other page content and can contain all types of content (text, images, etc.), but must provide some means of closing the dialog to return to the page. Typically, this will be provided by including one or more buttons on the modal dialog that will execute a script function when clicked to perform some action and to close the dialog.

A clickable button can be added to a web page or modal dialog with a **<button>** element. Text between **<button>** and **</button>** tags will appear on the button as its label. The opening **<button>** tag can include an **onclick** attribute to nominate a script function to be called when the button is clicked. Alternatively, the script can dynamically add an "event listener" for each button to recognize when the user clicks a button – creating a "click event".

dialog.html

1 Create an HTML document

2 Within the body section, add a button and an empty paragraph that each have a unique **id** for scripting
```
<button id="show">Show Dialog</button>
<p id="info"></p>
```

3 Next, add a dialog containing text, an image, and two buttons that each have a unique **id** for scripting
```
<dialog id="dlog">
```

Your Choices

dialog-qmark.svg

```
<img src="dialog-qmark.svg"
        height="64" width="64" alt="Question Mark">
<br>
<button id="cncl">Cancel</button>
<button id="conf">Confirm</button>

</dialog>
```

4 Now, add a script to add event listeners and event handler functions for each button

```
<script>

( function ( ) {
  const dlog = document.getElementById( 'dlog' )
  const info = document.getElementById( 'info' )
  const show = document.getElementById( 'show' )
  const cncl = document.getElementById( 'cncl' )
  const conf = document.getElementById( 'conf' )

  show.addEventListener( 'click',  function ( ) {
    dlog.showModal( )
    info.innerText = 'Modal Dialog Open' } )

  cncl.addEventListener( 'click',  function ( ) {
    dlog.close( )
    info.innerText = 'Modal Dialog Canceled' } )

  conf.addEventListener( 'click',  function ( ) {
    dlog.close( )
    info.innerText = 'Modal Dialog Confirmed' } )
} ) ( )

</script>
```

Hot tip

Although the **onclick** and **addEventListener** techniques are both correct, there are advantages in preferring event listeners. It cleanly separates script from HTML code and, unlike **onclick**, it allows you to have multiple listeners for the same event.

5 Save the HTML document, then open it in your browser and click the button to see the modal dialog

Beware

In Firefox you may have to open **about:config** and set **dom.dialog_element** to **enabled** to see the modal dialog.

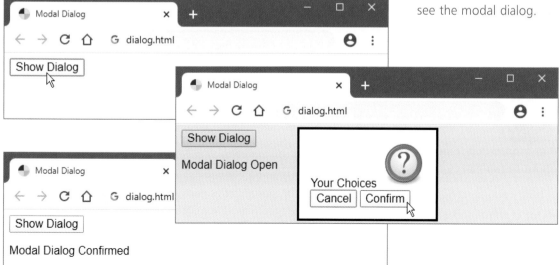

123

Paint Canvas

The HTML **<canvas> </canvas>** tags create a bitmap canvas area on the page in which JavaScript can paint shapes, text, and images. By default, the canvas area is 300 pixels wide and 150 pixels high but other dimensions can be specified to the **<canvas>** element's **width** and **height** attributes. Optionally, fallback text can be included between the **<canvas> </canvas>** tags that will only be displayed by browsers that do not support the canvas area.

In order to use the canvas, a script must first create a "CanvasRenderingContext2D" object. This snappily-named context object provides all the methods and properties needed to paint shapes and text in the canvas area. The context object is created using a **getContext( )** method of the canvas itself. For example, for a **<canvas>** element with an **id** of "canvas", like this:

```
const ctx = document.getElementById( 'canvas' ).getContext( '2d' )
```

Values can then be assigned to the context object's many properties and calls made to its many methods to paint on the canvas, such as these basic properties and methods listed below:

Property	Sets
fillStyle	fill color (default Black)
strokeStyle	stroke color (default Black)
lineWidth	stroke width (default 1)
font	font size and face (default 10px sans-serif)
Method	Paints
fillRect( )	a filled rectangle
strokeRect( )	an unfilled rectangle
fillText( )	filled text
strokeText( )	unfilled text

A canvas can be repainted at frequent intervals by a script to create animations, and a canvas can be used to create interactive games. In fact, the possibilities provided by a canvas are almost limitless, so a comprehensive exploration of the canvas element could fill another book. The example listed opposite merely gives a brief introduction to the canvas element using the basic properties and methods in the table above.

Hot tip

You can discover more about the canvas element's properties and methods online in the HTML Living Standard specifications at html.spec.whatwg.org/multipage/canvas.html

1 Create an HTML document with a canvas element

```
<canvas id="canvas" width="500" height="150">
[Fallback Text]</canvas>
```

canvas.html

2 Add a script with a self-invoking function that begins by initializing a context object and setting two properties

```
<script>
( function ( ) {
  const ctx =
  document.getElementById( 'canvas' ).getContext( '2d' )
  ctx.lineWidth = 2
  ctx.font = '5em Fantasy'

  // Statements to be inserted here.

} ) ( )
</script>
```

3 Next, insert statements to fill and stroke the entire canvas

```
ctx.fillStyle = 'Bisque'
ctx.fillRect( 0, 0, 500, 150 )
ctx.strokeStyle = 'Red'
ctx.strokeRect( 0, 0, 500, 150 )
```

4 Now, insert statements to fill and stroke some text

```
ctx.fillStyle = 'Orange'
ctx.fillText( 'HTML Canvas', 30, 100 )
ctx.strokeStyle = 'Black'
ctx.strokeText( 'HTML Canvas', 30, 100 )
```

5 Save the HTML document, then open it in your browser to see the fills and strokes painted onto the canvas

Hot tip

These arguments specify the X,Y coordinates of the top-left corner of the rectangle, followed by width and height sizes. These arguments specify the text and X,Y coordinates of the top-left corner of the text.

125

Summary

- The **<img>** tag places an image on the web page, and should preferably always include **src**, **width**, **height**, and **alt** attributes.

- The **<map>** **</map>** tags enclose **<area>** elements, to define the areas of an image map, and must include a **name** attribute.

- The **<figure>** and **<figcaption>** tags can be used to embed a captioned reference image within an HTML document.

- A **<picture>** element can contain several **<source>** tags to provide a variety of image sizes for different screen widths.

- The **<object>** **</object>** tags can be used to embed external resources within an HTML document.

- External resources can be embedded into an inline frame with an **<iframe>** element that sets the size of a display area.

- External audio resources can be embedded into an HTML document using **<audio>** **</audio>** tags, and external video resources can be embedded using **<video>** **</video>** tags.

- A **<video>** element can contain a nested **<track>** element to specify a subtitle file in the WebVTT format.

- The **<progress>** element can be used to provide a visual indicator of media playback.

- The **<template>** element can designate a group of elements that can be cloned to dynamically write content.

- A template can include **<slot>** **</slot>** elements whose content can differ in each instance of the template.

- The **<dialog>** **</dialog>** tags create a modal dialog on a layer above all other page content.

- The **<button>** **</button>** tags create a clickable button.

- The **<canvas>** element can be used to add graphics, animations, and interactive games onto a web page.

6

Create a Local Domain

Install Abyss

It is useful to have a web server installed on your system for web page development. There are several free web servers available, such as the Abyss Web Server X1 from Aprelium.

1 Launch your web browser and visit **aprelium.com**

2 Click the **Downloads** menu item, then choose **Free Download** and download the installer for your system

There are versions of Abyss for Windows, macOS, and Linux.

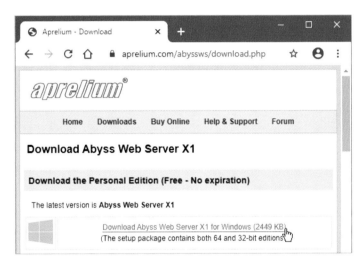

On a Windows system, double-click on the downloaded **.exe** file to run the installer.

3 Run the installer, accept the license agreement, and choose options – such as **64-bit** version, **SSL Support**, and **Start Menu Shortcuts**

4 Accept the suggested installation location and click the **Install** button

5 Choose how you prefer the web server to be started – such as **Install as a Windows Service** to continuously run in the background automatically

6 Click the **OK** button to open the Abyss Web Server Console

7 Select your language (**English**), then enter a memorable login name and password – you will need these later!

8 Click the **OK** button to save your credentials, then click the next **OK** button to see that the web server is running

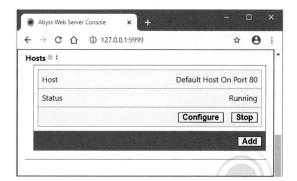

9 Now, type **localhost** into your browser's address field, then hit **Return** to see a default index web page appear

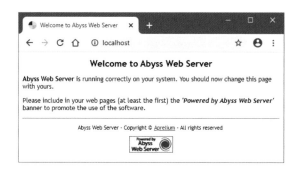

If your system has limited resources you may prefer to start the web server manually whenever you need it.

The default page is a file named **index.html** located in a folder named **htdocs** at the location where you installed Abyss. This folder is where you will place your web pages during development.

129

Install Python

A web server can run server-side scripts that respond to requests made from a web browser. The most popular server-side scripting languages include PHP, ASP.NET, Ruby, Perl, and Python.

In order to enable server-side scripting for the Abyss Web Server installed on your PC, you must first install the interpreter for a server-side scripting language – such as Python.

1 Launch your web browser and visit **activestate.com**

2 Sign in (or create an account and sign in), then select **Featured Projects & Languages** and download the latest Python build installer for your system

Hot tip

Python is available for free and there is no charge for creating an account at ActiveState.

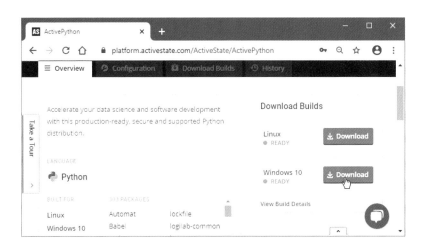

3 Run the installer, then click **Next** to begin setup

4 Click **Next** to accept the license agreement

5 Click **Next** to accept the suggested installation location and all options

Don't forget

The suggested installation folder name may include a version number, but you can change it to **C:\Python**.

...cont'd

6 Now, click the **Install** button on the next dialog to begin the installation process – sit back, this will take a while

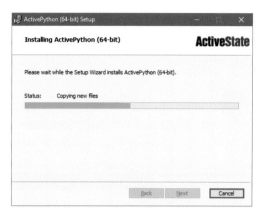

Installation is lengthy because the installer dynamically compiles C source code as it runs.

7 When installation has completed, click the **Finish** button to close the installer

You can find the Command Prompt launcher in the Windows System folder on the Windows 10 Start menu.

8 Now, open a Command Prompt or Terminal window, then type **python** and hit **Return** to open the Python Console – where you can interact with the interpreter

9 At the Python Console prompt, precisely type this line of Python code and hit **Return** to see the location of the interpreter on your system
import sys ; print(sys.executable)

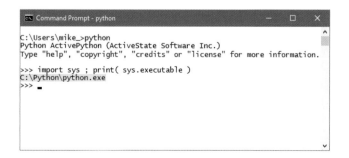

Note the interpreter location, as you will need it to configure Abyss for Python scripting.

Configure Abyss

In order for the Abyss Web Server to execute Python server-side scripts it must be configured to know the location on your system of the Python interpreter (**python.exe**) and to recognize that files with the file extension of **.py** are Python scripts.

1 With the Abyss Web Server running, launch your web browser and type **localhost:9999** into the address field then hit **Return** to open the Abyss Web Server Console

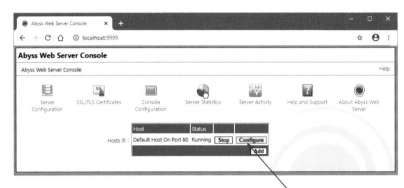

2 Enter your credentials, then click the **Configure** button

3 Now, click the **Scripting Parameters** icon

Hot tip

The domain name **localhost** is an alias for the IP (Internet Protocol) address **127.0.0.1** – so you could enter **127.0.0.1:9999** to open the Abyss Web Server Console.

4 A "Scripting Parameters" page will now appear – check the **Enable Scripts Execution** box

5 Now, click the **Add** button in the Interpreters table

...cont'd

6 An "Interpreters" page will now appear – set the Interface field to **CGI/ISAPI**

7 Now, click the **Browse** button in the Interpreter field, and go to the Python folder and select the **python.exe** file

8 Check the **Use the associated extensions to automatically update the Script Paths** box

9 Now, click the **Add** button in the Associated Extensions field and enter **py** in the Extension field

Hot tip

CGI (Common Gateway Interface) and ISAPI (Internet Server Application Programming Interface) allow data to be transferred between the web server and a script interpreter.

Don't forget

Your selections should look similar to those shown here.

10 Click the **OK** button, and click **OK** again, then click the **Restart** button to apply the new configuration

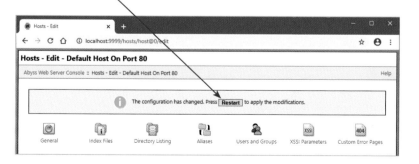

133

Echo Script

Having configured the Abyss Web Server for the Python interpreter, and for script files with the **.py** file extension, you can now create a Python script to be executed in response to a request from your web browser.

Many requests send data as key=value pairs to the web server, so a Python script could simply echo the pairs in an HTML response that places the keys and values in a table.

echo.py

1 Open a plain text editor, such as Windows' Notepad app, then type an instruction at the beginning of the first line to use a special Python module for server-side scripting
```
import cgi
```

2 Next, assign all key=value pairs to a variable, using a function supplied by the special Python module
```
form = cgi.FieldStorage( )
```

3 Now, use the Python built-in **print( )** function to write the HTML headers that will be sent to the browser
```
print( 'Content-Type:text/html; charset=utf-8' )
```

4 The headers must be separated from content, so add this line to write two carriage return and newline characters
```
print( '\r\n\r\n' )
```

5 Start writing the HTML document with a type declaration, title, and style sheet
```
print( '''<!DOCTYPE HTML>
<html><title>Web Server Response</title>
<style>tr,th,td{border:2px solid Gray}</style>''' )
```

Beware

Indentation is used in Python to group statements, instead of curly brackets, so these three lines must be indented alike.

6 Next, begin a table with two header cells
```
print( '<table style="width:500px"><tr><th>Key<th>Value' )
```

7 Then, add a loop to write any keys and values in table cells
```
for i in form.keys( ) :
    key = str( i )
    val = str( form.getvalue( key ) )
    print( '<tr><td>' + key + '<td>' + val )
```

…cont'd

8 Finally, add these lines to complete the table, to display the server icon, and to complete the HTML document
**print('''</tr></table>
<img src="pwrabyss.gif"></html>''')**

```
echo.py - Notepad                              —    □    ×
File  Edit  Format  View  Help
import cgi

form = cgi.FieldStorage( )

print('Content-Type:text/html; charset=utf-8')

print('\r\n\r\n' )

print('''<!DOCTYPE HTML>
<html><title>Web Server Response</title>
<style>tr,th,td{border:2px solid Gray}</style>''')

print( '<table style="width:500px"><tr><th>Key<th>Value' )

for i in form.keys( ):
   key = str( i )
   val = str( form.getvalue( key ) )
   print( '<tr><td>' + key + '<td>' + val )

print('''</tr></table>
<img src="pwrabyss.gif"> </html>''')
```

Hot tip

You can discover more about Python scripting with the companion book in this series: Python in easy steps.

9 Ensure that your script looks like the screenshot above

10 Save the file as **echo.py** in the **htdocs** folder of the Abyss Web Server location on your system – typically on Windows this is **C:\Abyss Web Server\htdocs**

11 With the Abyss Web Server running, open your browser then type **localhost/echo.py** into the address field and hit **Return** to see the script respond with an empty table

Hot tip

The **echo.py** script is used throughout Chapter 7 to demonstrate HTML form submission to the Abyss Web Server.

Test Environment

Now, with the Abyss Web Server installed and configured to execute the Python script on pages 134-135, the environment can be tested by sending data from the browser to the server.

Data can be sent to the server by appending a "query string" to the URL of the Python script. This begins with a **?** question mark separator followed by a key=value pair – for example, to send a single pair with **http://localhost/echo.py?Forename=Mike**

Multiple key=value pairs can be sent to the server with each pair separated by an **&** ampersand character in the query string, such as **http://localhost/echo.py?Forename=Mike&Surname=McGrath**

The data can be sent by entering the URL and query string directly into the browser's address field. It can also be sent from a hyperlink that targets the URL and query string, or from JavaScript that sets location to the URL and query string.

query-string.html

1 Create an HTML document

2 Next, within the body section, add a hyperlink to send data to the Python script
```
<a href="http://localhost/echo.py?CSS=Style">
Styling Web Pages</a>
```

3 Now, add a button in the body section
```
<button id="sender">Scripting Web Pages</button>
```

4 Finally, add a script to send data to the Python script when the user clicks the button
```
<script>

( function ( ) {
  const sender = document.getElementById( 'sender' )
  sender.addEventListener( 'click' , function ( ) {
  location='http://localhost/echo.py?JavaScript=Function' } )
} ) ( )

</script>
```

5 Save the HTML document in the server's **htdocs** folder, then open it in your browser and use the browser's address field, hyperlink, or button to send data

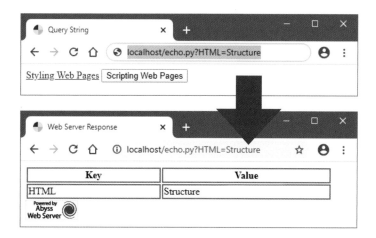

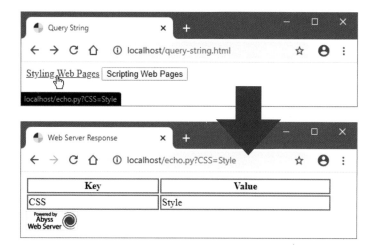

Hot tip

The Python script is performing as expected. Add more key=value pairs to the query string (each pair separated by an **&**) to see the response add further rows to the table.

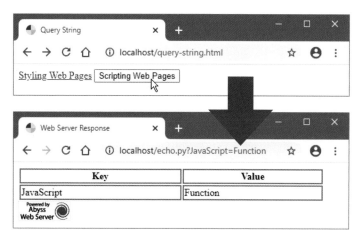

Summary

- The free Abyss Web Server X1 can be installed on your own PC for web development.

- Abyss can be started manually or set to continuously run in the background automatically.

- When Abyss is running it provides a domain named **localhost** that is an alias for the IP address **127.0.0.1**.

- A web server can call upon an interpreter to execute server-side scripts that respond to requests from a web browser.

- The most popular server-side scripting languages include PHP, ASP.NET, Ruby, Perl, and Python.

- When Python is installed you can directly interact with its interpreter (**python.exe**) via the Python Console.

- Abyss must be configured to know the location of the Python interpreter (**python.exe**) and to recognize that files with the file extension of **.py** are Python scripts.

- The URL **localhost:9999** and user credentials are needed to open the Abyss Web Server Console.

- The CGI/ISAPI interfaces allow data to be transferred between the web server and a script interpreter.

- The Abyss Web Server's location on your system contains a **htdocs** folder that is recognized by the **localhost** domain.

- HTML documents, server-side scripts, and other resource files should be placed in the Abyss **htdocs** folder.

- Data can be sent to a web server by appending a query string to a requested URL.

- Query strings begin with a **?** question mark separator.

- Query strings contain one or more key=value pairs, with each pair separated by an **&** ampersand character.

- A Python server-script can echo data sent to it from a browser request within a web server response.

7 Produce Input Forms

Submit Text

Web page forms are built from HTML elements that send data to a web server. Each element includes a **name** attribute and a **value** attribute so the data assigned to these attributes can be processed as key=value pairs. For example, where an element's **name** attribute is assigned "Brand" and its **value** attribute is assigned "Ford", the key=value pair represents the data as Brand=Ford.

Form elements are enclosed between **<form>** **</form>** tags. Each opening **<form>** tag should include a **method** attribute, specifying which HTTP method is to be used to submit the form, and an **action** attribute specifying the URL of a server-side script that is to be used to process the submitted data.

The **method** attribute can be assigned values of "GET" or "POST". Submission via the preferred **GET** method appends the data to the URL, whereas submission via the **POST** method encodes the data differently and can be used when the **GET** method fails.

Typically, an HTML form will have a "Submit" button that the user clicks to send the data for processing. This is created by assigning the value "submit" to a **type** attribute of an **<input>** tag. Additionally, this tag may include **name** and **value** attributes to submit data assigned to them as a name=value pair.

An HTML form can provide text boxes where the user can input data for submission. These are created by assigning the value "text" to the **type** attribute of an **<input>** tag, and a name to its **name** attribute. The data in the text box is sent as the value associated with the text box name as a key=value pair. Optionally, the **<input>** tag can include a **value** attribute to specify a default value. A text box for the input of a password is created by assigning the value "password" to the **type** attribute of an **<input>** tag. This functions like any other text box, but it does not display its contents as readable text. Both text and password **<input>** elements can optionally include these other attributes:

- **size** – the width of the text box in average character widths.
- **minlength** and **maxlength** – permissible number of characters.
- **min** and **max** – permissible range of numeric values.
- **placeholder** – provides a data entry hint to the user.
- **readonly** – the default value in the text box cannot be changed.
- **disabled** – the text box is grayed out and will not be submitted.

Don't forget

Data sent by the GET method is attached to the request as a query string, so may be visible in the browser's address field in the web server's response. You can submit by the POST method to prevent this for sensitive data.

…cont'd

1 Create an HTML document containing a form to send data to a server-side script using the GET method
```
<form method="GET" action="http://localhost/echo.py" >
<!-- Form components to go here. -->
</form>
```

textbox.html

2 Now, in the form element, insert text inputs and a submission button – whose value will appear on the button
```
<dl>
<dt>User Name:
<dd><input type="text" name="Name">
<dt>Password:
<dd><input type="password" name="Pwd">
<dt>Zip Code:
<dd><input type="text" name="Zip"
      size="5" maxlength="5">
</dl>
<input type="submit" name="Form" value="Sender">
```

The examples in this chapter send form data to the server-side script created on page 134.

3 Save the HTML document in the Abyss **htdocs** folder, then open it in your browser and submit some data

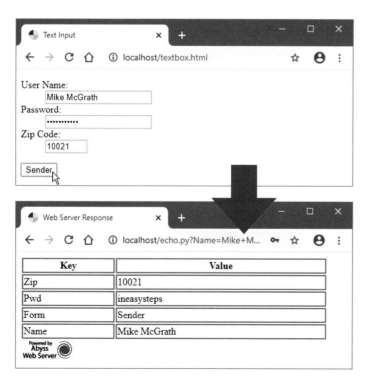

141

Key	Value
Zip	10021
Pwd	ineasysteps
Form	Sender
Name	Mike McGrath

Beware

Notice that the data in the response is not necessarily in the same order as the form input elements.

Input Types

An HTML form **<input>** tag can enforce its completion by including the **required** keyword. It can also control what the user is permitted to submit by the value assigned to its **type** attribute. Many of the input types listed in the table below prohibit submission of the form if the user enters a value that is not permitted and issue an error notice. Some also provide special controls that allow the user to easily select a permitted value.

Type	Permitted input
text	String of text
password	String of text (obscured by browser)
url	Valid URL protocol and domain address
email	Valid email address
date	Date in mm/dd/yyyy format
month	Month and year
week	Week number and year
time	Time in HH:MM format
datetime-local	Date and time as mm-dd-yy HH:MM
number	Numeric integer value
range	Numeric integer value (slider)
color	Color in #RRGGBB hexadecimal format
file	File path address (browse)

input-types.html

1 Create an HTML document containing a form with a submit button
```
<form method="GET" action="http://localhost/echo.py" >
<!-- Input elements to go here. -->
<p><input type="submit" value="Submit Form"></p>
</form>
```

2 Now, in the form, insert four controlling input elements
```
Color: <input type="color" name="color">
Range:
<input type="range" name="range" min="1" max="10">
Time: <input type="time" name="time"> <br>
URL:
<input type="url" name="url" size="54" required >
```

3 Save the HTML document in the Abyss **htdocs** folder, then try to submit the form to see it fail

4 Enter a valid URL into the **url** type input field

5 Now, enter permitted values using the special controls for the other inputs, then submit the form successfully

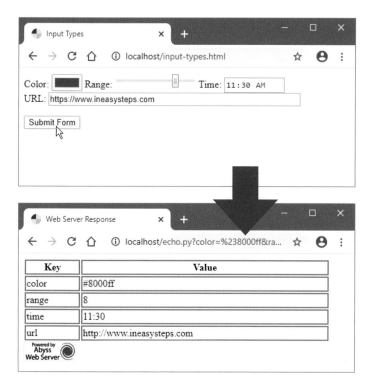

Key	Value
color	#8000ff
range	8
time	11:30
url	http://www.ineasysteps.com

Hot tip

Notice that special characters are converted to percentage Unicode values in the query string. Here the **#** symbol is converted to its Unicode value **%23**.

Text Areas

An HTML form can provide a multi-line text field where the user can input data for submission to the web server for processing. These are created by **<textarea> </textarea>** tags that may enclose default text content.

The **<textarea>** tag should include a **name** attribute that will be associated with the element's content upon submission as a key=value pair. Additionally, this tag must include a **rows** attribute, to specify the number of visible text lines, and a **cols** attribute to specify the field width in average character widths. Optionally, it may also include a **readonly** attribute to prevent the user editing its content.

When submitting large bodies of text you must be aware of some limitations of the **GET** method. This varies by browser, but may only allow the URL to append up to around 200 characters. The **POST** method provides much larger capacity as the text is sent as "Form Data" along with the HTTP header, not simply appended to the URL:

textarea.html

① Create an HTML document with a form element containing a submit button to send form data by the POST method
```
<form method="POST" action="http://localhost/echo.py" >
```

```
<!-- Text area element to go here. -->
```

```
<p><input type="submit" value="Submit Form"></p>
```

```
</form>
```

Don't forget

Unlike a text **<input>** element, the **<textarea>** element has no **value** attribute – as its content is treated as its value.

② Now, in the form element, insert a text input area that has 10 rows and is 65 average character widths wide
```
<textarea name="The Future Web"
                rows="8" cols="70">
</textarea>
```

③ Save the HTML document in the Abyss **htdocs** folder, then open the web page in your browser, enter some data, and submit the form

…cont'd

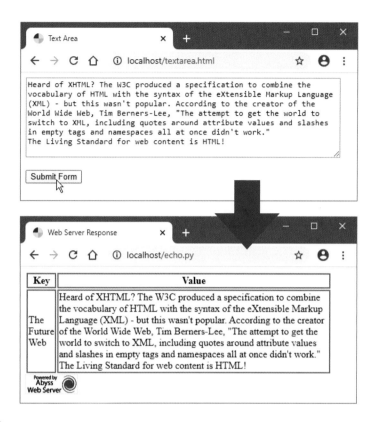

The average character width may vary between browsers – so the physical size of the text area field may vary too.

4 The text is not appended to the URL, so examine the response headers to see it has been sent as "Form Data"

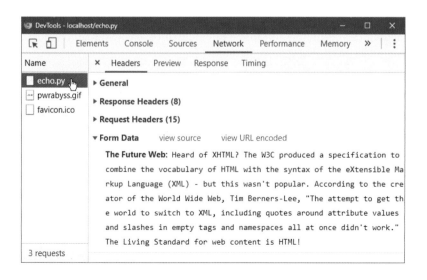

You can use the Developer Tools in the Google Chrome web browser to examine response headers. Hit **F12** then choose the **Network** tab and select the **echo.py** item in the left pane.

Check Boxes

An HTML form can provide a visual checkbox "on/off" switch that the user can toggle to include or exclude its associated data for submission to the server. When the box is checked, the switch is set to "on" and its key=value pair will be submitted.

A checkbox is created by assigning the value "checkbox" to the **type** attribute of an **<input>** tag. This tag must also include a **name** attribute and a **value** attribute to specify the key=value pair values. Optionally, this tag may also include a boolean **checked** attribute to set the initial state of the switch to "on" – so a check mark will automatically appear in the checkbox. Checkbox names may be individually unique, or several checkboxes can share a common name to allow the user to select multiple values for the same named property. In this case, the selected values are returned by the server as a comma-separated list where key=value,value,value.

A "radio button" is similar to a checkbox but is created by assigning the value "radio" to the **type** attribute of an **<input>** tag. Unlike checkboxes, radio buttons that share a common name are mutually exclusive, so when one radio button is selected, all others in that group are automatically switched off.

Multiple checkboxes and radio buttons can be visually grouped by surrounding their **<input>** elements with **<fieldset> </fieldset>** tags. These may also contain **<legend> </legend>** tags to state a common group name:

checkbox.html

1 Create an HTML document with a form element containing a submit button
```
<form method="GET" action="http://localhost/echo.py" >

   <!-- Checkbox and radio buttons to go here. -->

   <p><input type="submit"></p>
</form>
```

2 Now, in the form element, insert a paragraph containing two checkboxes
```
<p>Send details
<input type="checkbox" name="Send" value="Details">
Send prices
<input type="checkbox" name="Send" value="Prices">
</p>
```

3 Next, in the form element, insert a fieldset with a legend
```
<fieldset>
<legend>What kind of language is HTML?</legend>

<!-- Radio buttons to go here. -->

</fieldset>
```

4 Then, in the fieldset, insert radio buttons with one selected
```
Scripting <input type="radio"
        name="Definition" value="Scripting"> <br>
Markup <input type="radio"
        name="Definition" value="Markup"> <br>
Programming <input type="radio"
name="Definition" value="Programming" checked>
```

5 Save the HTML document in the Abyss **htdocs** folder, then open the web page, check both checkboxes, select the correct radio button answer, and submit the form

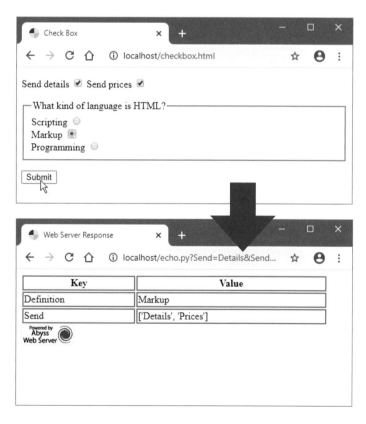

The **<fieldset>** element only groups the related elements it encloses for visual presentation – it does not associate them programmatically.

Check only one checkbox and submit the form to see only the checkbox's name and value are sent to the web server.

Hide Data

An HTML form can provide hidden elements that create no visible controls but allow additional data to be submitted to the server. Hidden form data is created by assigning the value "hidden" to the **type** attribute of an **<input>** tag. This tag must also include a **name** attribute, and may include a **value** attribute to specify static data that will be submitted as a name=value pair. Optionally, the **<input>** tag may include an **id** attribute and omit the **value** attribute so its value can be specified by script.

Hidden form data can also be used to perform a calculation and dynamically display the result in an **<output> </output>** element. The **<output>** tag must include an **id** attribute and a **for** attribute for reference in script. The **for** attribute can specify multiple element identities as a space separated list. These can be used in an assignment to the **<form>** tag's **oninput** attribute to perform a calculation whose result will appear in the **<output> </output>** element – but will not be submitted to the server:

HTML

hidden.html

Hot tip

Hidden data elements can be useful to maintain user data across a website – a user name entered on the first page can be recalled on any other page.

1 Create an HTML document containing an image displaying an item with sale price details
```
<img src="hidden-sale.png"
        width="200" height="120" alt="Sale">
```

2 Next, insert a form element
```
<form method="GET" action="http://localhost/echo.py" >

<!-- Hidden data, input, and output to go here -->

<input type="submit" name="Offer"
        value="Buy Teddy Bears">
</form>
```

3 Within the form element, insert a visible input element for user-entered data
```
Qty (60 Available) <input type="number" id="qty"
name="Quantity" min="1" max="60">
```

4 Now, in the form element, insert an invisible element for hidden data and an element to display a calculated result
```
<input type="hidden" id="price"
        name="Unit Price" value="24.99">
<output name="sum" for="qty price"></output> <br>
```

5 Then, insert another attribute in the **<form>** tag
oninput="sum.value=multiply(qty, price)"

6 Add a script to perform the calculation
<script>

function multiply(q, p) {

  let result=parseFloat(q.value) * parseFloat(p.value)

  if (isNaN(result) || result < 1) return ' '
  else return 'Total: $' + result.toFixed(2)
}

</script>

Beware

JavaScript is case-sensitive so you must use the correct case when copying script examples.

7 Save the HTML document in the Abyss **htdocs** folder, then open the web page in your browser, enter data, and submit the form

Don't forget

The hidden form **<input>** data gets submitted to the server, but the **<output>** element merely displays the result of the calculation.

149

Upload Files

An HTML form can provide a file selection facility, which calls upon the operating system's "Choose File" dialog, to allow the user to browse their local file system and select a file.

A file selection facility is created by assigning the value "file" to the **type** attribute of an **<input>** tag and a name to its **name** attribute. This element produces a text field and a "Browse" button to launch the Choose File dialog. After a file has been selected, its full path appears in the text field. When the form is submitted, the element name and the selected file's name are sent to the web server as a name=value pair.

Where a selected file is to be uploaded to the web server, the **<form>** tag must include an **enctype** attribute specifying the encoding type as "multipart/form-data". Also, its **method** attribute must specify the POST method – because Form Data cannot be appended to a URL using the GET method:

upload.html

1 Create an HTML document with a form element containing a submit button to send form data by the POST method and specify the encoding type for Form Data

```
<form  method="POST"
       action="http://localhost/upload.py"
       enctype="multipart/form-data" >

<!-- File input element to go here. -->

<input type="submit">
</form>
```

2 In the form element, insert a file element and a line break
```
<input type="file" name="Upload" size="70" > <br>
```

3 Save the HTML document in the Abyss **htdocs** folder, then open the web page in your browser, select a file on your system, and submit the form

4 Look in the Abyss **htdocs** folder to see a copy of the selected file is now placed there

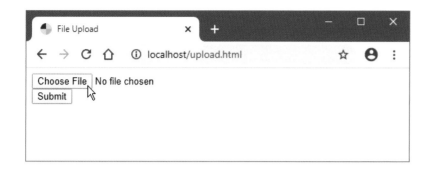

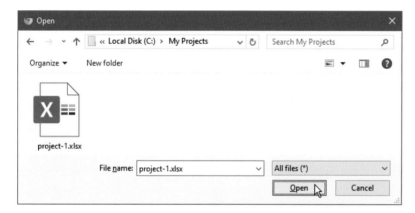

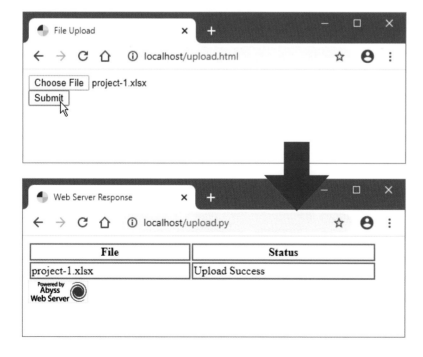

This example uses a Python script named **upload.py** placed in the Abyss **htdocs** folder. This script is provided in the download archive for this book, which is freely available from www.ineasysteps. com/resource-centre/ downloads

Push Buttons

An HTML form can provide push buttons for scripting purposes. When the user pushes a button, a "click event" occurs to which a script function can respond. This allows the user to dynamically interact with the form, and can be used to set attribute values. When a script designates a function to be called, whenever a button gets pushed it is said to attach a "behavior" to that button. A push button is created by specifying a "button" value to the **type** attribute of an **<input>** tag, and should also include an **id** attribute so the script can easily identify that element. Text assigned to the button's **value** attribute will appear on the face of the button.

Additionally, any HTML form can be returned to its original state by pushing a reset button that is created by specifying a "reset" value to the **type** attribute of an **<input>** tag:

button.html

1 Create an HTML document with a form element containing a reset button, a push button, and a submit button
<form method="GET" action="http://localhost/echo.py" >

<!-- Fieldset to go here. -->

<input type="reset" value="Reset Form">
<input type="button" value="Choose For Me" id="btn">
<input type="submit" value="Submit Form">

</form>

2 Within the form element, insert a fieldset containing a legend and a checkbox group
<fieldset>

<legend>Pizza Toppings</legend>

<input id="pepperoni" type="checkbox"
  name="Toppings" value="Pepperoni"> Pepperoni |

<input id="mushroom" type="checkbox"
  name="Toppings" value="Mushroom"> Mushroom |

<input id="bbqsauce" type="checkbox"
  name="Toppings" value="BBQ Sauce"> BBQ Sauce

</fieldset>

…cont'd

3 Add a script that attaches a behavior to the push button

```
<script>
( function ( ) {

const pep = document.getElementById( 'pepperoni ' )
const btn = document.getElementById( 'btn ' )

btn.addEventListener( 'click' , function ( ) {
                          pep.checked = true } )
} ) ( )
</script>
```

The mere presence of a boolean **checked** attribute in an HTML element checks the box, but in script the box's **checked** property needs to be assigned a **true** value to check the box.

4 Save the HTML document in the Abyss **htdocs** folder, then open the web page in your browser, and push the button to check a box

5 Now, push the reset button to clear the form, then check the other two boxes and submit the form

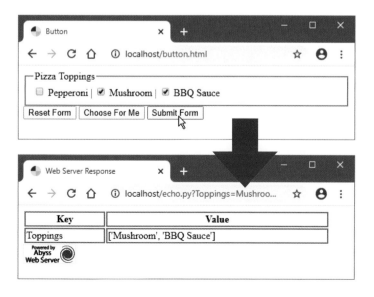

Key	Value
Toppings	['Mushroom', 'BBQ Sauce']

Image Buttons

An HTML form can use an image button to submit the form, in place of a regular submit button. An image button is created by specifying an "image" value to the **type** attribute of an **<input>** tag and including an **alt** attribute. When a form is submitted by an image button, the XY coordinates of the point at which the click occurred are automatically submitted as key=value pairs along with the rest of the form data.

Additionally, a regular **<img>** tag can be used as an image button by attaching a behavior with script. Where the behavior is to submit a form, the script function can usefully incorporate validation – for example, to ensure a user-entered email address is in the expected format:

ibutton.html

Note that the image button that will perform validation is given an identity so the script can attach a behavior to it.

1 Create an HTML document with a form element containing a text input field, which both have an identity for scripting
```
<form id="my-form"
      method="GET" action="http://localhost/echo.py" >
```

Please Supply Your Email Address:
```
<input id="adr"
       name="Address" type="text" size="45"> <br>
```

<!-- Image Buttons to go here. -->

```
</form>
```

2 Next, in the form element, insert an image button that will simply submit the form
```
<input type="image"
       src="ibutton.png"
       alt="Submit Button"
       title="Click to submit form">
```

3 Now, in the form element, insert an image button that will perform validation then submit the form
```
<img   id="btn"
       src="ibutton.png"
       alt="Submit Button"
       title="Click to submit with JavaScript validation">
```

4 Add a script that attaches a behavior to an image button

```
<script>
( function ( ) {

const btn = document.getElementById( 'btn' )
btn.addEventListener( 'click' , function ( ) {

  const myForm = document.getElementById( 'myForm' )
  const pattern =
  /^([a-zA-Z0-9_.-])+@([a-zA-Z0-9_.-])+\.([a-zA-Z])+([a-zA-Z])+/
  let adr = document.getElementById( 'adr' ).value
  if( ! pattern.test( adr ) ) alert( 'Invalid Email Address' )
  else myForm.submit( )
  } )

} ) ( )
</script>
```

Beware

The script in this example checks the input text against a regular expression pattern that describes the format of any valid email address. The pattern must appear on a single line – exactly as it is listed here.

5 Save the HTML document in the Abyss **htdocs** folder, then open it in your browser, enter an incomplete email address, and submit the form using each button

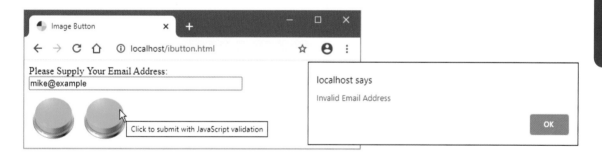

6 When validation fails using the button with scripted behavior, correct the email address then click the validating button again to submit the form successfully

Hot tip

Submit the form with the unscripted image button to also see coordinates in the web server response.

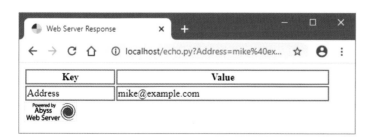

Add Logos

HTML can create push buttons that display small "logo" images using **<button> </button>** tags. These tags can then enclose an **<img>** element specifying the URL of the logo image, and text that will appear on the face of the button.

Each **<button>** tag should include a **type** attribute to specify whether the button is simply a scripting "button" type, a "submit" form type, or a "reset" form type. Scripting buttons can include an **onclick** attribute in the **<button>** tag to specify the function to be called when the button gets clicked, or directly specify a snippet of script to execute:

logo.html

1 Create an HTML document with a form element containing a fieldset with a legend and a text input field
<form method="GET" action="http://localhost/echo.py">

<fieldset>

<legend>Favorite Color</legend>
<input type="text" name="Color">

<!-- Logo Buttons to go here. -->

</fieldset>

</form>

2 In the fieldset, insert a scripting logo button specifying a snippet of script to execute when that button gets clicked
<button type="button"
onclick="alert('Enter your favorite color in the text box')">

<!-- Logo Image and Face Text to go here. -->

</button>

3 Now, within the button element, insert an image element and text that will appear on the face of the button
<img src="logo-help.png" alt="Help">Help

4 Next, add a button element to submit the form
<button type="submit">
<img src="logo-submit.png" alt="Submit">
Submit</button>

5 Finally, add a button element to reset the form
<button type="reset">
<img src="logo-reset.png" alt="Reset">Reset</button>

6 Save the HTML document in the Abyss **htdocs** folder, then open it in your browser and click the "Help" button

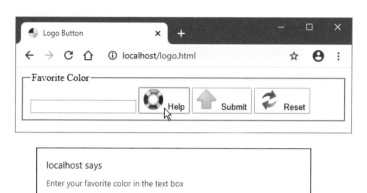

You can specify a default value for a text input to the **value** attribute of its **<input>** tag.

7 Enter a color in the text box, then click the reset logo button to clear the text box

8 Enter a color in the text box again, then submit the form

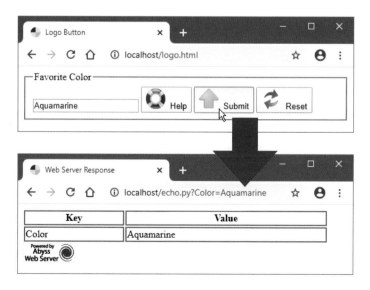

Select Options

An HTML form can provide a select option list, from which the user can select one option to include its associated data for submission to the server.

A select option list is created using **<select> </select>** tags. The opening **<select>** tag must include a **name** attribute specifying a list name. The **<select>** element encloses **<option> </option>** tags that define each option. Each opening **<option>** tag must include a **value** attribute specifying an option value. When the form is submitted, the list name and the selected option value are sent to the server as a name=value pair.

Optionally, one **<option>** tag may also include a boolean **selected** attribute to automatically select that option, and the **<option>** elements may be grouped by enclosure in **<optgroup> </optgroup>** tags. The opening **<optgroup>** tag may specify an option group name to a **label** attribute.

A select option list will normally appear as a single-line dropdown list unless a **size** attribute is included in the **<select>** tag to specify the number of rows to be visible:

select.html

1 Create an HTML document with a form element containing a submit button
```
<form method="GET" action="http://localhost/echo.py" >

<!-- Select option lists to go here. -->

<p>
<input type="submit">
</p>

</form>
```

2 Now, in the form element, insert a fixed height select option list with one option automatically selected
```
<select name="HTML List Type Selector One" size="4">

<optgroup label="List Type 1">
<option value="UL">Unordered List</option>
<option value="OL" selected>Ordered List</option>
<option value="DL">Description List</option>
</optgroup>

</select>
```

3 Next, in the form element, insert a dropdown select option list with one option automatically selected
<select name="HTML List Type Selector Two"**>**

<optgroup label="List Type 2"**>**
<option value="UL"**>Unordered List</option>**
<option value="OL"**>Ordered List</option>**
<option value="DL" selected**>Description List</option>**
</optgroup>

</select>

4 Save the HTML document in the Abyss **htdocs** folder, then open it in your browser

5 Open the dropdown list and submit the form to see the default option values get submitted

Always include a **selected** attribute to automatically select one option in each option list – to provide a default choice.

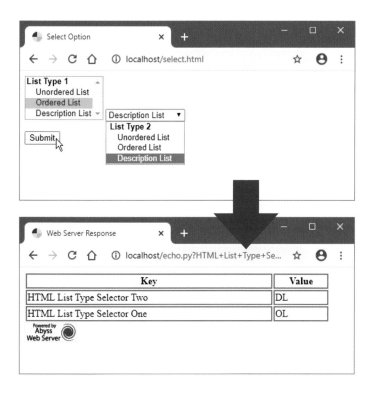

Datalist Options

A simple "autocomplete" feature can be provided for a text **<input>** using a **<datalist> </datalist>** element to enclose a number of pre-defined **<option>** values. The user may choose any one of the options, or enter text directly into the input field. In order to associate the **<input>** field with the list, the **<datalist>** tag must include an **id** attribute to specify a list name. The same name must then be specified to a **list** attribute within the **<input>** tag to create the association. The **<input>** tag must also include a name attribute to send to the server as usual.

datalist.html

The key=value pair submitted to the server is the specified list name and the input value selected from the options or entered directly by the user.

1 Create an HTML document with a form element containing a submit button
```
<form method="GET" action="http://localhost/echo.py">
```

```
<!-- Form data list and input field to go here. -->
```

```
<p><input type="submit" value="Submit Form"></p>
</form>
```

2 Next, insert a data list of pre-defined options with a specified **id** name
```
<datalist id="browsers">
```

```
<option value="Google Chrome">
<option value="Firefox">
<option value="Internet Explorer">
<option value="Opera">
<option value="Safari">
<option value="Microsoft Edge">
```

```
</datalist>
```

3 Now, insert a label that contains text and an input field that is associated with the data list above
```
<label>
```
Choose your browser from this list:
```
<input list="browsers" name="myBrowser">
</label>
```

4 Save the HTML document in the Abyss **htdocs** folder, then open the web page in your browser

5 Select the input field to see the pre-defined options appear in a dropdown list

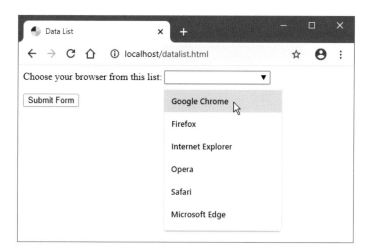

Hot tip

You may need to double-click the input field to override your browser's own autocomplete suggestions.

6 Select any option from the dropdown list, or type your own text into the input field to create a value

7 Submit the form to send the input field name and your chosen value to the server

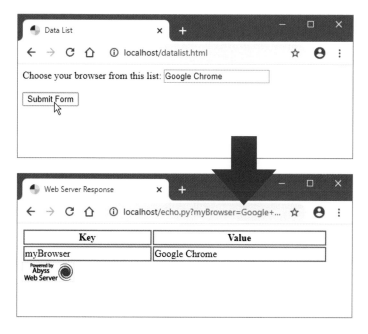

Label Controls

Text that is to be associated with an HTML form control can be enclosed between **<label>** **</label>** tags. The opening **<label>** tag can include a **for** attribute to specify the value assigned to the control's **id** attribute to make the association.

Alternatively, the **<label>** element can simply enclose both the text and the control element to make the association. This allows styling to be applied to the entire label – including the text and control. Often this is useful to distinguish the control associated with particular text.

Additionally, each form control element may include a **tabindex** attribute to specify its tabbing order within the document as a unique value between 0 and 32,767. Using the tab key, the user can then navigate through the document starting at the lowest **tabindex** value and proceeding through successively higher values:

label.html

Hot tip

A form "control" is any **<input>**,**<button>**, or **<textarea>** element. A **tabindex** attribute can be included in these tags and also in any **<a>**, **<area>**, **<object>**, or **<select>** tag.

1 Create an HTML document with a form element containing a fieldset with a legend
```
<form method="GET" action="http://localhost/echo.py">
<fieldset> <legend>Toolbox</legend>
<!-- Form Controls to go here. -->
</fieldset>
</form>
```

2 Now, in the fieldset, insert labels that each contain text and a checkbox with a specified tab order
```
<label>Hammer
<input type="checkbox" name="Toolbox"
       value="Hammer" tabindex="2" checked></label>
<label>Screwdriver
<input type="checkbox" name="Toolbox"
       value="Screwdriver" tabindex="3" ></label>
<label>Wrench
<input type="checkbox" name="Toolbox"
       value="Wrench" tabindex="4" checked></label>
<label>Drill
<input type="checkbox" name="Toolbox"
       value="Drill" tabindex="5"></label>
<label>Saw
<input type="checkbox" name="Toolbox"
       value="Saw" tabindex="6" checked></label>
```

3 Next, insert a logo submit button – in first tab place
```
<button type="submit" tabindex="1">
<img src="label-tools.png" alt="Tools">Submit</button>
```

4 Save the HTML document in the Abyss **htdocs** folder, then open it in your browser to see the text-control association is unclear

5 Edit the HTML document to add a class attribute to each alternate label tag for styling purposes
<label class="hilite">

6 Add a style sheet with a rule to distinguish the labels
<style>
label.hilite { background : Red ; color : White ; }
</style>

7 Save the HTML document again, then open the web page to see that the text-control association is now clear. Use the tab key to move between controls and the space bar to select checkboxes, then submit the form

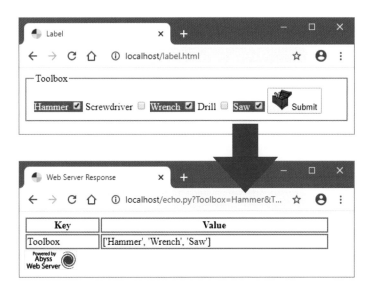

Summary

- HTML forms submit data to the web server as key=value pairs for processing by a specified server-side script.

- All form component elements are enclosed between **<form>** **</form>** tags, which must include an **action** attribute, to specify the URL of the processing script, and a **method** attribute to specify the submission method as **GET** or **POST**.

- Each **<input>** tag's **type** attribute specifies its component type, such as "text", "password", "checkbox", "radio", etc.

- An **<input>** tag can include **name** and **value** attributes to specify data for submission as a key=value pair.

- An **<input>** tag can enforce its completion by including the **required** keyword, but many automatically prohibit submission if the user enters a value that is not permitted.

- A multi-line text field is created by **<textarea>** **</textarea>** tags that require **rows** and **cols** attributes to specify its size.

- Radio button and checkbox inputs only submit their **name** and **value** attribute data if they are checked.

- Forms can contain "hidden" elements that allow static or script-generated data to be submitted to the server for processing.

- When a form is to upload files, the **<form>** tag must include an **enctype** attribute specifying encoding as "multipart/form-data".

- A form may be submitted by a regular submit **<input>** element, by an image **<input>** element, or by a **<button>** element.

- Logo images can be added to the button face by enclosing an **<img>** element between **<button>** **</button>** tags.

- An option list is created by enclosing a number of **<option>** elements between **<select>** **</select>** tags.

- Option lists can be enclosed between **<optgroup>** **</optgroup>** tags that can specify an option group name to a **label** attribute.

- An **<input>** tag can include a **list** attribute to associate it with the **id** of a **<datalist>** element to provide pre-defined options.

- Each form control can be enclosed between **<label>** **</label>** tags to visually group them with text for styling purposes.

8 Get Started in CSS

Meet CSS

Cascading Style Sheets (CSS) is a language used to control the presentation of elements within HyperText Markup Language (HTML) documents. Presentation is specified by "styles" that may be assigned "inline" to HTML element **style** attributes, or by "rules" within **<style> </style>** tags in the HTML document's head section, or as rules within separate style sheets. Each style rule selects specified elements then applies specified styles to them.

CSS was created by the World Wide Web Consortium (W3C) to regain control of document markup as HTML grew from the initial few "tags" that merely defined the structural elements of a document – headings, paragraphs, hyperlinks, lists, etc. As further tags were added controlling images, text color, font size and background color, it became recognized that the source code of many web pages often contained a great deal of markup for very little actual content.

The W3C offered a solution to regain control of document markup by separating their structural and presentational aspects. HTML tags would continue to control the structure but presentational aspects would now be controlled by "style rules" written in the Cascading Style Sheets (CSS) language. Besides distinguishing between structural and presentational aspects of a document, the CSS solution brings these additional benefits:

The W3C is an international consortium whose members work together to develop web standards. The CSS home page can be found on the W3C website at www.w3.org/Style/CSS

- **Easier maintenance** – a single style sheet can control multiple HTML documents, so changing appearance across an entire website is possible by editing just one style sheet.

- **Smaller file sizes** – removal of all presentational markup from HTML produces smaller files, which download faster.

- **Greater control** – margins, borders, padding, background color and background images to any HTML element, and the appearance of certain parts of the interface, such as the cursor, can now be specified.

The latest CSS specification (CSS3) is divided into modules that allow enhancements such as rounded borders, drop-shadows, gradient color-fills and animation effects – these and more are demonstrated by example in this book.

...cont'd

The term "Cascading" in CSS describes the manner in which style rules can fall from one style sheet to another. The cascade determines which style rule will have precedence over others and be the one applied to the selected HTML element.

There are three basic types of style sheet that can specify style rules to be applied to HTML elements:

- **Browser (default) style sheet** – browsers employ an intrinsic set of style rules that they apply to all web pages by default. These vary slightly between different browsers but all have common features such as black text and blue hyperlinks.

- **User style sheet** – some browsers allow the user to specify their own appearance preferences, which effectively creates a custom style sheet that overrides the browser's default style sheet.

- **Author style sheet** – where the HTML document specifies a style sheet created by the web page author, the browser will apply the style rules it contains, overriding both the user style sheet and the default browser style sheet.

CSS is the universally accepted style sheet language that is recognized by all modern web browsers.

167

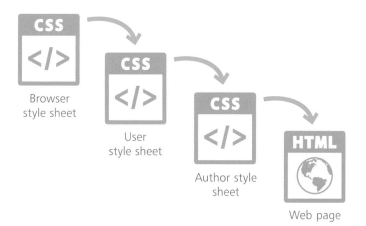

Browser style sheet

User style sheet

Author style sheet

HTML

Web page

Final precedence of style rules that target the same element is determined by their "specificity" weight – see pages 180-181.

So the cascade means that the browsers will typically apply the style rules in an author style sheet, if present, otherwise it will apply the style rules in a user style sheet, if present, otherwise it will apply the style rules in the browser's style sheet by default.

Create Rules

In CSS each style rule is comprised of two main parts:

1 **Selector** – specifying which element/s of the HTML document are the target of that rule.

2 **Declaration Block** – specifying how properties of the selected target element should be styled.

A style rule (or "style rule set") begins with the selector, followed by the declaration block within a pair of curly brackets (braces). The braces contain one or more declarations that each specify a property and a valid value for that property, as in this example:

Typically, the selector targets (selects) a particular HTML element for styling – such as all **<h1>** heading elements in the document using the style rules example above.

Hot tip

The **background** property is a "shorthand" property for **background-color** and several other CSS properties that are described on page 184.

The declaration block in the example above contains two declarations to specify the foreground and background colors of the selected target elements. The CSS **color** property is assigned a **Blue** value – so each **<h1>** heading element will have blue foreground text. Similarly, the CSS **background** property is assigned a **Yellow** value – so each **<h1>** heading element will have a yellow background.

Notice how the CSS declaration uses a : colon character to assign a value to a property. Notice also that each declaration is terminated by a ; semicolon character.

Strictly speaking, the final declaration in the declaration block does not need to be terminated by a semicolon but most web page authors prefer to habitually terminate all CSS declarations – so they need not remember to add a separating semicolon when adding further declarations to an existing style rule set.

...cont'd

1 When creating a new CSS style rule, the author must initially specify a selector to target the HTML element to which the rule will be applied – the CSS selector is everything that appears before the opening brace of the declaration block
h1

2 Next, the declaration block must be created by adding a pair of braces after the selector
h1 {   }

3 Now, a declaration can be inserted within the declaration block to assign a value to a property
h1 { color : Blue ; }

4 A second declaration can then be added within the declaration block, separated from the first by a semicolon
h1 { color : Blue ; background : Yellow ; }

5 The style rule set is now complete but can also be applied to another HTML element by extending the selector to become a comma-separated list
h1, h2 { color : Blue ; background : Yellow ; }

6 Further style rule sets can then be added below the first style rule set to target other elements
h1, h2   { color : Blue ; background : Yellow ; }
p   { color : Red ; }

rules.html

Whitespace (spaces, tabs, line feeds, and carriage returns) is permitted within style rules to allow the author to format the style rules to their own preference.

169

Style rule sets with fewer than four declarations are written on a single line, otherwise they are written across multiple lines for clarity – typically the selector and **{** opening brace will appear on the first line, followed by declarations on individual lines, then the **}** closing brace on the final line. Code is listed in this book more concisely formatted due to limited page space.

In the browser window:

Rules × +

← → C ⌂ G rules.html

Heading styled by CSS

Sub-heading styled by CSS

Paragraph styled by CSS

Apply Rules

A style sheet is simply a collection of style rules to be applied to an HTML document. An internal style sheet can be created by inserting the style rules between **<style>** and **</style>** tags in the head section of the HTML document.

Additionally, the head section of each HTML document should include a **<meta>** tag to set up the "viewport" for the page. This tag determines the visible area of the web page to suit the device on which the page is being viewed, and looks exactly like this:

<meta name="viewport"
      content="width=device-width, initial-scale=1.0" >

- The **width=device-width** part sets the width of the page to match the screen-width of the viewing device.

- The **initial-scale=1.0** part sets the initial zoom level of the browser to 100% when the web page is first loaded.

apply.html

The viewport's <meta> tag does not need to be spread across two lines. It is shown like that here due to space constraints.

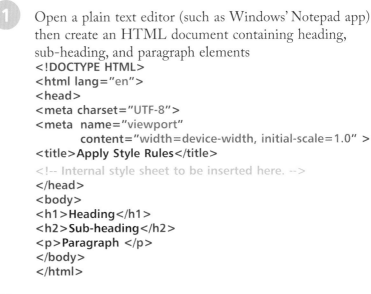

1. Open a plain text editor (such as Windows' Notepad app) then create an HTML document containing heading, sub-heading, and paragraph elements

```
<!DOCTYPE HTML>
<html lang="en">
<head>
<meta charset="UTF-8">
<meta  name="viewport"
        content="width=device-width, initial-scale=1.0" >
<title>Apply Style Rules</title>
<!-- Internal style sheet to be inserted here. -->
</head>
<body>
<h1>Heading</h1>
<h2>Sub-heading</h2>
<p>Paragraph </p>
</body>
</html>
```

2. In the document's head section, insert an internal style sheet containing style rules for the heading element

```
<style>
h1      { color : Blue ;  background : Yellow ; }
</style>
```

3. Save the HTML file then open it in your web browser to see the internal style sheet rules applied to the heading

...cont'd

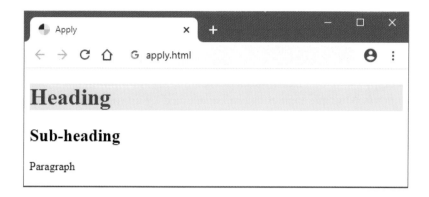

Style rules can also be applied by assigning "inline" properties and values to the **style** attribute of an element:

4 Edit the sub-heading tag to add an inline rule set
`<h2 style="color : White ; background : Green ;" >`

Style rules can also be applied from an external style sheet:

5 Open a plain text editor, then type the style rules below and save it as an external style sheet named "external.css"
`p { color : Yellow ; background : Red ; }`

6 Edit the HTML file to link the external style sheet by inserting this tag in the document's head section
`<link rel="stylesheet" href="external.css" type="text/css">`

7 Save the HTML file then reopen it in your web browser to see the inline and external style sheet rules applied

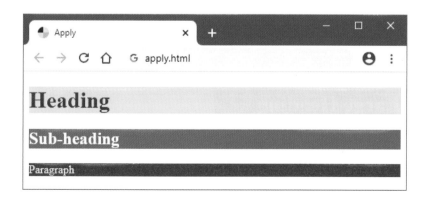

Inline rules may override rules specified by other style sheets, as inline rules are the last to be applied by the browser.

external.css

External style sheets are great to maintain consistent styles across multiple web pages, so authors can change a single rule that will be instantly applied across all pages. Internal style sheets are used by most examples in this book so that each HTML document is a standalone example.

Select Type

The selector part of a style rule selects elements in an HTML document to be styled according to the values specified in that rule's declaration block.

A "type" selector selects all elements in the page that match the selector. Multiple elements can be selected by a type selector that specifies a comma-separated list of element types.

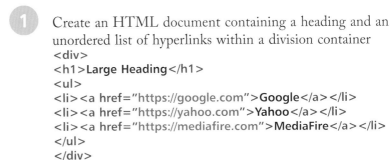

type.html

1 Create an HTML document containing a heading and an unordered list of hyperlinks within a division container
```
<div>
<h1>Large Heading</h1>
<ul>
<li><a href="https://google.com">Google</a></li>
<li><a href="https://yahoo.com">Yahoo</a></li>
<li><a href="https://mediafire.com">MediaFire</a></li>
</ul>
</div>
```

2 Add a style sheet with a style rule setting the width of the container element at half the page width
```
<style>
div { width : 50% ; }
</style>
```

3 Add style rules setting the background color of all hyperlinks, the heading, and list elements
```
a { background : Yellow ; }
h1, ul { color: White ; background : Blue ; }
```

Beware

Remember that there must be a comma between the element types in a selector targeting multiple element types.

4 Save the HTML file then open the web page in a browser to see the elements styled by type selectors

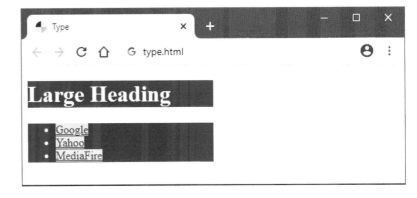

...cont'd

The CSS * universal selector can be used to select elements of all types within an HTML document – as if it was a selector listing all element types as a comma-separated list:

5 Add a style rule with a universal selector to make all text italic, then save the HTML file again and refresh the browser to see both heading and list text become italic
`* { font-style : italic ; }`

Hot tip

You will discover many more CSS font properties in Chapter 10 of this book.

The * universal selector can also be used to select elements of any type contained within a specified element type:

6 Add a style rule with a universal selector to add a 2-pixel wide border around all elements within the "div" container, then save the HTML file once more and refresh the browser to see borders around the elements
`div * { border : 2px solid Red ; }`

Don't forget

The **div *** selector selects elements of all types within the div container, but not the **<div>** element itself.

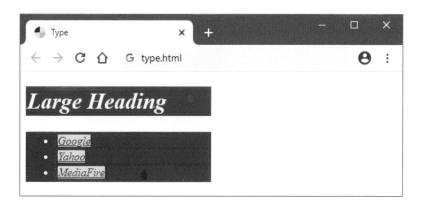

Select Class

As an alternative to selecting elements by type, a class selector can select HTML elements that contain a **class** attribute that has been assigned a value matching the selector. The class selector begins with a . period character followed by the **class** value to match. This is especially useful to apply the style rule across a number of specific elements of different type.

Additionally, a class selector can be combined with a type selector to select specific instances of a class. In this case, the selector first specifies the element type, followed by a . period character and the **class** value to match:

class.html

1. Create an HTML document containing a paragraph and two spanned words – which all have a common **class** value
   ```
   <p class="frame">You can fool all the people
   <span class="frame">some</span> of the time, and
   <span class="frame">some</span> of the people all the
   time, but you cannot fool all the people all the time.</p>
   ```

2. Add a style sheet with a style rule drawing red borders around each element using the **class** value
   ```
   <style>
   .frame { border : 2px solid Red ; }
   </style>
   ```

3. Now, add a style rule overriding the previous one for the paragraph element only – to draw a blue border around the paragraph and to set its width
   ```
   p.frame { border : 2px solid Blue ; width : 50% ; }
   ```

4. Save the HTML document then open the web page in a browser to see elements styled by the class selectors

Hot tip

If two rules select the same element, the lower rule in the style sheet will be applied. But it doesn't matter in which order these rules appear in the style sheet. The class selector that is combined with the type selector will be applied as it is more specific. See page 180 to discover how specificity is calculated.

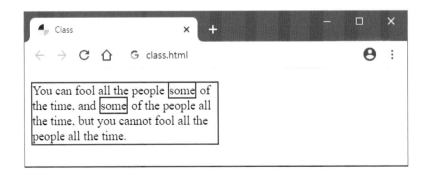

Select Identity

Similar to a class selector, an identity selector can select HTML elements that contain an **id** attribute that has been assigned a value matching the selector. The identity selector begins with a **#** hash character followed by the **id** value to match. This is mostly useful to apply the style rule to one specific element, as each **id** attribute value must be unique within the HTML document.

Optionally, an identity selector can be combined with a type selector simply to identify the element type. In this case, the selector first specifies the element type, followed by a hash character and the **id** value to match:

1   Create an HTML document containing a paragraph and two spanned phrases – which all have a unique **id** value

```
<p id="para1">You may only be someone
<span id="span1">in the world</span><br>
but to someone else you may
<span id="span2">be the world</span></p>
```

identity.html

2   Add a style sheet with style rules painting colored backgrounds behind the text in each **span** element

```
<style>
#span1 { color : White ; background : Red ; }
#span2 { color : White ; background : Lime ; }
</style>
```

3   Now, add a style rule to paint a colored background behind the rest of the paragraph and to set its width

```
p#para1 { background : Yellow ; width : 70% ; }
```

4   Save the HTML document then open the web page in a browser to see elements styled by the identity selectors

175

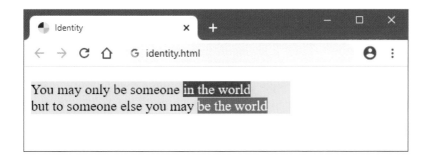

Select Relatives

In addition to selecting target elements by type, class or identity (as described on pages 172-175) CSS allows selectors to be combined to select elements relative to other elements in the HTML document. These "combinators" provide four options:

Descendant Selector (*space*)

This selects all elements that are descendants of a parent element. The CSS selector first specifies the parent element, then a space, followed by the descendant element. For example, to select all **<p>** paragraph elements within a **<div>** division element <u>at any level</u> of descendancy:

div p { }

Child Selector (>)

This selects all elements that are children of a parent element. The CSS selector first specifies the parent element, then a > angled bracket character, followed by the child element. For example, to select all **<p>** paragraph elements whose <u>direct parent</u> is a **<div>** division element:

div > p { }

Adjacent Sibling Selector (+)

This selects all elements that are adjacent siblings immediately following a parent element. The CSS selector first specifies the parent element, then a + plus character, followed by the sibling element. For example, to select all **<p>** paragraph elements that are placed <u>immediately after</u> each **<div>** division element:

div + p { }

General Sibling Selector (~)

This selects all elements that are siblings immediately following a parent element. The CSS selector first specifies the parent element, then a ~ tilde character, followed by the sibling element. For example, to select all **<p>** paragraph elements that <u>follow</u> a **<div>** division element:

div ~ p { }

A child selector will target all child elements of the parent – even if there are other element levels between them.

Sibling elements must have the same parent. Adjacent siblings must immediately follow the parent element, but general siblings are all those contained directly within the parent.

...cont'd

1 Create an HTML document containing a heading, several divisions and paragraphs, plus an aside element

```
<h3>Heading</h3>
<div>Content</div> <div>More content</div>

<div>   <p>Para 1</p> <p>Para 2</p>
        <aside> <p>Para 3</p> </aside>
</div>
```

relative.html

2 Add a style sheet with style rules selecting all paragraphs, and only the division element that immediately follows the heading element

```
<style>
div p { color : White ; background : Blue ; }
h3 + div { background : Yellow ; }
</style>
```

You can specify more than one descendant to further refine a descendant selector, such as **div p span { }**

3 Save the HTML document then open the web page in a browser to see elements styled by the relative selectors

Adjacent sibling

177

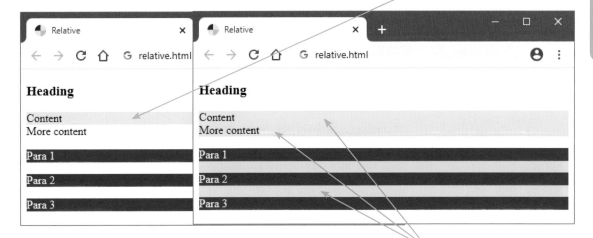

General siblings

4 Edit the style rules to select only paragraphs whose direct parent is a division element, and all division elements that follow the heading element

```
div > p { color : White ; background : Blue ; }
h3 ~ div { background : Yellow ; }
```

5 Save the HTML document once more, then refresh the browser to see the changes

Select Attributes

In addition to selecting target elements by type, class, identity or by relationship (as described on pages 172-177) CSS selectors can target HTML elements that have specific attributes or particular attribute values. Attribute selectors have seven options:

Attribute Name Selector [*attribute*]

This selects all elements that have a specified attribute, by stating an element followed by an attribute name in [ ] brackets:

ol[*attribute*]

Attribute Value Selector [*attribute="value"*]

This selects all elements that have a specified attribute and a specified value, stated within the [ ] brackets:

li[class=*"value"*]

Attribute Value Item Selector [*attribute~="value"*]

This selects all elements that have a specified attribute and a list of values that contain a specified word:

li[class~=*"item"*]

Attribute First Word Selector [*attribute|="value"*]

This selects all elements that have a specified attribute and a value that begins with a specified word:

li[class|=*"word"*]

Attribute Substring Selector [*attribute*="value"*]

This selects all elements that have a specified attribute and a value that includes a specified substring anywhere in a value or list:

li[class*=*"substring"*]

Attribute First Substring Selector [*attribute^="value"*]

This selects all elements that have a specified attribute and a value that begins with a specified substring anywhere in a value or list:

li[class^=*"substring"*]

Attribute Final Substring Selector [*attribute$="value"*]

This selects all elements that have a specified attribute and a value that ends with a specified substring anywhere in a value or list:

li[class$=*"substring"*]

Beware

The first word selector will only select the element if the attribute value is a single whole word or hyphenated – for example, selecting **[class="top"]** with values of "topcat", or "top-cat".

1 Create an HTML document containing an ordered list in which all elements include attributes

```
<ol id="list">
<li class="reptile">Alligator</li>
<li class="domestic animal">Dog</li>
<li class="animal wild">Tiger</li>
<li class="cat-family">Lion</li>
<li class="sea fish">Barracuda</li>
<li class="topcat">Cartoon</li>
<li class ="domestic bird">Budgerigar</li>
</ol>
```

attribute.html

2 Add a style sheet with a style rule that selects the list element by its attribute

```
<style>
ol[ id ]  { border : 2px solid Red ; }
</style>
```

3 Now, add style rules that select all the list items by their attribute values

```
li[class="reptile"]      { background : Red ; }
li[class~="animal"]      { background : Blue ; }
li[ class|="cat" ]       { background : Green ; }
li[class*="fi"]          { background : Yellow ; }
li[class^="top"]         { background : Orange ; }
li[class$="ird"]         { background : Purple ; }
```

The value specified to the three substring selectors does not need to be a whole word.

4 Save the HTML document then open the web page in a browser to see elements styled by the attribute selectors

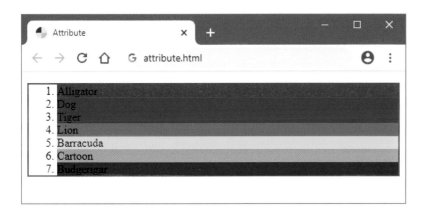

Weigh Importance

Where more than one style rule targets properties of the same element, the CSS cascade evaluates their importance by examining their selector's "specificity" – to consider how specifically each one targets the element to determine their relative importance.

There are four categories that define the importance of a selector. These are, in descending order of importance, as follows:

- **Inline:** a style rule declared to the **style** attribute directly within an element – for example, **style="color:White;"**

- **Identity:** a selector that targets the **id** attribute of an element – for example, **h2#header**

- **Class, Attribute:** a selector that targets the **class** or **[attribute]** of an element – for example, **h2.head**

- **Element:** a selector that targets the type of an element by name – for example, **h2**

The specificity evaluation process awards points for each selector component, which get stored in four weight "registers" for later comparison against the specificity value of conflicting selectors. So the specificity value can be expressed as a comma-separated list – in which **0,0,0,0** is a zero specificity value. The selector component points are awarded like this:

- For inline **style** attribute declarations, add **1,0,0,0**

- For each **id** attribute in the selector, add **0,1,0,0**

- For each **class** attribute in the selector or attribute value selection, add **0,0,1,0**

- For each element (or pseudo-element) in the selector, add **0,0,0,1**

If two selectors have the same specificity weight rating, the "latest rule counts" so the lower rule in the style sheet will be applied.

Embedded style sheet rules take precedence over those in external style sheets, and the * universal selector has a zero specificity value of **0,0,0,0**

Pseudo elements are described on page 230.

1 Create an HTML document containing three headings

```
<h2 style="color:White;" >Element Style</h2>

<h2 id="header">Identity Style</h2>

<h2 class="head">Class Style</h2>
```

specificity.html

2 Add a style sheet with a style rule that selects all heading elements by type

```
<style>
h2 { color : Yellow ; }
</style>
```

Hot tip

The /* */ syntax may be used to add single and multi-line comments within a CSS style sheet.

3 Now, add style rules that each target the heading elements' background property in different ways

```
h2        { background : Red ; }     /* 0,0,0,1 */
body h2 { background : Blue ; }      /* 0,0,0,2 */

#header   { background : Green ; }    /* 0,1,0,0 */
h2#header { background : Red ; }      /* 0,1,0,1 */

h2.head        { background : Red ; }   /* 0,0,1,1 */
body h2.head { background : Green ; }  /* 0,0,1,2 */
```

4 Save the HTML document then open the web page in a browser to see the elements styled after considering specificity to rate their importance

Hot tip

See that the first heading's color is applied from the inline declaration – overriding the type selector in the style sheet. Each heading's background is applied by the rule with most weight points.

181

Paint Colors

Web browsers recognize all the color names listed in these tables. You can use these names in CSS rules to set the color of HTML elements. The names are not case-sensitive so they may also be written in all lowercase letters – for example, **background : aqua ;**

Colors can also be written as the Red, Green, Blue components that make up the color – for example, the color red is **rgb(255, 0, 0)**. Alternatively, colors can be written as hexadecimal numbers – for example, the color red is hexadecimal **#FF0000**, which is Red **FF** (decimal 255), **00** (decimal 0) Green, and **00** (decimal 0) Blue.

AliceBlue	AntiqueWhite	Aqua
Aquamarine	Azure	Beige
Bisque	Black	BlanchedAlmond
Blue	BlueViolet	Brown
BurlyWood	CadetBlue	Chartreuse
Chocolate	Coral	CornflowerBlue
Cornsilk	Crimson	Cyan
DarkBlue	DarkCyan	DarkGoldenRod
DarkGray	DarkGreen	DarkKhaki
DarkMagenta	DarkOliveGreen	DarkOrange
DarkOrchid	DarkRed	DarkSalmon
DarkSeaGreen	DarkSlateBlue	DarkSlateGray
DarkTurquoise	DarkViolet	DeepPink
DeepSkyBlue	DimGray	DodgerBlue
FireBrick	FloralWhite	ForestGreen
Fuchsia	Gainsboro	GhostWhite
Gold	GoldenRod	Gray
Green	GreenYellow	HoneyDew
HotPink	IndianRed	Indigo
Ivory	Khaki	Lavender
LavenderBlush	LawnGreen	LemonChiffon
LightBlue	LightCoral	LightCyan

LightGoldenRodYellow	LightGray	LightGreen
LightPink	LightSalmon	LightSeaGreen
LightSkyBlue	LightSlateGray	LightSteelBlue
LightYellow	Lime	LimeGreen
Linen	Magenta	Maroon
MediumAquamarine	MediumBlue	MediumOrchid
MediumPurple	MediumSeaGreen	MediumSlateBlue
MediumSpringGreen	MediumTurquoise	MediumVioletRed
MidnightBlue	MintCream	MistyRose
Moccasin	NavajoWhite	Navy
OldLace	Olive	OliveDrab
Orange	OrangeRed	Orchid
PaleGoldenRod	PaleGreen	PaleTurquoise
PaleVioletRed	PapayaWhip	PeachPuff
Peru	Pink	Plum
PowderBlue	Purple	RebeccaPurple
Red	RosyBrown	RoyalBlue
SaddleBrown	Salmon	SandyBrown
SeaGreen	SeaShell	Sienna
Silver	SkyBlue	SlateBlue
SlateGray	Snow	SpringGreen
SteelBlue	Tan	Teal
Thistle	Tomato	Turquoise
Violet	Wheat	White
WhiteSmoke	Yellow	YellowGreen

Hot tip

Colors can also be written as their Hue, Saturation, Lightness values – for example, the color full red is specified as **hsl(0, 100%, 50%)**

Hot tip

Optionally, a fourth Alpha value can be added to the color specification to determine the opacity of the color – for example, a half-transparent full red color specified as **rgba(255, 0, 0, 0.5)** or as **hsla(0, 100%, 50%, 0.5)**

Set Backgrounds

Just as each element can have a background color specified to its **background** property, a background image can be specified to its **background** property, as a **url(*filename*)** value. Here, the *filename* is the path to an image file – for example, **background : url(bg.png) ;**

The **background** property can also be used to specify both a background image and color as space-separated values – for example, **background : LightBlue url(bg.png) ;**
Background images are placed on a layer above the background's color layer so specifying an image with transparent areas will allow the background color to shine through the image.

Any specified background image will normally be positioned at the top-left corner of the element and the browser will, by default, repeatedly "tile" the image row-by-row across the element area. This behavior can be modified by assigning different values to the **background** property where values of **repeat-x** restricts the tiling pattern to one horizontal row and **repeat-y** restricts the tiling pattern to one vertical column. Tiling can also be prevented by assigning a **no-repeat** value so that a single copy of the image appears at the top-left corner of the content box.

The position of a background image can be specified to the **background** property to control its horizontal position with values of **left**, **center**, and **right**, and to control its vertical position with values of **top**, **center**, and **bottom**. Combining horizontal and vertical values together with a **no-repeat** value lets you set a single version of the image at a given position within the element area – for example, **background : url(bg.png) no-repeat top right ;**

The **background** property has a **scroll** value by default that relates to the viewport, not the element, so by default a background image will scroll along with the page. Should you prefer to attach a background page image, so it does not scroll along with the page, you can specify a **fixed** value to the **background** property so the background image will remain at a specified position relative to the viewport when the page gets scrolled.

All background values can be specified in a space-separated list to the **background** shorthand property, or individually to properties of **background-color, background-image, background-repeat, background-position** and **background-attachment**

When choosing a background image be sure it will not make text content difficult to read.

Use the **background** shorthand property rather than the various individual properties – to keep the style sheet more concise. The list of values should appear in the order in which they are listed here, but optionally any of these values may be omitted.

...cont'd

1 Create an HTML document containing two paragraphs
```
<p class="repeat"></p>
<p class="repeat-y"></p>
```

background.html

2 Add a style sheet with rules that set the dimensions and background properties of each paragraph
```
<style>
p.repeat { width : 384px ; height : 128px ;
 background : LightBlue url( crab.png ) ; }

p.repeat-y { width : 384px ; height : 128px ; background :
 DeepSkyBlue url( crab.png ) repeat-y top right ;  }
</style>
```

3 Now, add a style rule that attaches a background image to the page at a fixed position
```
body { background : url( crab.png )
        no-repeat bottom right fixed ; }
```

crab.png – 64px x 64px
Gray areas are transparent.

4 Save the HTML document, then open the web page in a browser to see the backgrounds – scroll the page to see the fixed page background image

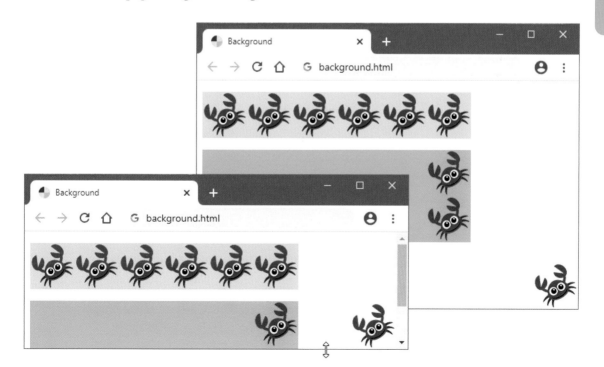

Summary

- CSS is a language provided by the W3C to regain control of markup by separating document structure from presentation.

- The cascade allows style rules to fall from one style sheet to another and determines which style rule will be applied.

- Each style rule comprises a selector and a declaration block.

- Each declaration specifies a property and a value to be applied to that property – separated by a : colon character.

- A style rule set may contain multiple declarations – each terminated by a ; semicolon character.

- Style rules can be specified in an internal style sheet, inline to an HTML element's **style** attribute, or in an external style sheet.

- Type selectors select all elements that match the selector.

- Class selectors select all elements that contain a **class** attribute that has been assigned a value matching the selector.

- Identity selectors select all elements that contain an **id** attribute that has been assigned a value matching the selector.

- Relative selectors are combinators that select elements relative to other elements as descendants, children, or siblings.

- Attribute selectors select elements that have specific attributes or particular attribute values.

- The cascade evaluates the selector's specificity to rate importance by how specifically each one targets the element.

- Color values can be specified by name, hexadecimal value, Red Green Blue value or Hue, Saturation, Lightness value.

- The **background** shorthand property can specify an element's background color, image, repeat, position, and attachment.

9 Manage the Box Model

Recognize Boxes

Content on a web page is displayed in a number of invisible rectangular boxes that are generated by the browser. These content boxes may be either "block level" or "inline".

Block-level content boxes normally have line breaks before and after the box, such as paragraph, heading, and division elements.

Inline content boxes, on the other hand, do not add line breaks but are simply created within lines of content, such as span, emphasis, and hyperlink elements.

Each block-level content box comprises a core content area surrounded by optional areas for padding, border, and margins:

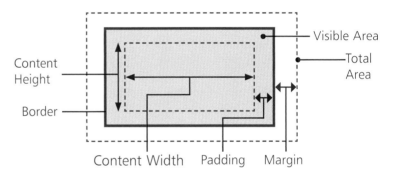

Style rules can specify values for the **padding**, **border**, and **margin** properties to control the appearance of content boxes. These all apply to block-level boxes but some properties, such as **width** and **height**, do not apply to inline boxes. Additionally, the **margin** and **padding** properties of inline boxes only apply to either side of the content – not the areas above and below the content.

When the **padding**, **border**, and **margin** properties all have a zero width, the content box will be the same size as the content area, determined by the dimensions of the content.

Any **padding**, **border**, and **margin** areas that have a non-zero width are added outside the content area, so the content size remains the same but the box size increases.

The **padding** property extends the area around the content and inherits the background color of the content area. The **border** property extends the area around the content and any padding. The **margin** property extends the area around the content, any padding, and any border, with a transparent background.

Content is the area filled by text or images. **Padding** is a transparent area around the content. **Border** surrounds the content and padding. **Margin** is a transparent area outside the border.

...cont'd

1 Create an HTML document with four simple paragraphs, three with assigned class attribute values

```
<p>Content Box</p>
<p class="pad">Content + Padding</p>
<p class="pad bdr">Content + Padding + Border</p>
<p class="pad bdr mgn">
        Content + Padding + Border + Margin</p>
```

box.html

2 Add a style sheet with a rule that sets the background color of the core content area and its width at 300 pixels

```
p { background : MistyRose ; width : 300px ; }
```

3 Next, add a style rule to add padding of 10 pixels around all sides of the content

```
p.pad { padding : 10px ; }
```

4 Now, add a style rule to add a border of 5 pixels around all sides of the padded content area

```
p.bdr { border : 5px solid Tomato ; }
```

5 Finally, add a style rule to add a margin of 20 pixels around all sides of the border

```
p.mgn { margin : 20px ; }
```

6 Save the HTML document then open the web page in a browser to see the content boxes with added padding, borders, and margin

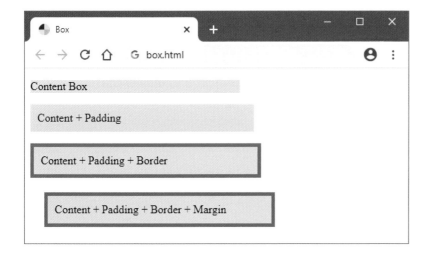

The HTML **<style>** and **</style>** tags are omitted from the steps in all further examples to save book page space. Instructions on how to add style sheets to an HTML document are provided on page 170.

If you specify the width and height of an element you only set the width and height of the content area. You must add any padding, border, and margin areas to calculate the total space occupied by the element. In this case, the total width occupied by the element is **300px** (width) + **20px** (left and right padding) + **10px** (left and right border) + **40px** (left and right margin) = 370 pixels.

Display Inline

A web page relies upon the creation of block-level content boxes, to determine its general layout, and the creation of inline content boxes within the blocks to determine its precise layout.

This places great emphasis on whether an element is considered block-level or inline to determine the display format. Generally, the default display format for each element will be the most appropriate. For example, it's generally desirable to display list items on individual lines in a block-level list.

Don't forget

Assigning a non-default display type to an element only changes the way it gets displayed – in the document tree inline elements are always descendants of block-level elements.

The display format of an element can also be explicitly determined by a style rule that assigns the **block** or **inline** keywords to that element's **display** property. This means that content can be displayed in a different format without changing the HTML tags. For example, list items can be displayed on a single line with a **display : inline ;** declaration.

Additionally, an inline content-box can have its **display** property assigned an **inline-block** value to allow it to be displayed somewhat like a block-level content box. The inline-block still appears inline, as usual, but unlike regular inline content boxes its **width** and **height** properties can be assigned values to control its size.

Hot tip

List items can be made to display horizontally, rather than vertically, if each list item element is made into an inline-block. This is often used to create a navigation bar of horizontal links – see page 248.

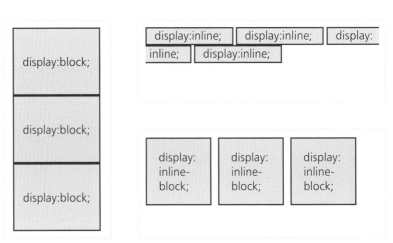

With a **display:inline ;** declaration, top and bottom margins and paddings are not applied – but they are with inline-blocks. Additionally, note that a **display : block ;** declaration will add a line break after the element – but inline-blocks will not.

...cont'd

1 Create an HTML document with three unordered lists

```
<ul class="block">
        <li>Block</li><li>Block</li><li>Block</li></ul>
<ul class="inline" >
        <li>Inline</li><li>Inline</li><li>Inline</li></ul>
<ul class="inline-block" >
<li>Inline Block</li><li>Inline Block</li><li>Inline Block</li>
</ul>
```

display.html

2 Add a style sheet with rules to style each list's border and list item elements

```
ul      { border : 2px solid Tomato ; }
ul > li { background : MistyRose ; margin : 10px ;
          padding : 5px ; width : 100px ; height : 20px ; }
```

3 Now, add style rules to specify the display type for each list's item elements

```
ul.block > li { display : block ; }
ul.inline > li { display : inline ; }
ul.inline-block > li { display : inline-block ; }
```

4 Save the HTML document then open the web page in a browser to see the content displayed in specific formats

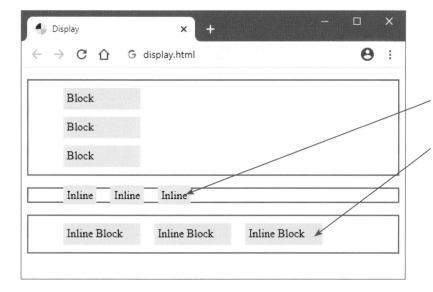

Beware

Inline boxes will not include top and padding or margin values.
Inline Block boxes will include top and padding or margin values.

Define Dimensions

When assigning any non-zero value to a property, the declaration must include a two-letter unit name to specify which unit of measurement to apply. The CSS specification provides the following unit names representing real world measurement:

Unit	Description	Example
in (inches)	American standard unit of length measurement	div { width : 1in ; }
cm (centimeters)	Metric unit of length where 2.54 centimeters is equivalent to 1 inch	div { height : 2.54cm ; }
mm (millimeters)	Metric unit of length (one tenth of one centimeter) where 25.4 millimeters is equivalent to 1 inch	div { height : 25.4mm ; }
pt (points)	Typographical unit of font height where 72 points is equivalent to 1 inch	div { font-size : 12pt ; }
pc (picas)	Typographical unit of font height where 6 picas is equivalent to 1 inch	div { font-size : 2pc ; }

The CSS specification also provides the following unit names representing relative values according to the viewing device:

Unit	Description	Example
em (font size)	Abstract typographical unit of font size where 1em is equivalent to the height of a given font	div { font-size : 12pt ; } (1em = 12pt)
ex (font size)	Abstract typographical unit of font size where 1ex is equivalent to the height of lowercase "x" in a font (often 50% of 1em)	div { font-size : 12pt ; } (1ex = 6pt)
px (pixels)	Abstract unit representing the dots on a computer monitor where there are 1024 pixels on each line when the monitor resolution is 1024x768	div { height : 100px ; }

Don't forget

Zero values can be assigned using just a "0" number – without specifying a unit name.

Hot tip

A percentage value can also specify a relative size – where a value of 50% makes the target element half the size of its containing element.

...cont'd

1 Create an HTML document containing four division elements

```
<div id="absolute">3in x &half;in</div>
<div id="container">400px x 150px
  <div id="percent">50% x 50%</div>
  <div id="relative">20em x 2em</div>
</div>
```

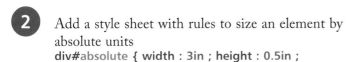

dimensions.html

2 Add a style sheet with rules to size an element by absolute units

```
div#absolute { width : 3in ; height : 0.5in ;
                              background : Tomato ; }
```

3 Next, add rules to size an element by monitor resolution

```
div#container { width : 400px ; height : 150px ;
                              background : MistyRose ; }
```

4 Now, add rules to size an element by percentage

```
div#percent { width : 50% ; height : 50% ;
                              background : Tomato ; }
```

5 Then, add rules to size an element relative to font height

```
div#relative { width : 20em ; height : 2em ;
                              background : LightSalmon ; }
```

6 Save the HTML document then open the web page in a browser to see the element sizes

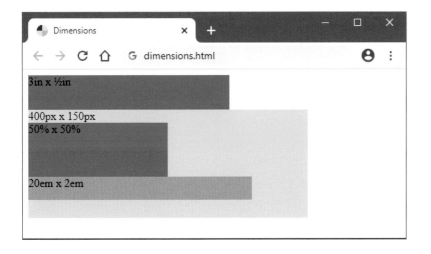

The name of the **em** unit originates from typography, where it represented the width of the letter "M" in the current font set. It is different in CSS though, as it represents the height of the current font. It is often considered good practice to use **em** units for text size wherever possible – for maximum flexibility.

Control Borders

Each content box can have a border comprising **border-width**, **border-color**, and **border-style** properties. A value can be specified to each of these individual properties to apply a uniform border to all four sides of the content box, or a space-separated list of values can be specified to apply different borders to each side:

- When two values are listed, the first is applied to the top and bottom borders.

- When three values are listed, the first is applied to the top border, the second is applied to the left and right borders, and the third is applied to the bottom border.

- When four values are listed, they are applied clockwise to the top, right, bottom, and left borders.

The default **border-width** value is **medium** (a computed value), and the default **border-color** value is inherited from the element's **color** property, but the default **border-style** is **none**. This means that the border will not be visible until a value is assigned – possible **border-style** values are **solid**, **double**, **dotted**, **dashed**, **groove**, **ridge**, **inset**, **outset**, **hidden**, and **none**.

Rather than creating separate style rules for the **border-width**, **border-color**, and **border-style** properties, it is simpler to use the CSS shorthand technique that specifies a value for each of these three properties to a **border** property as a space-separated list. This uniformly styles each side of the content box with a border of the specified width, color, and style. For example, a style rule declaration of **border : 0.5in dotted Red ;** would apply a half-inch wide red dotted border to all four sides of the content box.

If it is desirable to have different styles, the borders on each side of a content box can be individually styled by creating rules for the element's **border-top**, **border-right**, **border-bottom**, and **border-left** properties. The CSS shorthand technique can also be used with these properties to specify a width, color, and style for the individual side as a space-separated list. For example, a style rule declaration of **border-bottom : 0.5in red dotted** would apply a half-inch wide red dotted border to just the bottom side of the content box.

Hot tip

The **outset** border style can be used to create the appearance of a raised button – and the **inset** border style can be used to create the appearance of a depressed button.

1 Create an HTML document containing four paragraphs
```
<p id="no1">Solid - Inherit - Medium</p>
<p id="no2">Top: Dotted - LightSalmon - 0.5em
        <br>Bottom: Dashed - DarkSalmon - 0.5em</p>
<p id="no3">Ridge Double - MistyRose - 1em</p>
<p id="no4">Outset - Tomato - 1em</p>
```

border.html

2 Save the HTML document then create a linked style sheet with rules to add a border that inherits a color
```
p#no1 { color : Tomato ; border : solid ; }
```

3 Next, add rules with shorthand declarations to create a border above and below the content area only
```
p#no2 { border-top : 0.5em dotted LightSalmon ;
        border-bottom : 0.5em dashed DarkSalmon ; }
```

4 Now, add rules creating a border from separate properties
```
p#no3 { border-width : 1em ;
        border-style : ridge double ;
        border-color : MistyRose ; }
```

5 Then, add a rule creating a border on all four sides using the recommended CSS shorthand technique
```
p#no4 { border : 1em outset Tomato ; }
```

6 Save the HTML document then open the web page in a browser to see the borders

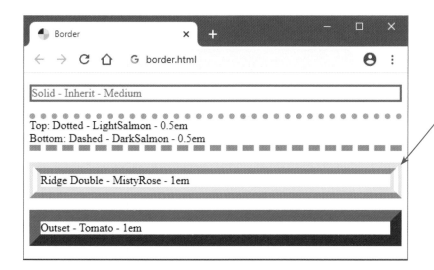

Hot tip

Notice how the browser miters the borders diagonally where they meet – this offers some creative possibilities.

Add Padding

Each content box can have "padding" space added around the core content area by a style rule assigning a value to the **padding** property. A single value can be specified to apply a uniform padding width to all four sides of the content area, or a space-separated list of values can be specified to apply different padding widths to each side:

- When two values are listed, the first is applied to the top and bottom sides and the second is applied to the left and right.

- When three values are listed, the first is applied to the top side, the second is applied to the left and right sides, and the third is applied to the bottom side.

- When four values are listed, they are applied clockwise to the top, right, bottom, and left sides.

The padding area surrounds the core content area and extends to the outer edges of the border area if a border is specified – right up to the beginning of the margin area. The element's background fills the core content area and the padding area, so that any specified background color gets automatically applied to both the core content area and the padding area.

The **padding** property can be specified as a unit value or as a percentage value. When a percentage is specified, the padding width is calculated using the width and height of the containing element – and the padding area size will be adjusted if the size of the containing element gets changed.

Typically, a padding area is specified when adding a border to an element to increase the space between the content and the border.

If it is desirable to have different padding widths on each side of a content box, the padding can be individually styled by creating rules for the element's **padding-top**, **padding-right**, **padding-bottom**, and **padding-left** properties. For example, style rule of **padding-top : 0.5in ; padding-bottom : 0.5in ;** would apply a half-inch padding area to top and bottom sides. Alternatively, the same result can be achieved using the CSS shorthand with a declaration of **padding : 0.5in 0 0.5in 0 ;**

Beware

Setting padding as a percentage may produce undesirable results when the user resizes the browser window – you can specify unit values to avoid this.

Hot tip

The padding width for each side can always be set using the CSS **padding** shorthand by setting sides requiring no padding to zero – always use the shorthand.

1 Create an HTML document containing three paragraphs that each include a span element and are separated by horizontal ruled lines

```
<p>Horizontally
<span id="pad-h">Padded</span> Content.</p> <hr>
<p>Vertically
<span id="pad-v">Padded</span> Content.</p> <hr>
<p>Horizontally and Vertically
<span id="pad-hv">Padded</span> Content.</p>
```

padding.html

2 Add a style sheet with rules to color the paragraph and span elements

```
p { background : LightSalmon ; }
span { background : MistyRose ;
        border : 0.3em dashed Tomato ; }
```

3 Next, add a style rule to add padding to the left and right sides of the first span content box

```
span#pad-h { padding : 0 3em 0 3em ; }
```

4 Now, add a style rule to add padding to the top and bottom sides of the second span content box

```
span#pad-v { padding : 1em 0 1em 0 ; }
```

5 Then, add a style rule to add uniform padding to all sides of the third span element

```
span#pad-hv { padding : 1em ; }
```

6 Save the HTML document then open the web page in a browser to see the added padding

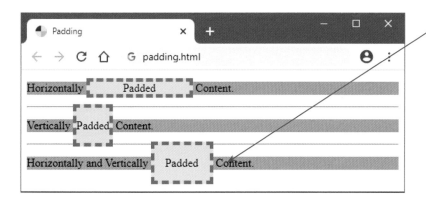

Notice how the background color fills the content area and padding area – extending right up to the outer edge of the border area.

Set Margins

Each content box can have outer transparent "margin" space added around the entire content, padding, and border areas by a style rule assigning a value to the **margin** property. A single value can be specified to apply a uniform margin width to all four sides of the content box, or a space-separated list of values can be specified to apply different margin widths to each side:

- When two values are listed, the first is applied to the top and bottom sides and the second is applied to the left and right.

- When three values are listed, the first is applied to the top side, the second is applied to the left and right sides, and the third is applied to the bottom side.

- When four values are listed, they are applied clockwise to the top, right, bottom, and left sides.

The **margin** property has a default value of zero but in reality the browser applies its own intrinsic default values to allow spacing between elements. For example, heading elements always allow a margin area before a following paragraph element.

The margin width for each side can always be set using the CSS **margin** shorthand by setting sides requiring no margin to zero – always use the shorthand.

The **margin** property can be specified as a unit value, or as a percentage value, or with the **auto** keyword to have the browser compute a suitable margin. When the **auto** keyword is specified to an element's **margin** property, the browser first calculates the distance to the left and right of that element, up to the boundaries of its containing element, then divides the total in half to compute the value of each side margin. For example, applying a **margin : auto ;** rule to a paragraph element of 80px width, that is contained within an outer division element of 400px width, the browser divides the total difference of 320px in half then applies 160px wide margins to each side of the paragraph element – so it gets positioned centrally within the containing division element.

If it is desirable to have different margin widths on each side of a content box, the margin can be individually styled by creating rules for the element's **margin-top**, **margin-right**, **margin-bottom**, and **margin-left** properties. For example, style rule declarations of **margin-top : 0.5in ; margin-bottom : 0.5in ;** would apply a half-inch margin area to top and bottom sides. Alternatively, the same result can be achieved using the CSS shorthand with a declaration of **margin : 0.5in 0 0.5in 0 ;**

1 Create an HTML document with an outer division element that contains three inner division elements
```
<div class="container"> Centered Block
<div class="zero">Default Position</div>
<div class="center">Centered Block</div>
<div class="offset">Offset Block</div>
</div>
```

margin.html

2 Add a style sheet with rules to center the outer division within the page, and create a border around the division
```
div.container { margin : auto ;
               border : 0.3em dashed Tomato ; }
```

3 Next, add style rules to remove all margins from the first inner division, and to color its background
```
div.zero { margin : 0 ; width : 10em ;
          background : LightSalmon ; }
```

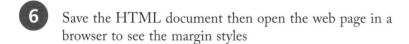

4 Now, add style rules to center the second inner division, to create a border, and to color its background
```
div.center { margin : auto ; border : 0.3em dashed Tomato ;
            width : 10em ; background : MistyRose ; }
```

The ability to automatically compute the margin size is essential for centering content.

5 Then, add style rules to add top and left margins to the third inner division, and to color its background
```
div.offset { margin : 20px 0 0 20px ;
            background : LightSalmon ; }
```

6 Save the HTML document then open the web page in a browser to see the margin styles

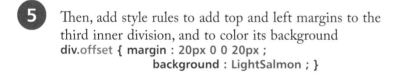

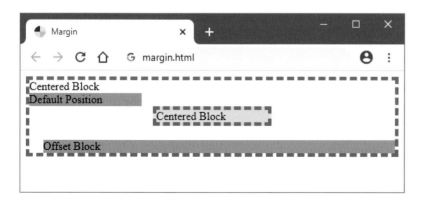

Notice that **margin:auto;** centers the block but not the text within that block. See page 222 for text alignment styles.

Position Boxes

When laying out the element content boxes of a web page, the CSS **position** property has a default value of **static** – representing the normal flow positioning scheme. Assigning a different value to an element's **position** property allows that element's place to move from the normal flow so it can be positioned independently.

Alternatives to the default **static** value can be specified using the **absolute, relative, fixed**, and **sticky** keywords to specify an alternative positioning scheme to that of the normal flow layout.

The **absolute, relative, fixed**, and **sticky** positioning schemes each use one or more of the CSS "offset" properties **top, right, bottom**, and **left**, to define the element's position.

When the position property is specified as **absolute**, the positioning scheme places the element at the specified offset distance from the boundaries of its containing element. For example, an absolutely positioned division element with **top** and **left** values of **100px** will be positioned 100 pixels below and to the right of the boundaries of its containing element.

When the position property is specified as **relative**, the positioning scheme adjusts the position of an element relative to the place it would originally occupy in the normal flow layout. For example, specifying a **top** value of **-18px** moves the selected element up, and specifying a **left** value of **100px** moves it to the right – but crucially, the space occupied by its original layout position is preserved. Applying these relative position values to a span element within a paragraph has this effect:

a repositioned span element

There is   on this line, but it pays no heed to other paragraph content for it is an inline content box.

Notice how the original content is shifted from its normal flow layout position into a newly-created content box positioned at the specified distance relative to its original position. This relative position will be maintained, even when the position of the outer containing element is changed.

So while **absolute** positioning may typically control the position of the outer element, the **relative** positioning scheme is often useful to control the position of nested inner elements.

Don't forget

Absolutely positioned elements and relatively positioned elements move along with the rest of the page when the page gets scrolled.

Beware

Notice how a negative value is used here – these can be used with other properties too but may sometimes produce unexpected results.

1 Create an HTML document with two division elements that each contain a span element
```
<div class="left">
<span>Normal Flow Element</span></div>

<div class="right">
<span class="offset">Relatively Positioned Element
</span></div>
```

position.html

2 Add a style sheet with rules to specify the size of the division elements, and to add borders to all elements
```
div { width : 250px ; height : 100px ; }
div,span { border : 2px solid Tomato ; }
```

3 Next, add style rules to absolutely position the division elements
```
div.left { position : absolute ; top : 20px ; left : 20px ; }
div.right { position : absolute ; top : 80px ; left : 245px ; }
```

4 Now, add style rules to relatively position a span element
```
span.offset { position : relative ; top : 70px ; left : 25px ; }
```

5 Save the HTML document then open the web page in a browser to see the division elements positioned at absolute coordinates on the page, and to see a span positioned relative to the borders of its container

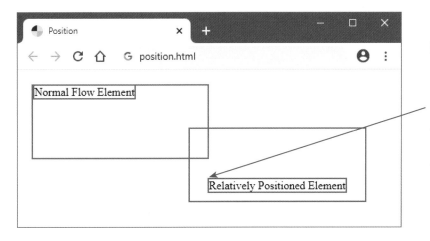

Hot tip

Remember that the position values specify the position of the top-left corner of the target element. Here, it's offset 70 pixels down and 25 pixels to the right.

Fix Positions

A **fixed** positioning scheme, like the **absolute** positioning scheme, completely removes the selected element's content box from the normal flow layout. But unlike **absolute** positioning, where offset values relate to the boundaries of the containing element, in **fixed** positioning the offset values relate to the viewport – the position is relative to the browser window, not to any part of the document.

Usefully, element positions can be fixed to emulate a frame-style interface where some frames remain at a constant position regardless of how the regular page is scrolled. For example, a logo frame could be fixed at a bottom corner of the page so it remains constantly visible even when the page is scrolled.

A **sticky** positioning scheme can also be used to ensure an element remains visible when the user scrolls the page. This initially places an element relative to other elements on the page and maintains this position when the page gets scrolled until it reaches a specified offset position in the viewport. At that point, the element assumes a fixed position and sticks in place. Scrolling back to the specified offset position causes the element to resume its relative positioning.

As with fixed positioning, element positions can be sticky to emulate a frame-style interface. For example, a banner frame could stick at the top of the viewport so it remains constantly visible even when the page is scrolled.

To use the **sticky** positioning scheme you must specify a threshold offset position to at least one of the element's **top**, **bottom**, **left**, or **right** properties, otherwise it will remain relatively positioned when the user scrolls the page.

fixed.html

1 Create an HTML document containing a heading, two divisions, and a tall image
```
<h1>Fixing Elements</h1>
<div class="sticky">Sticky Banner Element</div>
<div class="fixed">Fixed Logo Element</div>
<img src="ruler.png" alt="Tall Ruler">
```

2 Add a style sheet with rules to specify the size and colors of the division elements
```
div { width : 150px ; padding : 10px ;
        background :  Tomato ; color : White ; }
```

3 Next, add style rules to make the first division element stick centered at the top of the page when scrolled
div.sticky { position : sticky ; top : 10px ; margin : auto ; }

4 Now, add style rules to fix the second division element at the bottom right of the page when scrolled
div.fixed { position : fixed ; bottom : 0px ; right : 0px ; }

5 Save the HTML document then open the web page in a browser and scroll the page to see the division elements remain visible

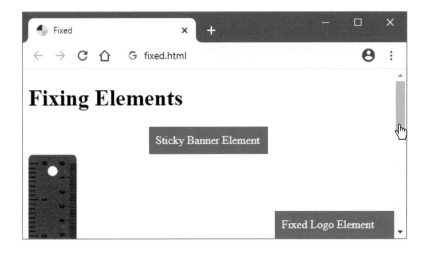

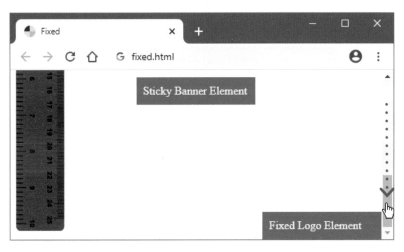

ruler.png – 70px x 525px

Stack Boxes

Changing from the **static** default positioning scheme, by assigning the **absolute** value to the **position** property, allows elements to overlap – stacking one above the other in the same order they are listed in the HTML code.

The stacking order can be explicitly specified, however, in CSS by assigning an integer value to the **z-index** property of each element. The element with the highest value appears uppermost, then beneath that appears the element with the next highest value, and so on.

So the **absolute** positioning scheme allows element position to be precisely controlled in three dimensions using XYZ coordinates – along the X axis with the **left** and **right** offset properties, along the Y axis using the **top** and **bottom** offset properties, and along the Z axis using the **z-index** stacking order property.

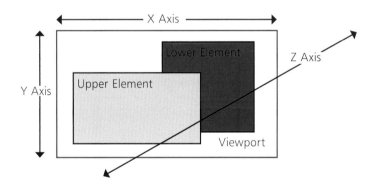

stack.html

Specifying a value to the **z-index** property of stacked elements allows you to control whether elements should appear in front or behind other elements – regardless of the order in which they are listed in the HTML document.

It is often useful to stack elements containing text above an image element to add text labels to the image.

1 Create an HTML document containing three division elements and an image element
```
<div class="container">
<img src="scene.png" alt="Street Scene">
<div class="btm-label">Street Scene</div>
<div class="top=label">Paris, 1966</div>
</div>
```

...cont'd

2 Add a style sheet with rules to position the outer division element at the bottom of a stack

div.container { **position** : absolute ;
           top : 0px ; **left** : 0px ; **z-index** : 0 ; }

3 Next, add rules to position a division element on the next level in the stack

div.top-label { **position** : absolute ; **color** : Red ;
           top : 10px ; **right** : 20px ; **z-index** : 1 ; }

4 Now, add rules to position a division element on the uppermost level in the stack

div.btm-label { **position** : absolute ; **color** : Red ;
           bottom : 10px ; **left** : 220px ; **z-index** : 2 ; }

5 Save the HTML document then open the web page in a browser to see the elements positioned in all three dimensions to add text labels above the image

scene.png
500px x 350px

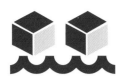

Float Boxes

The CSS **float** property allows a content box to be positioned at the side boundary of its containing element – using the **left** or **right** keywords to specify the preferred side. Typically, this feature is used to flow text around images that have been floated to the side of a containing paragraph element.

You can also explicitly prevent text flowing alongside a floated content box using the CSS **clear** property – specifying **left, right,** or **both** keywords to determine which side must be clear, so that text will begin below the floated content box.

float.html

viper-front.png
150px x 128px

viper-rear.png
155px x 115px

1 Create an HTML document containing three paragraphs and two images
<p>Massive acceleration - the forbidden fruit! It's easy to avoid such unlawful
<img src="viper-front.png" alt="Viper Front">
activities in a normal vehicle. But there is an evil serpent; a Viper that tempts you to take a bite out of the asphalt. With a tasty 500-hp V10 powering a mere 3,300-lb roadster, the Dodge Viper SRT-10 tricks you into playing music with the loud pedal.</p>

<p>This car is too excessive, too epic for most people to use on a daily basis.
<img src="viper-rear.png" alt="Viper Rear">
But for otherwise nice couples who need only two seats this is the car that will shame those who come up against them.</p>

<p class="clear">If you can afford to...
                Buy one. You'll like it.</p>

2 Add a style sheet with a rule to color all paragraph backgrounds
p { background : LightSalmon ; }

3 Next, add style rules to float the first image to the right side of its containing paragraph element and add a border
img[src="viper-front.png"] {
        float : right ; border : 2px dashed Tomato ; }

4 Now, add style rules to float the second image to the left side of its containing paragraph element and add a border
img[src="viper-rear.png"] {
        float : left ; border : 2px dashed Tomato ; }

...cont'd

5 Save the HTML document then open the web page in a browser to see the floated images

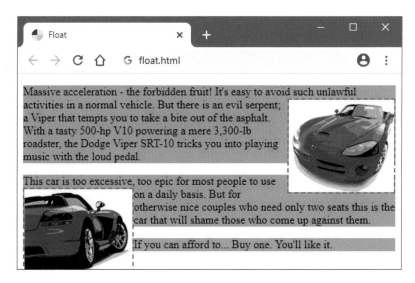

Hot tip

Floated content boxes are not removed from normal flow layout but merely repositioned within it – the space at their original position gets filled with surrounding content.

6 Edit the style sheet to add a rule that prevents the final paragraph flowing alongside the second floated image
p.clear { clear : both ; }

7 Save the HTML document again and refresh the browser to see the final paragraph is now below the second image

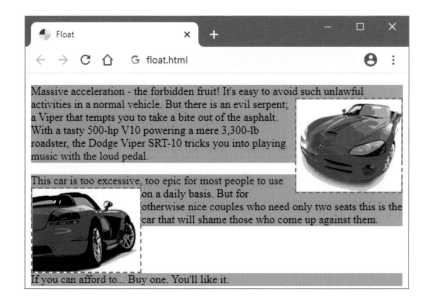

Don't forget

With CSS any element can be floated to the side of its containing element by setting its **float** property.

Handle Overflow

Although CSS provides many controls to specify the precise size and position of content boxes, there is no guarantee that their content will fit neatly within their boundaries in all circumstances. For example, consider the effect of increasing the font size of text content that fits snugly within a block-level content box – the text may then "overflow" outside the box boundaries.

Overflowing content is generally **visible** by default, but the CSS **overflow** property can specify alternative handling behaviors using the **hidden** or **scroll** keywords. With **overflow : hidden ;** the overflowing content will be invisible, but with **overflow : scroll ;** the browser will provide horizontal and vertical scrollbars that the user can use to view the overflowing content.

You can control whether the browser provides only a horizontal scrollbar, or only a vertical scrollbar, for the user to view hidden content with **overflow-x** and **overflow-y** properties. These accept a value of **hidden** to hide the individual scrollbar, or a value of **scroll** to provide an individual scrollbar. For example, with the style rule **overflow-x : hidden ;** the horizontal scrollbar is not provided, whereas **overflow-y : scroll ;** provides a vertical scrollbar.

Text content will normally wrap to the next line within a block-level content box at word breaks, as the **whitespace** property is set to **normal** by default. You can, however, disable text wrapping with a **whitespace : nowrap ;** style rule. As overflowing content is generally **visible** by default, the text will then appear on a single line extending beyond the boundary of the content box.

If it is undesirable to display overflowing text, you can hide it with the **overflow : hidden ;** rule as with other content. Additionally, you can specify how overflowing text is treated with a style rule using a **text-overflow** property. This can accept a **clip** value, which truncates the text characters without regard to word breaks, or it can accept an **ellipsis** value, which replaces the final truncated letters with an ... ellipsis – to indicate that text has overflowed.

Beware

The **overflow** property is only effective for block elements that have a specified height, otherwise the block will automatically accommodate the content.

overflow.html

1 Create an HTML document with six division elements
```
<div class="vis"><img src="berry.png" alt="Berry"></div>
<div class="hid"><img src="berry.png" alt="Berry"></div>
<div class="scr"><img src="berry.png" alt="Berry"></div>
<div class="ver"><img src="berry.png" alt="Berry"></div>
<div class="hor"><img src="berry.png" alt="Berry"></div>
<div class="txt">CSS for Cascading Style Sheets</div>
```

2 Add a style sheet with rules that specify the block type and size of the divisions – as less than the image size

```
div { display : inline-block ; width : 80px ; height : 130px ;
border : 2px dashed Tomato ; margin-right : 60px ; }
```

3 Next, add style rules to handle the image overflow

```
div.vis { overflow : visible ; }
div.hid { overflow : hidden ; }
div.scr { overflow : scroll ; }
```

berry.png
100px x 130px

4 Now, add style rules to control individual scrollbars

```
div.ver { width : 120px ;
        overflow-x : hidden ; overflow-y : scroll ;  }
div.hor { height : 150px ;
        overflow-x : scroll ; overflow-y : hidden ;  }
```

5 Then, add style rules to handle the text overflow

```
div.txt { white-space : nowrap ;
        overflow : hidden ; text-overflow : ellipsis ; }
```

Hot tip

Notice the different treatment of overflow...
Visible
Hidden
Scroll

6 Save the HTML document then open the web page in a browser to see how the overflow has been handled

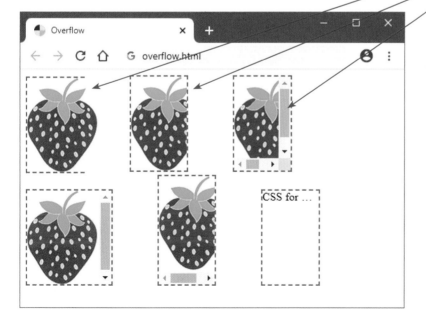

Layout Pages

The arrangement of content boxes on a web page can create many different layouts, but one of the most common layout schemes divides the web page into a header, a navigation bar, side bars, main content, and a footer – as illustrated below.

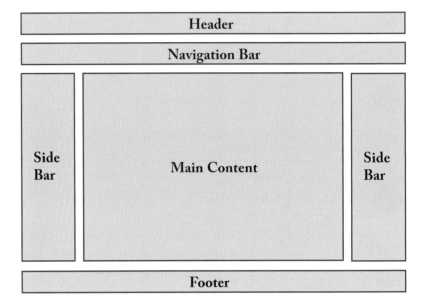

- **Header** – the name of the website and often a logo image.

- **Navigation Bar** – hyperlinks to pages of the website.

- **Main Content** – the most important part of the web page.

- **Side Bars** – supplemental information or advertisements.

- **Footer** – details such as copyright and contact information.

To best achieve a web page layout it is important to include a universal **margin : 0px ;** style rule to override the browser's default margin size.

You should also include a universal **box-sizing : border-box ;** style rule that allows the content boxes' padding and border to be included within each element's total width and height. This means that borders and padding will not be added outside the size you specify for each element – so you have better control.

Hot tip

You can discover more about the **box-sizing** property on page 282.

...cont'd

1 Create an HTML document with six division elements
```
<div>Header</div>
<div>Navigation Bar</div>
<div class="column side">Side<br>Bar</div>
<div class="column main">Main Content</div>
<div class="column side">Side<br>Bar</div>
<div class="footer">Footer</div>
```

layout.html

2 Add a style sheet with universal overriding rules
```
* { margin : 0px ; box-sizing : border-box ; }
```

3 Next, add style rules to add padding and borders to each division element – now included within their total size
```
div { padding : 5px ; border : 1px solid Tomato ; }
```

You can adjust the percentage values of the three column divisions, but added together they must total 100%.

4 Now, add rules to size and float three division elements
```
div.column { float : left ; height : 200px ; }
div.side { width : 15% ; }
div.main { width : 70% ; }
```

5 Finally, add a style rule to position the final division
```
div.footer { clear : both ; }
```

6 Save the HTML document then open the web page in a browser to see the layout

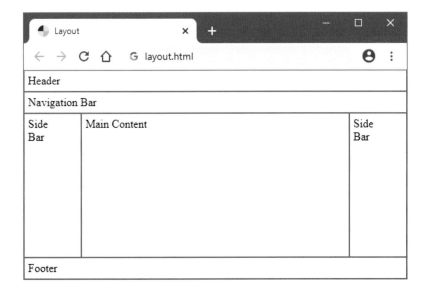

This is the traditional CSS method to create a 3-column layout, but you will discover more modern responsive layout methods later in this book.

211

Summary

- Content on a web page is displayed within invisible rectangular boxes that are either block-level or inline.

- Block-level content boxes add line breaks before and after the box and have optional areas for **padding**, **border**, and **margin**.

- Inline content boxes do not add line breaks or support rules for width, height, top/bottom margin, and padding.

- Inline-blocks appear inline but unlike regular inline content boxes they do support rules for **width** and **height**.

- When assigning any non-zero value to a property, the declaration must include a two-letter unit name.

- A **border** can be added around a content box by a rule specifying a width, a color, and a border style.

- A **padding** space can be added around the core content area by a rule specifying a padding size.

- Padding and borders are added outside the core content area that is set by a rule specifying an element's **width** and **height**.

- Transparent **margin** space can be added around the content, **padding**, and **border**, by a rule specifying a margin size.

- Content boxes can be placed on the web page at **absolute**, **relative**, or **fixed** positions.

- The stacking order of overlapping content boxes can be determined by a rule specifying a **z-index** integer value.

- A content box to be positioned at the side boundary of its containing element by a rule specifying a left or right side.

- Overflowing content is generally visible but can be made invisible by a rule specifying a **hidden** or **scroll** option.

- To best achieve a web page layout it is important to include a universal rule to override the browser's default **margin** size.

- Padding and borders can be included in an element's width and height by a rule specifying **box-sizing** as **border-box**.

10 Manipulate Text Content

Above are serif (left) and sans-serif (right) versions of a letter – the serif decorations are circled. Serif font characters are generally considered to be more readable but sans-serif is better for small font sizes and for text aimed at children.

Develop the habit of enclosing all named fonts within quotes.

Suggest Font

A CSS style rule can suggest a specific font to be used by the browser for the display of text content in a selected element by specifying the font name to its **font-family** property. The browser will use the specified font if it is available on the user's system – otherwise it will display the text using its default font.

The default font may not be the best choice for the author's purpose, so CSS additionally allows the **font-family** property to suggest a generic font family from those in the table below:

Font Family	Description	Example
serif	Proportional fonts where characters have different widths to suit their size, and with serif decorations at the end of the character strokes	Times New Roman
sans-serif	Proportional fonts without serif decorations	Arial
monospace	Non-proportional fonts where characters are of fixed width, similar to type-written text	Courier
cursive	Fonts that attempt to emulate human hand-written text	Segoe Script
fantasy	Decorative fonts with highly graphic appearance	Castellar

The browser will first try to apply the named font, but in the event that it is unavailable will select a font from those available that most closely matches the characteristics of the generic preference. In this way, the appearance of the text should at least approximate the author's intention, even without specific font-matching.

In a style rule **font-family** declaration, the preferred font name should appear before the generic font family preference separated by a comma. Multiple named fonts can be specified as a comma-separated list – all before the generic font family preference. Font names that include spaces must be enclosed within quote marks or they will not be recognized by the browser.

1 Create an HTML document containing a paragraph with several spanned sections of text

```
<p>The <span class="serif">City of New York</span>
was introduced to professional football on the same day
that the city was introduced to the
<span class="fantasy">New York Giants</span>.
It was a clear sunny
<span class="mono">October afternoon in 1925</span>
when the Giants took the field to play against the
<span class="cursive">Frankford Yellow Jackets</span>.
</p>
```

family.html

2 Add a style sheet containing a rule suggesting a default font for the entire paragraph

```
p { font-family : "Arial Narrow", sans-serif ; }
```

3 Next, add style rules suggesting fonts for the spanned text

```
span.serif { font-family : "Times New Roman", serif ; }
span.fantasy { font-family : "Castellar", fantasy ; }
span.mono { font-family : "Courier", monospace ; }
span.cursive { font-family : "Segoe Script", cursive ; }
```

4 Save the HTML document then open the web page in a browser to see the sections of text appear in the named fonts or in a generic family font

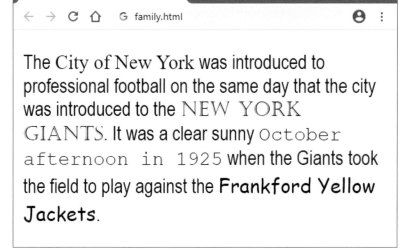

It is good practice to specify a generic font family preference in every **font-family** declaration.

Set Size

CSS provides a number of ways to specify the size of text in a style rule declaration by assigning values to the **font-size** property. The most obvious way is as an absolute size using any of the units listed on page 192 – for example, **font-size : 12pt ;**. Additionally, CSS provides a number of keywords to specify a relative size:

Keyword	Equivalent
xx-large	24pt
x-large	17pt
large	13.5pt
medium	12pt
small	10.5pt
x-small	7.5pt
xx-small	7pt

Using the keywords listed in the table on the left, the **medium** size is the browser's default font size, and the rest are computed relative to that size.

Where the browser's default font size is **12pt**, the computed values might look something like those listed in the table.

It is preferable to use **em** units or percentage values to specify sizes relative to the browser's default font size. For example, where the browser's default font size is **12pt**, a value of **1em** (or **100%**) is equivalent to a font size of 12 points – so **1.5em** (or **150%**) would be equivalent to a font size of 18 points in that case.

A further refinement is to specify the **font-size** property with values in **vw** ("viewport width") units, where a value of **1vw** is 1% of the current viewport width. This allows the size of text to resize to suit the size of viewing device or browser window.

The thickness or "weight" of text can be easily adjusted using the CSS **font-weight** property and the **bold** and **normal** keywords.

Specifying a **bold** value to a selected element's **font-weight** property causes normally weighted text to appear in a heavier font, and specifying a **normal** value causes heavily weighted text to appear in a lighter font. In reality, the browser uses two different fonts to achieve this effect – for **normal** text it uses a regularly weighted font (for example "Verdana") but it switches to the heavier weighted variant of that font if one is available (such as "Verdana Bold") for **bold** text.

Hot tip

Use relative values rather than absolute values to specify font sizes for maximum flexibility. The W3C recommend using **em** units for font sizes.

1 Create an HTML document containing four paragraphs

```
<p>Medium sized text at the default size</p>
<p class="lg">Large sized text at 150%</p>
<p class="sm">Small sized sans text at 60%</p>
<p class="huge">Bold text at double size</p>
```

size.html

2 Add a style sheet containing a rule to specify the browser's default font size relative to the viewport

```
body { font-size : 4vw ; }
```

3 Next, add a rule to specify font size for the second paragraph

```
p.lg { font-size : 1.5em ; }
```

4 Now, add rules to specify font size and a generic font family for the third paragraph

```
p.sm { font-size : 0.6em ; font-family : sans-serif ; }
```

Sans-serif fonts are considered to be more readable for smaller text.

5 Finally, add rules to specify font size and font weight for the fourth paragraph

```
p.huge { font-size : 200% ; font-weight : bold ; }
```

6 Save the HTML document then open the web page in a browser to see each paragraph's font size and weight

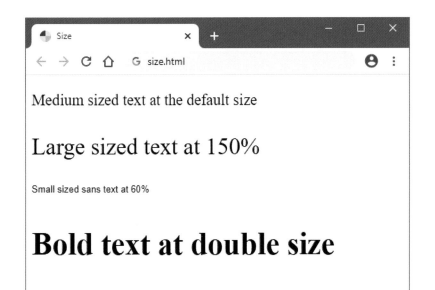

With this example you can resize the browser window to see the font size change to suit the current viewport area.

F F

Vary Style

Slanting text

A CSS **font-style** property can request the browser to use a slanting variant of the current font by specifying the **italic** or **oblique** keywords – these are subtly different.
When the **italic** keyword is specified, the browser seeks an italicized variant of the current font in its font database. This is an actual font set, similar to the current upright font but graphically different to produce slanting versions of each upright character.

When the **oblique** keyword is specified, the browser seeks an oblique variant of the current font in its font database. This may be an actual font set – a slanting version of the current upright font – or alternatively, it may be a generated version in which the browser has computed a slanting version of the upright font. Either may be mapped to the **oblique** keyword in the browser's font database and called upon by the CSS **font-style** property.

In reality, using either **italic** or **oblique** keywords typically produces the same italicized text appearance, and in each case upright text can be resumed by specifying the **normal** keyword to the element's **font-style** property.

Small capitals

A CSS property called **font-variant** can specify a **small-caps** value to allow text characters to be displayed in a popular small capitals format using uppercase characters of two different sizes. Uppercase text in the selected element will appear as large capital characters, but lowercase text will appear as smaller capitals. The browser may achieve the small capitals effect using a smaller capital from the font set, or by generating a computed smaller version. Once again, regular text can be resumed by specifying the **normal** keyword as the **font-variant**.

Hot tip

You can specify the **small-caps** value to the **font-variant** property of heading elements to make document headings more interesting.

1 Create an HTML document containing four headings

```
<h1>A Heading with Regular Font Style</h1>
<h1 class="ital">A Heading with Italic Font Style</h1>
<h1 class="caps">A Heading with Small Capitals</h1>
<h1 class="caps">A Heading
<span class="norm">with Mixed</span> Variants</h1>
```

variant.html

2 Add a style sheet containing a rule to specify an italic font style for the second heading

```
h1.ital { font-style : italic ; }
```

3 Next, add a rule to specify a small capitals font variant for the third heading

```
h1.caps { font-variant : small-caps ; }
```

4 Now, add rules to specify that part of the fourth heading should return to normal from a small capitals font variant, and add a background to emphasize the change

```
span.norm { font-variant : normal ;
                  background : LightGreen ; }
```

5 Save the HTML document then open the web page in a browser to see each heading's font style and variant

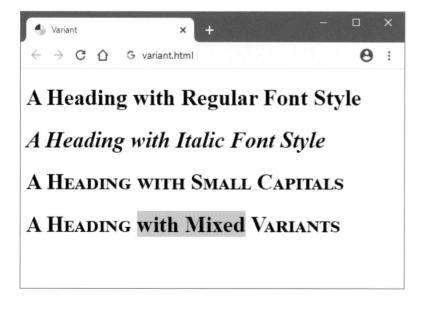

Use Shorthand

Usefully, CSS provides a **font** property to which various font preferences can be specified in a combined single rule stating:

font-style | font-variant | font-weight | font-size | font-family

Appropriate values can be assigned to each part of the combined **font** shorthand property – for example, like this:

p { font : italic small-caps bold medium "Times", serif ; }

The **font-size** and **font-family** values are mandatory, but the first three values for **font-style**, **font-variant**, and **font-weight** properties are optional and may appear in any order. Values for each one of these three optional properties may be completely omitted and a **normal** value will be automatically assumed.

It is important to recognize that values not explicitly specified will still have a **normal** value applied – no value is inherited from the containing element, and this can produce some unexpected results. For example, a style rule selecting a span element within a containing paragraph element styled by the rule above might look like this:

span { font : large cursive ; }

The values explicitly specified in this rule will be applied to the **font-size** and **font-family** properties of the span element, and a **normal** value will be applied to its **font-style**, **font-variant**, and **font-weight** properties – so text within the span element does not inherit the **italic**, **small-caps**, or **bold** values from the paragraph.

One further possibility available with a combined **font** rule is the option to specify a **line-height** (the spacing between each line) by adding a forward slash and unit value after the **font-size** value. This is useful to establish a common standard line spacing where various font sizes appear.

Beware

Remember that a **normal** value is applied for each part of a combined **font** rule unless explicitly specified – and this will override the current parent element value.

font.html

① Create an HTML document containing a paragraph with several spanned sections of text

```
<p>
<span class="head">The Sneakers Game</span><br>
In 1934 the
<span class="giant">New York Giants</span> beat the
<span class="bears">Chicago Bears</span>, by
<span class="score">30-13</span>,
in nine-degree temperatures [
```

```
<span class="venue">at the Polo Grounds</span>
] in a game that has become famous as the "Sneakers
Game." With the <span class="giant">Giants</span>
trailing <span class="score">10-3</span> at the half,
head coach <span class="coach">Steve Owen</span>
provided his squad with basketball shoes to increase
traction on the icy turf. The team responded with four
touchdowns in the second half to turn the game into a
<span class="giant">Giants</span> rout. </p>
```

2 Add a style sheet with font rules for the paragraph and
for each of the span elements

```
p { font : normal small/1.3em "Courier",monospace ; }
span.head { font : 350% "Pristina", cursive ; }
span.giant { font : small-caps large "Castellar", fantasy ; }
span.bears { font : large "Arial", sans-serif ; }
span.score { font : bold small "Verdana", sans-serif ; }
span.venue { font : italic medium "Arial", sans-serif ; }
span.coach { font : medium "Comic Sans MS", cursive ; }
```

3 Save the HTML document then open the web page in a
browser to see the styles applied using the font shorthand

Always use the **font**
shorthand property
rather than the individual
font-style, **font-variant**,
font-weight, **font-size**,
and **font-family**
properties.

Align Text

English language text in a paragraph is normally horizontally aligned to the left edge of the paragraph, and this is the default behavior to display text in a paragraph element's content box.

Additionally, CSS provides a **text-align** property that can explicitly specify how text should be horizontally aligned within the paragraph element's content box using the keywords **left**, **center**, **right**, or **justify**. As expected, the **left** value aligns each line to the paragraph's left edge, the **right** value aligns each line to the paragraph's left edge, and the **center** value aligns each line centrally between both edges.

Perhaps more interestingly, the **justify** value aligns each full line to both left and right edges of the content box and adjusts the spacing between characters and words to make each line the same length.

In displaying lines of text, the browser automatically computes the line height to suit the content size – typically this will be the height of the font x 1.2. The browser then displays the text vertically centered in invisible "line boxes" of the computed height.

The CSS **vertical-align** property can explicitly specify how text should be vertically aligned using the keywords **baseline**, **sub**, and **super**. The **baseline** value specifies central vertical alignment: the default behavior. The **sub** and **super** values increase the boundaries of the outer container in which the line box exists, and shift the text down or up respectively to display subscript or superscript.

Content can also be shifted up or down by specifying positive or negative unit values, or percentage values, to the **vertical-align** property. Alternatively, the **top**, **middle**, and **bottom** keywords can specify vertical alignment with top-most, middle, or bottom-most content.

Two other keywords of **text-top** and **text-bottom** can be specified to the **vertical-align** property in order to vertically align other inline content boxes, such as those of image elements, to the top or bottom edge of a line box.

The **text-align** property only controls alignment of text within a content box – it is not used to center content boxes. See page 198 for details on how to center content boxes.

Usually subscript and superscript is much smaller than the text – create the vertical shift by specifying **sub** or **super** values then apply a **font** rule to reduce the shifted text's size.

…cont'd

1 Create an HTML document containing three paragraphs
```
<p>Enjoy the sunsets, the restaurants, the fishing, the
diving... the lifestyle of the Florida Keys!</p>
<p class="just">Enjoy the sunsets, the restaurants, the
fishing, the diving... the lifestyle of the Florida Keys!</p>
<p>Line <span class="up">Superscript</span>
<span class="down">Subscript</span>
<span class="top">Top</span></p>
```

align.html

2 Add a style sheet with rules to specify font and colors
```
p, span { font : medium monospace ;
background : LightGreen ; border : 1px solid LimeGreen ; }
```

3 Next, add a rule to horizontally justify the text within the second paragraph's content box
```
p.just { text-align : justify ; }
```

4 Now, add rules to adjust the vertical alignment of spanned text within the third paragraph
```
span.up { vertical-align : super ; }
span.down { vertical-align : sub ; }
span.top { vertical-align : top ; }
```

5 Save the HTML document then open the web page in a browser to see the alignments

223

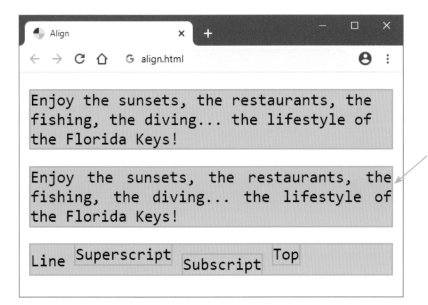

Hot tip

Notice how the **justify** keyword aligns each full line to the edge of the content box and adjusts the spacing between characters and words.

Control Space

One of the most common features of printed text is the indentation of the first line of each paragraph to improve readability. This can be easily accomplished for text in HTML paragraphs using the **text-indent** property to specify an indentation size, such as **5em**.

Alternatively, the indentation value may be specified as a percentage where the browser will indent an amount relative to the total line length. For example, given a paragraph element within a division container element of **500px** width, specifying a **text-indent** value of **10%** would indent the start of the first line by **50px** (500 x 10% = 50).

It is also possible to specify negative values for the **text-indent** property, but this can produce inconsistent results so is best avoided.

The amount of space between each word can be adjusted from the **normal** default spacing by explicitly specifying a value to the CSS **word-spacing** property. Note that the specified value is added to the default spacing to increase the space. For example, specifying a unit value of **5em** increases the space to **normal+5em**, not a spacing of **5em** overall.

Similarly, the amount of space between each letter can be adjusted from the **normal** default spacing by explicitly specifying a value to the CSS **letter-spacing** property. This also adds the specified value onto the default spacing to determine the total space. For example, specifying a unit value of **5em** increases the space to **normal+5em**, not a spacing of **5em** overall.

Both **word-spacing** and **letter-spacing** properties accept the **normal** keyword to resume normal spacing. Also, they may both be overridden by the **text-align** property, described on page 222, that has precedence in determining the appearance of the entire line.

The **word-spacing** and **letter-spacing** properties can both accept negative values – to produce some interesting results.

...cont'd

space.html

1 Create an HTML document with two paragraphs containing spanned text

```
<p>The Geologic Story at the
<span class="spread">Grand Canyon</span>
attracts the attention of the world for many reasons, but
perhaps its greatest significance lies in the geologic record
preserved and exposed here.</p><p>The rocks at
<span class="spread">Grand Canyon</span>
are not inherently unique but the
<span class="space">variety of rocks clearly exposed
present a complex geologic story.</span> </p>
```

2 Add a style sheet containing a rule to indent the start of each paragraph

```
p { text-indent : 5em ; }
```

3 Next, add style rules to increase the letter spacing and set a background color on two spanned sections of text

```
span.spread { letter-spacing : 1em ;
                background : LightGreen ; }
```

4 Now, add style rules to increase the word spacing and set a background color on the other spanned text

```
span.space { word-spacing : 1.5em ;
                background : LawnGreen ; }
```

5 Save the HTML document then open the web page in a browser to see the indentations and spacing

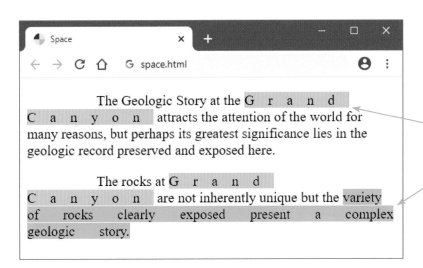

Hot tip

Notice the increased letter spacing and increased word spacing.

Decorate Text

Style rules can add decorative lines to text content using the CSS **text-decoration** property with keywords **underline**, **overline**, and **line-through**. These behave as expected adding a line below, a line above, and a line through the text respectively.

Usefully, the CSS **none** keyword can be specified to the **text-decoration** property to prevent unwanted decorations appearing – this is particularly popular for displaying hyperlinks without their usual default underline.

Multiple keywords can be specified to the **text-decoration** property as a space-separated list to apply multiple decorations to the text.

An additional way to enhance text with CSS is available using the **text-transform** property to specify capitalization in the selected element with the keywords **uppercase**, **lowercase**, or **capitalize**.

decor.html

Some users may not recognize hyperlinks if their default underline is removed.

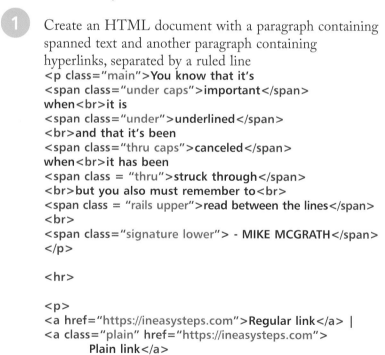

1 Create an HTML document with a paragraph containing spanned text and another paragraph containing hyperlinks, separated by a ruled line

```
<p class="main">You know that it's
<span class="under caps">important</span>
when<br>it is
<span class="under">underlined</span>
<br>and that it's been
<span class="thru caps">canceled</span>
when<br>it has been
<span class = "thru">struck through</span>
<br>but you also must remember to<br>
<span class = "rails upper">read between the lines</span>
<br>
<span class="signature lower"> - MIKE MCGRATH</span>
</p>

<hr>

<p>
<a href="https://ineasysteps.com">Regular link</a> |
<a class="plain" href="https://ineasysteps.com">
        Plain link</a>
</p>
```

226

…cont'd

2 Add a style sheet with rules to specify fonts and colors

```
p.main { font : medium "Courier", monospace ;
                                background : LightGreen ; }
span.signature { font : 2em "Lucida Handwriting", cursive ;
                                color : Green ; }
```

3 Next, add style rules to decorate spanned text with lines

```
span.under { text-decoration : underline ; }
span.thru { text-decoration : line-through ; }
span.rails { text-decoration : overline underline ; }
```

4 Now, add style rules to transform the case of spanned text

```
span.lower { text-transform : lowercase ; }
span.upper { text-transform : uppercase ; }
span.caps { text-transform : capitalize ; }
```

5 Finally, add a style rule to remove the default underline from a hyperlink

```
a.plain { text-decoration : none ; }
```

6 Save the HTML document then open the web page in a browser to see the text decorations and case transformations

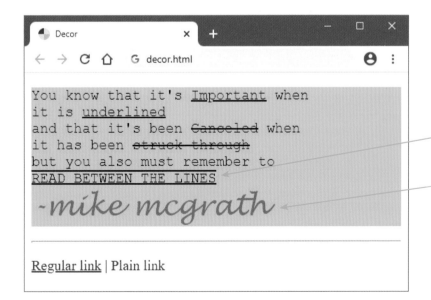

Hot tip

Notice how lowercase has been transformed to uppercase, and how uppercase has been transformed into lowercase.

Change Direction

The default treatment of whitespace within text content is to collapse multiple spaces into a single space, but this can be controlled with the CSS **white-space** property. Specifying the **pre** (preserve) keyword preserves all spaces as they appear in the original text, including any line breaks. Conversely, the automatic wrapping of text in a block can be prevented by specifying the **no-wrap** keyword. Additionally, the **pre-wrap** keyword can be specified to preserve spaces while still allowing text to wrap normally, or the **pre-line** keyword can be specified to collapse multiple spaces while preserving line breaks.

The default left-to-right direction of text lines can be changed to right-to-left by specifying the **rtl** keyword to the CSS **direction** property, and the normal direction resumed with the **ltr** keyword.

Interestingly, when the line direction is changed with the **rtl** keyword, the words appear from right-to-left but the order of English language characters is preserved so that each word still reads correctly left-to-right.

This intelligent feature also allows text to be presented in different directions on a single line – for example, to incorporate words in languages that are read right-to-left such as Hebrew and Arabic. The browser examines the Unicode value of each character using a complex Bidirectional algorithm to determine which direction each word should be displayed – those characters from right-to-left languages are automatically displayed in that direction, even if written logically from left-to-right in the HTML source code. The automatic Bidirectional algorithm can be turned off, however, by specifying the **bidi-override** keyword to a **unicode-bidi** property.

Hot tip

You can discover more about Unicode online at **www.unicode.org** and more on character entities online at www.w3.org

HTML

direction.html

1 Create an HTML document with a paragraph containing Hebrew character entities and stepped whitespace
```
<p>Hebrew "Congratulations" with mazel tov:
&#1502;&#1494;&#1500;  [mazel]
  + &#1496;&#1493;&#1489;  [tov]
    = &#1502;&#1494;&#1500;  &#1496;&#1493;&#1489;
</p>
```

2 Next, begin a definition list with the same entities
```
<dl>
<dt>LTR Default Direction (lines begin at the LEFT):</dt>
<dd class="ltr">&#1502;&#1494;&#1500; [mazel]
&#1496;&#1493;&#1489; [tov]</dd>
```

...cont'd

3 Now, add two more definitions to complete the list, again featuring the same Hebrew character entities

```
<dt>RTL Custom Direction (lines begin at the RIGHT):</dt>
<dd class="rtl">&#1502;&#1494;&#1500; [mazel]
&#1496;&#1493;&#1489; [tov]</dd>
<dt>LTR Explicit Direction + Bidirectional Override:</dt>
<dd class="bidi-off ltr">No longer reads as mazel tov :
&#1502;&#1494;&#1500; &#1496;&#1493;&#1489;</dd>
</dl>
```

4 Add a style sheet with rules to color element backgrounds and preserve whitespace in paragraphs

```
p,dd { background : LightGreen ; }
p { whitespace : pre ; }
```

5 Now, add style rules to set the text directions of each definition in the list

```
dd.ltr { direction : ltr ; }
dd.rtl { direction : rtl ; }
dd.bidi-off { unicode-bidi : bidi-override ; }
```

6 Save the HTML document then open the web page in a browser to see the preserved whitespace and changing directions of the text

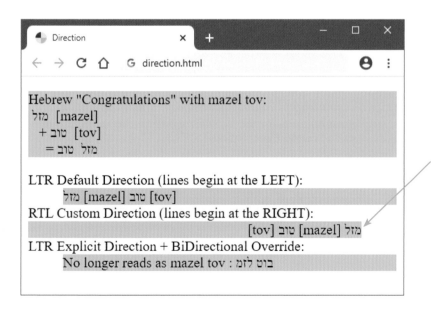

Generally, the default treatment of right-to-left language characters achieves the desired effect. In practice, overriding the Unicode Bidirectional algorithm is seldom needed.

Notice that the **rtl** value displays the characters in the correct order reading from right to left.

Enhance Text

CSS provides five "pseudo-elements" of ::**before**, ::**after**, ::**first-letter**, ::**first-line** and ::**selection** that can be included in the style rule selector to enhance the content of a selected element.

The ::**first-letter** and ::**first-line** pseudo-elements are used to add a style to the beginning of text. The ::**selection** pseudo element is used to add style to text that has been selected by the user.

The ::**before** and ::**after** pseudo-elements are used to insert content around the original content. For example, a selector of **p::before** inserts content before the start of each paragraph.

The ::**before** and ::**after** pseudo-elements specify the content to be inserted to a **content** property in the style rule declaration. Most simply, this can specify a string of text to be inserted. The string must be enclosed in quote marks, but these will not be included in the inserted text – although spaces in the string will be preserved in the inserted text. The **content** property can, however, specify the keywords **open-quote** or **close-quote** to explicitly insert quotes.

Generated content is not limited to text strings, as the CSS **url( )** function can be used to specify non-textual content to the **content** property by stating the path to a resource within the parentheses.

Additionally, the CSS **attr( )** function can be used to specify to the **content** property the name of an attribute within the selected element whose assigned value should be inserted as content.

Multiple items to be inserted can be specified to the **content** property as a space-separated list – using any of the above.

In CSS, all pseudo-elements begin with two colon characters.

pseudo.html

info.pdf

1 Create an HTML document with a heading and four paragraphs that each contain a link to the same resource
```
<h1>Pseudo Elements</h1>
```

```
<p>Get more <a href="info.pdf">info</a> here</p>
```

```
<p>Get more
    <a href="info.pdf" class="quote">info</a> here</p>
```

```
<p>Get more
    <a href="info.pdf" class="pdf">info</a> here</p>
```

```
<p>Get more
    <a href="info.pdf" class="att">info</a> here</p>
```

2   Add a style sheet containing rules to style the heading's
first letter and selected text – if selected by the user
h1::first-letter { color : ForestGreen ; }
h1::selection { background : LawnGreen ; }

3   Next, add rules to insert text characters on colored
backgrounds before and after the content of each paragraph
p::before { content : "*" ; background : LightGreen ; }**
p::after { content : "!!!" ; background : LawnGreen ; }

4   Now, add rules to insert colored quotes around a link
a[href].quote::before { content : open-quote ; color : Blue ; }
a[href].quote::after { content : close-quote ; color : Blue ; }

5   Then, add a rule to insert an image after a link
a[href].pdf::after { content : url(pdf-ico.png) ; }

pdf-ico.png
32px x 32px

6   Finally, add rules to insert a colored attribute value after a
link to display the name of the linked resource file
a[href].att::after { content : "(" attr(href) ")" ; color : Blue ; }

7   Save the HTML document then open the web page in
a browser and select part of the heading's text to see the
content inserted by CSS style rules

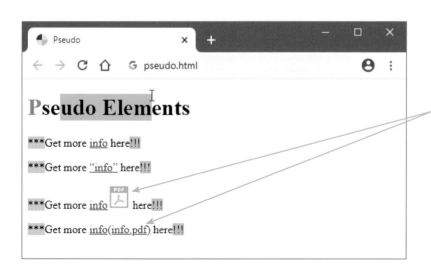

Inserted content is added inside the content box of the selected element – so the enhancements to the links in this example become part of the link.

231

Number Sections

The CSS ::**before** pseudo-element, introduced in the example on page 230, can insert generated content to automatically number sections of an HTML document using the CSS **counter( )** function. This specifies the name of a counter to be inserted into content within its ( ) parentheses.

A counter to count the instances of a selected element must first be created by specifying a chosen name and an incremental value to the **counter-increment** property as a space-separated list.

The counter will begin counting from zero by default and will increment by the specified incremental value for every instance of the selected element. Optionally, the explicitly specified incremental value may be omitted from the rule so the value of 1 will be assumed as the incremental value. For example, a declaration of **counter-increment : num ;** creates a counter named "num" that will start counting from zero and increment by one.

Additionally, the counter can be made to resume counting from a number other than the current count number by specifying the counter name and an integer value from which to count as a space-separated list to the **counter-reset** property. Typically, this will specify a zero integer value to resume counting afresh.

Once a counter has been created it can be inserted before a selected element as generated content by a CSS pseudo-element.

counter.html

1 Create an HTML document with various headings of two different sizes
```
<h2>Topic</h2>
        <h3>Section</h3>
        <h3>Section</h3>
        <h3>Section</h3>

<h2>Topic</h2>
        <h3 class="restart">Section</h3>
        <h3>Section</h3>
        <h3>Section</h3>
```

2 Add a style sheet containing a rule to create a counter for the larger heading elements, which will increment by one
```
h2 { counter-increment : num 1 ; }
```

3 Next, add style rules to create a counter for the smaller heading elements, which will increment by one
h3 { counter-increment : sub 1 ; text-indent : 10% ; }

4 Now, add style rules to insert the current larger heading counter value before each larger heading and set the counter's foreground and background colors
h2::before { content : counter(num) " " ;
                  background : Green ; color : White ; }

5 Then, add style rules to insert both the current larger and smaller heading counter value before each smaller heading and set that background color
h3::before { content : counter(num) "." counter(sub) " " ;
                  background : LawnGreen ; }

6 Finally, add a style rule to reset the smaller heading counter after each larger heading element
h3.restart { counter-reset : sub 0 ; }

7 Save the HTML document then open the web page in a browser to see the generated counter values inserted before each heading

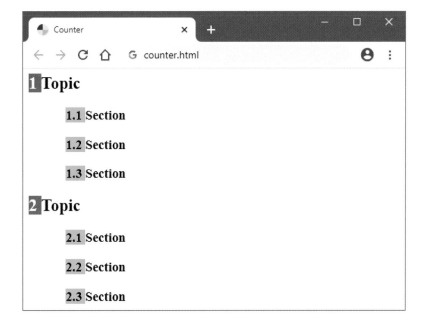

Notice that the generated content in this example includes a space for formatting purposes.

Summary

- Style rules can suggest specific **font** by name and a generic **font-family** as **serif, sans-serif, monospace, cursive**, or **fantasy**.

- A **font-size** can be specified using keywords or absolute sizes, but it is recommended to use relative sizes for flexibility.

- A **font-weight** can be specified as **bold** or **normal**.

- A **font-style** can be specified as **italic** or **normal**.

- A **font-variant** can be specified as **small-caps** or **normal**.

- The **font** shorthand property can be used to specify values for text style, variant, weight, size, and font family.

- The **font-size** and **font-family** values are required when using the **font** shorthand property, but the other values are optional.

- Text can be horizontally aligned within a content box by specifying **text-align** as **left, center, right**, or **justify**.

- Text can be vertically aligned within a content box by specifying **vertical-align** as **top, middle**, or **bottom**.

- The spacing between text can be specified as a unit value to the **text-indent, word-spacing**, and **letter-spacing** properties.

- Text can be decorated by specifying **text-decoration** as **underline, overline**, or **line-through**.

- Text can be transformed by specifying **text-transform** as **uppercase, lowercase**, or **capitalize.**

- Multiple spaces in text are normally collapsed into a single space, but can be preserved using the **white-space** property.

- The default left-to-right direction of text lines can be changed to right-to-left using the **direction** property.

- CSS pseudo-elements can be included after the style rule selector to enhance the content of a selected element.

- Sections of a web page can be automatically numbered using the CSS **counter( )** function.

11 Organize Tables & Lists

Construct Columns

Although web page authors are now discouraged from using HTML tables for page layout, in favor of CSS, tables remain an invaluable format for the presentation of information within the content of a page.

When displaying an HTML table, the browser will, by default, automatically create a table layout sized to accommodate its content. This invariably produces a table with columns of varying width, where each column width is determined by the widest content of any cell in that column. This process requires the browser to examine the table content in some detail before it can compute the optimum table layout and, especially for large tables, can take some time before the browser is able to draw the table.

CSS provides an alternative that allows the browser to quickly compute a suitable table layout without examining the content of the entire table – a fixed layout can be specified to the **table-layout** property of a table element with the **fixed** keyword.

In a **fixed** layout the browser need only consider the **width** value of the table itself and the **width** value of the columns and cells on its first row to determine the table layout, like this:

- The overall table width will be its specified **width** value or the sum of its column **width** values – whichever is the greater.

- A specified column **width** value sets the width for that column.

- When there is no specified column **width** value, a specified cell **width** value sets the width for that column.

- Any columns that have no specified **width** values, for either column or cell, will be sized equally within the table width.

Specify the first column width and a fixed layout rule to create a first column of custom width and other columns of equal width to each other.

Alternatively, a style rule can explicitly specify that the default table layout scheme should be used, in which the browser computes the column widths according to their content by assigning an **auto** value to the **table-layout** property.

Where tables include a caption element, the position of the caption can be suggested by specifying keywords of **top** or **bottom** to the table element's CSS **caption-side** property.

...cont'd

columns.html

1 Create an HTML document containing two tables with similar content
```
<table><caption>Auto Layout</caption>
<tr><td>Text content</td>
<td>This is text content wider than 130px</td>
<td>Text content</td></tr></table>

<table class="fixed"><caption>Fixed Layout</caption>
<tr><td>Text content</td>
<td>This is text content wider than 130px</td>
<td>Text content</td></tr></table>
```

2 Add a style sheet containing rules to specify table width and its features
```
table { width : 500px ; border : 2px dashed DeepPink ;
caption-side : top ; text-align : center ; margin : 0 0 30px ; }
```

The **caption-side** property can suggest where a caption might appear but the actual treatment of captions is browser-specific.

3 Next, add style rules to color each table cell and caption
```
td { border : 2px solid DeepPink  ; }
caption { background : Pink ; }
```

4 Now, add a style rule to specify a fixed size column scheme for the second table
```
table.fixed { table-layout : fixed ; }
```

5 Save the HTML document then open the web page in a browser to see tables drawn with both automatic and fixed layout schemes

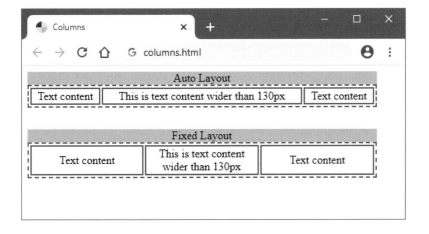

Space Cells

The distance between table cell borders can be specified as a unit value to the CSS **border-spacing** property. This easily allows cells to be spread some distance apart throughout a table.

A single specified **border-spacing** value will be applied uniformly to all cell separations – in much the same way as with the HTML cellspacing attribute.

CSS provides greater flexibility, however, by allowing two values to be specified to the **border-spacing** property as a space-separated list. The first will be applied to the horizontal spacing, at the left and right of each table cell, and the second will be applied to the vertical spacing at the top and bottom of each cell. This means that different distances can be specified for the horizontal and vertical spacing throughout a table.

Another possibility offered by CSS is the ability to hide table cells that contain no content. These frequently occur due to the grid format of tables, which does not always conveniently match the number of cells required – for example, displaying nine content items in a table of five rows and two columns.

Creating a style rule with the CSS **empty-cells** property specifying a **hide** value will cause the browser to not display the border and background of any cell that contains absolutely no content. Cells that contain any content at all, even if it's simply a ** ** (non-breaking space entity), will still be visible.

Conversely, a style rule can explicitly ensure that empty cells are displayed by specifying a **show** value to the **empty-cells** property.

Empty cells that are hidden do continue to have a presence in the table layout inasmuch as their **border-spacing** values are preserved. For example, where the **border-spacing** property is set to **20px**, and the **empty-cells** property specifies a **hide** value, a single empty cell is not displayed, but the surrounding cells remain 40 pixels apart – rather than just a distance of 20 pixels that would exist if the hidden cell did not exist.

Negative values cannot be specified to the **border-spacing** property.

The **empty-cells** property does not apply when a **collapse** value is specified to the **border-collapse** property – see page 240.

1 Create an HTML document containing two tables with similar content – including one empty cell

```
<table>
<tr><td>1</td><td></td><td>3</td></tr>
</table>

<table class="space">
<tr><td>1</td><td></td><td>3</td></tr>
</table>
```

hide.html

2 Add a style sheet containing rules to specify table width and its features

```
table { width : 500px ;
        margin : 20px ; border : 2px dashed DeepPink ; }
```

3 Next, add a style rule to color each table cell and border

```
td { border : 2px solid DeepPink ; }
```

4 Now, add style rules to specify the border spacing and hide empty cells in the second table

```
table.space { border-spacing : 20px ; empty-cells : hide ; }
```

5 Save the HTML document then open the web page in a browser to see tables drawn with both visible and hidden empty cells

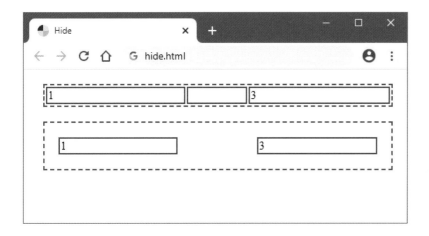

Collapse Borders

The borders of adjacent table borders, and table cell borders, can be made to "collapse" into a single border by specifying the **collapse** keyword to the CSS **border-collapse** property. This requires the browser to perform a series of evaluations, comparing the existing borders, to determine how the collapsed border should appear:

- **Visibility Evaluation:** where one of the borders to be collapsed has a **border-style** value of **hidden**, that value takes precedence – so the collapsed border at that location will be hidden.

- **Width Evaluation:** where two visible borders with different **border-width** values are to be collapsed, the highest value takes precedence – so the collapsed border will be the greater width.

- **Style Evaluation:** where two visible borders of equal width are to be collapsed, their **border-style** value sets the precedence in the descending status order of **double, solid, dashed, dotted, ridge, outset, groove, inset** – so the collapsed border at that location will be in the style of highest status. For example, a **double** style wins out over a **solid** style.

- **Color Evaluation:** where two visible borders of equal width and identical style are to be collapsed, the **border-color** value is determined in the descending status order of cell, row, row group, column, column group, table – so that collapsed border will be in the color of highest status. For example, the cell **border-color** wins out over the table **border-color** value.

Don't forget

The **separate** keyword can also be specified to the **border-collapse** property – to explicitly prevent collapsing borders.

The effect of collapsing borders where a table **border-width** of **2px** is compared to a cell **border-width** of **5px** means that the collapsed **border-width** will be 5 pixels – the greater width.

In comparing adjacent **border-style** values of **dotted** and **double**, the collapsed **border-style** will be double – the higher status.

Similarly, comparing adjacent **border-style** values of **dotted** and **solid**, the collapsed **border-style** will be solid – the higher status.

1 Create an HTML document containing two tables with similar content

```
<table><tr>
<td class="twin">1</td>
<td class="dots">2</td>
<td class="full">3</td> </tr></table>

<table class="fold"><tr>
<td class="twin">1</td>
<td class="dots">2</td>
<td class="full">3</td> </tr></table>
```

collapse.html

2 Add a style sheet containing rules to specify table width and its features

```
table { width : 500px ; height : 60px ; margin : 20px ; }
```

3 Next, add style rules to specify the size and color of the table border and each table cell

```
table { border : 2px solid DeepPink ; }
td.twin { border : 5px double DeepPink ; }
td.dots { border : 5px dotted DeepPink ;  }
td.full { border : 5px solid DeepPink ;  }
```

4 Now, add a style rule to collapse the borders of the second table

```
table.fold { border-collapse : collapse ; }
```

5 Save the HTML document then open the web page in a browser to see tables drawn with both regular and collapsed borders

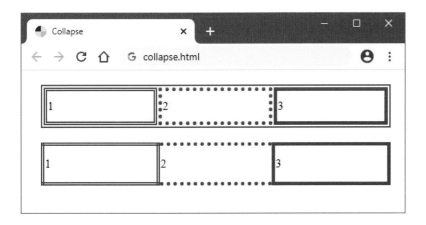

Assign Features

The CSS **display** property can accept a range of values to specify that a selected element should be treated as a table component – emulating the default behavior of HTML tags that a browser automatically applies to table components:

HTML Tag	CSS Equivalent
<table>	table
<tr>	table-row
<thead>	table-header-group
<tbody>	table-row-group
<tfoot>	table-footer-group
<col>	table-column
<colgroup>	table-column-group
<th>	} table-cell
<td>	
<caption>	table-caption

The CSS values that can be specified to the **display** property are listed in the table above, together with the HTML tag they most closely represent. These can be used to specify table features to elements of an XML document so a browser will display their content as if it was an HTML table.

xtable.xml

 Create an XML document that nominates a CSS style sheet to format its element content

```
<?xml version="1.0" encoding="UTF-8"?>
<?xml-stylesheet href="xtable.css" type="text/css"?>
<league><caption>La Liga Top 3</caption>
 <headers>
  <lbl>Position</lbl> <lbl>Team</lbl> <lbl>Points</lbl>
 </headers>
 <rows>
  <team> <pos>1</pos> <name>Barcelona</name>
  <pts>84</pts> </team>
  <team> <pos>2</pos> <name>Real Madrid</name>
  <pts>80</pts> </team>
  <team> <pos>3</pos> <name>Villareal</name>
  <pts>65</pts> </team>
 </rows>
</league>
```

2 Save the XML document then create a style sheet with rules that assign table characteristics to the XML tags

```
caption { display : table-caption ; }

league { display : table ; }

headers { display : table-header-group ; }

rows { display : table-row-group ; }

team { display : table-row ; }

name, pos, pts, lbl { display : table-cell ; }
```

xtable.css

3 Next, add style rules that specify the table features

```
league { margin : auto ; margin-top : 20px ; width : 300px ;
 border-spacing : 3px ; border : 8px ridge DeepPink ; }
```

4 Now, add style rules to color the headers and row cells

```
headers { background : DeepPink ; color : White ; }
rows { background : Pink ; }
```

5 Save the style sheet alongside the XML document then open the XML document in a browser to see the table

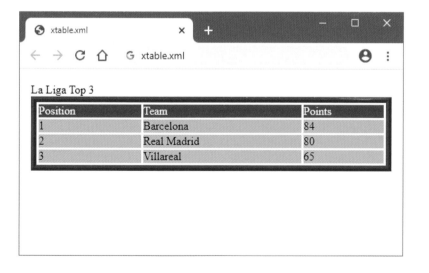

Choose Markers

A list "marker" indicates the beginning of an item in a list – typically a bullet in an unordered **<ul>** list, or an incrementing number in an ordered **<ol>** list. The browser conducts an item count in each case, but usually only uses this to number the items in an ordered list display.

The CSS **list-style-type** property can specify an alternative type of marker for any list – so unordered lists can have numbered markers, and ordered lists can have bullet-points if so desired.

Keywords allow the bullet marker type to be specified as **disc**, **circle**, or **square**, and number marker types as **lower-roman**, **upper-roman**, **decimal**, or **decimal-leading-zero**.

Alphabetical marker types can be specified with the **lower-latin**, **upper-latin**, and **lower-greek** keywords. Additionally, the CSS specification provides keywords for other alphabets such as **armenian** and **georgian** – but a suitable font is needed for the marker to be displayed correctly by the web browser.

The **list-style-type** property can also specify a **none** value to explicitly suppress the markers so they will not be displayed, although they do remain in the item count.

Optionally, an image may be specified as a marker by stating its path in the parentheses of the CSS **url( )** function to the **list-style-image** property.

markers.html

1 Create an HTML document containing three headings and several ordered lists

```
<h3>Alphabetical list marker types:</h3>
<ol id="list-0"><li>lower-latin<li>...<li>...</ol>
<ol id="list-1"><li>upper-latin<li>...<li>...</ol>
<ol id="list-2"><li>lower-greek<li>...<li>...</ol>

<h3>Bullet list marker types:</h3>
<ol id="list-3"><li>disc<li>...<li>...</ol>
<ol id="list-4"><li>circle<li>...<li>...</ol>
<ol id="list-5"><li>square<li>...<li>...</ol>
<ol id="list-6"><li>image<li>...<li>...</ol>

<h3>Numerical list marker types:</h3>
<ol id="list-7"><li>lower-roman<li>...<li>...</ol>
<ol id="list-8"><li>upper-roman<li>...<li>...</ol>
<ol id="list-9"><li>decimal<li>...<li>...</ol>
<ol id="list-10"><li>decimal-leading-zero<li>...<li>...</ol>
```

2   Add a style sheet with rules to specify heading and list features

```
h3 { clear : left ; margin : 0 ; }
ol {      margin : 0 5px 0 0 ; border : 2px solid DeepPink ;
          float : left ;
          background : Pink ; padding : 0 0 0 10px ; }
li { margin : 0 0 0 20px ; background : White ; }
```

3   Next, add style rules to specify alphabetical list markers

```
ol#list-0 { list-style-type: lower-latin ; }
ol#list-1 { list-style-type: upper-latin ; }
ol#list-2 { list-style-type: lower-greek ; }
```

4   Now, add style rules to specify bullet list markers

```
ol#list-3 { list-style-type: disc ; }
ol#list-4 { list-style-type: circle ; }
ol#list-5 { list-style-type: square ; }
ol#list-6 { list-style-image : url(tick.png) ; }
```

5   Finally, add style rules to specify numerical list markers

```
ol#list-7 { list-style-type: lower-roman ; }
ol#list-8 { list-style-type: upper-roman ; }
ol#list-9 { list-style-type: decimal ; }
ol#list-10 { list-style-type: decimal-leading-zero ; }
```

tick.png – 20px x 20px
Gray areas are transparent.

6   Save the HTML document then open the web page in a browser to see the list markers

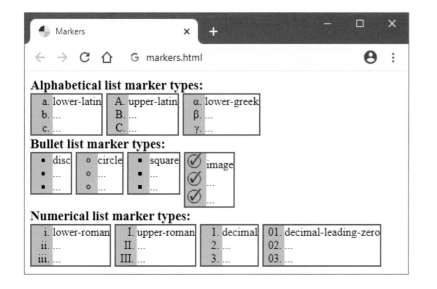

Both numerical and alphabetical markers display the incrementing item count.

Position Markers

Typically, to display a list the browser creates a block-level content box for the entire list and inline content boxes for each list item. Typically, an automatic left margin insets the list item content boxes and each marker appears up against the right edge of this margin area – outside the list item content boxes.

The position of the marker may be explicitly specified to the **list-style-position** property using **inside** or **outside** keywords to determine whether the markers should appear inside the list item content boxes.

Rather than creating separate style rules for the **list-style-type**, **list-style-image**, and **list-style-position** properties, it is simpler to use the CSS shorthand technique that may specify a value for each property as a space-separated list to the **list-style** property. The values may appear in any order, and where any value is omitted the default value for that property will be assumed.

Lists of either type may be nested with their marker position and type specified independently:

list.html

1   Create an HTML document containing three lists plus one nested list
```
<ol class="outside-markers">
 <li>List<li>Markers<li>Outside content box
</ol>

<ol class="inside-markers">
 <li>List<li>Markers<li>Inside content box
</ol>

<ul>
 <li>List<li>Style
 <ol class="inside-markers">
 <li>List<li>Markers<li>Inside content box
 </ol><li>Shorthand
</ul>
```

Hot tip

Nested lists can specify they should adopt the **list-style** of the containing element using the **inherit** keyword or suppress markers with the **none** keyword.

2   Add a style sheet containing rules to show the list boundaries
```
li { background : Pink ; }
ol,ul { border : 2px solid DeepPink ; }
```

3 Next, add a style rule to specify that some ordered list markers should appear outside the list item content boxes
ol.outside-markers **{ list-style-position : outside ; }**

4 Now, add a style rule to specify that other ordered list markers should appear inside the list item content boxes
ol.inside-markers **{ list-style-position : inside ; }**

5 Finally, add a shorthand style rule that specifies the position, image, and bullet type for the unordered list
ul { list-style : url(star.png) outside square ; }

6 Save the HTML document then open the web page in a browser to see the lists

star.png – 20px x 20px
Gray areas are transparent.

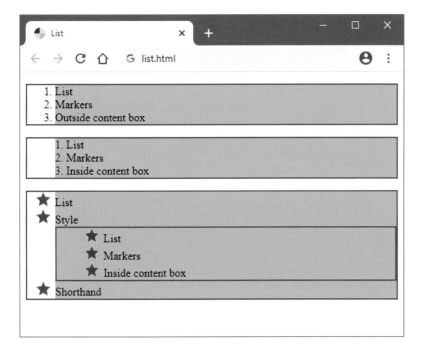

The **square** marker type specified by the shorthand rule will be used when the specified image is not available.

Provide Navigation

A navigation bar is simply a list of hyperlinks with particular CSS style rules applied to an HTML list element. Markers are not required, so the **list-style-type** property is specified as **none**, and the browser's default margins and paddings are removed. The hyperlinks in the list are then styled with **display : block ; ,** so that their entire content box is clickable (not just the link text), and **text-decoration : none ;** – to remove the default underlines.

Hyperlinks can indicate status by adding a class for styling, to indicate the current location on the website, and by adding a **:hover** pseudo-class after the selector.

Vertical navigation bars typically specify a fixed **width** value for the list, whereas horizontal navigation bars can instead **float** the list items and hide the **overflow** to maintain visibility of the bar.

navigation.html

1 Create an HTML document containing a list with four hyperlink items
```
<ul>
<li><a href="#home" class="current">Home</a></li>
<li><a href="#info">Information</a></li>
<li><a href="#extra">Extra</a></li>
<li><a href="#contact">Contact</a></li>
</ul>
```

2 Add a style sheet containing rules to remove the markers, margin, and padding, then specify a color and fixed width
```
ul { list-style-type : none ; margin : 0 ; padding : 0 ;
        background : Pink ; width : 150px ; }
```

3 Next, add style rules to display the hyperlinks in blocks and specify how they should appear
```
li a { display : block ; text-align : center ;
        text-decoration : none ;
        color : Black ;  padding : 10px ; }
```

4 Now, add style rules to indicate the hyperlinks' status
```
li a.current { background : HotPink ; }
li a:hover { background : DeepPink ; color : White ; }
```

5 Save the HTML document then open the web page in a browser to see the vertical navigation bar

Hot tip

Pseudo-classes are used to indicate the state of a hyperlink with **a:link** (default), **a:visited**, **a:hover**, and **a:active**.

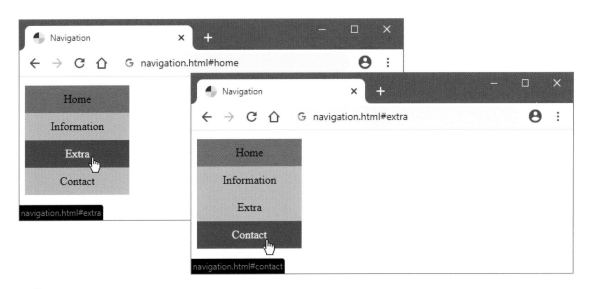

6 Edit the rules in Step 2 to replace width with overflow
ul { list-style-type : none ; margin : 0 ; padding : 0 ;
    background : Pink ; overflow : hidden ; }

7 Also edit the rules in Step 3 to add a float rule
li a { display : block ; text-align : center ;
    text-decoration : none ;
    color : Black ; padding : 10px ; float : left ; }

8 Save the HTML document again, then refresh the web
page in your browser to see the horizontal navigation bar

You can discover how to automatically display appropriate navigation for different device sizes on page 300.

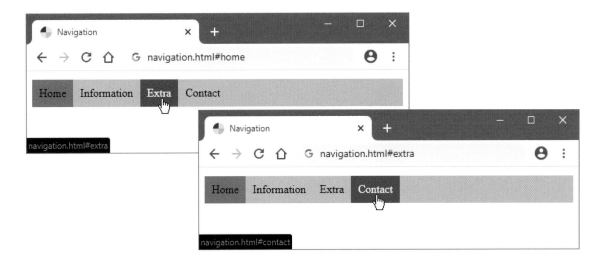

Make Dropdowns

A dropdown box is a content box that is hidden until the user places the cursor over an active element, at which point the box appears to offer further information, a larger image when placing the cursor over a thumbnail image, or a list of clickable options.

The active element should be styled with a **position : relative** ; rule so that the dropdown box can be positioned directly beneath it with a **position : absolute** ; rule. Additionally, the dropdown box should have a specified **z-index** value to place it above any existing content on the page.

It is also useful to include a universal **box-sizing : border-box** ; rule that allows padding and border to be included within the total width and height of the active element and of the dropdown box.

dropdown.html

1 Create an HTML document with a heading, a division element containing two inner divisions, and a paragraph
<h1>Banner</h1>

```
<div class="container">
  <div class="active">Dropdown Menu</div>
  <div class="dropdown">
    <a href="#option-1">Option 1</a>
    <a href="#option-2">Option 2</a>
    <a href="#option-3">Option 3</a>
  </div>
</div>

<p>Random text content:
        Remains below the dropdown menu.</p>
```

Hot tip

You can discover more about the **box-sizing** property on page 282.

2 Add a style sheet containing a rule to include padding and borders in all elements' total width and height
* { box-sizing : border-box ; }

3 Next, add a rule to create a border around the heading, just to reveal its overall width and height
h1 { border : 2px dashed DeepPink ; }

4 Now, add rules to position the outer division as an inline-block beneath the heading
div.container { position : relative ; display : inline-block ; }

5 Then, add rules to style the first inner division – this will be the active element for the dropdown
div.active { padding : 15px ; background : Pink ; }

6 Next, add rules to position and hide the second inner division – this will be the dropdown content
**div.dropdown { position : absolute ; width : 100% ;
border : 2px solid Pink ; background : White ;
z-index : 1 ; display : none ; }**

If you do not specify a **background** value for the dropdown content it may be transparent – so the content beneath will remain visible.

7 Now, add rules to make each link's content box clickable
**div.dropdown a { display : block ; padding : 15px ;
text-decoration : none ; color : Black ; }**

8 Then, add rules to change the link's appearance when the user places the cursor over the link
**div.dropdown a:hover { background : DeepPink ;
color : White ; }**

9 Finally, add a style rule to reveal the dropdown box when the user places the cursor over the active element
div.container:hover div.dropdown { display : block ; }

10 Save the HTML document then open it and put your cursor over the active element to see the dropdown appear

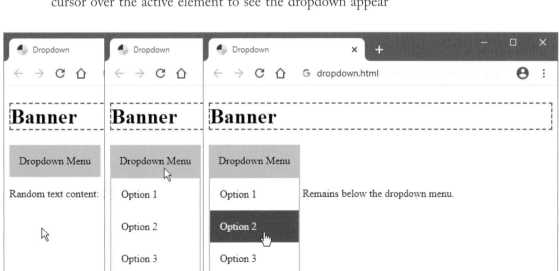

Summary

- A web browser can quickly draw a fixed layout table by assessing the width of the table and its first row of cells.

- A table **caption-side** can be specified as **top** or **bottom**.

- A **border-spacing** can specify the distance between table cell borders as a uniform distance or as horizontal and vertical.

- The **empty-cells** property can hide any cell that contains absolutely no content.

- The **border-collapse** property can combine adjacent borders of a table and its cells into a single border.

- The **display** property can specify that a selected element should be treated by the browser as a table component.

- A **list-style-type** can specify the type of marker to be used for list items as bullets, numbers or letters.

- The CSS **url( )** function can specify the path to an image for use as a list marker.

- A **list-style-position** can specify whether markers should appear inside or outside the list's content box.

- A navigation bar is a list of hyperlinks with particular CSS style rules applied to an HTML list element.

- When a hyperlink is displayed as a **block**, its entire content box is clickable.

- Pseudo-classes can be used to indicate the status of hyperlinks.

- Vertical navigation bars specify a list width, but horizontal navigation bars **float** the list items and hide the **overflow**.

- A dropdown box is a content box that is **hidden** until the user places the cursor over an active element.

- A dropdown's active element should be relatively positioned so the dropdown box can be absolutely positioned beneath it.

12 Generate Effects

This chapter demonstrates how to produce stylish effects in HTML documents.

Choose Cursors

The CSS **cursor** property can specify the type of cursor to display when the pointer hovers over a selected element. Its default value of **auto** allows the browser to determine which cursor to display, but specifying a **default** keyword will explicitly force the browser to use the operating system's default cursor.

Alternative cursor keywords, together with the cursor icons they represent in the Windows operating system, are listed below:

Don't forget

By default, Windows uses the same resize icon for each diagonal (north-south) but these can be individually different.

Keyword	Cursor	Keyword	Cursor
default		n-resize	
pointer		ne-resize	
crosshair		e-resize	
move		se-resize	
text		s-resize	
wait		sw-resize	
progress		w-resize	
help		nw-resize	

Hot tip

The **wait** cursor means that the user should not proceed until the current task has completed, whereas the **progress** cursor allows the user to proceed without delay.

Traditionally, the **pointer** cursor icon indicates a hyperlink, the **move** cursor icon indicates an item that can be dragged, and the **text** cursor icon indicates a component in which text can be selected. As most users are familiar with these cursor conventions, it is best to adhere to them.

In addition to system cursor icons, the **cursor** property can specify an image for use as a custom cursor icon by stating its path within the parentheses of the CSS **url( )** function. Multiple images may be specified, as a comma-separated list, but the list should always end with a regular cursor keyword to specify which system cursor icon to use if the specified images are unavailable.

...cont'd

1 Create an HTML document containing two paragraphs

```
<p class="help-cursor">Browser defined help cursor</p>
<p class="target-cursor">
        Custom cursor (or browser default)</p>
```

cursor.html

2 Add a style sheet with rules to specify border, paragraph height, and color

```
p { border : 2px solid DarkOrange ;
        height : 60px ; background : Bisque ; }
```

3 Next, add style rules to specify cursors for the paragraphs

```
p.help-cursor { cursor : help ; }
p.target-cursor{ cursor : url(target.cur), default ; }
```

4 Save the HTML document then place the pointer over each paragraph to see the cursors

target.cur – 32px x 32px
Gray areas are transparent.

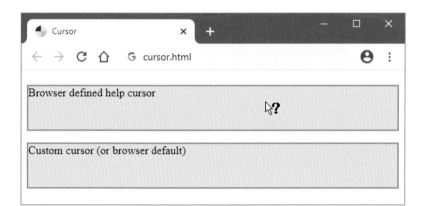

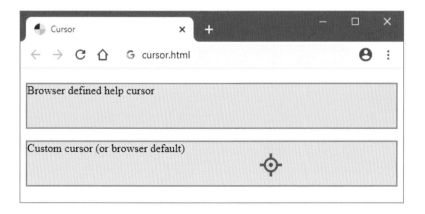

Show Focus

Interactive components of an HTML document comprise those elements that can accept keyboard input, such as a text field, and those that can be activated by a user action, such as a push button or hyperlink. When one of these interactive components is selected by the user, typically by a mouse click or tab key, it is ready to be activated and is said to have "focus".

CSS provides the :focus pseudo-class that can be used to apply styling to the element with current focus in a document – in recognition of the user's selection. The styling is removed from that element when the focus shifts to another element, as the user selects a different interactive component.

Indicating the element with current focus is especially useful in lengthy forms with many input fields, as it acts as a marker that easily identifies the progress through the form.

focus.html

1 Create an HTML document containing a form with several interactive components
```
<form action="echo.py">
<fieldset>
<legend>Send for details</legend>
<label for="addr">Enter your email address: </label>
<input id="addr" type="text"><br>
<input type="submit" value="Send">
<a href = "http://samples">Samples Page</a>
</fieldset>
</form>
```

2 Add a style sheet with a rule to color input elements when in focus
```
input:focus { background : DarkOrange ; }
```

3 Next, add a style rule to color hyperlinks when in focus
```
a:focus { background : Orange ; }
```

4 Save the HTML document then open the web page in a browser and select each interactive component in turn to see the styles applied

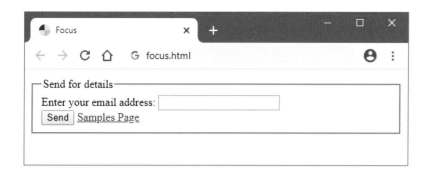

Hot tip

Repeatedly hit the Tab key to move through the interactive components.

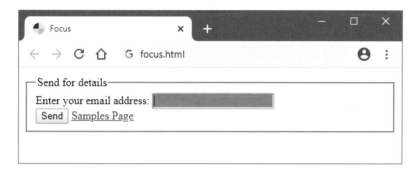

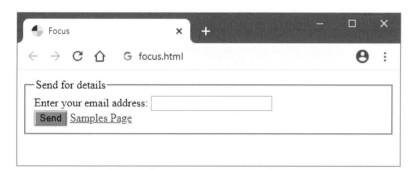

Don't forget

Focus only relates to interactive elements that can receive keyboard input or be somehow activated by the user.

Roll Over

User actions cause interface "events" to which the three dynamic pseudo-classes :**focus**, :**hover**, and :**active** can react. For example, when a user clicks on a text input, the Focus event occurs – to which the :**focus** pseudo-class can react by applying styles. Perhaps more interestingly, when the user moves the cursor onto any element, the MouseOver event occurs – to which the :**hover** pseudo-class can react by applying styles. The applied styles are removed when the cursor moves off the element, as the MouseOut event occurs, creating a dynamic "rollover" effect.

Typically, the rollover will highlight the selected element by changing its content color or background color to become more prominent. A rollover might also specify a different background image to create an image-swap – but this may not work too well on slower connections that need to wait for the new image to download.

A better image-swap alternative is to combine the images for both MouseOver and MouseOut states into a single image file, then have the rollover reveal the appropriate half of the image by specifying a different background position for each state.

prints.png
Gray areas are transparent.

1 Create an image file of 150x100 pixels containing top and bottom image areas on a transparent background

rollover.html

2 Next, create an HTML document containing two empty division elements with **id** attributes for style reference
<div id="active"></div> <div id="prints"></div>

3 Add a style sheet with rules to set the divisions' position and size – with height exactly half that of the image
div { position : absolute ; top : 10px ;
width : 150px ; height : 50px ; }
div#active { left : 10px ; }
div#prints { left : 170px ; }

4 Next, add style rules to color the backgrounds, and set the background position at the top-left corner of the image, when the cursor is not over the div elements
div#active { background : Bisque ; }
div#prints { background : url(prints.png) 0 0 Bisque ; }

5 Now, add style rules to change the background colors and set the background position at the center-left of the image, when the cursor is over the division elements
div#active:hover { background-color : DarkOrange ; }
div#prints:hover {
background : url(prints.png) 0 -50px DarkOrange ; }

6 Save the HTML document then open the web page in a browser and roll the cursor over the division elements to see their backgrounds change

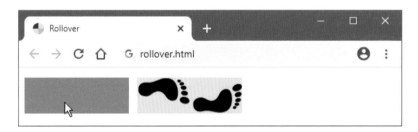

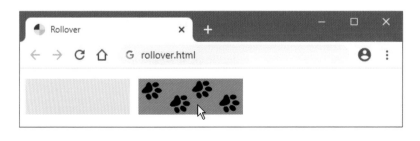

The **:focus** pseudo-class only relates to elements that can receive input – but the **:hover** pseudo-class relates to almost ANY element.

Push Buttons

A rollover effect, as described in the example on page 258, can be used with almost any HTML element to create CSS push buttons – for links, scripting, or form submission.

echo.py   buttons.html & target.html

1   Create an HTML document with a form that contains three inner elements that will be styled as buttons

```
<a class="button" href="target.html" >Link Button</a>
<button class="button"
        onclick="alert(this.innerText + ' Clicked')">
        Script Button</button>
<form method="GET" action="http://localhost/echo.py">
<input class="button" type="submit"
        name="CSS" value="Submit Button">
</form>
```

2   Add a style sheet with rules to style each of the three inner elements – removing any default styles

```
.button { display : inline-block ; font : 16px sans-serif ;
        background : Orange ; color : White ;
        border : none ; padding : 16px 32px ; margin : 5px ;
        text-align : center ; text-decoration : none ;
        cursor : pointer ; }
```

Hot tip

Notice how the selector only specifies the class in this example, to apply the same style rules to various types of element.

3   Next, add rules to create a rollover effect on each button and to simply align the form

```
.button:link, .button:visited { color : White ; }
.button:hover { background : Coral ; }
.button:active { background : OrangeRed ; }
form { display : inline-block ; }
```

4   Save the HTML document then open it in a browser to see the rollover effect on each button

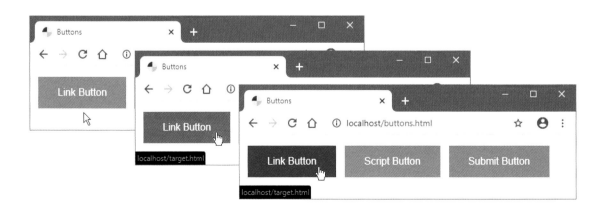

5 Click the link button to open its target page, then return to the buttons page

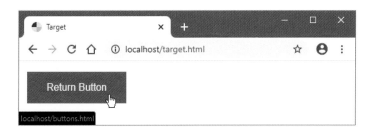

6 Click the script button to execute the snippet of code assigned to its **onclick** attribute, then close the dialog box

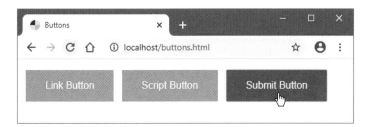

7 Click the submit button to see the web server response

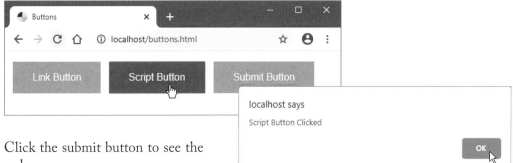

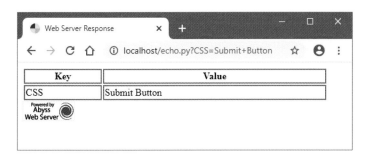

Reveal Elements

A dropdown box can be used to reveal larger versions of thumbnail images and, optionally, additional descriptive text. This technique is similar to that used to display the dropdown menu on page 250, so the thumbnail element should be styled with a **position : relative ;** rule so that the dropdown box can be positioned directly beneath it with a **position : absolute ;** rule. Additionally, the dropdown box should have a specified **z-index** value to place it above any existing content on the page.

reveal.html

html.png
& css.png
& js.png – all
330px x 464px

Don't forget

If you do not specify a **background** value for the dropdown content it may be transparent – so the content beneath will remain visible.

1 Create an HTML document with a division that contains a thumbnail image, plus an inner division containing a larger version of the image and some descriptive text
```
<div class="thumbnail">
<img src="html.png" alt="logo" width="35" height="50">
<div class="dropdown">
<img src="html.png" alt="logo" width="135" height="190">
<span class="label">HyperText Markup Language</span>
</div>
```

2 Next, copy and paste the elements in Step 1, then in the copies replace both image sources with **css.png** and replace the descriptive text with **Cascading Style Sheets**

3 Once again, copy and paste the elements in Step 1, then in these copies replace both image sources with **js.png** and replace the descriptive text with **JavaScript**

4 Add a style sheet with rules to position the thumbnail – this will be the active element for the dropdown
```
div.thumbnail { position : relative ; display : inline-block ; }
```

5 Next, add rules to position and hide the second inner division – this will be the dropdown content
```
div.dropdown { position : absolute ; padding : 2px ;
               border : 2px dashed DarkOrange ;
               background : White ;
               z-index : 1 ; display : none ; }
```

6 Now, add a rule to reveal the dropdown content when the user places the cursor over the thumbnail
```
div.thumbnail:hover div.dropdown { display : block ; }
```

...cont'd

7 Finally, add rules to style the descriptive text
   span.label **{ display : block ; padding : 15px ;**
   text-align : center ;
   background : DarkOrange ; color : White ; }

8 Save the HTML document then place the cursor over
   each thumbnail to reveal the dropdown content

Hot tip

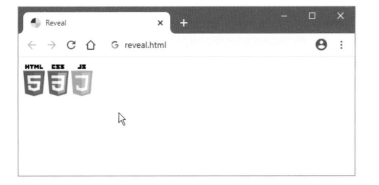

Alternatively, elements can be hidden with a **visibility : hidden ;** rule and revealed with a **visibility : visible ;** rule. With these, the content still occupies space on the page even when hidden, whereas with a **display : none ;** rule, the content is totally removed from the page flow layout.

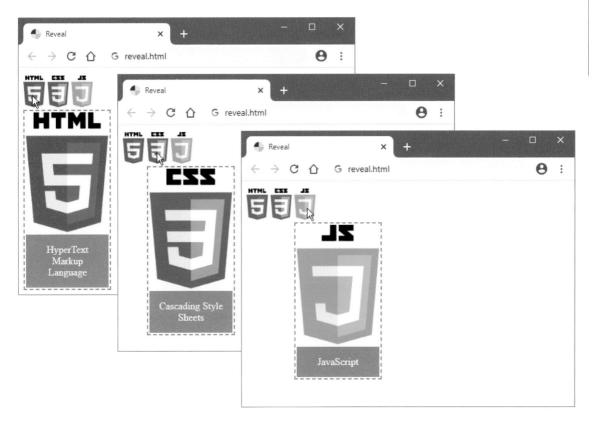

Draw Corners

The appearance of content box borders can be enhanced by rounding their corners with the CSS **border-radius** property. Where all corners are to have the same radius, this property can specify the radius size as a distance from the corner point in both horizontal and vertical directions – for example, as a value of **20px**.

Individual corners may also be rounded by specifying a radius size to **border-top-left, border-top-right, border-bottom-right,** and **border-bottom-left** properties.

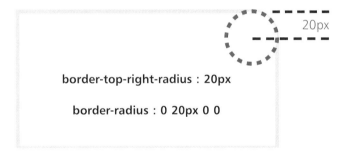

Hot tip

You can create an ellipsis by setting **border-radius** to 50% on an oblong content box.

Alternatively, individual corners may be rounded by using **border-radius** as a shorthand property to specify four values – one value for each corner in the order **border-top-left, border-top-right, border-bottom-right, border-bottom-left.** Where a zero value is specified for any corner, no radius will be produced. Individual corners may also be curved by specifying two values to define an ellipse so the horizontal and vertical directions get a different radius. The first value specifies the horizontal x radius and the second value specifies the vertical y radius. For example, **border-top-right-radius : 20px 50px** defines an ellipse.

Circles can be created by setting the **border-radius** property to exactly half the size (including borders) of a square content box.

1 Create an HTML document with three outer divisions, which each contain one inner division element
**<div class="outer all"><div class="inner">
All Rounded Corners</div></div>**

**<div class="outer ind"><div class="inner">
Individual Corners</div></div>**

**<div class="outer cir"><div class="inner">
Circle</div></div>**

radius.html

2 Next, add a style sheet with rules to specify the position and appearance of each element
div.outer, div.inner { width : 120px ; height : 120px ; }

**div.outer { display : inline-block ; margin : 10px ;
  border : 5px solid DarkOrange ; background : Bisque ; }**

**div.inner { display : table-cell ; text-align : center ;
  vertical-align : middle ; border : 2px dashed Orange ; }**

Hot tip

Notice here how the **table-cell** display style allows the text to be centered horizontally and vertically.

3 Now, add rules to adjust the corners of the outer divisions
div.all { border-radius : 40px ; }

div.ind { border-radius : 50px 0 50px 0 ; }

div.cir { border-radius : 65px ; }

265

4 Save the HTML document then open it in a browser to see the rounded corners

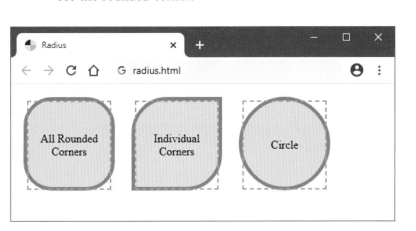

Don't forget

The second outer division in this example could alternatively be styled with individual rules **border-top-left-radius : 50px ; border-bottom-right-radius : 50px ;**

Cast Shadows

The appearance of content boxes can be enhanced by adding drop-shadow effects with the **box-shadow** property, and text can be similarly enhanced with the **text-shadow** property.

Horizontal and vertical offset values must be specified to position the shadow. Where these are positive values, the shadow will be positioned to the right and below the item. Conversely, negative values can be specified to position the shadow to the left and above respectively – for example, positive values of **20px 10px**.

20px

10px

Optionally, the **box-shadow** and **text-shadow** properties can have a third value to specify a blur distance that determines how blurred the shadow's edge will be – the higher the value, the more blurred. For example, a blur value of **20px** expands the shadow to blur its edge in an area that is 10 pixels either side of the original offset.

Beware

Although specifying a color is not strictly required, it is recommended to avoid inconsistencies between web browsers.

Additionally, a fourth optional value can specify a spread distance, to determine how far the shadow should extend beyond the offset, and the **inset** keyword can be used to create an inner shadow.

You can also add multiple shadows to text by specifying a comma-separated list of shadow values to the **text-shadow** property.

...cont'd

1 Create an HTML document with three outer divisions, which each contain one inner division element

```
<div class="outer drop">
        <div class="inner">HTML</div></div>
<div class="outer glow">
        <div class="inner">CSS</div></div>
<div class="outer inset">
        <div class="inner">JS</div></div>
```

shadow.html

2 Next, add a style sheet with rules to specify the position and appearance of each element

```
div.outer, div.inner { width : 120px ; height : 120px ; }
div.outer { display : inline-block ; margin : 20px ;
  border : 2px solid Black ; background : White ; }
div.inner { display : table-cell ; text-align : center ;
  vertical-align : middle ; font : bold 2em sans-serif ; }
```

3 Now, add rules to apply shadows to boxes and text

```
div.drop { box-shadow : 10px 10px 10px DarkOrange ; }
div.drop > div.inner { text-shadow : 2px 2px DarkOrange ; }

div.glow { box-shadow : 0 0 10px 10px DarkOrange ; }
div.glow > div.inner { color : White ;
                text-shadow : 2px 2px 4px Black ; }

div.inset { box-shadow : 10px 10px 30px DarkOrange inset ; }
div.inset > div.inner { color : Bisque ; text-shadow :
-1px 0 Black , 0 1px Black , 1px 0 Black , 0 -1px Black ; }
```

4 Save the HTML document then open it in a browser to see the shadows

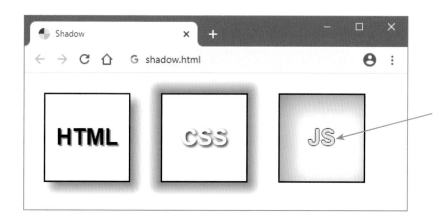

Hot tip

Notice how the multiple shadow rules create a border around the text.

Blend Gradients

CSS provides four functions to create gradient fills, which the browser blends smoothly from one specified color to another – **linear-gradient( )**, **repeating-linear-gradient( )**, **radial-gradient( )** and **repeating-radial-gradient( )**.

The **linear-gradient( )** function creates the color transition along a linear path blending from one "color stop" point to another. Each color stop may be specified in the function's parentheses simply as comma-separated color values, or as comma-separated color and position value – for example, as **Red, Yellow** or as **Red 50%, Yellow 100%** to define color stops at the path's mid-point and end. There must be at least two color stops, but you can specify multiple color stops for more elaborate gradient effects that employ more colors.

The default direction of the **linear-gradient( )** function's path is top-to-bottom, but you can define a different direction by including an optional first value as a combination of keywords **to top bottom left right** – for example, for a diagonal gradient starting at the top left with **to bottom right** keywords. For more precise control of the direction, the optional first value may be specified as an angle, such as **45deg** or **90deg**. In this case, the value specifies the angle between a horizontal edge and **linear-gradient( )** path. For example, **45deg** creates a diagonal path from the bottom left corner to the top right corner, and **90deg** produces a horizontal path from left to right. You can also specify negative values. For example, **-90deg** creates a horizontal path from right to left (as does **270deg**).

The **radial-gradient( )** function also blends from one color stop to another, but the path spreads out from a center point. By default, it begins at the center of the element and is circular. Optionally, the **ellipse** keyword can be specified along with length and position values to define a different radial shape and different center point. You can define a different center point by including an optional first value as a combination of keywords **closest-side**, **farthest-side**, **closest-corner**, **farthest-corner**, **at** and percentage values for the x-axis and y-axis – for example, for a radial gradient starting to the right and below center with **closest-side at 60% 60%**.

The **repeating-linear-gradient( )** and **repeating-radial-gradient( )** functions accept the same values as their non-repeating counterparts, but automatically repeat the gradient after the final specified color stop has been reached.

Don't forget

Each gradient must have at least two color stops.

...cont'd

1 Create an HTML document with four division elements
```
<div class="linear"></div>
<div class="linear-repeat"></div>
<div class="radial"></div>
<div class="radial-repeat"></div>
```

gradient.html

2 Next, add a style sheet with rules to specify the position and appearance of each element – including a default background color
```
div { display : inline-block ; width : 100px ; height : 100px ;
      margin : 10px ; border : 2px solid Black ;
      background : Orange ; }
```

Beware

Some browsers may not support gradients so it's useful to specify a default single color.

3 Now, add rules to apply gradient backgrounds for browsers that support gradients
```
div.linear { background :
      linear-gradient( 45deg , DarkOrange, Bisque ) ; }

div.linear-repeat { background :
      repeating-linear-gradient( DarkOrange 20%,
            Bisque 40%, OrangeRed 50% ) ; }
div.radial { background :
      radial-gradient( DarkOrange 20%,
            Bisque 40%, OrangeRed 50% ) ; }

div.radial-repeat { background :
      repeating-radial-gradient( DarkOrange 20%,
            Bisque 40%, OrangeRed 50% ) ; }
```

4 Save the HTML document then open it in a browser to see the gradients

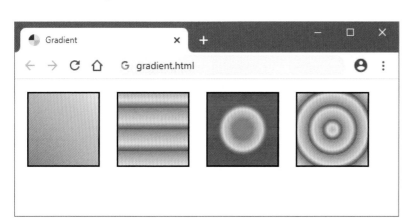

Hot tip

You can specify the same color for the first and last color stops in a repeating gradient to avoid abrupt changes.

Decorate Borders

CSS provides a **border-image** property that allows you to specify an image source to the CSS **url( )** function for decoration of borders. This is the only required value and will position the image within a specified border area, at each corner of a content box.

The **border-image** property can specify additional values, after the image source, to decorate the border areas between the corners – but this works in an unusual manner.

The **border-image** property slices the image into nine sections, like those of a tic-tac-toe board. The first additional value can specify at which points to slice the image from the top, right, bottom, and left edges. For example, a **33%** value will slice one third from each edge. The four corner slices are then placed at each

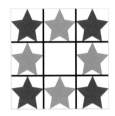

corner of the border, and the four middle slices are then stretched, by default, to decorate the border areas between the corners.

A second additional value can explicitly specify how to decorate the border areas between the corners using these keywords:

- **stretch** – the middle slices stretch to fill the areas (the default).

- **repeat** – the middle slices tile to fill the areas, dividing if necessary.

- **round** – the middle slices tile to fill the areas, rescaling if necessary to avoid dividing.

The **border-image** property is a shorthand property for individual **border-image-source**, **border-image-slice**, and **border-image-repeat** properties. There are also further additional values that can be specified for **border-image-width**, to specify the widths of the border image, and **border-image-outset**, to specify how far the image can extend outside the border area.

All browsers that support the **border-image** property also support gradients. This means that, besides images, you can specify any type of gradient to decorate a border.

Beware

The **border-image** will only be applied if a **border** property has been specified.

1 Create an HTML document with four division elements
```
<div class="image"></div>
<div class="round"></div>
<div class="stretch"></div>
<div class="gradient"></div>
```

decorate.html

2 Next, add a style sheet with rules to specify the position and appearance of each element – including a border
```
div { display : inline-block ; width : 175px ; height : 100px ;
      margin : 10px ; border : 30px solid transparent ;
      background : Bisque ; }
```

3 Now, add rules to decorate the border of each division
```
div.image { border-image : url( stars.png) ; }
div.round { border-image : url( stars.png) 33% round ; }
div.stretch { border-image : url( stars.png) 33% stretch ; }
div.gradient { border-image : repeating-linear-gradient
              ( 45deg, OrangeRed, Orange 20% ) 33% ; }
```

stars.png – 90px x 90px
Gray areas are transparent.

4 Save the HTML document then open it in a browser to see the decorated borders

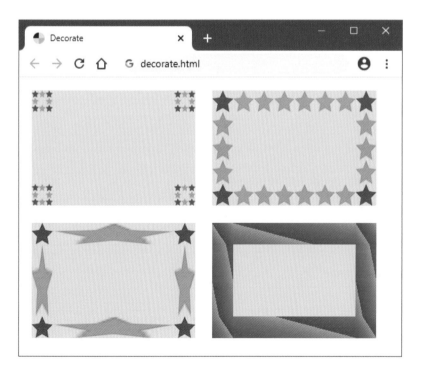

Transform Shapes

CSS can dynamically manipulate content boxes to change their size, position or orientation by specifying one of the transformation functions below to their **transform** property.

Function	Transform
scale(*n1,n2*)	Scales X and Y axis all by the ratio *n1 n2*
scaleX(*n*)	Scales X axis by the ratio *n*
scaleY(*n*)	Scales Y axis by the ratio *n*
skew(*n1,n2*)	Scales X and Y axis all by the angle *n1 n2*
skewX(*n*)	Scales X axis by the angle *n*
skewY(*n*)	Scales Y axis by the angle *n*
rotate(*n*)	Rotates by the angle *n* amount
rotateX(*n*)	Rotates X axis by the angle *n* amount
rotateY(*n*)	Rotates Y axis by the angle *n* amount
rotateZ(*n*)	Rotates Z axis by the angle *n* amount
translate(*n1,n2*)	Moves X and Y axis by *n1 n2* amount
translateX(*n*)	Moves X axis by n amount
translateY(*n*)	Moves Y axis by *n* amount
matrix(*n,n,n,n,n,n*)	Scales by *n, n*, skews by *n, n* translates by *n, n*

Hot tip

You can also specify just one single value to the **scale( )** function to be applied to both the X axis and Y axis.

The **matrix( )** function is seldom used but it allows you to rotate, scale, move, and skew elements all at once. Its six values, in (somewhat confusing) order, represent the individual functions **scaleX( )**, **skewY( )**, **skewX( )**, **scaleY( )**, **translateX( )**, and **translateY( )**.

A "transform origin" is the point around which a transformation is performed and is, by default, the center of the element. You can, however, specify an alternative to a **transform-origin** property as units, percentage values, or keywords **top**, **bottom**, **left**, **right**, and **center**. For example, with **rotate( )** and **transform-origin : top left ;** the element will pivot around its top-left corner, instead of its center point.

Beware

The **transform-origin** property can only be used in conjunction with the **transform** property.

Transformations can be specified to the element's **:hover** pseudo-class so the transformation will be performed when the user places the cursor over the element, and will resume its normal state when the user moves the cursor off the element.

…cont'd

1 Create an HTML document with three division elements
```
<div class="rotate">Rotate</div>
<div class="scale">Scale</div>
<div class="skew">Skew</div>
```

transform.html

2 Next, add a style sheet with rules to specify the position and appearance of each element
```
div { display : inline-block ; margin : 50px 0 0 50px ;
       padding : 15px ; background : DarkOrange ;
       color : White ; font : 1.5em sans-serif ; }
```

3 Now, add rules to transform each division when the user places the cursor over the content box
```
div.rotate:hover { transform : rotate( 45deg ) ; }
div.scale:hover { transform : scale(  2.0, 2.0 ) ; }
div.skew:hover { transform : skew( 15deg, 15deg ) ; }
```

4 Save the HTML document then open it in a browser and place the cursor over each element to see transformations

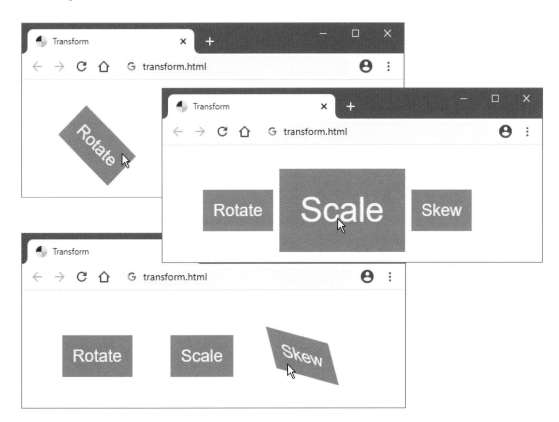

Make Transitions

CSS can dynamically modify property values to change their color, size, position, orientation, etc. over a specified period of time to create simple animated effects with the **transition** property.

The **transition** property must specify the CSS property that is to be modified, and the duration of the effect – for example, a style rule **transition : width 5s ;** to modify the width of an element over a period of five seconds. Multiple properties can be specified as a comma-separated list of property and duration pairs, such as **transition : width 5s, height 3s ;** to modify both width and height.

You can control the "acceleration curve" of the effect by assigning one of the functions below to a **transition-timing-function** property.

Don't forget

A transition will not run unless you specify a duration period.

274

Function	Transition
linear	Consistent speed from start to end
ease	Increases from start to reach full speed then decreases at end (default)
ease-in	Increases at start only
ease-out	Decreases at end only
ease-in-out	Increases at start and decreases at end
steps(*n*)	Jump to *n* number of intervals
cubic-bezier(*x1,y1,x2,y2*)	Elastic or bounce between coordinates

Additionally, you can specify a **transition-delay** time value, such as **1s** for one second, so the effect will not begin immediately.

Hot tip

The **steps( )** function jumps to pauses in the transition, so that **steps(5)** pauses each second in a five second effect.

The **transition** property is a shorthand property for individual **transition-property, transition-duration, transition-timing-function,** and **transition-delay** properties. Values for these may be specified to each individual property or values for all four may be specified, in this order, to the shorthand property – for example, to modify a width, over five seconds, at a consistent speed, after a half second delay with **transition : width 5s linear 0.5s ;**. You can also specify multiple transitions in a comma-separated list of grouped values.

The final value of the property to be modified can be specified to an element's **:hover** pseudo-class – so the transformation will be performed when the user places the cursor over the element.

...cont'd

1 Create an HTML document with one division element
`<div class="expand">Transition</div>`

transition.html

2 Next, add a style sheet with rules to specify the position and appearance of the element
```
div { margin : 50px ; padding : 15px ;
      color : White ; font : 1.5em sans-serif ;
      background : Orange ;
      width : 100px ; height : 30px ; }
```

3 Now, add a rule to modify the background, width, and height properties in a five-second transition effect
```
div.expand { transition : background 5s linear 0.5s ,
             width 5s ease-out 0.5s ,
             height 5s steps(5) 0.5s ; }
```

Hot tip

4 Then, add rules to specify the final values of the background, width, and height at the end of the effect
```
div.expand:hover { background : OrangeRed ;
                   width : 350px ; height : 100px ; }
```

The element will resume its original values when the user moves the cursor off the active element – automatically running the transition effect in reverse.

5 Save the HTML document then open it in a browser and place the cursor over the element to see the transition

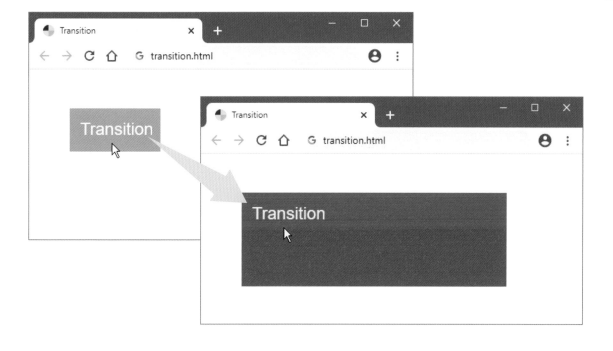

Animate Elements

CSS can dynamically modify property values over a specified period of time with the **transition** property, as described on page 274, but can also nominate "keyframes" to determine property values at particular points for the **animation** property.

Keyframes are created by a CSS **@keyframes** ("at keyframes") rule that defines an animation name and selects points using percentages or **from** (0%) and **to** (100%) keywords – for example, naming an animation "bounce" and selecting three points, like this:

```
@keyframes bounce {

                    from      { top : 100px ; }
                    50%       { top : 150px ; }
                    to        { top : 300px ; }

}
```

The **animation** property can specify, in this order, the animation name (defined by the **@keyframes** rule), duration, timing function, delay, iteration count, and direction.

Duration and delay are specified as with transitions, where a value of **5s** represents a period of five seconds.

Timing functions that control the acceleration curve are the same as those for transitions, such as **ease-in-out**, and the iteration count may be an integer or the keyword **infinite**.

Interestingly, the direction can be specified as **normal** (the default), **reverse**, or **alternate** – alternating between playing forward and reverse on successive iterations.

The **animation** property is a shorthand property for individual **animation-name, animation-duration, animation-timing-function, animation-delay, animation-iteration-count, animation-direction** properties. Values for these may be specified to each individual property or values for all six may be specified, in this order, to the shorthand property – for example, to bind a keyframe named "bounce" to a five-second animation, at a consistent speed, after a one-second delay, to repeat infinitely, in alternating directions, with **animation : bounce 5s linear 1s infinite alternate ;**

An **animation-fill-mode** can also be added for animations that run for a set number of iterations. This can specify **forwards**, so that the element will retain the values of the final keyframe, **backwards**, so it will get the style values of the first keyframe, or **both**.

Keyframes determine what styles one or more properties will have at various points during an animation.

You can combine transitions and animations to create some great effects.

1 Create an HTML document with one division element that contains an inner division element
```
<div class="ball">
<div class="label">Animation</div></div>
```

animation.html

2 Next, add a style sheet with rules to specify the position and appearance of the outer division element
```
div.ball { position : absolute ; top : 10px ; width : 120px ;
height : 120px ; color : White ; font : 1.5em sans-serif ;
background : Orange ; border-radius : 50% ; }
```

3 Now, add rules to specify the appearance of the inner division element
```
div.label { display : table-cell ; width : 120px ;
height : 120px ; text-align : center ; vertical-align : middle ; }
```

4 Then, add a keyframe rule to define an animation name and specify points for the animation
```
@keyframes bounce { from { top : 10px ; }
50% { top : 40px ; } to { top : 100px ; } }
```

Hot tip

No animation delay is required in this example, so its value is omitted from the style rule and the browser uses its zero default delay value.

277

5 Finally, add a rule to bind the animation to the outer division element
```
div.ball { animation : bounce 2s linear infinite alternate ; }
```

6 Save the HTML document then open it in a browser to see the animation

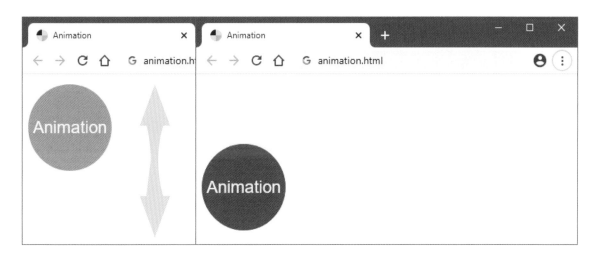

Fit Objects

CSS provides a number of ways in which you can manipulate image or video content. These can be centered within a container simply by making the **<img>** or **<video>** element into a block and setting its left and right margins to the **auto** value.

More interestingly, you can specify how image or video content fits into the **<img>** or **<video>** element itself, using a CSS **object-fit** property. This can determine whether the content should be stretched, squeezed, scaled, or clipped by specifying any of the values listed below:

Value	Fit
fill	Content is stretched or squeezed to fill the element's content box (the default)
contain	Content is scaled up or down to maintain its aspect ratio and fit inside the element's content box
cover	Content is scaled to maintain its aspect ratio and fill the element's content box, so may be clipped
scale-down	Content is scaled down to maintain its aspect ratio in smaller content boxes
none	Content is not resized, so may be clipped

Probably the best way to understand how these values affect how the object fits into its content box is by comparison:

fit.html

run.png
150px x 120px

1 Create an HTML document with six elements that will display the same image – but fit differently
<img src="run.png" alt="Run">

<img class="scale-down short" src="run.png" alt="Run">

<img class="none short" src="run.png" alt="Run">

<img class="fill tall" src="run.png" alt="Run">

<img class="contain tall" src="run.png" alt="Run">

<img class="cover tall" src="run.png" alt="Run">

...cont'd

2 Add a style sheet with rules to specify the appearance and set the width of each element to match the image width
img { display : inline-block ; border : 2px solid DarkOrange ; margin : 5px ; width : 150px ; }

3 Next, add style rules to set some content boxes shorter, and some taller, than the image height of 120 pixels
img.short { height : 80px ; }
img.tall { height : 200px ; }

4 Now, add rules to specify how the images should fit their respective content boxes
img.scale-down { object-fit : scale-down ; }
img.none { object-fit : none ; }
img.fill { object-fit : fill ; }
img.contain { object-fit : contain ; }
img.cover { object-fit : cover ; }

5 Save the HTML document then open it in a browser to compare how the objects fit within each content box

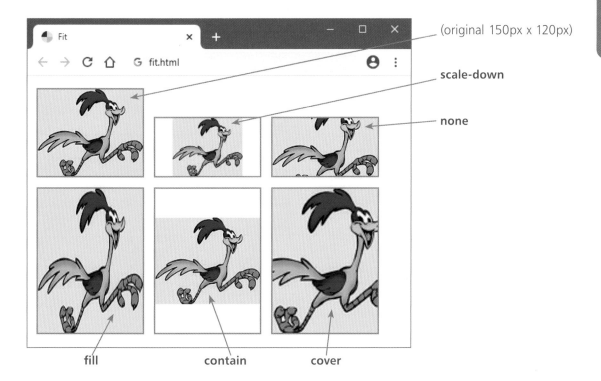

(original 150px x 120px)

scale-down

fill   contain   cover

Summary

● The type of **cursor** icon to display when the pointer hovers over a selected element can be specified using a keyword.

● A currently-selected interactive component of a page can be indicated by specifying a value to the CSS **:focus** pseudo-class.

● Interface events caused by user actions are recognized by the CSS **:focus**, **:hover**, and **:active** pseudo-classes.

● The MouseOver and MouseOut states can be used to create rollover effects for links, scripting, or form submission buttons.

● A relatively positioned thumbnail element can reveal a larger element that is absolutely positioned directly beneath it.

● Content box borders can have rounded corners by specifying a radius size to the **border-radius** property.

● Content boxes and text can have shadows by specifying offset values to the **box-shadow** or **text-shadow** property.

● Linear and radial gradients fill content boxes with colors blended between specified color stop points.

● Content box borders can be decorated by stretching or tiling a sliced image specified to the **border-image** property.

● Transformations manipulate content boxes to change their size, position or orientation.

● Transitions modify property values over a specified period of time to create simple animated effects.

● Animations modify property values over a period of time and nominate keyframes to specify values at particular points.

● Images and videos can be stretched, squeezed, scaled or clipped to fit inside a content box.

13 Control the Web Page

Change Models

Web browsers apply default element styles, contained in their "user agent style sheet", that apply margins and padding values automatically to some elements. For example, the **<body>** element typically gets an 8-pixel margin by default. You can inspect this in most browsers by hitting the F12 key, to open a Developer Tools window, and selecting the body element:

default.html

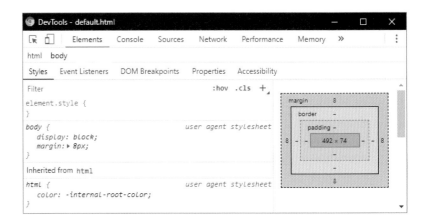

The default value for the CSS **box-sizing** property is **content-box**.

Additionally, the browser's default box model will apply your specified padding and borders outside your specified element size, so the overall size of the element becomes larger than your specification. For example, an **<ul>** list element specified to have a 2-pixel border and a size of 100 x 70 pixels typically gains a 16-pixel margin top and bottom, 40-pixel left padding (for the list markers), and the 2-pixel border outside the content box. This makes the overall size of the element 144 x 106 pixels:

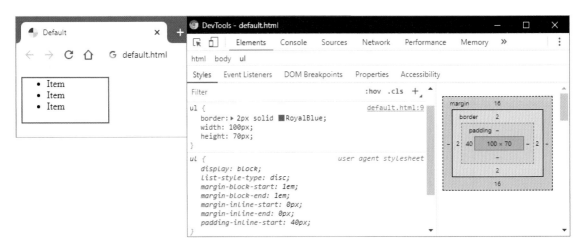

...cont'd

In order to gain control of these default browser behaviors, you can begin each one of your style sheets with these universal rules:

* { margin : 0 ; padding : 0 ; box-sizing : border-box ; }

This overrides the browser's default styles so margins and padding values are no longer automatically applied to elements:

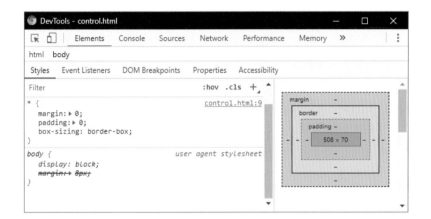

control.html

Additionally, the browser's default box model will no longer apply your specified padding and borders outside your specified element size, so the overall size of the element is exactly as you specified. For example, an **<ul>** list element specified to have a 2-pixel border and a size of 100 x 70 pixels, now gains no margins or padding, and the 2-pixel border is now inside the content box. This makes the overall size of the element 100 x 70 pixels, as intended by your specification:

Hot tip

You now have control and could add a left padding for the list markers if required.

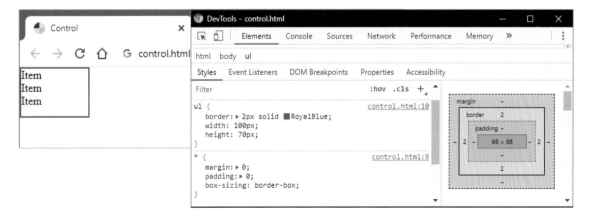

Draw Outlines

CSS provides three properties that can be applied to the user interface, complementing the regular box model. The first two of these can be used to add outlines around an element. The **outline** property accepts the same values that can be specified to the **border** property – for example, **outline : 2px solid RoyalBlue ;** to draw a 2-pixel blue outline around an element.

Crucially, unlike a border, an outline is not part of the element's dimensions, so an element's total width and height is unaffected by the addition of an outline. An outline is drawn on a different level of the Z axis, so may overlap other content.

Additionally, you can add space between an outline and the edge, (or border) of an element by specifying a distance value to an **outline-offset** property – for example, **outline-offset : 5px ;** to add a 5-pixel space between the edge of an element and an outline.

The third property that can be applied to the user interface can be used to allow the user to resize an element, typically by dragging its bottom-right corner. The **resize** property can allow the user to resize an element's size both horizontally and vertically when it specifies a **both** value.

If the user resizes an element to reduce its dimensions, the contents may well overflow, so when using the **resize** property it should be accompanied by an **overflow** style rule to handle the content overflow. It is important that the overflow should be specified as **scroll**, **auto**, or **hidden**, because the **resize** property will not be applied to inline or block elements whose overflow is set to a **visible** value.

Where you want to restrict the user's ability to resize an element in both directions, you can specify a **horizontal** value to the **resize** property – so that the user can only adjust the width of an element by dragging its corner.

Conversely, you can specify a **vertical** value to the **resize** property – so that the user can only adjust the height of an element by dragging its corner.

Don't forget

Setting all elements' **box-sizing** property to **border-box** means that the edge of the element is the same as the edge of any border it has.

...cont'd

outline.html

1 Create an HTML document containing a division element
`<div class="outline resize">This division has a blue outline and can be resized by dragging its bottom-right corner.</div>`

2 Add a style sheet with rules to control the web page
`* { margin : 0 ; padding : 0 ; box-sizing : border-box ; }`

3 Next, add rules to specify the appearance of the division
`div { width : 420px ; margin : 20px ; padding : 10px ; border : 2px solid Black ; background : LightSteelBlue ; font : 1.25em sans-serif ; }`

4 Now, add rules to surround the division with an outline
`div.outline {    outline : 10px solid RoyalBlue ; outline-offset : 5px ; }`

5 Then, add a rule to make the division resizable
`div.resize { resize : both ; overflow : auto ; }`

6 Save the HTML document, then open it in a web browser to see the outline and resize the element

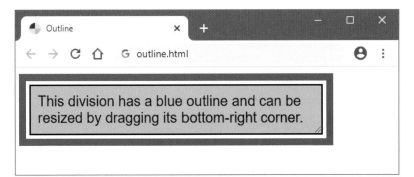

Outlines can overlap page contents.

285

Use Columns

CSS provides a number of properties that make it simple to create multiple-column layouts for text – like those in newspapers.

First, you need to specify an integer value to a **column-count** property to determine the number of columns you want the text divided into – for example, **column-count : 3** ; for three columns. Typically, this will create a gap ("gutter") between each column that is **1em** wide by default – equivalent to the height of the font. You can also choose your own gutter size by specifying a distance to a **column-gap** property – for example, **column-gap : 50px** ; to create a gap of 50-pixels width between the columns.

With a wider gutter, you can then add a vertical ruled line by specifying width, style, and color values to a **column-rule** property. This accepts the same values as the **border** property, so that a rule of **column-rule : 5px solid RoyalBlue** ; would add blue lines. The **column-rule** property is a shorthand property for individual **column-rule-width**, **column-rule-style**, and **column-rule-color** properties. It must at least specify a style to display a vertical ruled line using default initial values for width and color.

multicol.html

1 Create an HTML document with a division element that contains one heading and some text content
<div class="newspaper">

<h1>The CSS Reporter</h1>
Cascading Style Sheets (CSS) is a style sheet language used for describing the presentation of a document written in a markup language. Although most often used to set the visual style of web pages and user interfaces written in HTML and XHTML, the language can be applied to any XML document, including plain XML, SVG and XUL, and is applicable to rendering in speech, or on other media.

</div>

2 Add a style sheet with rules to control the web page
* { margin : 0 ; padding : 0 ; box-sizing : border-box ; }

3 Next, add rules to add a margin to the division and to specify the appearance of a two-column layout
div.newspaper { margin : 15px ;
            column-count : 2 ;
            column-gap : 50px ;
            column-rule : solid ; }

4 Save the HTML document, then open it in a web browser to see the multiple-column layout

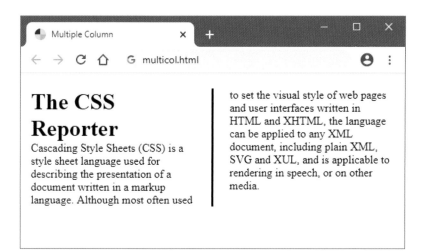

The default **column-rule-color** value here is derived from the text color – adding a color rule for the text will also change the vertical line color to match – for example, **color : Red ;** to change text and line.

5 Edit the rules in Step 3 – to change the appearance to a three-column layout with dotted gutter lines

```
div.newspaper { margin : 15px ;
               column-count : 3 ;
               column-gap : 50px ;
               column-rule : 5px dotted RoyalBlue ; }
```

6 Save the HTML document again, then refresh the web browser to see the new multiple-column layout

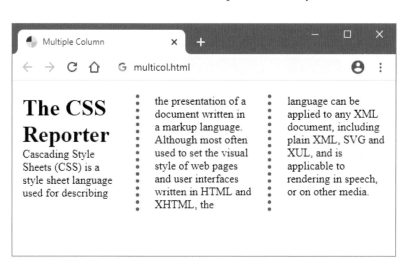

Beware

Setting this example to have many columns will cause the heading to overlap other content – a solution is demonstrated in the example overleaf.

Span Columns

In addition to the **column-count**, **column-gap**, and **column-rule** properties introduced in the example on page 286, CSS provides three further properties for use in column layouts.

Where you prefer elements such as headings to span across columns, you can specify how many columns to span as an integer value, or using the keyword **all**, to a **column-span** property.

You can also state a preferred width for the columns by specifying a size to a **column-width** property – but the browser only treats the specified value as a minimum width suggestion. If it cannot fit at least two columns at the specified width, it will revert to a single-column layout.

Lastly, there is a shorthand **columns** property that can be used to specify both **column-width** and **column-count** values. Using both the **columns** and **column-rule** shorthand properties lets you specify a large number of column layout values very concisely.

spancol.html

1 Create an HTML document with a division that contains text content and two headings
```
<div class="newspaper">
```

```
<h1>Professional Word Documents</h1>
To make your document look professionally produced,
Word provides header, footer, cover page, and text box
designs that complement each other. You can add a
matching cover page, header, and sidebar. Click Insert and
then choose the elements you want from the different
galleries.
```

```
<h2>Coordinated Document Styles</h2>
Themes and styles also help keep your document
coordinated. When you click Design and choose a new
Theme, the pictures, charts, and SmartArt graphics change
to match your new theme. When you apply styles, your
headings change to match the new theme.
```

```
</div>
```

2 Add a style sheet with rules to control the web page
```
* { margin : 0 ; padding : 0 ; box-sizing : border-box ; }
```

...cont'd

3 Next, add rules to add left and right margins to the division and to specify the appearance of a three column layout – with a suggested column width of 100 pixels
div.newspaper {
  margin : 0 15px ;
  column-gap : 50px ;
  column-rule : 5px solid LightSteelBlue ;
  columns : 100px 3 ; }

4 Now, add rules to specify the appearance of the headings and to have both headings span across all columns
h1, h2 {
  padding : 10px 10px 10px ;
  margin : 20px 0 0 ;
  background : LightSteelBlue ;
  column-span : all ; }

5 Save the HTML document, then open it in a web browser to see the multiple column layout and headings that span across the columns

The **column-rule** property is shorthand for **column-width**, **column-style** and **column-color** properties.

289

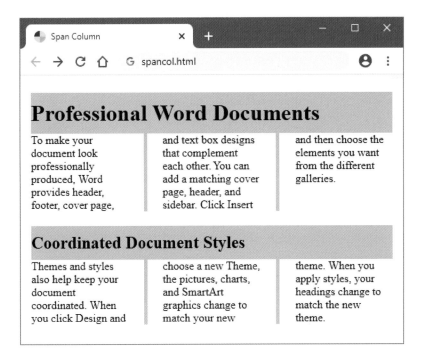

Use Flexbox

Previous examples in this book have displayed content using absolute or relative positioning, and by floating content. These are important, but not ideally suited to create a flexible layout that will respond to various browser screen sizes. To answer this need, CSS introduced the flexible box ("flexbox") layout scheme.

To create a flexible box you must first define an element to be a "flex container" by specifying a **flex** value to its **display** property.

Any inner elements ("flex items") within a flex container will appear on a single row. If the length of the row exceeds the width of the browser, the row will not, by default, wrap onto the next row – unless you specify a **wrap** value to a **flex-wrap** property.

You can also reverse the order of the flex items in the row by specifying a **wrap-reverse** value to the **flex-wrap** property.

So, to create a flexible box that will wrap items onto rows, you will need to specify values to both **display** and **flex-wrap** properties.

Hot tip

Refer back to the absolute and relative positioning example on page 200 and the float layout on page 206.

flexbox.html

Hot tip

All modern browsers support flexbox since:

 Chrome 29.0

 Edge 11.0

 Firefox 22.0

 Safari 10

 Opera 48

1 Create an HTML document with a division element that contains five inner divisions
```
<div class="flex-container">
        <div>One</div>
        <div>Two</div>
        <div>Three</div>
        <div>Four</div>
        <div>Five</div>
</div>
```

2 Add a style sheet with rules to control the web page
`* { margin : 0 ; padding : 0 ; box-sizing : border-box ; }`

3 Next, add rules to make the outer division flexible
```
div.flex-container {        display : flex ;
                            flex-wrap : wrap ;
                            border : 2px dashed RoyalBlue ; }
```

4 Now, add rules to specify the appearance of the flex items
```
div.flex-container > div {
            padding : 10px 40px ;
            background : LightSteelBlue ;
            border : 2px solid RoyalBlue ;
            font : 1.25em sans-serif ; }
```

5 Save the HTML document, then open it in a web browser to see the flexbox layout

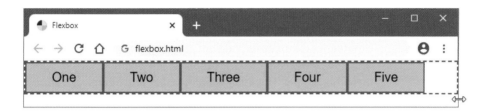

6 Drag one side of the browser window to make it narrower and see the layout wrap flex items onto the next row

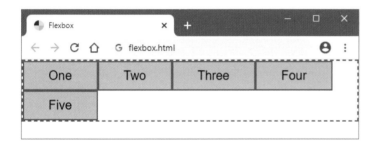

7 Edit the rules in Step 3 – to reverse the wrapping order

div.flex-container {   **display** : flex ;
                 flex-wrap : wrap-reverse ;
                 background : RoyalBlue ; }

8 Save the HTML document again, then refresh the web browser to see the flex items appear in reverse order

The default value for the **wrap** property is **nowrap**.

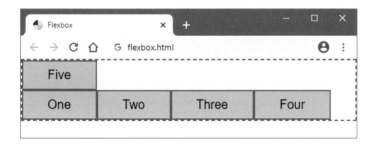

Align Items

The flexbox examples on page 290 have stretched the flex items within the confines of their lines in the flex container. This is the default behavior, but you can control how the flex items align along their lines using a CSS **justify-content** property to specify **center**, **flex-start**, **flex-end**, **space-evenly**, **space-around**, or **space-between**. The **center** value aligns items around the center of the line, but **flex-start** and **flex-end** aligns them at the start or end of the container. The **space-evenly** value adds even space around each item; **space-around** adds space between, but half-space before and after the items; and **space-between** only adds space between.

You can also control how the flex items align vertically within their lines using an **align-items** property to specify **center**, **flex-start** (start of the line), or **flex-end** (end of the line).

Similarly, you can control how the lines align within the flex container using an **align-content** property to specify **center**, **flex-start** (start of the container) or **flex-end** (end of the container).

If you want to align individual flex items vertically within their line, you can reference each inner child element by specifying its index number in the parentheses of an **:nth-child( )** pseudo-class selector, and specify your preferred value to an **align-self** property.

Hot tip

For perfect centering use **justify-content : center ; align-items : center ;** style rules.

alignment.html

1 Create an HTML document with a division element that contains five inner divisions
```
<div class="flex-container">
        <div>One</div>
        <div>Two</div>
        <div>Three</div>
        <div>Four</div>
        <div>Five</div>
</div>
```

2 Add a style sheet with rules to control the web page
```
* { margin : 0 ; padding : 0 ; box-sizing : border-box ; }
```

3 Next, add rules to make the outer division flexible and specify how the flex items should align
```
div.flex-container { display : flex ; flex-flow : row wrap ;
                     border : 2px dashed RoyalBlue ;
                     height : 200px ;
                     justify-content : space-between ;
                     align-items : center ; }
```

...cont'd

4 Now, add rules to specify the appearance of the flex items

div.flex-container > div {
        padding : 10px 40px ; background : LightSteelBlue ;
        border : 2px solid RoyalBlue ;
        font : 1.25em sans-serif ; }

5 Save the HTML document, then open it in a web browser to see the flex item alignment

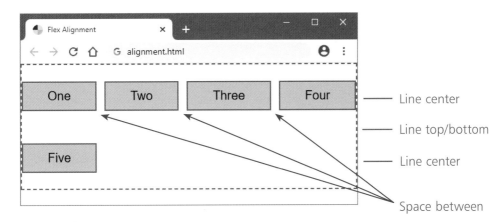

6 Now, add rules to change the alignment of two flex items

div.flex-container > div:nth-child(2) { **align-self : flex-end ; }**
div.flex-container > div:nth-child(3) { **align-self : flex-start ; }**

7 Save the HTML document again, then refresh the web browser to see the changed flex items alignment

The **align-self** property overrides the alignment specified to the **align-items** property.

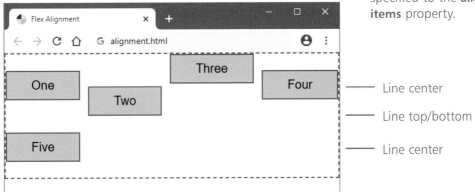

Draw Grid

The CSS flexible box layout scheme, described on pages 290-293, is a 1-dimensional system, which can automatically wrap its flex item lines to the next row or column in small display areas. By contrast, the CSS grid layout scheme is a 2-dimensional system, which places "grid items" in columns and rows.

To create a grid layout you must first define an element to be a "grid container" by specifying a **grid** (or **inline-grid**) value to its **display** property. All direct child elements within a grid container then automatically become the grid items.

You can specify how many columns the grid should have as a space-separated list of width values to a **grid-template-columns** property. For example, **grid-template-columns : 20% 60% 20% ;**. Similarly, you can specify how many rows the grid should have as a space-separated list of height values to a **grid-template-rows** property – for example, **grid-template-rows : 20% 40% 40% ;**

The **auto** keyword can also be used to specify any column width or row height – for example, to create three columns and rows of equal size with **grid-template-columns : auto auto auto ;** and with **grid-template-rows : auto auto auto ;**

	Column	Column	Column
Row			
Row			
Row			

The CSS **repeat( )** function can specify a large number of columns or rows as repeating fragment **fr** units. This function accepts two arguments to specify the number of repetitions and the number of grid track fragments – for example, to create ten columns of equal size with **grid-template-columns : repeat(10, 1fr) ;**

 Chrome 57.0

 Edge 16.0

 Firefox 52.0

 Safari 10

 Opera 44

...cont'd

1 Create an HTML document with a division element containing seven inner divisions

```
<div class="grid-container">
  <div>One</div> <div>Two</div> <div>Three</div>
  <div>Four</div> <div>Five</div> <div>Six</div>
  <div>Seven</div>
</div>
```

grid.html

2 Add a style sheet with rules to control the web page

```
* { margin : 0 ; padding : 0 ; box-sizing : border-box ; }
```

3 Next, add rules to make the outer division into a grid of three columns and two rows

```
div.grid-container {
  display : grid ;
  grid-template-columns : auto 250px auto ;
  grid-template-rows : auto 100px ;
  border : 2px dashed RoyalBlue ; }
```

4 Now, add rules to specify the appearance of the grid items

```
div.grid-container > div {
  background : LightSteelBlue ;
  border : 2px solid RoyalBlue ;
  padding : 10px 40px ;
  font : 1.25em sans-serif ; }
```

5 Save the HTML document, then open it in a web browser to see the grid layout

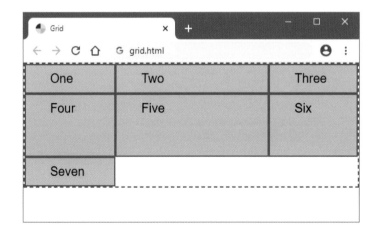

Hot tip

Notice that the second row and column is larger, and a third row is automatically added. Subsequent rows would all use only the first row template values.

Place Items

With grid containers, the lines at the leading edge between the columns and rows are known as "column lines" and "row lines".

Line numbers can be used to place grid items at a specific position in a grid container. The **grid-column** and **grid-row** shorthand properties can

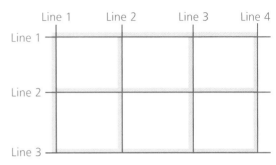

specify horizontal and vertical positioning as single line numbers, such as **grid-column : 1 ; grid-row : 2 ;** for the bottom left corner of the grid shown above.

Alternatively, two "/" forward slash-separated values can specify start and end line numbers to have the item span rows or columns – for example, **grid-column : 1 / 3 ;** would span the first two columns of the grid shown above. Additionally, the **span** keyword can achieve the same result with **grid-column : span 2 ;**

gridlines.html

Hot tip

Notice that the **justify-content**, **align-items**, and **align-content** properties can be used for item alignment in grids in the same way as with a flexbox layout.

1 Create an HTML document with a division element that contains three inner divisions
```
<div class="grid-container">
  <div>One</div> <div>Two</div> <div>Three</div>
</div>
```

2 Add a style sheet with rules to control the web page and to make the outer division into a grid container
```
* { margin : 0 ; padding : 0 ; box-sizing : border-box ; }

div.grid-container {
  display : grid ; height : 200px ;
  grid-template-columns : 100px 100px 100px ;
  grid-template-rows : 100px 100px ;
  justify-content : space-evenly ;
  align-items : center ; align-content : center ;
  border : 2px dashed DeepSkyBlue ; }
```

3 Now, add rules to specify the appearance of the grid items
```
div.grid-container > div {
  padding : 10px 30px ; background : LightBlue ;
  border : 2px solid DeepSkyBlue ; font : 1.25em sans-serif ; }
```

4 Save the HTML document, then open it in a web browser to see the grid item alignment

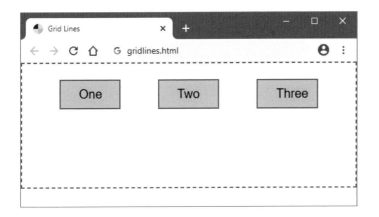

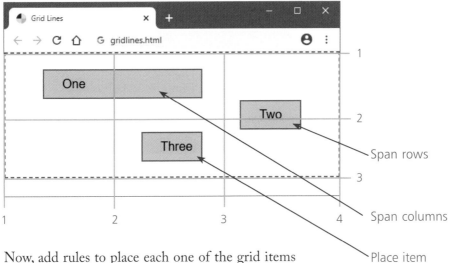

Span rows

Span columns

Place item

5 Now, add rules to place each one of the grid items

```
div.grid-container > div:nth-child( 1 ) {
  grid-column : span 2 ; grid-row : 1 ; }

div.grid-container > div:nth-child( 2 ) {
  grid-column : 3 ; grid-row : 1 / 3 ; }

div.grid-container > div:nth-child( 3 ) {
  grid-column : 2 ; grid-row : 2 ; }
```

6 Save the HTML document once more, then refresh the browser to see the position and extent of the grid items

Query Media

CSS has the ability to discover the capabilities of the viewing device by making "media queries" to apply appropriate style rules. The syntax of a CSS media query looks like this:

@media *media-type* **and** (*media-feature*) { *style-rules* }

The media type can be specified using any of the keywords below:

Keyword	Description
all	Detect all media types
print	Detect printers
screen	Detect PC desktop, tablet, and phone screens
speech	Detect screenreaders

A media query can check for many types of media feature, but the most useful are those that detect the width of the display area and orientation of the device using these keywords:

Keyword	Description
min-width	Minimum width of the display area, such as the width of the browser window
max-width	Maximum width of the display area, such as the width of the browser window
orientation	Orientation of the viewport, as either landscape mode or portrait mode

When a specified media feature is detected on the specified media type, the media query will report as true, so style rules within its curly brackets will be applied – otherwise they will be ignored. For example, to apply a background color only on devices whose display area is 600 pixels wide or less with this media query:

```
@media screen and ( max-width:600px ) {
        body { background : Blue ; }
}
```

Hot tip

A media query can check for the existence of multiple media features by adding further **and** (*media-feature*) parts to the query.

...cont'd

1 Create an HTML document with a style sheet that specifies a default background color for wide display areas
body { background : Tomato ; }

mediaquery.html

2 Next, add a media query to specify a background color for medium-width display areas
@media screen and (min-width:600px)
                        and (max-width:992px) {
  body { background : DarkOrange ; }
}

Notice that there are no spaces around the colon character in the media-feature specifications.

3 Now, add media queries for small-width display areas and different orientations
@media screen and (max-width:600px)
                        and (orientation:landscape) {
      body { background : LimeGreen ; }
}

@media screen and (max-width:600px)
                        and (orientation:portrait) {
      body { background : RoyalBlue ; }
}

4 Save the HTML document then open it in desktop, tablet, and cellphone devices to see appropriate colors

The values specified for screen widths here are typical breakpoints used to target small, medium, and large devices.

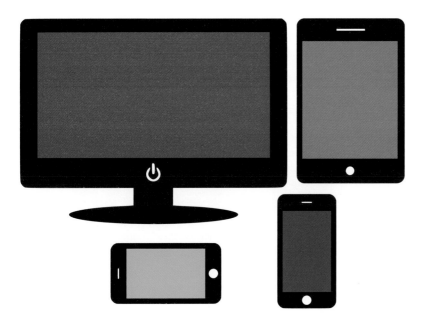

Switch Navigation

Media queries allow appropriate navigation to be provided for large and small devices. Typically, a horizontal navigation bar is provided for wide display areas, whereas a vertical navigation list is more suitable for smaller screens.

Vertical navigation bars will specify a fixed **width** value for the list, whereas horizontal navigation bars can instead **float** the list items and hide the **overflow** to maintain the visibility of the bar.

medianav.html

1 Create an HTML document containing a list with four hyperlink items
```
<ul>
<li><a href="#home" class="current">Home</a></li>
<li><a href="#info">Information</a></li>
<li><a href="#extra">Extra</a></li>
<li><a href="#contact">Contact</a></li>
</ul>
```

2 Add a style sheet with rules to control the web page
```
* { margin : 0 ; padding : 0 ; box-sizing : border-box ; }
```

3 Next, add rules to remove the markers, margin, and padding, then specify a color, fixed width, and font
```
ul {     list-style-type : none ;
         margin : 0 ;
         padding : 0 ;
         background : LightSteelBlue ;
         width : 150px ;
         font : 1.25em sans-serif ; }
```

4 Now, add style rules to display the hyperlinks in blocks and specify how they should appear
```
li a {    display : block ;
          text-align : center ;
          text-decoration : none ;
          color : Black ;
          padding : 10px ; }
```

5 Then, add style rules to indicate the hyperlinks' status
```
li a.current { background : CornflowerBlue ; }
li a:hover { background : RoyalBlue ; color : White ; }
```

6 Finally, add a media query that will apply new rules when the display area is 600 pixels or more in width
@media screen and (min-width:600px) {

       ul { overflow : hidden ; width : 100% ; }
       li a { float : left ; }

}

7 Save the HTML document then open the web page in a desktop web browser to see the horizontal navigation bar

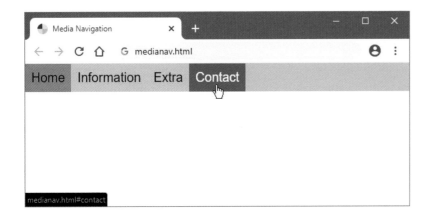

Hot tip

This example is similar to that on page 248 but automates the switch of navigation type.

8 Drag the edge of the browser to reduce its size to see the navigation bar automatically switch to a vertical list

Summary

- A universal style rule can be used to override the browser's default styles for **margin** and **padding**.

- An element's total width and height is unaffected by the addition of an **outline**.

- Elements that can be resized should specify how to handle any content **overflow**.

- A **column-count** can specify the number of columns into which text content should be divided.

- A **column-gap** can specify the gutter width between columns.

- A **column-rule** shorthand can specify the width, style, and color of a vertical ruled line to appear between columns.

- A **column-span** can specify the number of columns to span.

- The flexbox scheme first requires a flex container element be created by specifying a **flex** value to its **display** property.

- Inner elements within a **flex** container are flex items that will appear on a single row by default.

- A **justify-content** can align flex items horizontally and an **align-items** can align flex items vertically on the line.

- The grid layout scheme first requires a grid container element be created by specifying a **grid** value to its **display** property.

- The grid layout scheme is a 2-dimensional system, which places grid items in columns and rows.

- The **grid-column** and **grid-row** shorthand properties can specify horizontal and vertical positioning of grid items.

- A media query can be used to discover the capabilities of the viewing device to apply appropriate style rules.

- A media query can specify a **screen** media type to detect PC desktop, tablet, and phone screens.

- A media query can check for many types of media feature to discover the display area's width and **orientation** of the device.

14 Design for Devices

Adapt Layouts

Web pages are viewed on a variety of devices that have different-sized display areas and different features. In fact, since 2015, more web pages are now viewed on mobile devices than desktop PCs. This means it is important that web pages are designed to look great on a variety of devices and screen sizes.

Responsive Web Design ("RWD") aims to ensure optimum usability for user satisfaction by designing web pages that present content well, and perform well, across all devices.

Web pages designed with RWD adapt their layout to suit the viewing device using only HTML and CSS – no JavaScript.

The key to Responsive Web Design is the use of CSS media queries to determine the size and capabilities of the viewing device. Having recognized the device's features, the layout can be adapted to suit the viewing environment by the use of fluid proportion-based grids and flexible images to create a responsive layout:

Hot tip

Flexible images in RWD are sometimes referred to as "context-aware".

- **CSS Media Queries** – allow the web page to use style sheets containing rules that are appropriate for the screen size of the viewing device or width of the browser window.

- **Fluid Grid Layout** – requires the web page sizes to be specified in relative units, such as percentages and em values (rather than in absolute units such as pixel and point values), so that items can stretch or shrink.

- **Flexible Images** – requires image sizes to be specified in relative units, such as percentages, so they will not overflow their containing element on smaller viewing devices.

- **Responsive Layouts** – will automatically adapt to suit the size of the viewing device and adjust when the user resizes the browser window.

Pages optimized for Responsive Web Design <u>must</u> include the **<meta>** viewport tag in the document's head section, as described on page 170, to instruct the web browser how to control the page's dimensions and scaling. This tag's **width=device-width** value tells the browser to match the screen's width in device-independent pixels, and the tag's **initial-scale=1.0** value tells the browser to establish a 1:1 relationship between CSS pixels and device-independent pixels – irrespective of the device's orientation.

...cont'd

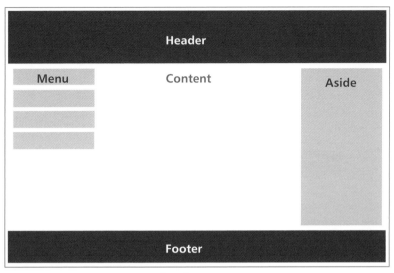

Desktop

Frequently, a Responsive Web Design will provide a 3-column web page layout for larger devices, similar to the one shown above. It will also provide a 2-column layout for medium sized devices, and a 1-column layout for smaller devices, like those shown below.

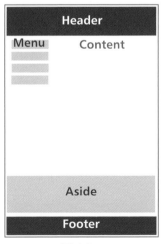

Tablet

Phone

Looking at the layouts illustrated above it should, hopefully, be apparent that the requirements of Responsive Web Design can be satisfied using the CSS flexbox and grid layout schemes.

Hot tip

The Google Chrome web browser has a facility that lets you simulate how a web page will look on different devices. Open the web page in Google Chrome, then press the **F12** key and click the ⬚ button in the "DevTools" window to open the device toolbar in the browser window. Choose any device to simulate from the dropdown options in the device toolbar menu.

Compare Schemes

In deciding which layout scheme is best suited for an RWD web page design, it is useful to compare the flexbox and grid schemes.

First, recall that flexbox is intended for 1-dimensional layouts, whereas grid is intended for 2-dimensional layouts. This means that if you want to lay out items in a row, such as buttons in a horizontal navigation bar, then choose the flexbox scheme.

Conversely, if you want to lay out items in two dimensions, with both rows and columns, then choose the grid layout scheme.

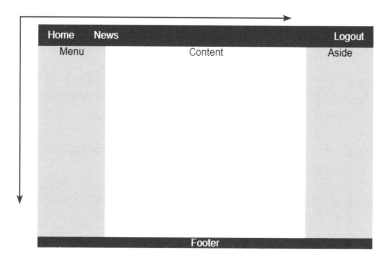

The straightforward choice of scheme for the header items in the illustrations above would then be for the flexbox layout scheme. It is, however, a useful exercise to build the header using each scheme to compare them:

flexvgrid.html

 Create an HTML document containing two similar headers, separated by a line break

```
<header class="flex-container">
<div>Home</div><div>News</div><div>Logout</div>
</header>
<br>
<header class="grid-container">
<div>Home</div><div>News</div><div>Logout</div>
</header>
```

2. Next, add a style sheet with rules to control the page and to specify the appearance of the headers

```
* { margin : 0 ; padding : 0 ; box-sizing : border-box ; }
header { background : Purple ; color : White ;  }
header > div { font : 1em sans-serif ; padding : 0 1em ; }
```

3. Now, add rules to create a flexbox layout and position its final item at the far right

```
header.flex-container { display : flex ; }
header.flex-container > div:nth-child(3) {
                                    margin : 0 0 0 auto ; }
```

4. Then, add rules to create a grid layout with ten columns, and position its final item at the far right

```
header.grid-container { display : grid ;
      grid-template-columns : repeat( 10, 1fr ) ; }
header.grid-container > div:nth-child(3) {
                                    grid-column : 10 ; }
```

Hot tip

Notice that the flexbox layout easily positions the final item to the far right by adding a left margin, whereas the grid layout must explicitly place it in the 10th column of the grid.

5. Save the HTML document, then open it in a browser to see that the headers appear to be identical

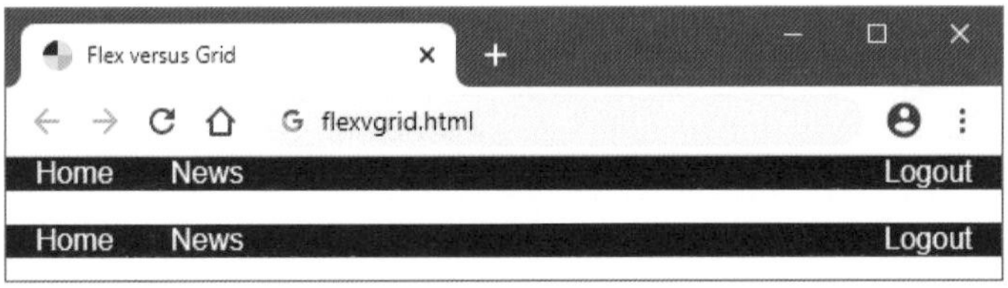

6. Open the browser's Developer Tools, then inspect each header to see how they compare

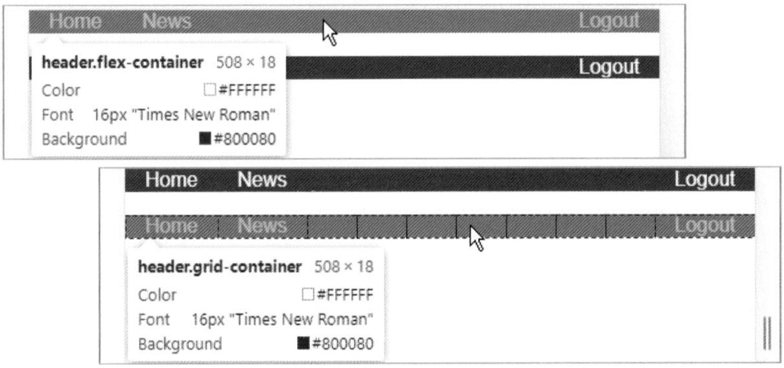

Hot tip

Open the web page in Google Chrome, then press the **F12** key and click the button in the "DevTools" window to open the device toolbar in the browser window. Place the cursor over any element to inspect it.

Combine Schemes

The optimum solution for an RWD web page design invariably uses a combination of the grid and flexbox layout schemes. Overall page layout is best governed by grid layout and the flexbox layout is best suited for horizontal components – such as items in a navigation bar.

As more web pages are now viewed on mobile devices than desktop PCs it is good practice to design for mobile first.

responsive.html

1 Create an HTML document with a division containing header, menu, content, aside, and footer elements

```
<div class="grid-container">

    <header>
          <div>Home</div>
          <div>News</div>
          <div>Logout</div>
    </header>

    <nav>Menu</nav>
    <main>Content</main>
    <aside>Aside</aside>
    <footer>Footer</footer>

</div>
```

2 Add a style sheet with rules to control the web page and the appearance of all its text

```
* { margin : 0 ; padding : 0 ; box-sizing : border-box ;
        font : 1em sans-serif ; text-align :  center ; }
```

3 Next, add rules to specify the appearance of some page elements

```
header, footer { background : Purple ; color : White ;  }
nav, aside { background : Thistle ; }
```

Hot tip

The **vw** and **vh** units are viewport dimensions of 100% width and height.

4 Now, add rules to make the division element into a grid layout of 10 columns and 5 rows that fill the viewport

```
div.grid-container {
  display : grid ;
  width : 100vw ;
  height : 100vh ;
  grid-template-columns : repeat(10, 1fr ) ;
  grid-template-rows: 10% 15% 60% 10% 5% ;
}
```

5 Then, add rules to position element items in the grid
```
header  { grid-column : span 10 ; }
nav     { grid-column : span 10 ; }
main    { grid-column : span 10 ; }
aside   { grid-column : span 10 ; }
footer  { grid-column : span 10 ; }
```

6 Next, add rules to make the header element into a flexbox layout with items vertically centered
```
header { display : flex ; align-items : center ; }
```

7 Now, add rules to pad each side of the flexbox header items and position its final item at the far right
```
header > div { padding : 0 1em ; }
header > div:nth-child(3) { margin : 0 0 0 auto ; }
```

8 Save the HTML document then open it in a browser to see the combined layouts

Hot tip

Adjust the size of the browser window horizontally and vertically to see the grid layout and flexbox layout are both maintained.

Add Breakpoints

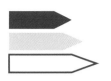

The responsive web page created on page 308 can now be made to adapt its layout for devices that have larger display areas by adding media queries to the style sheet. These will change the grid layout from the 1-column web page layout for small devices to a 2-column layout for medium-sized devices, and a 3-column layout for large devices.

breakpoints.html

1 Make a new copy of the "responsive.html" document from page 308 and save it as "breakpoints.html"

2 In the style sheet, after the existing rules, add a media query for medium-sized devices with rules to change the layout by decreasing the number of rows from five to four
```
@media screen  and ( min-width:600px )
                and ( max-width:992px ) {

        div.grid-container {
        grid-template-rows : 10% 75% 10% 5% ; }

        nav      { grid-column : span 2 ; }
        main     { grid-column : span 8 ; }
}
```

3 Next, add another media query to change the layout for large devices by decreasing the number of rows from five to three
```
@media screen  and ( min-width:992px ) {

        div.grid-container {
        grid-template-rows : 10% 85% 5% ; }

        nav      { grid-column : span 2 ; }
        main     { grid-column : span 6 ; }
        aside    { grid-column : span 2 ; }
}
```

4 Now, save the HTML document, then open it in a variety of devices to see how the breakpoints adapt the layout

...cont'd

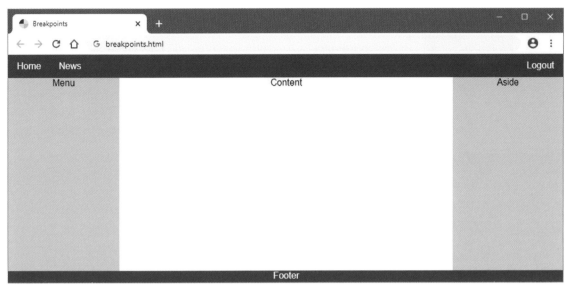

Desktop

Phone

Tablet

Scale Images

Responsive Web Design should recognize that images and video content on a web page should also adapt to suit viewing devices of different size.

Background images can be made to scale down and maintain their aspect ratio between width and height, by specifying the **contain** keyword to the **background-size** property and the **no-repeat** keyword to the **background-repeat** property – for example:

```
div {
        width : 100% ;
        height : 400px ;
        background-image : url(ferrari.png) ;
        background-size : contain ;
        background-repeat : no-repeat ;
}
```

But this technique will only scale down the image within its containing element – its container maintains the specified height.

If the image file size is a concern, you could specify different versions of the image for different devices using media queries to provide smaller image files to small devices for better performance. Remembering to design for mobile first, initially specify a small image file for small devices, then add media queries to specify increasingly larger image files for medium-sized and large devices.

More simply, images and video can easily be made to scale up or down using CSS rules to assign their **width** property a percentage value, and by specifying the **auto** keyword to their **height** property.

scale.html

ferrari.png
800px x 400px

1 Create an HTML document containing a division element and a single image
`<img class="scale" src="ferrari.png" alt="Ferrari">`

2 Add a style sheet with rules to control the web page
`* { margin : 0 ; padding : 0 ; box-sizing : border-box ; }`

3 Now, add rules to scale the image
`img.scale { width : 100% ; height : auto ;`
`                border : 5px dashed Purple ; }`

4 Save the HTML document, then open it in different devices to see the image scale to suit the display area

...cont'd

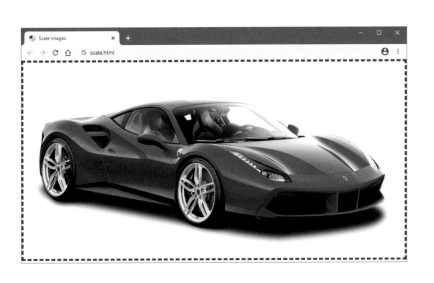

Desktop

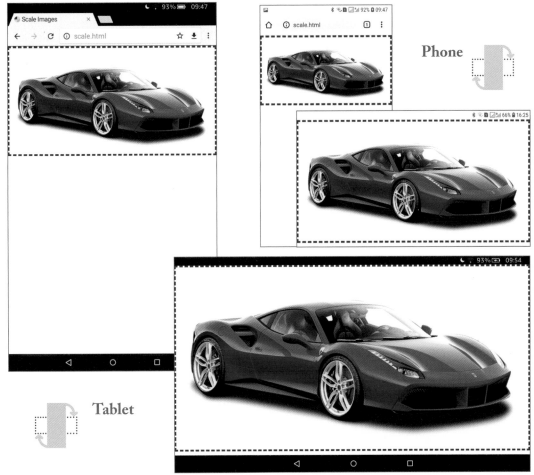

Phone

Tablet

Hide Content

CSS provides a number of ways in which web page content can be hidden from view, but with varying consequences:

- **display : none ;** – entirely removes content from the page flow, no page space reserved, and invisible to screen readers.

- **visibility : hidden ;** – remains in the page flow, page space is reserved, but content is invisible to users and screen readers.

- **opacity : 0 ;** – remains in the page flow, page space is reserved, the content is visually hidden but is visible to screen readers.

With Responsive Web Design content should, ideally, not be omitted from web pages viewed on small devices. You can, however, remove content visually from the page flow, but have it remain visible to screen readers to aid accessibility, by absolutely positioning the content outside the display area.

hide.html

orchid.png
200px x 200px

1 Create an HTML document with a division containing an image and a paragraph
```
<div class="flex-container">
<img src="orchid.png" alt="Orchid Photo.">
<p class="screen-reader-text">The orchid is the official national flower of Hong Kong.</p>
</div>
```

2 Add a style sheet with rules to control the web page
```
* { margin : 0 ; padding : 0 ; box-sizing : border-box ; }

body { background : Black ; }
```

3 Next, add rules to create a flexible row
```
div.flex-container {
  display : flex ;
  justify-content : center ;
}
```

4 Now, add rules to specify the appearance of the paragraph
```
p.screen-reader-text {
  font : 2em sans-serif ;
  padding : 1em ;
  color : Thistle ;
}
```

...cont'd

5 Then, add rules to hide the paragraph on small screens and center the image

```
@media screen and ( max-width:600px ) {

        p.screen-reader-text {
        position : absolute ; width : 1px ; height : 1px ;
        left : -10000px ;
        overflow : hidden ;  }
}
```

Hot tip

ChromeVox is a screen reader extension for the Google Chrome browser – available from chrome.google.com/webstore/category/extensions

6 Save the HTML document then open it in a web browser and enable a screen reader

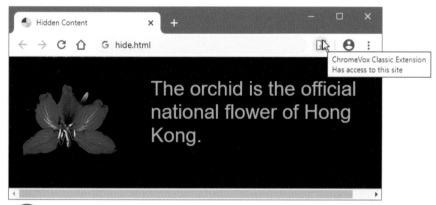

7 Drag the edge of the browser window to narrow its width – see the paragraph get hidden and the image centered

8 Click on the page to hear the screen reader read the image name and the hidden paragraph text

"Orchid Photo. The orchid is the official national flower of Hong Kong."

Summary

- Responsive Web Design (RWD) aims to ensure web pages present content well and perform well across all devices.

- Responsive Web Design uses media queries to determine the size and capabilities of the viewing device.

- Pages optimized for Responsive Web Design must include the **\<meta\>** viewport tag in the document's head section.

- Responsive Web Design requirements can be satisfied using the flexbox layout scheme and grid layout scheme.

- The flexbox layout scheme places items in rows, but the grid layout scheme places items in both rows and columns.

- The optimum solution for Responsive Web Design invariably uses a combination of the grid and flexbox layout schemes.

- It is good practice to design for mobile first, as more web pages are now viewed on mobile devices than desktop PCs.

- A responsive web page can be made to adapt its layout for devices that have larger display areas by adding media queries.

- Media queries can be used to specify different versions of an image for devices of different size.

- Background images can be made to scale down by specifying the **contain** keyword to the **background-size** property, and the **no-repeat** keyword to the **background-repeat** property.

- Images and video can be made to scale up or down by specifying a percentage value to their **width** property and the **auto** keyword to their **height** property.

- Content can be hidden and removed from the page flow by specifying the **none** keyword to the **display** property.

- The **visibility** and **opacity** properties can be used to hide content but they each reserve space on the web page.

- Content can be hidden from view and remain visible to screen readers without reserving page space by absolutely positioning the content outside the display area.

15 Get Started in JavaScript

Meet JS

JavaScript ("JS") is an object-based scripting language whose interpreter is embedded inside web browser software such as Google Chrome, Microsoft Edge, Firefox, Opera, and Safari. This allows scripts contained in a web page to be interpreted when the page is loaded in the browser to provide functionality. For security reasons, JavaScript cannot read or write files, with the exception of "cookie" files that store minimal data.

Created by Brendan Eich at Netscape, JavaScript was first introduced in December 1995, and was initially named "LiveScript". It was soon renamed, however, to perhaps capitalize on the popularity of Sun Microsystem's Java programming language – although it bears little resemblance.

Before the introduction of JavaScript, web page functionality required the browser to call upon "server-side" scripts, resident on the web server, where slow response could impede performance. Calling upon "client-side" scripts resident on the user's system, overcame the latency problem and provided a superior experience.

JavaScript quickly became very popular but a disagreement arose between Netscape and Microsoft over its licensing – so Microsoft introduced its own version named "JScript". Although similar to JavaScript, the new JScript version had some extended features. Recognizing the danger of fragmentation, the JavaScript language was standardized by the Ecma International standards organization in June 1997 as "ECMAScript". This helped to stabilize core features but the name, sounding like some kind of skin disease, is not widely used and most people will always call the language "JavaScript".

Brendan Eich, creator of the JavaScript language, also co-founded the Mozilla project and helped launch the Firefox web browser.

The JavaScript examples in this book describe three key ingredients:

- **Language basics** – illustrating the mechanics of the language syntax, keywords, operators, structure, and built-in objects.

- **Web page functionality** – illustrating how to use the browser's Document Object Model (DOM) to provide user interaction.

- **Web applications** – illustrating responsive web-based apps and JavaScript Object Notation (JSON) techniques.

Include Scripts

To include JavaScript code directly in an HTML document it must be inserted between **<script>** and **</script>** tags, like this:

```
<script>
document.getElementById( 'message' ).innerText = 'Hello World!'
</script>
```

An HTML document can include multiple scripts, and these may be placed in the head or body section of the document. It is, however, recommended that you place scripts at the end of the body section (immediately before the **</body>** closing tag) so the browser can render the web page before interpreting the script.

JavaScript code can also be written in external plain text files that are given a **.js** file extension. This allows several different web pages to call upon the same script. In order to include an external script in the HTML document, the file name of the script must be assigned to a **src** attribute of the **<script>** tag, like this:

```
<script src="external_script.js"> </script>
```

Again, this can be placed in the head or body section of the document, and the browser will treat the script as though it was written directly at that position in the HTML document.

Assigning only the file name of an external script to the **src** attribute of a **<script>** tag requires the script file to be located in the same folder (directory) as the HTML document. If the script is located in an adjacent folder you can assign the relative path address of the file instead, like this:

```
<script src="js/external_script.js"> </script>
```

If the script is located elsewhere, you can assign the absolute path address of the file, like this:

```
<script src="https://www.example.com/js/external_script.js">
</script>
```

You can also specify content that will only appear in the web page if the user has disabled JavaScript in their web browser by including a **<noscript>** element in the body of the HTML document, like this:

```
<noscript>JavaScript is Not Enabled!</noscript>
```

Hot tip

You may see a **type="text/javascript"** attribute in a **<script>** tag but this is no longer required as JavaScript is now the default scripting language for HTML.

Beware

Do not include **<script>** and **</script>** tags in an external JavaScript file, only the script code.

Don't forget

External script files can make code maintenance easier but almost all examples in this book are standalone for clarity, so include the script code between tags directly in the HTML document.

Console Output

JavaScript can display output by dynamically writing content into an HTML element. For example, with this code:

document.getElementById('message').innerText = 'Hello World!'

The element is identified by the value assigned to its **id** attribute and the **innerText** property specifies text to be written there.

Hot tip

Notice the use of the . period (full stop) operator to describe properties or methods of an object using "dot notation".

Additionally, JavaScript can display output by writing content into a pop-up dialog box, like this:

window.alert('Hello World!')

This calls the **alert( )** method of the **window** object to display the content specified within the ( ) parentheses in a dialog box.

Hot tip

The console provides helpful messages if an error occurs in your code – so is great for debugging the code.

When developing in JavaScript, and learning the language, it is initially better to display output in the browser's JavaScript console, like this:

console.log('Hello World!')

This calls the **log( )** method of the **console** object to display the content specified within the ( ) parentheses in a console window. All leading browsers have a JavaScript console within their Developers Tools feature – typically accessed by pressing the F12 keyboard key. As the Google Chrome web browser is statistically the most popular browser at the time of writing it is used throughout this book to demonstrate JavaScript, and initially its console window is used to display output.

1 Create an HTML document that includes an empty paragraph and a script to display output in three ways

```
<p id="message"></p>
<script>
document.getElementById( 'message' ).innerText =
                                        'Hello World!'
window.alert( 'Hello World!' )
console.log( 'Hello World!' )
</script>
```

output.html

2 Save the HTML document then open it in your browser to see the output written in the paragraph and displayed in a dialog box – as illustrated opposite

3 Next, hit the **F12** key, or use your browser's menu to open its Developers Tools feature

4 Now, select the **Console** tab to see the output written into the console window

There is also a **document.write( )** method that replaces the entire header and body of the web page, but its use is generally considered bad practice.

321

See that the console displays the output plus the name of the HTML document and the line number upon which the JavaScript code appears that created the output.

5 Click the ⬓ **Show/Hide** button to hide or show the sidebar, click the ⋮ **Customize** button to choose how the console window docks in the browser window, then click the ⊘ **Clear** button to clear all content from the console

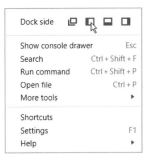

Make Statements

(.*)

JavaScript code is composed of a series of instructions called "statements", which are generally executed in top-to-bottom order as the browser's JavaScript engine proceeds through the script.

Each statement may contain any of the following components:

- **Keywords** – words that have special significance in the JavaScript language.

- **Operators** – special characters that perform an operation on one or more operands.

- **Values** – text strings, numbers, boolean **true** or **false**, **undefined**, and **null**.

- **Expressions** – units of code that produce a single value.

The JavaScript keywords are described on page 324 and you will learn about operators, values, and expressions later.

In earlier JavaScript code each statement had to be terminated by a ; semicolon character – just as each sentence must end with a . period (full stop) character in the English language. This is now optional so may be omitted unless you wish to write multiple statements on a single line. In that case, the statements do need to be separated by a semicolon, like this:

statement ; statement ; statement

An "expression" produces a value, whereas a "statement" performs an action.

Some JavaScript programmers still prefer to end each statement with a semicolon. The examples in this book choose to omit them for the sake of concision but the choice is yours.

The JavaScript interpreter ignores tabs and spaces ("whitespace") so you should use spacing to make your code more readable. For example, when adding two numbers:

total = 100 + 200 rather than **total=100+200**

JavaScript statements are often grouped together within **{ }** curly brackets ("braces") in function blocks that can be repeatedly called to execute when required. It is good practice to indent those statements by two spaces to improve readability, like this:

Use the space bar to indent statements, as tab spacing may be treated differently when viewing the code in text editors.

```
{
  statement
  statement
  statement
}
```

322

The rules that govern the JavaScript language is called "syntax", and it recognizes two types of values – fixed and variable. Fixed numeric and text string values are called "literals":

● **Number literals** – whole number integers, such as **100**, or floating-point numbers such as **3.142**.

● **String literals** – text within either double quotes, such as **"JavaScript Fun"**, or single quotes such as **'JavaScript Fun'**.

Variable values are called, quite simply, "variables" and are used to store data within a script. They can be created using the JavaScript **let** keyword – for example, **let total** creates a variable named "total". The variable can be assigned a value to store using the JavaScript = assignment operator, like this:

let total = 300

Other JavaScript operators can be used to form expressions that will evaluate to a single value. Typically, an expression may be enclosed within **( )** parentheses like this expression that comprises numbers and the JavaScript **+** addition operator and evaluates to a single value of 100:

(80 + 20)

Expressions may also contain variable values too, like this expression that comprises the previous variable value, the JavaScript - subtraction operator, and a number, to also evaluate to a single value of 100:

(total - 200)

JavaScript is a case-sensitive language so variables named **total** and **Total** are regarded as two entirely different variables.

It is good practice to add explanatory comments to your JavaScript code to make it more easily understood by others, and by yourself when revisiting the code later. Anything that appears on a single line following **//** double slashes or between **/*** and ***/** character sequences on one or more lines will be ignored.

let total = 100 // This code WILL be executed.

/* let total = 100
  This code will NOT be executed. */

Hot tip

Decide on one form of quotes to use in your code for string literals and stick with it for consistency. The examples in this book use single quotes.

323

Hot tip

It is often useful to "comment-out" lines of code to prevent their execution when debugging code.

Avoid Keywords

In JavaScript code you can choose your own names for variables and functions. The names should be meaningful and reflect the purpose of the variable or function. Your names may comprise letters, numbers, and underscore characters, but they may not contain spaces or begin with a number. You must also avoid these words of special significance in the JavaScript language:

JavaScript Keywords			
abstract	arguments	await	boolean
break	byte	case	catch
char	class	const	continue
debugger	default	delete	do
double	else	enum	eval
export	extends	false	final
finally	float	for	function
goto	if	implements	import
in	instanceof	int	interface
let	long	native	new
null	package	private	protected
public	return	short	static
super	switch	synchronized	this
throw	throws	transient	true
try	typeof	var	void
volatile	while	with	yield

JavaScript Objects, Properties, and Methods			
Array	Date	eval	function
hasOwnProperty	Infinity	isFinite	isNaN
isPrototypeOf	length	Math	NaN
name	Number	Object	prototype
String	toString	undefined	valueOf

...cont'd

HTML Names, Window Objects, and Properties			
alert	all	anchor	anchors
area	assign	blur	button
checkbox	clearInterval	clearTimeout	clientInformation
close	closed	confirm	constructor
crypto	decodeURI	decodeURIcomponent	defaultStatus
document	element	elements	embed
embeds	encodeURI	encodeURIcomponent	escape
event	fileUpload	focus	form
forms	frame	innerHeight	innerWidth
layer	layers	link	location
mimeTypes	navigate	navigator	frames
frameRate	hidden	history	image
images	offscreenBuffering	open	opener
option	outerHeight	outerWidth	packages
pageXOffset	pageYOffset	parent	parseFloat
parseInt	password	pkcs11	plugin
prompt	propertyIsEnum	radio	reset
screenX	screenY	scroll	secure
select	self	setInterval	setTimeout
status	submit	taint	text
textarea	top	unescape	untaint
window			

325

HTML Event Attributes For Example:			
onclick	ondblclick	onfocus	onfocusout
onkeydown	onkeypress	onkeyup	onload
onmousedown	onmouseup	onmouseover	onmouseout
onmousemove	onchange	onreset	onsubmit

Store Values

A "variable" is a container, common to every scripting and programming language, in which data can be stored and retrieved later. Unlike the "strongly typed" variables in most other languages, which must declare a particular data type they may contain, JavaScript variables are much easier to use because they are "loosely typed" – so they may contain any type of data:

Data Type	Example	Description
String	**'Hello World!'**	A string of text characters
Number	**3.142**	An integer or floating-point number
Boolean	**true**	A true (1) or false (0) value
Object	**console**	A user-defined or built-in object
Function	**log( )**	A user-defined function, a built-in function, or an object method
Symbol	**Symbol( )**	A unique property identifier
null	**null**	Absolutely nothing (not even zero)
undefined	**undefined**	A non-configured property

A variable name is an alias for the value it contains – using the name in script references its stored value.

Choose meaningful names for your variables to make the script easier to understand later.

A JavaScript variable can be declared using the **let, const,** or **var** keywords followed by a space and a name of your choosing. Variables declared with **let** can be reassigned new values as the script proceeds, whereas **const** (constant) does not allow this. The **var** keyword was used in JavaScript before the **let** keyword was introduced but is best avoided now as it does not prevent you declaring the same variable twice in the same context.

A **let** declaration of a variable in a script may simply create a variable to which a value can be assigned later, or may include an assignation to instantly "initialize" the variable with a value:

```
let myNumber                    // Declare a variable.
myNumber = 10                   // Initialize a variable.
let myString = 'Hello World!'   // Declare and initialize a variable.
```

Multiple variables may be declared on a single line too:

```
let i , j , k                   // Declare 3 variables.
let num =10 , char = 'C'        // Declare and initialize 2 variables.
```

Constant variables must, however, be initialized when declared:

```
const myName = 'Mike'
```

...cont'd

Upon initialization, JavaScript automatically sets the variable type for the value assigned. Subsequent assignation of a different data type later in the script can be made to change the variable type. The current variable type can be revealed by the **typeof** keyword.

① Create an HTML document with a script that declares several variables that are assigned different data types
```
const firstName = 'Mike'
const valueOfPi = 3.142
let isValid = true
let jsObject = console
let jsMethod = console.log
let jsSymbol = Symbol( )
let emptyVariable = null
let unusedVariable
```

variables.html

② Add statements to output the data type of each variable
```
console.log( 'firstName: ' + typeof firstName )
console.log( 'valueOfPi: ' + typeof valueOfPi )
console.log( 'isValid: ' + typeof isValid )
console.log( 'jsObject: ' + typeof jsObject )
console.log( 'jsMethod: ' + typeof jsMethod )
console.log( 'jsSymbol: ' + typeof jsSymbol )
console.log( 'emptyVariable: ' + typeof emptyVariable )
console.log( 'unusedVariable: ' + typeof unusedVariable )
```

The concatenation + operator is used here to output a combined text string.

③ Save the HTML document then open it in your browser and launch the console to see the data types in output

You should be surprised to see that the variable assigned a **null** value is described as being an **object** type, rather than a **null** type. This is a known error in the JavaScript language.

327

Create Functions

A function expression is simply one, or more, statements that are grouped together in { } curly brackets for execution, and it returns a final single value. Functions may be called as required by a script to execute their statements. Those functions that belong to an object, such as **console.log( )**, are known as "methods" – to differentiate them from built-in and user-defined functions. Both have trailing parentheses that may accept "argument" values to be passed to the function for manipulation – for example, an argument passed in the parentheses of the **console.log( )** method.

The number of arguments passed to a function must normally match the number of "parameters" specified within the parentheses of the function block declaration. For example, a user-defined function requiring exactly one argument looks like this:

```
function function-name ( parameter ) {
  // Statements to be executed go here.
}
```

Multiple parameters can be specified as a comma-separated list and you can, optionally, specify a default value to be used when the function call does not pass an argument, like this:

```
function function-name ( parameter , parameter = value ) {
  // Statements to be executed go here.
}
```

You choose your own parameter names following the same naming conventions as for variable names. The parameter names can then be used within the function to reference the argument values passed from the parentheses of the function call.

A function block can include a **return** statement so that script flow continues at the caller – no further statements in the function get executed. It is typical to finally return the result of manipulating passed argument values back to the caller:

```
function function-name ( parameter , parameter ) {
  // Statements to be executed go here.

  return result
}
```

It is common for statements within a function block to include calls to other functions – to modularize scripts into blocks.

① Create an HTML document with a script that declares a function to return the squared value of a passed argument

```
function square ( arg ) {
  return arg * arg
}
```

functions.html

② Next, add a function that returns the result of an addition

```
function add ( argOne, argTwo = 10 ) {
  return argOne + argTwo
}
```

③ Now, add a function that returns the result of squaring and an addition by calling each of the functions above

```
function squareAdd ( arg ) {
  let result = square( arg )
  return result + add( arg )
}
```

Don't forget

Notice that the default second parameter value (10) is used here when only one argument value is passed by the caller.

④ Finally, add statements that call the functions and print the returned values in output strings

```
console.log( '8 x 8: ' + square( 8 ) )
console.log( '8 + 20: ' + add( 8, 20 ) )
console.log( '8 + 10: ' + add( 8 ) )
console.log( '(8 x 8) + (8 + 10): ' + squareAdd( 8 ) )
```

⑤ Save the HTML document, then open it in your browser and launch the console to see values returned from functions

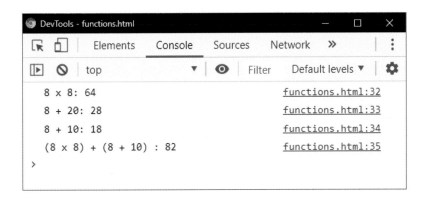

Hot tip

The * asterisk character is the arithmetical multiplication operator in JavaScript.

Assign Functions

Functions are really useful in JavaScript, as they can be called ("invoked") to execute their statements whenever required, and the caller can pass different arguments to return different results.

It is important to recognize that the JavaScript ( ) parentheses operator is the component of the call statement that actually calls the function. This means a statement can assign a function to a variable by specifying just the function name. The variable can then be used to call the function in a statement that specifies the variable name followed by the ( ) operator. But beware, if you attempt to assign a function to a variable by specifying the function name followed by ( ) the function will be invoked and the value returned by that function will be assigned.

Function Hoisting

Although scripts are read by the JavaScript interpreter in top-to-bottom order it actually makes two sweeps. The first sweep looks for function declarations and remembers any it finds in a process known as "hoisting". The second sweep is when the script is actually executed by the interpreter. Hoisting allows function calls to appear in the script before the function declaration, as the interpreter has already recognized the function on the first sweep. The first sweep does not, however, recognize functions that have been assigned to variables using the **let** or **const** keywords!

Anonymous Functions

When assigning a function to a variable, a function name can be omitted as the function can be called in a statement specifying the variable name and the ( ) operator. These are called anonymous function expressions, and their syntax looks like this:

let *variable* = function (*parameters*) { *statements* ; return *value* }

Anonymous function expressions can also be made "self-invoking" by enclosing the entire function within ( ) parentheses and adding the ( ) parentheses operator at the end of the expression. This means that their statements are automatically executed one time when the script is first loaded by the browser. The syntax of a self-invoking function expression looks like this:

(function ( ) { *statements* ; return *value* }) ( )

Self-invoking functions are used widely throughout this book to execute example code when the script gets loaded.

Hot tip

Variables that were declared using the older **var** keyword were also hoisted, but those declared with **let** or **const** are not hoisted.

Hot tip

Self-invoking function expressions are also known as Immediately Invoked Function Expressions (IIFE – often pronounced "iffy").

1 Create an HTML document with a script that calls a function that has not yet been declared
```
console.log( 'Hoisted: ' + add( 100, 200 ) )
```

anonymous.html

2 Next, add below the function that is called above
```
function add( numOne, numTwo ) {
  return numOne + numTwo
}
```

3 Now, add a function that assigns the function above to a variable, then calls the assigned function
```
let addition = add
console.log( 'Assigned: ' + addition( 32, 64 ) )
```

When assigning a named function to a variable, only specify the function name in the statement.

4 Then, assign a similar, but anonymous, function to a variable and call that assigned function
```
let anon = function ( numOne, numTwo ) {
  let result = numOne + numTwo ; return result
}
console.log( 'Anonymous: ' + anon( 9, 1 ) )
```

5 Finally, assign the value returned from a self-invoking function to a variable and display that value
```
let iffy = ( function ( ) {
  let str = 'Self Invoked Output' ; return str
} ) ( )
console.log( iffy )
```

6 Save the HTML document, then open it in your browser and launch the console to see values returned from functions

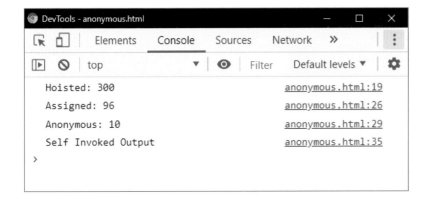

The significance of self-invoking functions may not be immediately obvious, but their importance should become clearer by the end of this chapter.

Recognize Scope

The extent to which variables are accessible in your scripts is determined by their "lexical scope" – the environment in which the variable was created. This can be either "global" or "local".

Global Scope

Variables created outside function blocks are accessible globally throughout the entire script. This means they exist continuously and are available to functions within the same script environment. At first glance this might seem very convenient, but has a very serious drawback in that variables of the same name can conflict. For example, imagine that you have created a global **myName** variable that has been assigned your name, but then also include an external script in which another developer has created a global **myName** variable that has been assigned his or her name. Both like-named variables exist in the same script environment, so conflict. This is best avoided so you should not create global variables to store primitive values (all data types except Object and Function) within your scripts.

Local Scope

Variables created inside function blocks are accessible locally throughout the life of the function. They exist only while the function is executing, then they are destroyed. Their script environment is limited – from the point at which they are created, to the final **}** curly bracket, or the moment when the function returns. It is good practice to declare variables at the very beginning of the function block so their lexical scope is the duration of the function. This means that like-named variables can exist within separate functions without conflict. For example, a local **myName** variable can exist happily inside separate functions within your script and inside functions in included external scripts. It is recommended that you try to create only local variables to store values within your scripts.

Best Practice

Declaring global variables with the older **var** keyword allows like-named conflicting variables to overwrite their assigned values without warning. The more recent **let** and **const** keywords prohibit this and instead recognize the behavior as an "Uncaught SyntaxError". It is therefore recommended that you create variables declared using the **let** or **const** keywords to store values within your scripts.

You will discover how to catch and handle errors on page 370.

1 Create an external script that calls a function to output the value of a global variable

```
let myName = 'External Script'
function readName( ) { console.log( myName ) }
readName( )
```

external.js

2 Create an HTML document that includes the external script and adds a similar script

```
<script src="external.js"></script>
<script>
let myName = 'Internal Script'
function getName( ) { console.log( myName ) }
getName( )
</script>
```

scope.html

3 Save both files in the same folder, then open the HTML document to see a conflict error reported in the console

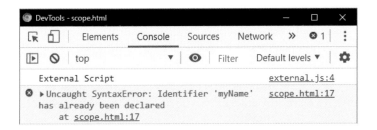

4 Edit both scripts to make the global variables into local variables then refresh the browser to see no conflict

```
function readName( ) {
  let myName = 'External Script' ; console.log( myName )
}
```

```
function getName( ) {
  let myName = 'Internal Script' ; console.log( myName )
}
```

The function calls **readName( )** and **getName( )** remain in the scripts without editing.

Use Closures

The previous example demonstrated the danger of creating global variables to store values in JavaScript, but sometimes you will want to store values that remain continuously accessible – for example, to remember an increasing score count as the script proceeds. How can you do this without using global variables to store primitive values? The answer lies with the use of "closures".

A closure is a function nested inside an outer function that retains access to variables declared in the outer function – because that is the lexical scope in which the nested function was created.

closure.html

1 Create an HTML document with a script that assigns a self-invoking anonymous function to a global variable
```
const add = ( function ( ) {
    // Statements to be inserted here.
} ) ( )
```

2 Next, insert statements to initialize a local variable and assign a function to a local variable in the same scope
```
let count = 0
const nested = function ( ) { return count = count + 1 }
```

3 Now, insert a statement to return the inner function – assigning the inner function to the global variable
```
return nested
```

4 Finally, add three identical function calls to the inner function that is now assigned to the global variable
```
console.log( 'Count is ' + add( ) )
console.log( 'Count is ' + add( ) )
console.log( 'Count is ' + add( ) )
```

5 Save the HTML document, then open it in your browser and launch the console to see values returned from a closure

Self-invoking function expressions are described on page 330. They execute their statements one time only. Here, you can use **console.log(add)** to confirm that the function expression has been assigned to the outer variable.

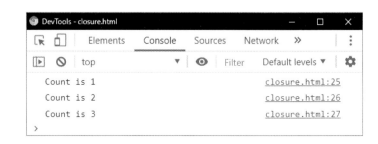

It can be difficult to grasp the concept of closures, as it would seem that the **count** variable in this example should be destroyed when the self-invoking function has completed execution. In order to better understand how closures work, you can explore the **prototype** property of the assigned function.

6   Add a statement at the end of the script to reveal how the assigned function has been constructed internally
console.log(add.prototype)

7   Save the HTML document, then refresh the browser and expand the "constructor" dropdown to see the scopes

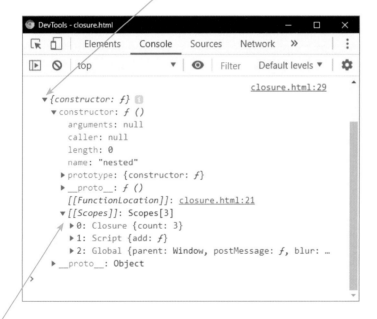

335

Closer inspection reveals that the assigned function has a special (Closure) scope in addition to the regular local (Script) scope and outer (Global) scope. This is how the **count** variable remains accessible via the assigned function yet, importantly, cannot be referenced in any other way.

The use of closures to hide persistent variables from other parts of your script is an important concept. It is similar to how "private" variables can be hidden in other programming languages and are only accessible via "getter" methods.

Summary

- JavaScript code can be included in an HTML document directly or from an external file using **<script> </script>** tags.

- JavaScript can display output in an HTML element in an alert dialog box or in the browser's console window.

- JavaScript statements may contain keywords, operators, values, and expressions.

- The JavaScript interpreter ignores tabs and spaces.

- JavaScript statements can be grouped in **{ }** curly bracket function blocks that can be called to execute when required.

- Variable and function names may comprise letters, numbers, and underscore characters, but must avoid keywords.

- JavaScript variables may contain data types of String, Number, Boolean, Object, Function, Symbol, **null**, and **undefined**.

- Variables declared with the **let** keyword can be reassigned new values, but the **const** keyword does not allow this.

- A function expression has statements grouped in **{ }** curly brackets for execution, and it returns a final single value.

- The **( )** parentheses of a function expression may contain parameters for argument values to be passed from the caller.

- A function block can include a **return** statement to specify data to be passed back to the caller.

- The JavaScript **( )** parentheses operator calls the function.

- Hoisting allows function calls to appear in the script before the function declaration.

- Anonymous function expressions have no function name.

- Lexical scope is the environment in which the variable was created and can be global, local, or closure.

- Local variables should be used to store values, but global variables can be assigned functions to create closures.

- A closure is a function nested within an outer function that retains access to variables declared in the outer function.

16 Perform Useful Operations

Convert Values

Before performing operations in JavaScript it is important to recognize the data types of the values you are working with in order to avoid unexpected results. For example, the value **42** is a number, but the value **'42'** is a string, so attempting to perform an addition with **'42' + 8** will return a string result of **'428'**, not the number **50**. Happily, JavaScript provides a number of ways to return versions of values in other data types – without changing the value's original data type.

Strings to Numbers

The JavaScript **parseInt( )** built-in function can return an integer whole number version, in the number data type, of a string specified within its parentheses. For example, **parseInt('42')** will return the number **42**, so **42 + 8** will return a number result of **50**.

Similarly, the JavaScript **parseFloat( )** built-in function can return a floating-point number version, in the number data type, of a string specified within its parentheses.

Both these methods allow alphabetic characters to follow the numeric part of the specified string and strip them from the result – for example, **parseInt('42nd Street')** returns number **42**.

If either of these functions cannot find a numeric value at the beginning of the specified string, the result will be **NaN** – a JavaScript property meaning "Not a Number". You can also check if a value is not a number by specifying the value within the parentheses of a JavaScript **isNaN( )** built-in function. This, too, will first attempt to find a number at the beginning of the specified value and return **false** if it finds a number (even from a specified string), otherwise it will return **true** if it cannot find a number.

Numbers to Strings

The JavaScript **String( )** method can return a string representation, in the string data type, of a number specified within its parentheses – for example, **String(42)** will return the number **'42'** as a string data type.

Alternatively, you can append a **toString( )** method call onto a variable name to return a string representation of a stored number data type. For example, where a variable named "num" has been assigned a number, **num.toString( )** will return a string version of that stored number.

Conversion of data types is known as "coercion", and it can be explicit or implicit. Where '42' + 8 returns the string '428' this is implicit coercion. Where String(42) returns the string '42' this is explicit coercion.

...cont'd

1 Create an HTML document with a self-invoking anonymous function block that declares three variables
(function ( ) {

```
let sum, net = '25', tax = 5.00
```

    // Statements to be inserted here.

```
} ) ( )
```

conversion.html

2 Next, insert statements that create versions of different data types and print the result in an output string

```
sum = net + tax
console.log( 'sum: ' + sum + ' ' + typeof sum )

sum = parseFloat( net ) + tax
console.log( 'sum: ' + sum + ' ' + typeof sum )

console.log( 'tax: ' + tax + ' ' + typeof tax )
tax = tax.toString( )
console.log( 'tax: ' + tax + ' ' + typeof tax )

net = '$' + net
console.log( 'net: ' + net + ' ' + parseInt( net ) )
console.log( 'net Not a Number? ' + isNaN( net ) )
```

Don't forget

If you try **isNan(net)** before the **'$'** prefix is added to the string the result is **false** – because the method finds the number at the beginning of the **'25'** string.

3 Save the HTML document, then open it in your browser and launch the console to see the different versions

Do Arithmetic

The arithmetical operators commonly used in JavaScript are listed in the table below, together with the operation they perform:

Operator	Operation
+	Addition of numbers Concatenation of strings
–	Subtraction
*	Multiplication
/	Division
%	Modulus
++	Increment
– –	Decrement
**	Exponentiation

Hot tip

The ** exponentiation operator returns the result of a first operand raised to the power of a second operand.

Hot tip

An example using the modulus operator to determine odd or even numbers can be found on page 349.

Values specified in operation statements are called "operands". For example, in the statement **5 + 2** the + operator is supplied operand values of five and two. Notice that the + operator performs two kinds of operation depending on the type of operands. Numeric operands are added to return a sum total, but string operands are concatenated to return a single joined string.

The % modulus operator divides the first operand by the second operand and returns the remainder. Dividing by two will return either one or zero to usefully determine whether the first operand is an odd number or an even number.

The ++ increment operator and -- decrement operator alter the value of a single operand by one, and return the new value. These operators are most commonly used to count iterations of a loop and can be used in two different ways to subtly different effect. When placed before the operand (prefixed) its value is immediately changed before the expression is evaluated, but when placed after the operand (postfixed) the expression is evaluated first then the value gets changed.

1 Create an HTML document with a self-invoking anonymous function block
(function ( ) {

// Statements to be inserted here.

}) ( )

arithmetic.html

2 Next, insert statements that assign values to variables using each arithmetical operator and print each result in an output string
let sum = 80 + 20 ; console.log('Addition: ' + sum)

let sub = sum - 50 ; console.log('Subtraction: ' + sub)

let mul = sum * 5 ; console.log('Multiplication: ' + mul)

let div = sum / 4 ; console.log('Division: ' + div)

let mod = sum % 2 ; console.log('Modulus: ' + mod)

let inc = ++sum ; console.log('Increment: ' + inc)

let dec = --sum ; console.log('Decrement: ' + dec)

3 Save the HTML document, then open it in your browser and launch the console to see the arithmetic results

```
DevTools - arithmetic.html                                    —    □    ×

  ⟲  ⧉ │ Elements   Console   Sources   Network   »   │   ⋮

  ▶  ⊘ │ top                ▼ │ ◉ │ Filter   Default levels ▼ │ ⚙

    Addition: 100                        arithmetic.html:19
    Subtraction: 50                      arithmetic.html:21
    Multiplication: 500                  arithmetic.html:23
    Division: 25                         arithmetic.html:25
    Modulus: 0                           arithmetic.html:27
    Increment: 101                       arithmetic.html:29
    Decrement: 100                       arithmetic.html:31
  >
```

Assign Values

The operators that are commonly used in JavaScript to assign values are all listed in the table below. All except the simple = assignment operator are shorthand forms of longer expressions, so each equivalent is also given for clarity.

Operator	Example	Equivalent
=	a = b	a = b
+=	a += b	a = (a + b)
–=	a –= b	a = (a – b)
*=	a *= b	a = (a * b)
/=	a /= b	a = (a / b)
%=	a %= b	a = (a % b)
**=	a **= b	a = (a ** b)

It is important to think of the = operator as meaning "assign" rather than "equals" to avoid confusion with the JavaScript === equality operator.

In the = example in the table, the variable **a** gets assigned the value contained in variable **b** to become its new stored value.

The combined += operator is most useful and can be employed to append a string onto an existing string. For example, with a variable string **let str = 'JavaScript'** and **str += ' Fun'** the variable now stores the combined string **'JavaScript Fun'**.

Numerically speaking, the += example in the table will add the value contained in variable **a** to that contained in variable **b** then assign the sum total to become the new value stored in variable **a**.

All other combined assignment operators work in a similar way to the += operator. They each perform the arithmetical operation on their two operands first, then assign the result of that operation to the first variable – so that becomes its new stored value.

Hot tip

The === equality operator compares values and is fully explained on page 344.

1 Create an HTML document with a self-invoking anonymous function that concatenates two strings
(function ( ) {

```
let msg = 'JavaScript' ; msg += ' Fun'
console.log( 'Add & concatenate: ' +  msg )
```

// Statements to be inserted here.

}) ( )

assignment.html

2 Next, insert statements that use combined operators to perform arithmetic and assign results for output
```
let sum = 5.00 ; sum += 2.50
console.log( 'Add & assign decimal: ' +  sum )

sum = 8 ; sum -= 4
console.log( 'Subtract & assign integer: ' +  sum )

sum = 8 ; sum *= 4
console.log( 'Multiply & assign integer: ' +  sum )

sum = 8 ; sum /= 4
console.log( 'Divide & assign integer: ' +  sum )

sum = 8 ; sum %= 4
console.log( 'Modulus & assign integer: ' +  sum )
```

3 Save the HTML document, then open it in your browser and launch the console to see the assigned values

---

DevTools - assignment.html — □ ✕

⬚ ⬚ | Elements **Console** Sources Network » ⋮

▷ ⊘ | top ▼ | 👁 | Filter Default levels ▼ | ⚙

```
Add & concatenate: JavaScript Fun          assignment.html:21
Add & assign decimal: 7.5                  assignment.html:24
Subtract & assign integer: 4               assignment.html:27
Multiply & assign integer: 32              assignment.html:30
Divide & assign integer: 2                 assignment.html:33
Modulus & assign integer: 0                assignment.html:36
>
```

Make Comparisons

The operators that are commonly used in JavaScript to compare two values are all listed in the table below:

Operator	Comparison
===	Equality
!==	Inequality
>	Greater than
<	Less than
>=	Greater than or equal to
<=	Less than or equal to

Hot tip

An example using the < less than operator in a loop structure can be found on page 362.

Beware

There is also a == equality operator and a != inequality operator, but these may produce unexpected results as, unlike === and !==, they do not ensure the values being compared are of the same data type. This means that **25 == '25'** returns **true**, whereas **25 === '25'** returns **false**. Always use the three-character versions so your scripts will make accurate comparisons.

The === equality operator compares two operands and will return a boolean **true** value if they are exactly equal, otherwise it will return a boolean **false** value. If the operands are identical numbers they are equal; if the operands are strings containing the same characters in the same positions they are equal; if the operands are boolean values that are both **true**, or both **false**, they are equal. Conversely, the !== inequality operator returns true if the two operands are not equal, using the same rules as the === equality operator.

Equality and inequality operators are useful in comparing two values to perform "conditional branching", where the script will follow a particular direction according to the result.

The > greater than operator compares two operands and returns **true** if the first is greater in value than the second. The < less than operator makes the same comparison but returns **true** when the first is less in value than the second. Adding the = character after the > greater than operator or the < less than operator makes them also return **true** when the two operands are equal.

The > greater than and < less than operators are frequently used to test the value of a counter variable in a loop structure.

1 Create an HTML document with a self-invoking anonymous function that declares three variables
(function ( ) {

```
let comparison, sum = 8, str = 'JavaScript'

// Statements to be inserted here.

} ) ( )
```

comparison.html

2 Next, insert statements that use comparison operators to assign boolean results for output

```
comparison = str === 'JAVASCRIPT'
console.log( 'String Equality? ' + comparison )

comparison = str === 'JavaScript'
console.log( 'String Equality? ' + comparison )

comparison = sum === 8
console.log( 'Number Equality? ' + comparison )

comparison = sum > 5
console.log( 'Greater Than? ' + comparison )

comparison = sum < 5
console.log( 'Less Than? ' + comparison )

comparison = sum <= 8
console.log( 'Less Than or Equal To? ' + comparison )
```

3 Save the HTML document, then open it in your browser and launch the console to see the assigned results

JavaScript is case-sensitive, so character capitalization must match for compared strings to be equal.

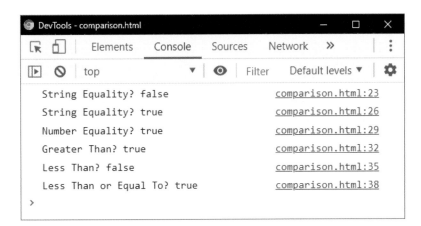

```
DevTools - comparison.html                          —    □    ×

[R] [□]    Elements    Console    Sources    Network   »        ⋮

[▷] [⊘]  | top                    ▼ | ⊙ | Filter   Default levels ▼ | ⚙

  String Equality? false              comparison.html:23
  String Equality? true               comparison.html:26
  Number Equality? true               comparison.html:29
  Greater Than? true                  comparison.html:32
  Less Than? false                    comparison.html:35
  Less Than or Equal To? true         comparison.html:38

>
```

Assess Logic

The three logical operators that can be used in JavaScript are listed in the table below:

Operator	Operation
&&	Logical AND
||	Logical OR
!	Logical NOT

The term "boolean" refers to a system of logical thought developed by the English mathematician George Boole (1815-1864).

The logical operators are typically used with operands that have a boolean value of **true** or **false** – or values that can convert to **true** or **false**.

The **&&** logical AND operator will evaluate two operands and return **true** only if both operands are themselves **true**. Otherwise, the **&&** AND operator will return **false**. This is often used in conditional branching where the direction of the script is determined by testing two conditions. If both conditions are satisfied, the script will follow a particular direction, otherwise it will follow a different direction.

Unlike the **&&** logical AND operator, which needs both operands to be **true**, the **||** logical OR operator will evaluate two operands and return **true** if either one of the operands is itself **true**. If neither operand is **true** then the **||** OR operator will return **false**. This is useful to have a script perform a certain action if either one of two test conditions is satisfied.

The third logical operator is the **!** logical NOT operator that is used before a single operand, and it returns the inverse value of the operand. For example, if variable named "tog" had a **true** value then **!tog** would return **false**. This is useful to "toggle" the value of a variable in successive loop iterations with a statement such as **tog = !a** so that the value is reversed on each iteration – like flicking a light switch on and off.

1 Create an HTML document with a self-invoking anonymous function that declares three variables
(function ( ) {

    let result, yes = true, no = false

    // Statements to be inserted here.

    }) ( )

logic.html

2 Next, insert statements that use logical operators to assign boolean results for output
```
result = yes && yes
console.log( 'Are both true? ' + result )

result = yes && no
console.log( 'Are both still true? ' + result )

result = yes || no
console.log( 'Are either true? ' + result )

result = no || no
console.log( 'Are either still true? ' + result )

console.log( 'Original value: ' + yes )
yes = !yes
console.log( 'Toggled value: ' + yes )
```

3 Save the HTML document, then open it in your browser and launch the console to see the returned results

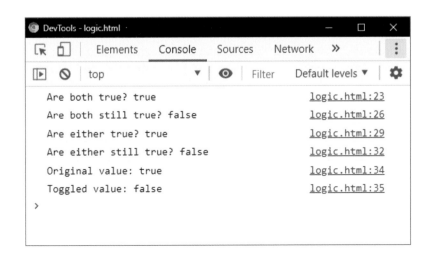

Hot tip

See that **false && false** returns **false**, not **true** – perhaps demonstrating the maxim "two wrongs don't make a right".

Examine Conditions

Possibly, the JavaScript author's favorite operator is the **?:** conditional operator. This operator is also known as the "ternary" operator – meaning composed of three parts.

The ternary operator evaluates a specified condition for a **true** or **false** value then executes one of two specified statements according to the result. Its syntax looks like this:

condition ? *if-true-do-this* **:** *if-false-do-this*

Where multiple actions are required to be performed, according to the result of the condition evaluation, each specified statement may be a function call to execute multiple statements in each function – for example, calling functions to execute multiple statements according to the boolean value of a variable named "flag", like this:

flag === true ? doThis( ) : doThat( )

In this example, the **===** equality operator and **true** keyword are actually superfluous, as operators that evaluate an expression for a boolean value automatically perform this assessment, so the example could be more simply stated as:

flag ? doThis( ) : doThat( )

Alternatively, the two statements specified to the ternary operator might assign a value to a variable according to the result of the condition evaluation, like this:

flag ? str = 'Go left' : str = 'Go right'

While this is syntactically correct, it can be more elegantly expressed by having the ternary operator assign an appropriate value to the variable in a single assignment statement, like this:

str = flag ? 'Go left' : 'Go right'

Where the condition evaluates the parity of a numeric value, the two statements can supply alternatives according to whether the evaluation determines the number to be even or odd.

Don't forget

The ternary operator has three operands – the one before the **?** and those either side of the **:** colon.

...cont'd

1 Create an HTML document with a self-invoking anonymous function that declares two variables
(function ( ) {

    const numOne = 8, numTwo = 3

    // Statements to be inserted here.

}) ( )

ternary.html

2 Next, insert statements to output a string with appropriate grammar for quantity
```
let verb = ( numOne !== 1 ) ? ' are ' : ' is '
console.log( 'There' + verb + numOne )
```

3 Now, insert statements to output strings correctly describing the parity of two variable values
```
let parity = ( numOne % 2 !== 0 ) ? 'Odd' : 'Even'
console.log( numOne + ' is ' + parity )

parity = ( numTwo % 2 !== 0 ) ? 'Odd' : 'Even'
console.log( numTwo + ' is ' + parity )
```

4 Finally, insert statements to output a string reporting the greater of two variable values
```
let max = ( numOne > numTwo ) ? numOne : numTwo
console.log( max + ' is the Greater Number' )
```

The ternary operator can return values of any data type – string, number, boolean, etc.

5 Save the HTML document, then open it in your browser and launch the console to see the string descriptions

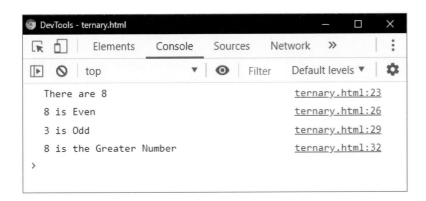

349

Juggle Bits

JavaScript "bitwise" operators regard their operands as a sequence of 32 bits in which each bit may contain a value of zero (0) or one (1). Each bit contributes a decimal component only when that bit contains a one. Components are designated right-to-left from the "Least Significant Bit" (LSB) to the "Most Significant Bit" (MSB). The binary number in the eight-bit pattern below represents decimal 50 as denoted by the bits set with a **1** value (2 + 16 + 32 = 50).

Bit No.	8	7	6	5	4	3	2	1
Decimal	128	64	32	16	8	4	2	1
Binary	0	0	1	1	0	0	1	0

It is possible to manipulate individual bits of the sequence using the JavaScript bitwise operators listed in the table below.

Operator	Name	Binary number operation:
|	OR	Return a **1** in each bit where either of two compared bits is a **1** Example: **1010 | 0101 = 1111**
&	AND	Return a **1** in each bit where both of two compared bits is a **1** Example: **1010 & 1100 = 1000**
~	NOT	Return a **1** in each bit where the bit is not **1**, and return **0** where the bit is **1** Example: **~ 1010 = 0101**
^	XOR	Return a **1** in each bit where only one of two compared bits is a **1** Example: **1010 ^ 0100 = 1110**
<<	Shift left	Push zeros in from the right, to move each bit a number of bits to the left Example: **0010 << 2 = 1000**
>>	Signed shift right	Push copies of the leftmost bit in from the left, to move each bit a number of bits to the right. Example: **1000 >> 2 = 0010**
>>>	Shift right	Push zeros in from the left, to move each bit a number of bits to the right Example: **1000 >> 2 = 0010**

Don't forget

Many JavaScript authors never use bitwise operators but it is useful to understand what they are and how they may be used.

Hot tip

A "byte" has 8 bits, and each half of a byte is known as a "nibble" (4 bits). The binary numbers in the examples in this table describe values stored in a nibble.

...cont'd

1 Create an HTML document with a self-invoking anonymous function that declares two variables
(function ( ) {

    let numOne = 10, numTwo = 5

    // Statements to be inserted here.

}) ( )

bitwise.html

2 Next, insert statements to simply output strings that confirm the initial values stored in each variable
console.log('numOne: ' + numOne)
console.log('numTwo: ' + numTwo)

3 Now, insert statements to swap the values stored in each variable using bitwise operations
numOne = numOne ^ numTwo
    // 1010 ^ 0101 = 1111 = (decimal 15)
numTwo = numOne ^ numTwo
    // 1111 ^ 0101 = 1010 (decimal 10)
numOne = numOne ^ numTwo
    // 1111 ^ 1010 = 0101 (decimal 5)

Hot tip

Notice how this example uses the special \n escape sequence to create a line break in the console output.

4 Finally, insert statements to output a line break and strings to confirm the final values stored in each variable
console.log('\n' + 'numOne: ' + numOne)
console.log('numTwo: ' + numTwo)

5 Save the HTML document, then open it in your browser and launch the console to see the swapped values

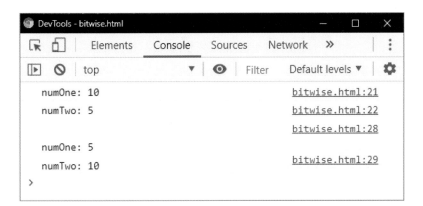

Force Order

JavaScript operators have different levels of priority to determine the order in which a statement containing multiple different operators gets evaluated – those with higher priority take precedence over those with lower priority. The table below lists each type of operator in order of highest to lowest priority from top to bottom of the table:

The [ ] operator is introduced in the section that demonstrates arrays beginning on page 380. Meanwhile, note that the . period (full stop) operator, used in dot notation such as **console.log( )**, is given high precedence for early recognition of the object and its member.

Priority

Operator	Operation
( )	Expression grouping
. [ ] ( )	Object Member Array Member Function Call
++ --	Postfix Increment, Postfix Decrement
++ -- ! ~	Prefix Increment, Prefix Decrement Logical NOT, Bitwise NOT
**	Exponentiation
* / %	Multiplication, Division, Modulus
+ –	Addition, Subtraction
<< >> >>>	Bitwise shift
< <= => >	Comparison
=== === !== !=	Equality, Inequality
&	Bitwise AND
^	Bitwise XOR
|	Bitwise OR
&&	Logical AND
||	Logical OR
?:	Ternary conditional
= += -= *= /= %= &= ^= |= <<= >>= >>>=	Assignment
,	Comma

1 Create an HTML document with a self-invoking anonymous function that initializes a variable with the result of an ungrouped expression and outputs its value

```
( function ( ) {

    let sum = 9 + 12 / 3              // Equivalent to 9 + 4.
    console.log( 'Ungrouped sum: ' + sum )

} ) ( )
```

precedence.html

2 Save the HTML document, then open it in your browser and launch the console to see the resulting value

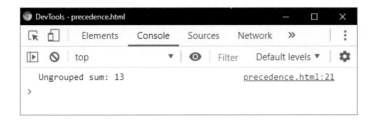

The evaluation first computes the division, as its operator has higher priority than the addition operator, so the result is 13. But you can force the order of precedence by grouping an expression within parentheses so it will be evaluated first, because the ( ) operator has the very highest priority of all operators.

3 Edit the statements within the function to force the order of evaluation so the addition is performed before division

```
    let sum = ( 9 + 12 ) / 3          // Equivalent to 21 / 3.
    console.log( 'Grouped sum: ' + sum )
```

4 Save the HTML document once more, then refresh your browser to see the new resulting value

Hot tip

Make a habit of using parentheses to group expressions and thereby set the precedence order of evaluation.

Summary

- **parseInt( )** and **parseFloat( )** can convert strings to numbers, but **String( )** and **toString( )** can convert numbers to strings.

- The **isNaN( )** function tests its argument for a **NaN** value.

- Arithmetic operators perform regular arithmetic plus **%** modulus, **++** increment, **--** decrement, and ****** exponentiation.

- When the **++** increment or **– –** decrement operator prefix the operand its value is changed immediately, but when they are postfixed after the operand the expression is evaluated first.

- The **=** operator can be combined with an arithmetic operator to perform an arithmetical operation then assign its result.

- The **+=** operator is useful to append to an existing string.

- Two operands can be compared for **===** equality, **!==** inequality, **>** greater than value, or **<** less than value.

- The **<=** and **>=** combined comparison operators also return **true** when both operands are equal.

- The logical **&&** AND operator evaluates two operands and returns **true** when both operands are **true**, but the logical **||** OR operator returns **true** when either operand is **true**.

- The logical **!** NOT operator can prefix a single operand to return its inverse value.

- Ternary operator **?:** evaluates a condition for **true** or **false** then executes one of two statements according to the result.

- JavaScript bitwise operators can manipulate individual bits of a binary sequence to perform binary arithmetic.

- JavaScript operators have different levels of priority to determine the order in which a statement gets evaluated.

- The order of precedence can be forced by grouping an expression within **( )** parentheses so it will be evaluated first.

17 Manage the Script Flow

Branch If

The progress of any script or computer program depends upon the evaluation of conditions to determine the direction of flow. Each evaluation may present one or more branches along which to continue according to the result of the evaluation.

In JavaScript, the basic conditional test is performed with the **if** keyword to test a condition for a boolean **true** or **false** value. When the result is **true**, a statement following the evaluation will be executed, otherwise this is skipped and flow continues at the next subsequent statement.

The syntax of an **if** statement demands that the condition to be tested is placed within parentheses after the **if** keyword, and looks like this:

if (*condition*) *execute-this-statement-when-true*

An **if** statement may also specify multiple statements to be executed when the result is true by enclosing those statements within braces, like this:

```
if ( condition )
{
  execute-this-statement-when-true
  execute-this-statement-when-true
  execute-this-statement-when-true
}
```

The evaluation of a condition and the execution of actions according to its result simply reflects the real-life thought process – for example, the actions you might execute on a summer day:

```
let temperature = readThermometer( )
const tolerable = 25

if ( temperature > tolerable )
{
  turn_on_air-conditioning( )
  get_a_cool_drink( )
  stay_in_shade( )
}
```

The conditional test is equivalent to **if(*condition* === true)**, but as it automatically performs the equality test for a **true** value there is no need to include **=== true** in the parentheses.

Hot tip

It is recommended that you enclose even single statements to be executed within braces – to maintain a consistent coding style.

...cont'd

1 Create an HTML document with a self-invoking function that begins by initializing a boolean variable
`let flag = true`

if.html

2 Next, insert statements to perform conditional tests of the variable's boolean value

```
if( !flag )
{
  console.log( 'Power is OFF' )
}

if( flag )
{
  console.log( 'Power is ON' )
}
```

Hot tip

The logical ! NOT operator is used here to invert the conditional test so it becomes equivalent to
`if( flag === false )`

3 Now, insert statements to perform conditional tests of an expression that compares two integers

```
if( 7 < 2 )
{
  console.log( 'Failure' )
}

if( 7 > 2 )
{
  console.log( 'Success' )
}
```

Hot tip

The script code that creates the function block is omitted from this example, and most further examples, to conserve page space. You can refer back to page 330 for instruction on how to create anonymous self-invoking functions.

4 Save the HTML document, then open it in your browser and launch the console to see which output statements get executed and which ones are ignored

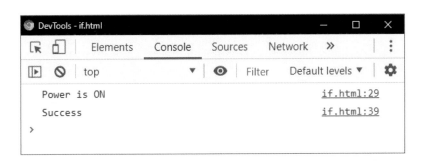

Branch Alternatives

An **if** statement, which tests a condition for a boolean value and only executes its statements when the result is **true**, provides a single branch that the script may follow. An alternative branch that the script can follow when the result is **false** can be provided by extending an **if** statement with the **else** keyword.

An **else** statement follows after the **if** statement, like this:

if (*condition*) *execute-this-statement-when-true*
else *execute-this-statement-when-false*

An **if else** statement may also specify multiple statements to be executed by enclosing those statements within braces, like this:

if (*condition*)
{
  execute-this-statement-when-true
  execute-this-statement-when-true
}
else
{
  execute-this-statement-when-false
  execute-this-statement-when-false
}

Multiple branches can be provided by making subsequent conditional **if** tests at the start of each **else** statement block, like this:

if (*condition*)
{
  execute-these-statements-when-true
}
else if (*condition*)
{
  execute-these-statements-when-true
}
else if (*condition*)
{
  execute-these-statements-when-true
}
else
{
  execute-these-statements-when-false
}

An **if else if** statement might repeatedly test a variable for a range of values or might test a variety of conditions. The final **else** statement acts as a default when no conditions are found to be **true**.

Hot tip

Once a condition is found to be **true** in an **if else** statement, its associated statements are executed, then flow continues after the **if else** statement – without evaluating subsequent **else** statements.

...cont'd

1 Create an HTML document with a self-invoking function that begins by initializing two variables

```
let flag = false
const num = 10
```

else.html

2 Next, insert statements to perform conditional tests of the first variable's boolean value

```
if( !flag )
{
  console.log( 'Power is OFF' )
}
else
{
  console.log( 'Power is ON' )
}
```

3 Now, insert statements to perform conditional tests of the second variable's numeric value

```
if( num === 5 )
{
  console.log( 'Number is Five' )
}
else if( num === 10 )
{
  console.log( 'Number is Ten' )
}
else
{
  console.log( 'Number is Neither Five nor Ten' )
}
```

The **else** statement specifies an alternative when a conditional test is **false**, but an **else if** statement specifies a new conditional test.

4 Save the HTML document, then open it in your browser and launch the console to see which output statements get executed and which ones are ignored

Switch Alternatives

Conditionally branching script flow using **if else** statements is fine for testing just a few conditions but can become unwieldy when there are a large number of conditions to test. In that situation it is often both more efficient and more elegant to use a **switch** statement rather than **if else** statements.

A **switch** statement works in an unusual way – it first evaluates a specified expression, then seeks a match for the resulting value. Where a match is found, the **switch** statement will execute one or more statements associated with that value, otherwise it will execute one or more statements specified as "default statements".

The **switch** statement begins by enclosing the expression to be evaluated within parentheses after the **switch** keyword. This is followed by a pair of **{ }** braces that contain the possible matches. Each match value follows a **case** keyword and employs a colon : character to associate one or more statements to be executed. Importantly, each **case** must end with a **break** statement to exit the **switch** statement after its associated statements have executed.

Beware

Omission of the **break** statement allows the script to also execute statements associated with subsequent unmatching **case** values.

Optionally, a **switch** statement may include a final **default** alternative to associate one or more statements to be executed when none of the specified **case** values match the result of the expression evaluation.

So the syntax of a **switch** statement looks like this:

```
switch ( expression )
{
    case value-1 : statements-to-be-executed-when-matched ; break

    case value-2 : statements-to-be-executed-when-matched ; break

    case value-3 : statements-to-be-executed-when-matched ; break

    default : statements-to-be-executed-when-no-match-found
}
```

There is no limit to the number of **case** values that can be included within a **switch** statement block, so this is an ideal way to match any one of tens, hundreds, or even thousands of different values.

...cont'd

1 Create an HTML document with a self-invoking function that begins by declaring a variable
let day

switch.html

2 Next, insert a switch statement to assign a value to the variable following the evaluation of an expression

```
switch( 5 - 2 )
{
  case 1 : day = 'Monday' ; break

  case 2 : day = 'Tuesday' ; break

  case 3 : day = 'Wednesday' ; break

  case 4 : day = 'Thursday' ; break

  case 5 : day = 'Friday' ; break

  default : day = 'Weekend'
}
```

String values offered as possible **case** matches must be enclosed within quotes like all other string values.

3 Now, insert a statement to output the value assigned by the case statement that found a match
console.log('It is ' + day)

4 Save the HTML document, then open it in your browser and launch the console to see the assigned value in output

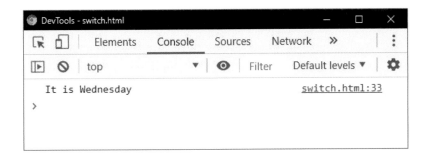

Loop For

A loop is a structure containing a test condition and one or more statements that are repeatedly executed while the test condition is met. Each single examination of the condition and execution of the statements is called an "iteration". When the test condition is not met, no further iterations are made and flow continues at the next statement following the loop structure.

Perhaps the most commonly used loop structure in JavaScript is the **for** loop, which has this syntax:

for (*initializer ; condition ; modifier*) { *statements-to-be-executed* }

The parentheses after the **for** keyword contain three expressions that control the number of iterations the loop will perform:

- **Initializer** – a statement that specifies the initial value of a variable that will be used to count the number of loop iterations . Traditionally, this trivial counter variable is simply named "i".

- **Condition** – an expression that is tested for a boolean **true** value on each iteration. When the evaluation returns **true**, the loop statements are then executed to complete that iteration. If the evaluation returns **false**, the statements are not executed and the loop ends. Typically, the condition examines the value of the loop counter variable.

Beware

Unless the modifier enables the evaluation to return **false** at some point, an infinite loop is created that will run forever.

- **Modifier** – a statement that modifies a value in the test condition so that at some point its evaluation will return **false**. Typically, this will increment, or decrement, the loop counter variable.

For example, a **for** loop structure to execute a set of statements one hundred times might look like this:

```
let i
for ( i = 0 ; i < 100 ; i++ ) { statements-to-be-executed }
```

In this case, the counter variable is incremented on each iteration until its value reaches 100, upon which the evaluation returns **false** and the loop ends.

...cont'd

1 Create an HTML document with a self-invoking function that begins by initializing a loop counter variable
let i = 0

2 Next, insert a **for** loop structure that will make 10 iterations and output the value of the loop counter on each iteration

```
for( i = 1 ; i < 11 ; i++ )
{
  console.log( 'Iteration Number: ' + i )
}
```

3 Save the HTML document, then open it in your browser and launch the console to see the loop iterations

for.html

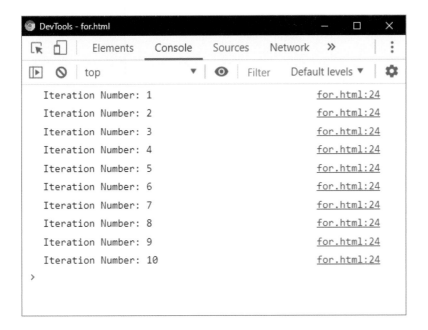

DevTools - for.html	— □ ✕

Elements Console Sources Network »

top ▼ ◉ Filter Default levels ▼ ⚙

```
Iteration Number: 1                for.html:24
Iteration Number: 2                for.html:24
Iteration Number: 3                for.html:24
Iteration Number: 4                for.html:24
Iteration Number: 5                for.html:24
Iteration Number: 6                for.html:24
Iteration Number: 7                for.html:24
Iteration Number: 8                for.html:24
Iteration Number: 9                for.html:24
Iteration Number: 10               for.html:24
>
```

Hot tip

This is the regular **for** loop. There is also a special **for in** loop that is used to iterate through properties of an object and is demonstrated later, on page 376.

Loop While

The **for** loop structure, described on pages 362-363, is ideal when the number of required iterations is a known quantity, but when this is unknown a **while** loop structure is often preferable. The syntax of a **while** loop looks like this:

```
while( condition )
{
  statements-to-be-executed
  modifier
}
```

The parentheses after the **while** keyword contain a condition that is evaluated for a boolean value upon each iteration. Statements to be executed on each iteration are enclosed within braces along with a statement that modifies a value in the test condition, so that at some point its evaluation will return **false** and the loop will exit. While the evaluation remains **true**, the statements will be executed on each iteration of the loop.

Where the condition evaluation is **false** on the first iteration, the loop exits immediately so the statements within its braces are never executed. Both **while** loops and **for** loops are sometimes referred to as "pre-test" loops because their test condition is evaluated before any statements are executed.

A **while** loop can be made to perform a specific number of iterations, like a **for** loop, by using a counter variable as the test condition and incrementing its value on each iteration. For example, a **while** loop structure to execute a set of statements 100 times might look like this:

```
let i = 0
while ( i < 100 )
{
  statements-to-be-executed
  i++ ;
}
```

The counter variable is incremented on each iteration until its value reaches 100, upon which the evaluation returns **false** and the loop ends.

Beware

Omitting a modifier from the **while** loop structure will create an infinite loop that will run forever.

...cont'd

1 Create an HTML document with a self-invoking function that begins by initializing a loop counter variable
let i = 10

while.html

2 Next, insert a **while** loop structure that will make iterations and output the value of the loop counter on each iteration until it reaches zero
```
while( i > -1 )
{
  console.log( 'Countdown Number: ' + i )
  i--
}
```

3 Save the HTML document, then open it in your browser and launch the console to see the loop iterations

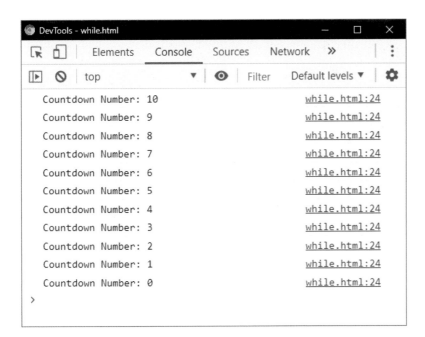

Hot tip

Each while loop must have braces as they contain at least two statements – one statement to execute and a modifier.

365

Do Loops

Another kind of loop available in JavaScript is the **do while** loop structure. This is like an inverted version of the **while** loop, described on pages 364-365, and is ideal when the statements it will execute on each iteration absolutely must be executed at least one time. Its syntax looks like this:

```
do
{
  statements-to-be-executed
  modifier
}
while ( condition )
```

The parentheses after the **while** keyword contain a condition that is evaluated for a boolean value after each iteration. Statements to be executed on each iteration are enclosed within braces along with a statement that modifies a value in the test condition, so that at some point its evaluation will return **false** and the loop will exit. While the evaluation remains **true**, the statements will be executed on each iteration of the loop.

Where the condition evaluation is **false** on the first iteration, the loop exits immediately so the statements within its braces have been executed once. The **do while** loop is sometimes referred to as a "post-test" loop because the test condition is evaluated after its statements have been executed.

A **do while** loop can be made to perform a specific number of iterations, like a **for** loop, by using a counter variable as the test condition and incrementing its value on each iteration. For example, a **do while** loop structure to execute a set of statements 100 times might look like this:

```
let i = 0
do
{
  statements-to-be-executed
  i++
}
while ( i < 100 )
```

The counter variable is incremented on each iteration until its value reaches 100, upon which the evaluation returns **false** and the loop ends.

Only use a **do while** loop if the statements absolutely must be executed at least once.

...cont'd

do.html

1 Create an HTML document with a self-invoking function that begins by initializing a loop counter variable **let i = 2**

2 Next, insert a **do while** loop structure that will make iterations and output the value of the loop counter on each iteration until it exceeds 1000

```
do
{
  i *= 2
  console.log( 'Multiplied Number: ' + i )
}
while( i < 1000 )
```

3 Save the HTML document, then open it in your browser and launch the console to see the loop iterations

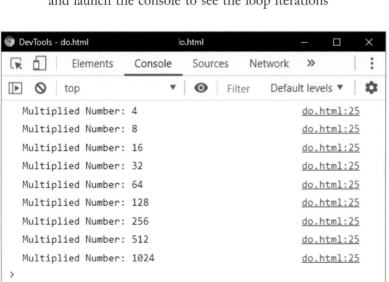

Don't forget

Notice that the final value exceeds the condition limit because it gets written in output before the test is made.

Break Out

The JavaScript **break** keyword can be used to exit from a loop when a specified condition is encountered. The conditional test should appear before all other statements to be executed so the loop will end immediately.

Where a **break** statement is used in a loop that is nested within an outer loop, flow resumes in the outer loop iteration.

The JavaScript **continue** keyword can be used to skip a single iteration of a loop when a specified condition is encountered.

Where a **continue** statement is used in a loop that is nested within an outer loop, flow resumes at the next iteration of the inner loop.

break.html

1 Create an HTML document with a self-invoking function that begins by initializing two loop counter variables

```
let i = 0
let j = 0
```

2 Next, insert a **for** loop containing an inner nested **for** loop

```
for ( i = 1 ; i < 3 ; i++ )
{
  console.log( 'Outer Loop: ' + i )

  for ( j = 1 ; j < 4 ; j++ )
  {

    // Statements to be inserted here.

    console.log( '\tInner Loop: ' + j )
  }

}
```

Hot tip

The **\t** escape sequence is used here to include a tab space in the output.

3 Save the HTML document, then open it in your browser and launch the console to see two iterations of the outer loop and three iterations of the inner loop

...cont'd

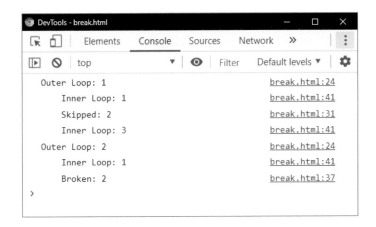

The **break** keyword is also used as a terminator in **switch** statements.

4 Next, insert statements in the inner loop to skip an iteration of the inner loop and break out of the outer loop

```
if( ( i === 1 ) && ( j === 2 ) ) {
  console.log( '\tSkipped: ' + j )
  continue
}

if( ( i === 2 ) && ( j === 2 ) ) {
  console.log( '\tBroken: ' + j )
  break
}
```

5 Save the HTML document again, then open it in your browser and launch the console to see an iteration skipped and the loop broken completely

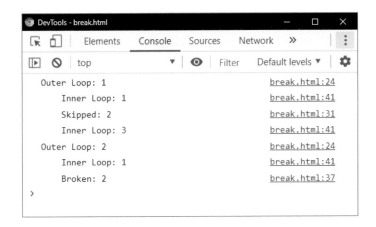

Don't be tempted to use **break** statements to exit loops in place of the regular conditional tests that form part of the loop structure.

369

Catch Errors

Sections of script in which it is possible to anticipate errors, such as those handling user input, may be enclosed in a **try catch** structure to handle "exception" errors. The statements to be executed are contained within the braces of a **try** block, and exceptions are passed as an argument to the ensuing **catch** block for handling. Optionally, this may be followed by a **finally** block, containing statements to execute after exceptions have been handled.

JavaScript recognizes error objects of **Error, EvalError, InternalError, RangeError, ReferenceError, SyntaxError, TypeError**, and **URIError**. These may be automatically created and passed to the catch block by the parser or manually created with the **new** keyword and a constructor method, then passed using the **throw** keyword.

Each error object can have a **name** property and a **message** property to allow the **catch** block to describe its nature. The message is specified as an argument to the constructor for error objects created manually, but is predefined otherwise.

Alternatively, a string may be passed to the **catch** block by the **throw** keyword to identify the error. An appropriate action can then be determined by examining the string value.

catch.html

1. Create an HTML document with a self-invoking function that begins by initializing a variable
   let day = 32

2. Next, insert a **try** block to recognize invalid integer values

```
try
{
  if( day > 31 )
  {
    throw new RangeError( 'Day Cannot Exceed 31' )
  }

  if( day < 1 )
  {
    throw 'invalid'
  }
}
```

3 Now, append a **catch** block to the **try** block, to handle invalid integer values

```
catch( err )
{
  if( err === 'invalid' )
  {
    console.log( 'Variable has invalid value of ' + day )
  }
  else
  {
    console.log( err.name + ' Exception: ' + err.message )
  }
}
```

4 Then, append a **finally** block to the **catch** block, to output a final message

```
finally
{
  console.log( 'The script has ignored the error...' )
}
```

5 Save the HTML document again, then open it in your browser and launch the console to see the error caught

6 Change the variable value to zero, then save the HTML document and refresh your browser to see the error caught

Hot tip

Delete or comment-out the **day** variable declaration then save and refresh this example to see an automatic **ReferenceError** get caught.

Summary

- The basic conditional test is performed with the **if** keyword to test a condition for a boolean **true** or **false** value.

- An alternative branch to the basic conditional test can be provided by extending an **if** statement with the **else** keyword.

- A large number of conditions can be tested for a boolean **true** or **false** value with a **switch** statement.

- In a **switch** block, each **case** statement must end with the **break** keyword to exit when a match is found.

- A **switch** block may contain a final **default** statement to execute when no match has been found.

- A **for** loop must specify an initializer, a condition to be tested for a boolean **true** or **false** value, and a modifier.

- A loop modifier must enable the tested condition to become **false** at some point in order to exit the loop.

- The **while** loops and **for** loops evaluate a test condition before any statements are executed.

- A **do while** loop evaluates a test condition after its statements have been executed.

- The **break** keyword can be used to exit from a loop when a specified condition is encountered.

- The **continue** keyword can be used to skip a single iteration of a loop when a specified condition is encountered.

- The **try catch** structure can be used to handle exception errors that occur in a script.

- Each error object can have a **name** property and a **message** property to allow the **catch** block to describe its nature.

- A string may be passed to the **catch** block by the **throw** keyword to identify the error.

- A **try catch** structure may be followed by a **finally** block containing statements to execute after exceptions are handled.

18 Use Script Objects

Custom Objects

Real-world objects are all around us, and they each have attributes and behaviors that we can describe:

● Attributes describe the features that an object has.

● Behaviors describe actions that an object can perform.

For example, a car might be described with attributes of "make" and "model", along with "accelerate" and "brake" behaviors.

Hot tip

Whitespace is ignored in the object's list of name:value pairs, but don't forget to put a comma between the pairs.

These features could be represented in JavaScript with a custom **car** object containing variable properties of **make** and **model**, along with **accelerate( )** and **brake( )** methods.

Values are assigned to the object as a comma-separated list of name:value pairs within **{ }** curly brackets, like this:

```
let car = { make: 'Jeep', model: 'Wrangler',

  accelerate: function ( ) { return this.model + ' drives away' } ,

  brake: function ( ) { return this.make + ' pulls up' }
}
```

You can reference the object property values in two ways – using dot notation syntax of ***objectName.propertyName*** or using the syntax of ***objectName['propertyName']***

The object methods can be called using dot notation syntax of ***objectName.methodName( )***

The **this** keyword can be used in object method definitions to refer to the object that "owns" the method. In the example above, **this** refers to the **car** object, so **this.model** references the **car.model** property and **this.make** references the **car.make** property.

...cont'd

1 Create an HTML document with a self-invoking function that begins by declaring a variable to contain an object definition
```
let car = {

    // Statements to be inserted here.

}
```

custom.html

2 Next, insert statements to define the object's properties
```
make: 'Jeep' ,
model: 'Wrangler' ,
```

3 Now, insert statements to define the object's methods
```
accelerate: function ( ) {
  return this.model + ' drives away' } ,
brake: function ( ) {
  return this.make + ' pulls up' }
```

4 Then, after the closing **}** of the variable declaration, add a statement to output a string containing the object property values – using each reference technique
```
console.log( 'Car is a ' + car.make + ' ' + car[ 'model' ] )
```

5 Finally, add statements to call each object method
```
console.log( car.accelerate( ) )
console.log( car.brake( ) )
```

Don't forget

You must include the trailing **( )** parentheses to call a method, otherwise it will simply return the function definition.

6 Save the HTML document, then open it in your browser and launch the console to see the object's property values and the strings returned from its methods

375

Extend Objects

Custom objects are very flexible and can easily be extended and updated at any time simply by assigning a new value, using dot notation to reference the property as **objectName.propertyName**

A special **for in** loop can be used to list all the property names and method names ('keys") of an object with this syntax:

for (*property* in *objectName*) { console.log(*property*) }

In order to reference the value of each property on each iteration, the property variable name can be enclosed within square brackets following the object name as **object-Name[*property*]**

extend.html

1 Create an HTML document with a self-invoking function that begins by initializing a variable that exactly recreates the object in the previous example
```
let property, car = {
  make: 'Jeep' ,
  model: 'Wrangler' ,
  accelerate: function ( ) {
    return this.model + ' drives away' } ,
  brake: function ( ) {
    return this.make + ' pulls up' }
}
```

Don't forget

The **property** variable in this example could, in fact, be given any valid variable name.

2 Add a loop statement to list the name and value of each property and method
```
for( property in car ) {
  console.log( property + ': ' + car[ property ] )
}
```

3 Save the HTML document, then open it in your browser and launch the console to see the object's keys and values

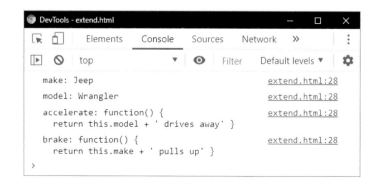

4 Next, add statements to assign new values to two existing object properties
```
car.make = 'Ford'
car.model = 'Bronco'
```

5 Now, add statements to extend the object with an additional property and an additional method
```
car.engine = 'V6'
car.start = function ( ) {
  return this.make + ' motor is running' }
```

6 Then, add statements to output strings containing the object property values – using each reference technique
```
console.log( '\nCar is a ' + car.make + ' ' + car[ 'model' ] )
console.log( 'Engine Type: ' + car.engine )
```

Hot tip

The **\n** escape sequence is used in this statement to include a newline (line break) in the output.

7 Finally, add statements to call each object method
```
console.log( car.start( ) )
console.log( car.accelerate( ) )
console.log( car.brake( ) )
```

8 Save the HTML document again, then refresh your browser to see the extended object's property values and the strings returned from its methods

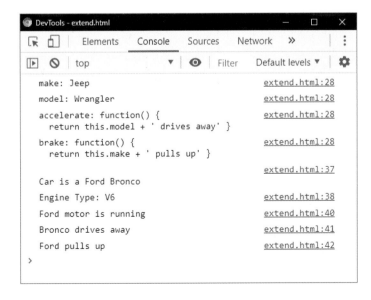

Built-in Objects

Object
String (an object only if created using the **new** keyword)
Number (an object only if created using the **new** keyword)
Boolean (an object only if created using the **new** keyword)
Object – an object defined by you
Date – an object containing date and time components
Array – an object storing indexed items of data
RegExp – an object describing a regular expression pattern
Math – an object providing math properties and methods
Error – an object supplying details of an error

Hot tip

If you're working through this book from the beginning you should already be somewhat familiar with **String**, **Number**, **Boolean**, **Error**, and **Object** objects. The **Array** object is introduced on page 380, the **Date** object is introduced on page 388, the **RegExp** object is introduced on page 396, and the **Math** object is introduced on page 406.

JavaScript provides the predefined built-in objects listed in the table above. Each of these objects, except for **Math**, has a like-named constructor method that can be used with the **new** keyword to create an object of that type – for example, to create a new **Date** object with **let now = new Date( )**.

It is, however, not recommended you use the **new** keyword and a constructor method for any object type other than **Error** and **Date**. JavaScript can intelligently recognize what type of object should be created by the value being assigned unless that value is a **string**, a **number**, or a **boolean**. These are each regarded as "primitive" literal values that have no properties or methods, so a **typeof** statement returns **string, number, boolean,** for these – not **object**.

All JavaScript built-in objects inherit properties and methods from a top-level **Object.prototype** object. For example, this provides a **toLocaleString( )** method to lower-level objects such as **Date.prototype**, so you can append that method call to a **Date** object to get a locally formatted date string.

You can also call inherited methods on the primitive **string, number,** and **boolean** literal values because JavaScript will automatically call the method from the equivalent object. This means you can append the **toLocaleString( )** method call to a **number** literal value to get a locally formatted number string.

...cont'd

builtin.html

1 Create an HTML document with a self-invoking function that begins by assigning primitive literal values to three variables

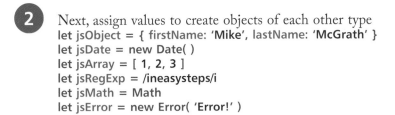
```
let jsString = 'Text'        // not, new String( 'Text' ).

let jsNumber = 125000  // not, new Number( 125000 ).

let jsBoolean = true       // not, new Boolean( true ).
```

2 Next, assign values to create objects of each other type

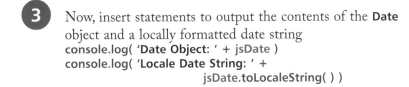
```
let jsObject = { firstName: 'Mike', lastName: 'McGrath' }
let jsDate = new Date( )
let jsArray = [ 1, 2, 3 ]
let jsRegExp = /ineasysteps/i
let jsMath = Math
let jsError = new Error( 'Error!' )
```

The **Math** object is the only JavaScript object that does not provide a constructor method.

3 Now, insert statements to output the contents of the **Date** object and a locally formatted date string
```
console.log( 'Date Object: ' + jsDate )
console.log( 'Locale Date String: ' +
                        jsDate.toLocaleString( ) )
```

4 Then, insert statements to output the primitive literal **number** value and a locally formatted numeric string
```
console.log( '\nPrimitive Number: ' + jsNumber )
console.log( 'Locale Number String: ' +
                        jsNumber.toLocaleString( ) )
```

5 Save the HTML document, then open it in your browser and launch the console to see the output strings

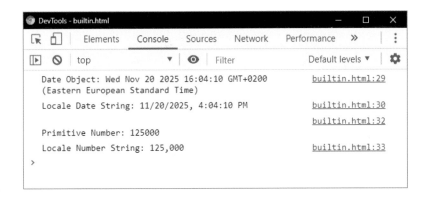

Create Arrays

An **Array** object is a JavaScript built-in object that can store multiple items (of various data-types) in individual "elements". An array is created by assigning [ ] square brackets to a variable, which can optionally contain a comma-separated list of values to initialize the array elements. Its syntax looks like this:

let *arrayName* = [*value1* , *value2* , *value3*]

Unlike custom objects, where each property is named, array elements are automatically numbered – starting at zero. So the first element is 0, the second is 1, the third is 2, and so on. This numbering system is often referred to as a "zero-based index".

The value stored within an array element can be referenced by enclosing its element index number within square brackets following the object name. For example, **colors[0]** would reference the value in the first element in an array named "colors".

Where array elements are not required to be initialized immediately, an empty array can be created and values assigned to its elements later, like this:

let colors = [ ]

colors[0] = 'Red'

colors[1] = 'Green'

colors[2] = 'Blue'

Although the Array object provides an **Array( )** constructor it should not be used as it can produce unexpected results – for example, creating an array initializing the first element, like this:

let jsArray = new Array(10)

You might reasonably expect **jsArray[0]** to reference an integer value of 10 within the first element, but it in fact returns an **undefined** value. What's going on? This is an anomaly that only occurs when you specify a single integer argument to the constructor method – which causes JavaScript to create an array of 10 empty elements! Creating the array with **jsArray = [10]** does not have that effect, and creates the array with its first element containing the integer value of 10 as expected.

380

Don't forget

All built-in object names begin with an uppercase character – so the constructor is named "Array", not "array".

1 Create an HTML document with a self-invoking function that begins by creating an array – the wrong way
```
let jsArray = new Array( 10 )
```

array.html

2 Next, add statements to output the value in the first array element and list the entire array
```
console.log( jsArray[ 0 ] )
console.log( jsArray )
```

3 Now, add a statement to declare a variable, and to declare a variable initialized with an array
```
let month, summer = [ 'June', 'July', 'August' ]
```

4 Then, add a loop to output the index number and value of each array element
```
for ( month in summer )
{
  if ( month !== ' ' )
  {
    console.log( month + ': ' + summer[ month ] )
  }
}
```

Hot tip

It's good practice to wrap the body of **for in** loops in an **if** statement – here, it ensures the element is not empty.

5 Finally, add statements to output the value in the first array element and list the entire array
```
console.log( 'Start of Summer: ' + summer[ 0 ] )
console.log( summer )
```

6 Save the HTML document, then open it in your browser and launch the console to see the array element contents

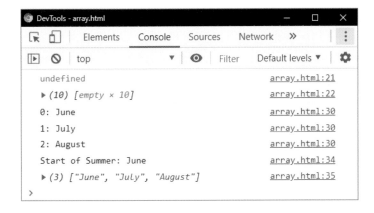

Loop Elements

Arrays and loops make great partners! Any kind of loop can be used to fill the elements of an array with values. The elements of even very large arrays can be "populated" in this way – and with surprisingly little code.

Similarly, loops can be used to quickly read the values in each array element and perform some action appropriate to that value on each iteration of the loop.

Usefully, each array has a **length** property that contains an integer record of the total number of elements in that array. As a result of zero-based indexing this will always be one greater than the final element's index number, so can be readily used in a conditional test to terminate the loop.

HTML

elements.html

1 Create an HTML document with a self-invoking function that begins by declaring three variables
```
let i, result, boolArray = [ ]
```

2 Next, output a simple heading
```
console.log( 'Fill Elements...' )
```

3 Now, add a loop to fill 10 elements with boolean values and output their index number and each stored value
```
for( i = 1 ; i < 11 ; i++ )
{
  boolArray[ i ] = ( i % 2 === 0 ) ? true : false
  console.log( 'Element ' + i + ': ' + boolArray[ i ] )
}
```

4 Then, output a second simple heading and initialize a variable with an empty string value
```
console.log( 'Read Elements...' )
result = ''
```

Hot tip

This array **length** property here has a value of 11 because the array has eleven elements – even though element zero has not been filled.

5 Next, add a loop to assign the index numbers of any elements containing a **true** value to a string
```
for( i = 1 ; i < boolArray.length ; i++ )
{
  if( boolArray[ i ] ) { result += i + ' | ' }
}
```

6 Now, output the string to reveal the index numbers of elements that contain a **true** value
```
console.log( 'True in Elements: ' + result )
```

7 Reset the string variable to contain an empty string
```
result = ''
```

8 Then, add a loop to assign the index numbers of any elements containing a **false** value to a string
```
for( i = 1 ; i < boolArray.length ; i++ )
{
  if( !boolArray[ i ] ) { result += i + ' | ' }
}
```

Don't forget

Conditional tests for a boolean value do not need to include the expression **=== true** as that is automatic.

9 Finally, output the string to reveal the index numbers of elements that contain a **false** value
```
console.log( 'False in Elements: ' + result )
```

10 Save the HTML document, then open it in your browser and launch the console to write and read array elements

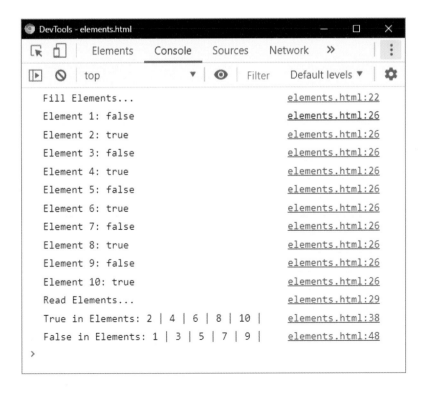

```
DevTools - elements.html                               —    □    ✕

⟨R  ⬚   Elements   Console   Sources   Network   »          ⋮

▷  ⊘   top              ▼  ◉  Filter   Default levels ▼     ✿

  Fill Elements...                      elements.html:22
  Element 1: false                      elements.html:26
  Element 2: true                       elements.html:26
  Element 3: false                      elements.html:26
  Element 4: true                       elements.html:26
  Element 5: false                      elements.html:26
  Element 6: true                       elements.html:26
  Element 7: false                      elements.html:26
  Element 8: true                       elements.html:26
  Element 9: false                      elements.html:26
  Element 10: true                      elements.html:26
  Read Elements...                      elements.html:29
  True in Elements: 2 | 4 | 6 | 8 | 10 |   elements.html:38
  False in Elements: 1 | 3 | 5 | 7 | 9 |   elements.html:48
>
```

Slice Arrays

JavaScript objects have properties and methods. In addition to the **length** property, each array object has methods that can be used to manipulate the elements in an array. These are listed in the table below, together with a brief description of the task they perform:

Method	Description
join(*separator*)	Unites all element values into a single string separated by a specified separator, or by a comma if no separator is specified
pop( )	Deletes the last element of the array, and returns its value
push(*value* , *value*)	Adds elements to the end of the array and returns the new length
reverse( )	Reverses the order of all elements in the array and returns the reordered value of each element
shift( )	Deletes the first element of the array, and returns its value
slice(*begin* , *end*)	Returns elements between specified index positions, or the end of the array if no end position is specified
sort( )	Sorts all elements in the array into alphabetical or numerical order and returns the reordered value of each element
splice(*position* , *number*, *value*, *value*)	Replaces a specified number of element values starting at a specified index position, and returns the replaced values
unshift(*value* , *value*)	Adds elements to the start of the array and returns the new length

Where no values are specified by the **push( )** or **unshift( )** methods, a single empty element gets added to the array. A comma-separated list of values can be specified to the **push( )**, **unshift( )**, and **splice( )** methods to change multiple elements.

Hot tip

The **join( )** method is faster for uniting a large number of element values into a single string, but the + concatenate operator is faster at uniting just a few element values.

Beware

The **slice( )** method returns the element values up to, but not including, the optional end index position.

1 Create an HTML document with a self-invoking function that begins by creating an array
```
let seasons = [ 'Spring', 'Summer', 'Fall', 'Winter' ]
console.log( 'Elements: ' + seasons )
```

2 Next, output a modified list of the elements
```
console.log( 'Joined: ' + seasons.join( ' & ' ) )
```

3 Now, extract the final element from the array
```
console.log( 'Popped: ' + seasons.pop( ) )
console.log( 'Elements: ' + seasons )
```

4 Then, put the final element back on the array
```
console.log( 'Pushed: ' + seasons.push( 'Winter' ) )
console.log( 'Elements: ' + seasons )
```

5 Next, output just two element values
```
console.log( 'Sliced: ' + seasons.slice( 1, 3 ) )
```

6 Finally, replace the value in the third element
```
console.log( 'Spliced: ' + seasons.splice( 2, 1, 'Autumn' ) )
console.log( 'Elements: ' + seasons )
```

7 Save the HTML document, then open it in your browser and launch the console to see the elements manipulated

slice.html

Hot tip

Use the **slice( )** method without a replacement value to delete a specified number of elements at a specified position and it will automatically renumber all remaining elements that follow in that array.

385

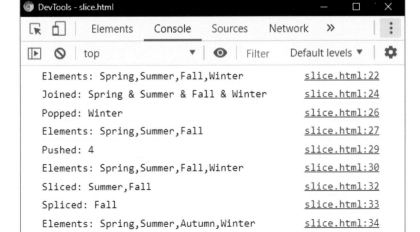

Don't forget

The **shift( )** and the **unshift( )** methods work like **pop( )** and **push( )** but on the first element rather than the last. The **reverse( )** and **sort( )** methods are used in the next example listed on pages 386-387.

Sort Elements

It is often desirable to arrange an array's element values in a particular order using the array **sort( )** method. This can optionally specify a comparison function argument to define the sort order.

When no comparison function is specified, the **sort( )** method will, by default, convert all element values to strings then sort them lexicographically in dictionary order – comparing each first character, then each second character, and so on. Where the elements contain matching strings that differ only by character case, the string with most uppercase characters gets a lower index position – appearing before that with fewer uppercase characters.

The **sort( )** method's default behavior of sorting into dictionary order is usually satisfactory for string values but is often not what you want when sorting numerical values. For example, in sorting three values 30, 100, 20, the result is 100, 20, 30 – because the first characters are different they are sorted by that comparison only. Typically, it is preferable to require all numerical element values to be sorted in ascending, or descending, numerical order so the **sort( )** method needs to specify the name of a custom comparison function to define the sort order.

A comparison function nominated by the **sort( )** method will be passed successive pairs of element values for comparison, and it must return an integer value to indicate each comparison's result. When the first value is greater than the second it should return a value greater than zero to indicate that the first value should be sorted to a higher index position – to appear after the second value. Conversely, the comparison function should return a value less than zero to indicate that the first value should be sorted to a lower index position – to appear before the second value. When both values are identical, zero should be returned to indicate that the element positions should remain unchanged. When all comparisons have been made, the elements will be arranged in ascending value order. If descending order is required, the array's **reverse( )** method can then be used to reverse the element order.

If a comparison function is comparing numerical element values it simply needs to return the result of subtracting the second passed value from the first passed value to have the desired effect.

Remember that **sort( )** does actually rearrange the values stored in the array elements.

The default behavior of the **sort( )** method is the equivalent of a comparison function comparing arguments **x** and **y** with these statements:
**if(x > y) return 1
else if(x < y) return -1
else return 0**

1 Create an HTML document with a self-invoking function that begins by creating two arrays
```
let hues = [ 'Red', 'RED', 'red', 'Green', 'Blue' ]
let nums = [ 1, 20, 3, 17, 14, 0.5 ]
```

sort.html

2 Next, output the values in each array, and output their element values sorted in dictionary sort order
```
console.log( 'Colors: ' + hues )
console.log( 'Dictionary Sort: ' + hues.sort( ) )
console.log( '\nNumbers: ' + nums )
console.log( 'Dictionary Sort: ' + nums.sort( ) )
```

3 Now, add a statement to output the numerical values sorted after calling a comparison function
```
console.log( 'Numerical Sort: ' + nums.sort( sortNums ) )
```

4 Finally, in the function block, add a statement to output the numerical values in descending order
```
console.log( 'Reversed Sort: ' + nums.reverse( ) )
```

5 Next, in the script, add the comparison function
```
function sortNums( numOne, numTwo ) {
  return numOne - numTwo
}
```

6 Save the HTML document, then open it in your browser and launch the console to see the elements sorted

Beware

When the **sort( )** method specifies a comparison function it must nominate it by function name only – do not include trailing brackets after the comparison function name in the argument to the **sort( )** method.

387

Get Dates

The built-in JavaScript **Date** object provides components representing a particular date, time, and timezone. An instance of a **Date** object is created using the **new** keyword, a **Date( )** object constructor, and a variable name assignment. Without specifying any arguments to the constructor, a new **Date** object represents the date and time of its creation based upon the system time of the computer on which the browser is running. There is no consideration given as to whether system time is accurate to the Universal Time Clock (UTC) or Greenwich Mean Time (GMT).

Computer date and time is measured numerically as the period of elapsed time since January 1, 1970 00:00:00 – a point in time often referred to as the "epoch". In JavaScript, the elapsed time is recorded as the number of milliseconds since the epoch. This figure can be extracted from **Date** object using its **getTime( )** method, and may be subtracted from that of another **Date** object to calculate an elapsed period between two points in a script – for example, to calculate the period taken to execute a loop.

A string of the components within a **Date** object can be extracted using its **toString( )** method, or an equivalent converted to UTC time using its **toUTCString( )** method.

JavaScript can determine in which time zone the user is located, assuming the system is correctly set to the local time zone, by examining the value returned by a current **Date** object's **getTimezoneOffset( )** method. This returns an integer value that is the number of minutes by which the current local time differs from UTC time. The calculation is performed in minutes rather than hours because some time zones are offset by other than one-hour intervals – for example, Newfoundland, Canada is UTC -3:30 (UTC -2:30 during periods of daylight saving time).

The time zone offset value can be used to provide localized customization for U.S. time zones but they must be adjusted by subtracting 60 (minutes) for periods of daylight saving time. The example opposite calls **getMonth( )** and **getDate( )** methods of a **Date** object to adjust the time zone offset value if daylight saving time is not in operation at the current date.

Hot tip

More examples follow on pages 390-395 that demonstrate how to use components of a **Date** object by calling its many methods.

...cont'd

1 Create an HTML document with a self-invoking function that begins by initializing three variables
```
const now = new Date( )
let offset = now.getTimezoneOffset( )
let dst = 60
```

2 Next, add statements to turn off daylight saving time from November 3 to March 10
```
if( ( now.getMonth( ) < 3 ) && ( now.getDate( ) < 10 ) )
{ dst = 0 }
if( ( now.getMonth( ) > 9 ) && ( now.getDate( ) > 2 ) )
{ dst = 0 }
```

3 Now, add a statement to establish a time zone
```
switch( offset )
{
  case ( 300 - dst ) : offset = 'East Coast' ; break
  case ( 360 - dst ) : offset = 'Central' ; break
  case ( 420 - dst ) : offset = 'Mountain' ; break
  case ( 480 - dst ) : offset = 'Pacific' ; break
  default : offset = 'All'
}
```

4 Finally, add statements to output date and time information, and an appropriate greeting message
```
console.log( 'System Time: ' + now.toString( ) )
console.log( 'UTC (GMT) Time: ' + now.toUTCString( ) )
console.log( '\nWelcome to ' + offset + ' Visitors' )
```

5 Save the HTML document, then open it in your browser and launch the console to see the elements sorted

date.html

The **getMonth( )** method returns a zero-based index number in which March is at position 2 – more on this in the next example on pages 390-391.

389

Discovery of the user's local time zone could be used to direct the browser to a page relevant to that time zone – for example, a page containing only Californian distributors for users in the Pacific time zone. But be aware that system time information can be easily changed by the user to any time, date, or time zone, so may not necessarily report their actual location.

```
DevTools - date.html                              —  □  ×
⬚ ⬚  | Elements  Console  Sources  Network  »  | ⋮
▷ ⊘ | top          ▼ | ◉ | Filter  Default levels ▼ | ⚙

System Time: Fri Nov 22 2025 01:49:21 GMT-    date.html:46
0800 (Pacific Standard Time)
UTC (GMT) Time: Fri, 22 Nov 2025 09:49:21 GMT  date.html:47
                                               date.html:48
Welcome to Pacific Visitors
>
```

Extract Calendar

A JavaScript **Date** object provides separate methods to extract each of its date components for the year, month name, day of the month, and the day name:

Method	Returns
getFullYear( )	Year as four digits (yyyy)
getMonth( )	Month as index number (0-11)
getDate( )	Day as number (1-31)
getDay( )	Weekday as index number (0-6)

The **Date** object's **getFullYear( )** method returns the year as a four-digit number, such as **2025**, and the **Date** object's **getDate( )** method returns the day number of the month – so that on the first day of the month it returns **1**.

For reasons of internationalization, **getMonth( )** and **getDay( )** return index number values that must be converted to the local language month and day names by the script. The conversion is easily made for month names by creating an array of all month names, starting with January, then using the index number returned by **getMonth( )** to reference the appropriate month name from the array element.

Similarly, the conversion is made for day names by creating an array of all day names, starting with Sunday, then using the index number returned by the **getDay( )** method to reference the appropriate day name from the array element.

The various components can then be assembled into a date string arranged according to the preferred date format of any locale.

...cont'd

1 Create an HTML document with a self-invoking function that begins by initializing three variables

```
const days = [ 'Sun', 'Mon', 'Tue', 'Wed', 'Thu', 'Fri', 'Sat' ]
const months = [ 'Jan', 'Feb', 'Mar', 'Apr', 'May', 'Jun',
                'Jul', 'Aug', 'Sep', 'Oct', 'Nov', 'Dec' ]
const now = new Date( )
```

calendar.html

2 Next, add statements to extract individual date components using methods of the **Date** object

```
let year = now.getFullYear( )
let month = now.getMonth( )
let dayNumber = now.getDate( )
let dayName = now.getDay( )
```

3 Now, add statements to convert the extracted index numbers to month name and day name values

```
month = months[ month ]
dayName = days[ dayName ]
```

4 Then, concatenate the date components into date strings – in both American and British date formats

```
let usDate = dayName + ', ' + month + ' ' +
             dayNumber + ', ' + year

let ukDate = dayName + ', ' + dayNumber + ' ' +
             month + ', ' + year
```

5 Finally, add statements to output each date string

```
console.log( 'U.S. Date: ' + usDate )
console.log( 'U.K. Date: ' + ukDate )
```

Month indexing starts at zero (0), not one (1) – so for example March is at index [2] not at [3].

6 Save the HTML document, then open it in your browser and launch the console to see the formatted date strings

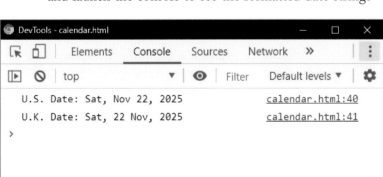

391

Extract Time

A JavaScript **Date** object provides separate methods to extract each of its time components for the hour, the minute, the second, and the millisecond:

Method	Returns
getHours( )	Hour as number (0-23)
getMinutes( )	Minute as number (0-59)
getSeconds( )	Second as number (0-59)
getMilliseconds( )	Millisecond as number (0-999)

The **Date** object's **getHours( )** method returns the hour in 24-hour format – as a value in the range 0-23. The **getMinutes( )** and **getSeconds( )** methods both return a value in the range 0-59. There is also a **getMilliseconds( )** method for even greater precision that returns a value in the range 0-999.

The values of each component can be concatenated into a time string but it is often preferable to add a leading zero to single minute and second values for better readability. For example, 10:05:02 is preferable to 10:5:2.

An appropriate greeting string can be created by examining the hour value to establish whether the user's system time is currently morning, afternoon, or evening.

For situations where a 12-hour time format is desirable, an "AM" or "PM" suffix can be created by examining the hour value and all PM hour values reduced by 12. For example, 13:00 can be transformed to 1:00 PM.

Beware

Time components are based upon the user's system time – which may not be accurate.

time.html

1 Create an HTML document with a self-invoking function that begins by initializing five variables

```
const now = new Date( )
let hour = now.getHours( )
let minute = now.getMinutes( )
let second = now.getSeconds( )
let millisecond = now.getMilliseconds( )
```

...cont'd

2 Next, add statements to prefix a zero to minute and
second values below 10
```
if( minute < 10 ) { minute = '0' + minute }
if( second < 10 ) { second = '0' + second }
```

3 Now, concatenate the time components into a string, then
output that string
```
let time = 'It is now: ' + hour + ':' + minute + ':' +
        second + ' and ' + millisecond + ' milliseconds'
console.log( time )
```

4 Then, output a greeting appropriate to the current time
add statements to output each date string
```
let greeting = 'Good Morning!'
if( hour > 11 ) { greeting = 'Good Afternoon!' }
if( hour > 17 ) { greeting = 'Good Evening!' }
console.log( greeting )
```

5 Finally, output the time in a 12-hour format
```
let suffix = ( hour > 11 ) ? ' P.M.' : ' A.M.'
if( hour > 12 ) { hour -= 12 }
console.log( 'Time is: ' + hour +':' + minute + suffix )
```

6 Save the HTML document, then open it in your browser
and launch the console to see the formatted time strings

The **Date** object also
provides methods
to retrieve the UTC
equivalent of each date
and time component –
for example, methods
getUTCMonth( ), and
getUTCHours( ).

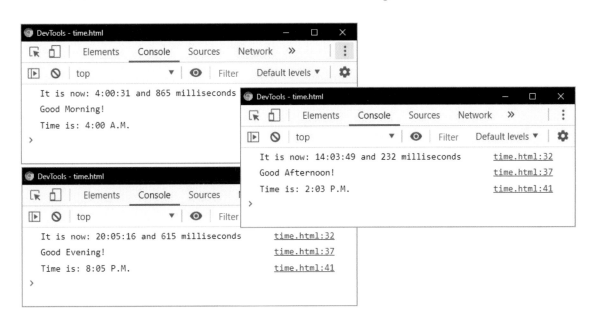

Set Dates

The JavaScript **Date( )** constructor can optionally specify two to seven arguments to set values for each of its components, like this:

new Date(*year, month, date, hours, minutes, seconds, milliseconds* **)**

When only the minimum year and month are specified, the date component is set to one (1), and all time components are set to zero (0).

The **Date** object also provides separate methods to specify the value of each of its date and time components individually:

Method	Sets
setDate( )	Day as number (1-31)
setFullYear( )	Year as four digits (yyyy)
setMonth( )	Month as number (0-11)
setHours( )	Hour as number (0-23)
setMinutes( )	Minute as number (0-59)
setSeconds( )	Second as number (0-59)
setMilliseconds( )	Millisecond as number (0-999)

The **setMonth( )** method sets the month numerically in the range where 0=January-11=December and, optionally, the **setFullYear( )** method can also set the month and day using this syntax:

date.setFullYear(*year* , *monthNumber* , *dayNumber*)

The values of each set component can be revealed by displaying the entire **Date** object. Additionally, all **Date** objects have methods to output a variety of strings displaying date and time. The **toString( )** method converts the date to a string value; the **toUTCString( )** method converts the date to its UTC equivalent; and the **toLocaleString( )** method displays the date using the computer's locale conventions. Useful **toDateString( )** and **toTimeString( )** methods can display date and time components.

Hot tip

The **toString( )** method returns the string value of any JavaScript object and has many uses.

...cont'd

1 Create an HTML document with a self-invoking function that begins by creating a 4th-of-July **Date** object

```
const holiday = new Date( 2025, 6, 4 )
console.log( 'Object: ' + holiday )
```

setdate.html

2 Next, add statements to modify individual date components to become a Christmas Day at noon

```
holiday.setFullYear( 2028 )
holiday.setMonth( 11 )
holiday.setDate( 25 )
holiday.setHours( 12 )
holiday.setMinutes( 0 )
holiday.setSeconds( 0 )
holiday.setMilliseconds( 0 )
```

3 Now, add statements to output the modified date and time and its equivalent UTC (GMT) time

```
console.log( 'String: ' + holiday.toString( ) )
console.log( 'UTC: ' + holiday.toUTCString( ) )
```

The **Date** object also has a **setTime( )** method that accepts an argument of the number of milliseconds since the epoch – each day has 86,400,000 milliseconds, so **setTime(86400000)** sets the date Jan 1, 1970.

4 Then, add statements to output the modified date and time in locale string, date string, and time string formats

```
console.log( 'Locale: ' + holiday.toLocaleString( ) )
console.log( 'Date: ' + holiday.toDateString( ) )
console.log( 'Time: ' + holiday.toTimeString( ) )
```

5 Save the HTML document, then open it in your browser and launch the console to see set date and time strings

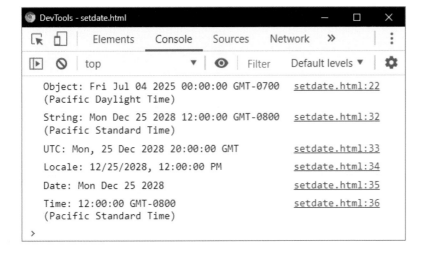

Match Patterns

The **RegExp** object is a JavaScript built-in object that can contain a "regular expression" pattern – describing a string of characters. Regular expressions are useful for text validation and for search-and-replace operations within text by matching their specified pattern to a section of the text.

A regular expression pattern may consist entirely of literal characters between **/ /** describing a character string to match. For example, the regular expression **/wind/** finds a match in "<u>wind</u>ows" – the pattern quite literally matches the string in the text. More typically, a regular expression pattern consists of a combination of literal characters and these "metacharacters":

Metacharacter	Matches	Example
.	Any Characters	ja..pt
^	First Characters	^ja
$	Final Characters	....pt$
*	Zero Or More Repetitions	ja*
+	One Or More Repetitions	ja+
?	Zero Or One Repetition	ja?
{ }	Multiple Repetitions	ja{ 3 }
[ ]	Character Class	[a-z]
\	Any Digits	\d
|	Either Optional Character	a | b
( )	Expression Group	(...)

Don't forget

The character class **[a-z]** matches only lowercase characters but **[a-z0-9]** also matches digits.

The pattern may also include an **i** modifier after the final **/** character, to perform a case-insensitive search, or a **g** modifier to perform a global search for all matches of the pattern.

A **RegExp** object has a **test( )** method that returns **true** when a match is found, or **false** otherwise. A **RegExp** object also has an **exec( )** method that returns a **null** value if no match was found, or the text found if the search was successful, and its **index** property, which contains the character position where the match begins.

1 Create an HTML document with a self-invoking function that begins by initializing three variables
```
const system = 'Windows', suite = 'Office' pattern = /ice/i
```

regexp.html

2 Next, add statements to output two search results
```
console.log( 'In ' + system +'? ' + pattern.test( system ) )
console.log( 'In ' + suite + '? ' + pattern.test( suite ) )
```

3 Now, add statements to output the text match and position, or a message if unsuccessful
```
let result = pattern.exec( suite )
if( result )
{
  console.log( 'Found: ' + result + ' at ' + result.index )
}
else { console.log( 'No Match Found' ) }
```

4 Then, add statements to output the result of an attempt to validate a badly formatted email address
```
let email = 'mike@example'
const format = /.+\@.+\..+/
console.log( email + ' Valid? ' + format.test( email ) )
```

The regular expression used here tests only the most basic email format requirements.

5 Finally, add statements to correct the address format and output the validation result
```
email += '.com'
console.log( email + ' Valid? ' + format.test( email ) )
```

6 Save the HTML document, then open it in your browser and launch the console to see regular expression matches

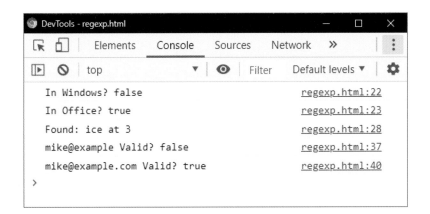

The character index begins at zero, so the fourth character is at index position 3.

Meet JSON

JavaScript Object Notation ("JSON") is a popular text format that is used to store and exchange data. It is a subset of the JavaScript language in which data is stored as a comma-separated list of key:value pairs within a JSON object. All keys must be of the String data type, enclosed in double quote marks, and their associated values may only be one of these data types:

- **String** – enclosed within double quotes, not single quotes.

- **Number** – either integer or floating point.

- **Object** – a JSON object.

- **Array** – but not a Function or a Date.

- **Boolean** – either true or false.

- **null** – but not undefined.

JSON key:value pairs are enclosed in curly brackets, like this:

{"name":"Alice","age":21,"city":"New York"}

You can easily convert a JavaScript object to a JSON object by specifying it as the argument to a **JSON.stringify( )** method.

Conversely, you can convert a JSON object to a JavaScript object by specifying it as the argument to a **JSON.parse( )** method.

Typically, JSON objects store data in a text file with a **.json** file extension as an online resource. A web page script may, therefore, receive data in JSON format from a web server.

After converting a JSON object to a JavaScript object, with the **JSON.parse( )** method, the data can be addressed as usual with dot notation, or with bracket notation.

Both JSON and XML (eXtensible Markup Language) can be used to receive data from a web server, but JSON is considered better because you need to loop through the elements to extract data from the XML format, whereas the **JSON.parse( )** method simply returns a string of all the data.

Usefully, JavaScript can fetch data from online JSON resources for use in web applications.

Hot tip

You can find a free JSON object validator online at jsonlint.com

...cont'd

1 Begin a script with a self-invoking function that creates a JavaScript object containing a String and an Array

```
let obj = { category : 'Fashion' ,
   models : [ { name : 'Alice', age : 21, city : 'New York' } ,
            { name : 'Kelly', age : 23, city : 'Las Vegas' } ] }
```

json.html

2 Next, create a JSON version of the JavaScript object and print it out

```
let json_obj = JSON.stringify( obj )
console.log( json_obj )
```

3 Now, create a JavaScript version of the JSON object and print it out for comparison

```
let new_obj = JSON.parse( json_obj )
console.log( new_obj )
```

4 Finally, print out selected values using both dot notation and bracket notation

```
console.log( new_obj[ 'category' ] )
console.log( new_obj.models[ 0 ].name )
console.log( new_obj[ 'models' ][ 1 ][ 'name' ] )
```

Hot tip

5 Save the HTML document then open it in a web browser and launch the Console in Developer Tools to compare the objects

See that the JSON object has all String values within double quotes.

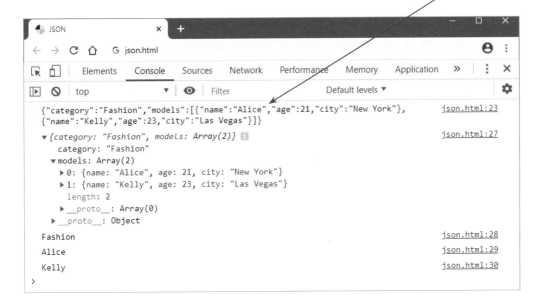

Make Promises

JavaScript is a single-threaded "synchronous" language. This means that only one operation can be executed at any given time. As the script proceeds, each operation is added to a "call stack", then executed (in top-down order) – then removed from the stack.

There are, however, some functions that are handled by a browser API ("Application Programming Interface"), rather than by the JavaScript engine. For example, the **setTimeout( )** method is handled by the browser – so that other operations can be executed while waiting for the timer to end. When the timer does end it passes the operation to a "callback queue", then (when it reaches the front of the queue) it gets executed. This entire process is controlled by an "event loop" that constantly monitors the state of the call stack and callback queue.

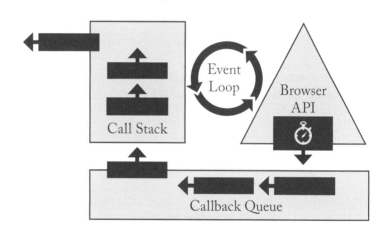

In JavaScript, a **Promise** object represents the eventual completion, or failure, of an asynchronous operation and its resulting value. Its status may be either pending, resolved (completed), or rejected (failed).

You create a promise using the JavaScript **new** keyword and the **Promise( )** constructor. This accepts a function as its argument, which in turn accepts the names of two functions that specify what to do when the promise is resolved or rejected.

Each JavaScript promise has **then( )** and **catch( )** methods that can be "chained" after the **Promise** object using dot notation. The **then( )** method can handle the resulting value of the asynchronous operation, and the **catch( )** method can handle errors if rejected.

1 Begin a script with a self-invoking function that creates a JavaScript **Promise** object that will execute one of two functions after a one-second delay

```
const promise = new Promise( function( resolve, reject ) {
  let random = Math.round( Math.random( ) * 10 )

  if ( random % 2 === 0 )
  { setTimeout( function( ) { resolve( random ) }, 1000 ) }
  else
  { setTimeout( function( ) { reject( random ) }, 1000 ) }
} )
```

promise.html

2 Next, add a statement with chained methods that display the promise status and handle the returned values

```
promise
  .then( console.log( promise ) )
  .then( function( res ) { console.log( res + ' Is Even' ) } )
  .catch( function( err )  { console.log( err + ' Is Odd' ) } )
```

3 Save the HTML document then open it in a web browser and launch the Console in Developer Tools to see the asynchronous operations

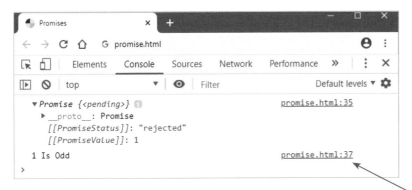

Notice how the Console provides the line number of the promise and of the function that handled the result.

Fetch Data

Web browsers support a Fetch API that can be used in JavaScript to grab resources over a network. The **fetch( )** method accepts a single argument, which is the URL of the resource to be grabbed.

The **fetch( )** method is asynchronous, so that means other operations can be executed while waiting for the resource to arrive. On completion, the **fetch( )** method returns a **Promise** object, which contains a response (an **HTTPResponse** object).

Typically, the **fetch( )** method can grab a JSON resource and parse it using a **json( )** method of the **HTTPResponse** object. The returned JSON data can then be passed as an argument to the next chained promise method, which can in turn pass the JSON data to a handler function. The syntax of the process looks like this:

```
fetch( url )
.then( function( response ) { return response.json( ) } )
.then( function( data ) { return handler( data ) } )
.catch( function( err ) { return console.log( err ) } )
```

Arrow Function Expressions
The function definitions above can, optionally, be written more concisely as JavaScript => arrow function expressions. This allows you to omit the **function** keyword, like this:
```
.then( ( response ) => { return response.json( ) } )
```

If the function body contains only one statement, and that statement returns a value, you can also omit the curly brackets and the **return** keyword from the => arrow function, like this:

```
.then( ( response ) => response.json( ) )
```

Any parameters can appear as a comma-separated list within the round ( ) brackets, as usual, but if there is only one parameter you can even omit the brackets from the => arrow function – so the entire syntax of the process can, optionally, look like this:

```
fetch( url )
.then( response => response.json( ) )
.then( data => handler( data ) )
.catch( err => console.log( err ) )
```

This is more readable, but you should be aware that => arrow functions treat the **this** keyword differently to regular functions.

Beware

With arrow functions, the **this** keyword represents the object in the originating context, whereas with regular functions, the **this** keyword represents the object that calls the function.

402

1 Open a plain text editor, such as Windows' Notepad app, then create a JSON document with an object containing five key:value pairs

weekdays.json

```
weekdays.json - Notepad                          —    □    ✕
File  Edit  Format  View  Help
{
  "DAY1":"Monday",  "DAY2":"Tuesday",  "DAY3":"Wednesday",
  "DAY4":"Thursday",  "DAY5":"Friday"
}
```

2 Save the JSON document in the "htdocs" folder of a web server – so it will be accessible over the network

3 Begin a script with an asynchronous HTTP request by creating a promise that must be resolved by grabbing data

```
fetch( 'http://localhost/weekdays.json' )
  .then( response => response.json( ) )
  .then( data => list( data ) )
  .catch( err => console.log( err ) )
```

fetch.html

4 Now, create the function to print out the data

```
function list( data ) {
  const values = Object.values( data )
  let i = 0
  while( i < values.length ) { console.log( values[ i ] ) ; i++ }
}
```

5 Save the HTML document alongside the JSON document, then open the web page via HTTP and launch the Console in Developer Tools to see the data

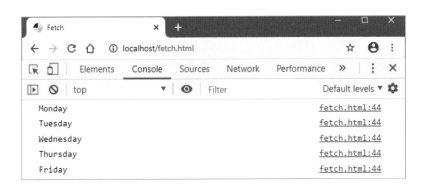

Summary

- Custom objects are assigned properties as a comma-separated list of name:value pairs within **{ }** curly brackets.

- Object property values can be referenced using dot notation syntax or by quoting their name between **[ ]** square brackets.

- Object methods are called by appending **( )** parentheses after the object's method name.

- The JavaScript built-in **Array** object stores items in individual elements that are numbered starting at zero.

- Values can be assigned to an array as a comma-separated list within **[ ]** square brackets.

- The value in an array element is referenced by enclosing its index number in **[ ]** square brackets after the object name.

- Each **Array** object has a length property and methods that can be used to manipulate the elements in the array.

- The JavaScript built-in **Date** object provides separate methods to extract each of its date and time components.

- The JavaScript **Date( )** constructor can optionally specify two to seven arguments to set values for each of its components.

- The **Date** object also provides separate methods to set the value of each of its date and time components individually.

- The JavaScript built-in **RegExp** object can contain a regular expression pattern that describes a string of characters.

- The **RegExp** object has **test( )** and **exec( )** methods that search a specified string argument for a match to its pattern.

- The JavaScript **JSON** object stores data as a comma-separated list of key:value pairs where each key must be a String type.

- The **JSON** object has **parse( )** and **stringify( )** methods that convert between JavaScript and JSON object types.

- The **Promise** object represents the eventual completion or failure of an asynchronous operation and its resulting value.

- The **then( )** and **catch( )** methods can be chained after a **Promise** object or the **fetch( )** method to handle results.

19 Control Strings & Numbers

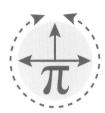

Calculate Areas

JavaScript has a built-in **Math** object that provides a number of useful methods and constant mathematical values. The constants are listed in the table below, together with their approximate value:

Constant	Description
Math.E	Constant E, base of the natural logarithm, with an approximate value of 2.71828
Math.LN2	The natural logarithm of 2, with an approximate value of 0.69315
Math.LN10	The natural logarithm of 10, with an approximate value of 2.30259
Math.LOG2E	The base-2 logarithm of constant E, with an approximate value of 1.44269
Math.LOG10E	The base-10 logarithm of constant E, with an approximate value of 0.43429
Math.PI	The constant PI, with an approximate value of 3.14159
Math.SQRT1_2	The square root of 0.5, with an approximate value of 0.70711
Math.SQRT2	The square root of 2, with an approximate value of 1.41421

Hot tip

All the **Math** methods are listed on page 408.

There is no need to create an instance of the **Math** object as it is globally available by default, so **Math** constants and methods are accessible from anywhere in your script via the **Math** object and dot notation syntax.

The **Math** constants are mostly used in scripts that have a particular mathematical purpose, but all the **Math** constants are listed above for completeness.

...cont'd

1 Create an HTML document with a self-invoking function that begins by initializing a variable

```
let radius = 4
console.log( '\nRadius of Circle: ' + radius )
```

constants.html

2 Next, add statements to perform a mathematical calculation and display the result in output

```
let area = Math.PI * ( radius * radius )
console.log( '\nArea of Circle: ' + area )
```

3 Now, add statements to perform another mathematical calculation and display the result in output

```
let circumference = 2 * ( Math.PI * radius )
console.log( '\nPerimeter of Circle: ' + circumference )
```

4 Then, add statements to perform a final mathematical calculation and display the result in output

```
let cube = ( radius * radius * radius )
let volume = ( ( 4 / 3 ) * Math.PI ) * cube
console.log( '\nVolume of Sphere: ' + volume )
```

5 Save the HTML document, then open it in your browser and launch the console to see the mathematical results

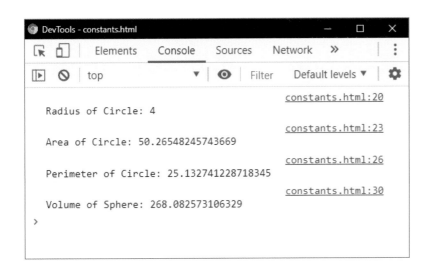

Beware

All **Math** constant names must be stated in uppercase – for example, be sure to use **Math.PI** rather than **Math.pi**.

407

Compare Numbers

The built-in **Math** object provides these useful methods:

Method	Returns
Math.abs( )	An absolute value
Math.acos( )	An arc cosine value
Math.asin( )	An arc sine value
Math.atan( )	An arc tangent value
Math.atan2( )	An angle from an X-axis point
Math.ceil( )	A rounded-up value
Math.cos( )	A cosine value
Math.exp( )	An exponent of constant E
Math.floor( )	A rounded-down value
Math.log( )	A natural logarithm value
Math.max( )	The larger of two numbers
Math.min( )	The smaller of two numbers
Math.pow( )	A power value
Math.random( )	A pseudo-random number
Math.round( )	The nearest integer value
Math.sin( )	A sine value
Math.sqrt( )	A square root value
Math.tan( )	A tangent value

1 Create an HTML document with a self-invoking function that begins by initializing two variables

```
let square = Math.pow( 5, 2 )   // 5 to power 2 ( 5 x 5 )

let cube = Math.pow( 4, 3 )     // 4 to power 3 ( 4 x 4 x 4 )
```

math.html

2 Next, add statements to display the largest and smallest of these two positive variable values in output

```
console.log( '\nLargest Positive: ' +
                    Math.max( square, cube ) )
console.log( '\nSmallest Positive: ' +
                    Math.min( square, cube ) )
```

3 Now, add statements to reverse the numerical polarity of each variable – making positive values into negative values

```
square *= -1
cube *= -1
```

4 Then, add statements to display the largest and smallest of these two negative variable values in output

```
console.log( '\nLargest Negative: ' +
                    Math.max( square, cube ) )
console.log( '\nSmallest Negative: ' +
                    Math.min( square, cube ) )
```

5 Save the HTML document, then open it in your browser and launch the console to see the numerical comparisons

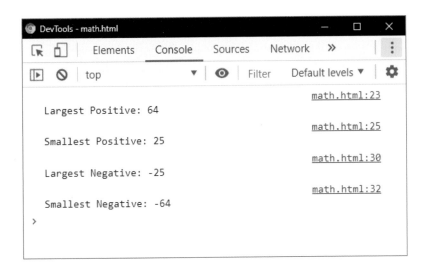

Don't forget

The largest negative value is the one closest to zero.

Round Decimals

The built-in JavaScript **Math** object provides three methods for rounding floating-point numbers to integer values. Each method takes the floating-point value as its argument and returns an integer. The **Math.ceil( )** method rounds up, the **Math.floor( )** method rounds down, and the **Math.round( )** method rounds up or down to the nearest integer.

When handling floating-point values it is important to recognize a discrepancy that exists between the prevailing computer floating-point math standard, as defined by the IEEE (Institute of Electrical and Electronics Engineers), and generally accepted mathematical accuracy. This exists because some decimal numbers cannot be exactly translated into binary form. For example, the decimal number 81.66 cannot be exactly translated to binary, so – the expression **81.66 * 15** returns **1224.8999999999999** rather than the mathematically accurate figure of **1224.9**.

Some programming languages provide automatic rounding to overcome floating-point discrepancies, but JavaScript does not so care must be taken, especially with monetary values, to avoid mathematically erroneous results. The recommended procedure is to first multiply the floating-point value by 100, then perform the arithmetical operation, and finally divide the result by 100 to return to the same decimal level.

A similar procedure can be used to commute long floating-point values to just two decimal places. After multiplying a value by 100, the **Math.round( )** method can be employed to round the value, then division by zero returns to two decimal places.

Procedures that multiply, operate, then divide, can be written as individual steps or parentheses can be used to determine the order in a single succinct expression. For example, commuting a long floating-point value in a variable named "num" can be written as:

```
num = num * 100
num= Math.round( num )
num /= 100
```

or alternatively as:

```
num = ( Math.round( num * 100 ) ) / 100
```

Hot tip

The **Math.round( )** method rounds up by default – so **Math.round(7.5)** returns 8, not 7 and **Math.round(-7.5)** returns -7, not -8.

...cont'd

round.html

1 Create an HTML document with a self-invoking function that begins by initializing a variable
`let bodyTemp = 98.6`

2 Next, add statements to display closest integers to the floating-point value
```
console.log( 'Ceiling: ' + Math.ceil( bodyTemp ) )
console.log( 'Floor: ' + Math.floor( bodyTemp ) )
console.log( 'Round: ' + Math.round( bodyTemp ) )
```

3 Now, add statements to display an incorrectly calculated result of an expression and a corrected equivalent
```
console.log( '\nImprecision: ' + ( 81.66 * 15 ) )

console.log( 'Corrected: ' + ( ( ( 81.66 * 100 ) * 15 ) / 100 ) )
```

4 Then, add statements to display a long floating-point value and a commuted equivalent
```
console.log( '\nFloat: ' + Math.PI )

console.log( 'Commuted: ' +
                ( ( Math.round ( Math.PI * 100 ) / 100 ) ) )
```

5 Save the HTML document, then open it in your browser and launch the console to see the rounded numbers

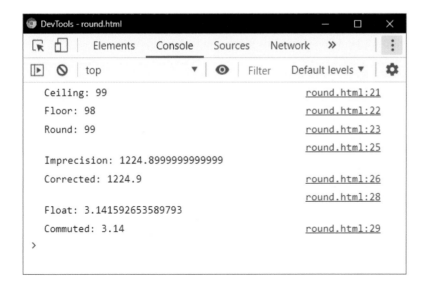

Don't forget

Expressions in innermost parentheses are evaluated first.

Generate Randoms

The JavaScript **Math.random( )** method returns a random floating-point number between 0.0 and 1.0. This can be used for a variety of web page effects that require a generated random number. Multiplying the random floating-point value will increase its range. For example, multiplying it by 10 increases the range to become 0.0-10.0.

Generally, it is useful to round the random value up with the **Math.ceil( )** method so that the range becomes 1-10.

The process of specifying the range for a random number value can be written as individual steps, or parentheses can be used to determine the order in a single expression. For example, specifying a range of 1-10 for a variable named "rand" can be written as:

```
let rand = Math.random( )
rand *= 10
rand = Math.ceil( rand )
```

or alternatively as:

```
let rand = Math.ceil( Math.random( ) * 10 )
```

A series of unique random numbers can be generated within a specified range. For example, to produce a random lottery numbers selection within the range 1-59:

random.html

1 Create an HTML document with a self-invoking function that begins by declaring five variables
```
let i, rand, temp, nums = [ ]
let str = '\n\nYour Six Lucky Numbers: '
```

2 Next, add a loop to fill array elements 1-59 with their respective index number
```
for( i = 1 ; i < 60 ; i++ ) { nums[ i ] = i }
```

3 Now, add a loop to randomize the numbers in the array elements
```
for( i = 1 ; i < 60 ; i++ )
{
  rand = Math.ceil( Math.random( ) * 59 )
  temp = nums[ i ]
  nums[ i ] = nums[ rand ]
  nums[ rand ] = temp
}
```

Hot tip

Step 3 contains an algorithm that shuffles the numbers and ensures no two elements contain the same number.

...cont'd

4 Then, add a loop to append a hyphenated list of six element values to the string variable

```
for( i = 1 ; i < 7 ; i++ )
{
  str += nums[ i ]
  if( i !== 6 ) { str += ' - ' }
}
```

5 Finally, add a statement to output the string variable

```
console.log( str )
```

6 Save the HTML document, then open it in your browser and launch the console to see a unique selection of random numbers within the specified range each time the script is executed

Here, the random numbers are in the range 1 to 59 – to play the UK Lotto game or the US New York Lotto game.

Unite Strings

JavaScript has a **String** object that provides useful methods to manipulate string values. There is, however, no need to create instances of the **String** object with the **new** keyword and the **String( )** constructor, as its methods can simply be applied to string variables using dot notation. For example, **str.toUpperCase( )** returns all characters of a string variable named "str" in uppercase, whereas **str.toLowerCase( )** returns all its characters in lowercase.

There is also a string **length** property that stores the total number of characters in a string.

Many of the examples listed earlier use the **+** concatenation operator to unite multiple strings but, alternatively, the string **concat( )** method can be used to append one or more strings supplied as a comma-separated list of arguments.

The **eval( )** built-in function is also used to unite strings and variables by some script authors – but this absolutely should be avoided. The **eval( )** function directly calls the JavaScript compiler to compile its string argument into a JavaScript statement:

- If the string represents an expression, **eval( )** will evaluate that expression – for example, **eval('1 + 1')** returns 2.

- If the string represents a statement, or sequence of statements, **eval( )** will evaluate the last statement – for example, the code **eval('let num = 100 ; alert(num)')** produces an alert dialog.

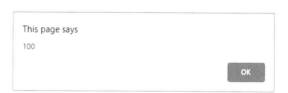

This page says
100
OK

This use of **eval( )** incurs a large cost in script performance and is unnecessary in almost every case as there is usually a more efficient and elegant solution. Furthermore, the **eval( )** function can have security implications if the script allows user input to be evaluated as a JavaScript instruction. This provides the opportunity to execute malicious code. For example, the code **eval('while(true) ; alert( )')** will produce an infinite loop that locks the browser.

1 Create an HTML document with a self-invoking function that begins by declaring three variables
```
let topic = 'JavaScript'
let series = 'in easy steps'
let title = ''
```

string.html

2 Next, add statements to display converted case versions of the first two string variable values
```
console.log( topic + ' > ' + topic.toLowerCase( ) )
console.log( series + ' > ' + series.toUpperCase( ) )
```

3 Now, add statements to append a space and the second string onto the first string, then assign it to the third variable and output the concatenated string
```
title = topic.concat( ' ', series )
console.log( 'Title: ' + title )
```

4 Then, add statements to display the length of each string in output
```
console.log( '\n' + topic + ' - Length: ' + topic.length )

console.log( series + ' - Length: ' + series.length )

console.log( title + ' - Length: ' + title.length )
```

5 Save the HTML document, then open it in your browser and launch the console to see the string output

```
DevTools - string.html                              —   □   ×
┌⟋ □      Elements   Console   Sources   Network  »    ⋮
▷ ⊘   top                ▼  👁  Filter  Default levels ▼   ⚙

  JavaScript > javascript                    string.html:28
  in easy steps > IN EASY STEPS              string.html:29
  Title: JavaScript in easy steps            string.html:32
                                             string.html:34
  JavaScript - Length: 10
  in easy steps - Length: 13                 string.html:35
  JavaScript in easy steps - Length: 24      string.html:36
>
```

Split Strings

There are several string methods that allow a specified part of a string to be copied from the full string. These treat each string like an array, in which each element contains a character or a space, and can be referenced by their index position. As with arrays, the string index is zero-based, so the first character is at position zero.

The start at which to begin copying a "substring" can be specified by stating its index position as an argument to the string's **substring( )** method. This will copy all characters after that position right up to the end of the string. Optionally, a second argument may be supplied to the string's **substring( )** method to specify a subsequent index position as the end of the substring. This will then copy all characters between the start and end positions.

An alternative way to copy substrings is provided by the string **substr( )** method. Like the **substring( )** method, this can take a single argument to specify the index position at which to begin copying, and will copy all characters after that position right up to the end of the string. Unlike the **substring( )** method, the **substr( )** method may optionally be supplied with a second argument to specify the number of characters to copy after the start position.

Similarly, the string **slice( )** method can be used to return all characters after a start position, specified by a single argument, or all characters between two positions, specified as two arguments.

It is sometimes useful to copy parts of a string that are separated by a particular character. The separator character can be specified as an argument to the string **split( )** method, which will return an array of all substrings that exist between occurrences of that character. Optionally, the **split( )** method may be supplied with a second argument specifying the size of the array it should return. In this case, each substring that exists between the specified separator character is returned until the limit is reached, and the rest of the string is ignored.

None of these string methods modify the original string but merely make a copy of a particular part of the original string.

The **substr( )** method is invariably easier to use than the **substring( )** method – because you need only calculate the start position and the substring length, not an end position.

The **split( )** method is used to separate cookie data in the example on page 454.

...cont'd

① Create an HTML document with a self-invoking function that begins by initializing a variable
**let definition = 'JavaScript is the original dialect of \
the ECMAScript standard language.'**

split.html

② Next, add statements to assign selected slices of the string to a second variable, then output its value
let str = definition.slice(0, 27)
str += definition.slice(62, 70)
console.log(str)

Hot tip

A \ backslash character lets you continue the string on the next line.

③ Now, add a statements to output four individual words of the slices
console.log(str.split(' ', 4)

④ Then, add statements to assign selected substrings of the original string to the second variable, then output its value
str = definition.substring(42, 52)
str += definition.substring(10, 17)
str += definition.substr(52, 70)

console.log(str)

⑤ Save the HTML document, then open it in your browser and launch the console to see the split string output

```
DevTools - split.html                          —  □  ×
⌖  ⧉    Elements  Console  Sources  Network  »      ⋮
▶  ⦸   top            ▼  ◉  Filter  Default levels ▼  ⚙
  JavaScript is the original language.      split.html:23
                                            split.html:27
  ▼ (4) ["JavaScript", "is", "the", "original"] ⓘ
     0: "JavaScript"
     1: "is"
     2: "the"
     3: "original"
     length: 4
   ▶ __proto__: Array(0)
  ECMAScript is the standard language.      split.html:33
  >
```

Don't forget

Specify '' (an empty string without any space) as the separator to the **split( )** function to return an array of individual characters.

Find Characters

The JavaScript **String** object provides a number of methods that allow a string to be searched for a particular character or substring. The string **search( )** method takes a substring as its argument and returns the position at which that occurs in the searched string, or a **-1** value if it is not found. Alternatively, the substring can be specified as the argument to a string **match( )** method that will return the substring if it is present, or the JavaScript **null** value if it is absent.

The string **indexOf( )** method takes a substring as its argument and returns the index position of the first occurrence of the substring when it's present, or **-1** when it's absent. The **lastIndexOf( )** method works in the same way but searches backwards, from the end of the string, reporting the last occurrence of the substring.

To discover the character at a particular index position in a string, its index value can be specified as an argument to a **charAt( )** method, or its numerical Unicode value can be revealed by specifying its index value to the **charCodeAt( )** method. Conversely, one or more Unicode values can be specified as arguments to the **String.fromCharCode( )** method to return their character values.

Additionally, all occurrences of a character or substring can be replaced by specifying their value as the first argument to the string **replace( )** method, and a replacement value as its second argument.

Beware

The **null** keyword is not equivalent to a zero value, as **null** has no value whatsoever.

418

find.html

Hot tip

Use double quotes to include quote marks in a string surrounded by single quotes.

1 Create an HTML document with a self-invoking function that begins by initializing a variable with a string value
let str = 'JavaScript in easy steps'

2 Next, add statements to output the results of two case-sensitive string searches
console.log('"Script" Search: ' + str.search('Script'))
console.log('"script" Search: ' + str.search('script'))

3 Now, add statements to output the results of two case-sensitive string matches
console.log('\n"Script" Match: ' + str.match('Script'))
console.log('"script" Match: ' + str.match('script'))

...cont'd

4 Add statements to output the first and last index positions of a character if found within the string

```
console.log( '\nindexOf "s": ' + str.indexOf( 's' ) )
console.log( 'indexOf "m": ' + str.indexOf( 'm' ) )
console.log( '\nlastIndexOf "s": ' + str.lastIndexOf( 's' ) )
console.log( 'lastIndexOf "m": ' + str.lastIndexOf( 'm' ) )
```

Hot tip

Unicode uppercase A-Z values are 65-90, and lowercase a-z values are 97-122.

5 Then, add statements to output the first character in the string and its Unicode value, plus four characters specified by their Unicode values

```
console.log( '\ncharAt 0: ' + str.charAt( 0 ) )
console.log( 'charCodeAt 0: ' + str.charCodeAt( 0 ) )
console.log( 'fromCharCode: ' +
            String.fromCharCode( 74, 97, 118, 97 ) )
```

6 Finally, add statements to output the original string and a modified version of that string

```
console.log( '\nOriginal: ' + str )
console.log( 'Replaced: ' + str.replace( 'easy', 'simple' ) )
```

Don't forget

7 Save the HTML document, then open it in your browser and launch the console to see the results output

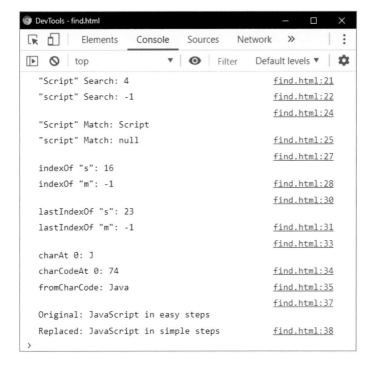

The **replace( )** method returns a modified version of the original string but does not actually change the original string.

419

Trim Strings

The JavaScript **String** object provides a **trim( )** method that removes whitespace from both ends of a string. This is especially useful to ensure that user input does not have spaces, tabs, or newline characters accidentally included by the user.

Having trimmed whitespace from a string, you can verify its first characters using a **startsWith( )** method, and verify its last characters using an **endsWith( )** method. These each accept a character or substring as their argument and seek a case-sensitive match within the string. If a match is found they will return **true**, otherwise they will return **false** if no match is found.

An individual character can be referenced by stating its index position within [ ] square brackets after the string variable name – for example, **str[0]** to reference the first letter of a string in a variable named "str".

You can also perform a case-sensitive match within a string by specifying a character or substring as the argument to an **includes( )** method. If a match is found, this will return **true**, otherwise it will return **false** if no match is found.

If you wish to construct a new string containing multiple copies of an existing string, simply specify an integer argument to a **repeat( )** method to determine how many times the existing string should be repeated in the newly created string.

Hot tip

The **split( )** method is used to remove whitespace from cookie data in the example on page 454.

420

HTML

trim.html

1 Create an HTML document with a self-invoking function that begins by initializing a variable – with a value that contains whitespace at both ends of a string
`let str = '   Love For All, Hatred For None.   '`

2 Next, add statements to output the string and test its beginning and end
`console.log( 'String: ' + str )`
`console.log( 'Starts With "L" ? ' + str.startsWith( 'L' ) )`
`console.log( 'Ends With "." ? ' +str.endsWith( '.' ) )`
`console.log( 'First Letter: ' + str[ 0 ] )`

3 Now, add a statement to assign a trimmed version of the string to the variable
`str = str.trim( )`

...cont'd

4 Then, add statements to output the trimmed string and test its beginning and end, as before

```
console.log( 'Trimmed: ' + str )
console.log( 'Starts With "L" ? ' + str.startsWith( 'L' ) )
console.log( 'Ends With "." ? ' +str.endsWith( '.' ) )
console.log( 'First Letter: ' + str[ 0 ] )
```

5 Add statements to see substrings within the string

```
console.log( '\nIncludes "Hat" ? '+ str.includes( 'Hat' ) )
console.log( 'Includes "hat" ? '+ str.includes( 'hat' ) )
```

6 Finally, add a statement to output 10 copies of the trimmed string

```
console.log( '\nRepeat:\n' + str.repeat( 10 ) )
```

7 Save the HTML document, then open it in your browser and launch the console to see the results output

Hot tip

Character matching can alternatively be performed with the equality operator, such as **str[0] === 'L'**

Don't forget

Matching with these methods is case-sensitive.

421

Summary

- The **Math** object provides mathematical constants, such as **Math.PI**, and mathematical methods, such as **Math.max( )**

- Floating-point numbers can be rounded to the nearest integer using **Math.floor( )**, **Math.ceil( )**, and **Math.round( )** methods.

- JavaScript does not provide automatic rounding to overcome floating-point discrepancies.

- Multiply floating-point values by 100, perform the arithmetic, then divide the result by 100 to avoid discrepancy errors.

- The **Math.random( )** method returns a random floating-point number between 0.0 and 1.0.

- Multiplying a random floating-point number by 10 and rounding the result with **Math.ceil( )** makes the range 1-10.

- The **String** object provides useful methods to manipulate string values, such as **toUpperCase( )** and **toLowerCase( )**

- Each string has a **length** property containing an integer that is the total number of characters in that string.

- Strings can be joined together using the + concatenation operator or the string **concat( )** method.

- The **eval( )** built-in function can have security implications so is best avoided.

- The **slice( )** and **substring( )** method arguments specify start and end positions, but those of the **substr( )** method specify the start position and the number of characters to copy.

- The **split( )** method returns an array of all substrings that exist between occurrences of the character specified as its argument.

- The **search( )**, **match( )**, **indexOf( )**, **lastIndexOf( )**, and **charAt( )** methods can be used to seek characters within a string.

- The **trim( )** method removes whitespace from both ends of a string.

- The **startsWith( )**, **endsWith( )**, and **includes( )** methods seek a case-sensitive match within a string.

- The **replace( )** and **repeat( )** methods create modified strings.

20 Address the Window Object

This chapter describes and demonstrates methods of the top-level Window object of a web browser environment.

Meet DOM

The browser represents all components of a web page within a hierarchical tree called the "Document Object Model" (DOM). Each component appears below the top-level **window** object, and the tree contains branches like those illustrated below:

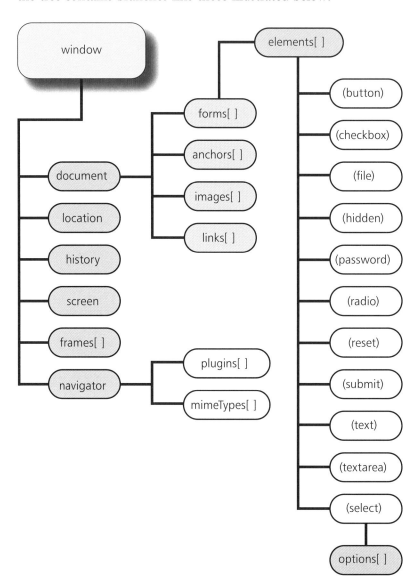

Hot tip

Items followed by square brackets are array objects, and those within regular parentheses are various types of form elements.

A **for in** loop can be used to list all properties of the **window** object provided by the browser. The list will contain fundamental properties that are common to all modern browsers, plus minor properties that are browser-specific.

1 Create an HTML document with an empty list element
```
<ol id="props" style="column-count:3"> </ol>
```

HTML

dom.html

2 Next, in a script element, create a self-invoking function that begins by initializing two variables
```
const list = document.getElementById( 'props' )
let property = null
```

3 Now, add a loop to populate the list element with items that are direct properties of the browser's **window** object
```
for( property in window )
{
  if( property ) { list.innerHTML += '<li>' + property }
}
```

Closing **</li>** tags are optional so are omitted in this loop.

4 Save the HTML document, then open it in your browser to see the **window** object's properties and method names

Scroll down the list to examine all **window** properties and methods – on this occasion there was a total of 204 items. The important properties in the tree illustration opposite are highlighted in this screenshot.

425

Document Object Model × +

← → C ⌂ G dom.html

1. postMessage	69. ondrag	137. onoffline
2. blur	70. ondragend	138. ononline
3. focus	71. ondragenter	139. onpagehide
4. close	72. ondragleave	140. onpageshow
5. parent	73. ondragover	141. onpopstate
6. opener	74. ondragstart	142. onrejectionhandled
7. top	75. ondrop	143. onstorage
8. length	76. ondurationchange	144. onunhandledrejection
9. frames	77. onemptied	145. onunload
10. closed	78. onended	146. performance
11. location	79. onerror	147. stop
12. self	80. onfocus	148. open
13. window	81. oninput	149. alert
14. document	82. oninvalid	150. confirm
15. name	83. onkeydown	151. prompt
16. customElements	84. onkeypress	152. print
17. history	85. onkeyup	153. queueMicrotask
18. locationbar	86. onload	154. requestAnimationFrame
19. menubar	87. onloadeddata	155. cancelAnimationFrame
20. personalbar	88. onloadedmetadata	156. captureEvents
21. scrollbars	89. onloadstart	157. releaseEvents
22. statusbar	90. onmousedown	158. requestIdleCallback
23. toolbar	91. onmouseenter	159. cancelIdleCallback
24. status	92. onmouseleave	160. getComputedStyle
25. frameElement	93. onmousemove	161. matchMedia
26. navigator	94. onmouseout	162. moveTo
27. origin	95. onmouseover	163. moveBy
28. external	96. onmouseup	164. resizeTo
29. screen	97. onmousewheel	165. resizeBy
30. innerWidth	98. onpause	166. scroll

Inspect Properties

The top-level DOM **window** object has a **screen** child object that provides properties describing the user's monitor resolution in pixel measurement. Overall screen dimensions can be found in the **window.screen.width** and **window.screen.height** properties.

Similarly, the usable screen dimensions, excluding the space occupied by the desktop task bar, can be found in the **window.screen.availWidth** and **window.screen.availHeight** properties.

The screen's color capability can be discovered from the **window.screen.colorDepth** property that contains a bit value describing the range of possible colors that screen can display:

- **8-bit** – Low Color can display only 256 colors.

- **16-bit** – High Color can display 65,536 colors.

- **24-bit** – True Color can display millions of colors.

- **32-bit** – Deep Color can display a gamut comprising a billion or more colors.

Modern computers use 24-bit or 32-bit hardware for color display, but older computers use 16-bit hardware. Only very old computers and old cellphones use 8-bit hardware for color display.

There is also a **window.screen.pixelDepth** property that contains the screen's pixel depth, but on modern computers this is the same value as in the **window.screen.colorDepth** property – always use **window.screen.colorDepth** to discover the color capability.

Some browsers now support a **window.screen.orientation** object that has a **type** property describing the current orientation of the screen as either landscape or portrait, and whether this is the screen's primary or secondary usual orientation.

As the **window** object is the top-level global object in the browser's scripting environment, its name can optionally be omitted when referencing its child objects and their properties. For example, you can simply write **screen.colorDepth** to reference the **window.screen.colorDepth** property.

Beware

Notice the "camelCase" capitalization of these property names.

...cont'd

1 Create an HTML document with an empty paragraph
`<p id="props" style="font:1.5em sans-serif"></p>`

screen.html

2 Next, in a script element, create a self-invoking function that begins by initializing six variables
```
const info = document.getElementById( 'props' )
let width = window.screen.width + 'px'
let height = window.screen.height + 'px'
let availW = window.screen.availWidth + 'px'
let availH = window.screen.availHeight + 'px'
let colors = 'Unknown'
```

3 Now, add a statement to describe the color capability
```
switch( window.screen.colorDepth )
{
  case 8 : colors = 'Low Color' ; break
  case 16 : colors = 'High Color' ; break
  case 24 : colors = 'True Color' ; break
  case 32 : colors = 'Deep Color' ; break
}
```

The **colorDepth** property can be used to deliver low resolution images within a document for browsers with limited color capabilities.

4 Then, add statements to display screen information
```
info.innerHTML  = 'Screen Resolution: ' +
                  width + ' x ' + height + '<br>'
info.innerHTML += 'Available Screen Size: ' +
                  availW + ' x ' + availH + '<br>'
info.innerHTML += 'Color Capability: ' + colors + '<br>'
if( window.screen.orientation )
{
  info.innerHTML += 'Orientation: ' +
                  window.screen.orientation.type
}
```

427

5 Save the HTML document, then open it in your browser to see the screen information

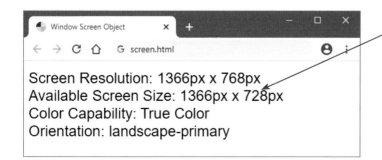

The available height here is 40 pixels less than the screen height because the desktop taskbar is 40 pixels high.

Show Dialogs

The top-level DOM **window** object provides three methods with which JavaScript can display dialog messages to the user. A simple warning message string can be specified as the argument to the **window.alert( )** method. This gets displayed on a dialog box with just an "OK" button, which merely closes the dialog box.

More usefully, a message can be specified as the argument to the **window.confirm( )** method to request a decision from the user. This gets displayed on a dialog box with an "OK" button and a "Cancel" button. Either button will close the dialog box when pushed, but the "OK" button returns a **true** value, whereas the "Cancel" button returns a **false** value.

A message can also be specified as the argument to the **window.prompt( )** method to request input from the user. This gets displayed on a dialog box with an "OK" button, a "Cancel" button, and a text input field. Either button will close the dialog box when pushed, but the "OK" button returns the value in the text field, whereas the "Cancel" button returns a **null** value. A second argument can also be supplied to the **window.prompt( )** method to specify default content for the text field.

HTML

dialogs.html

1 Create an HTML document with an empty paragraph
<p id="response" style="font:1.5em sans-serif"></p>

2 Next, in a script element, create a self-invoking function that begins by initializing one variable reference
const info = document.getElementById('response')

3 Now, add a statement to display a message on a simple dialog box
window.alert('Hello from JavaScript')

4 Then, add a statement to request a decision from the user and write the response in the paragraph
info.innerHTML = 'Confirm: ' +
          window.confirm('Go or Stop?')

5 Next, add a statement to request text input from the user and write the text response into the paragraph
**info.innerHTML += '
Prompt: ' +**
          window.prompt('Yes or No?', 'Yes')

6 Save the HTML document, then open it in your browser to see the message appear on a simple dialog box

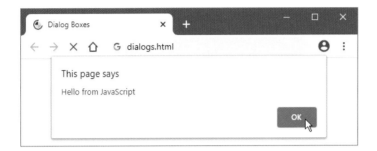

7 Click the OK button on each dialog box to close them in turn, then see the response appear in the paragraph

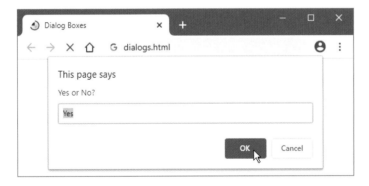

The **confirm** dialog can be used with an **if** statement to branch a script – for example, **if(confirm('OK?')) { ... } else { ... }**

If the script is to use text input from a **prompt** dialog it is good practice to trim whitespace from the ends of the string – see page 420.

Scroll Around

The DOM **window** object has a **scrollBy( )** method that allows the window to be scrolled horizontally and vertically when content overflows the window in either orientation. This method requires two arguments to specify the number of pixels to shift along the X and Y axes.

When content overflows the window vertically, a scroll bar appears along the right edge of the browser window. The **scrollBy( )** method will scroll by the number of pixels specified as its first argument – or until it reaches the extreme of the content.

Similarly, when content overflows the window horizontally, a scroll bar appears along the bottom of the browser window. The **scrollBy( )** method will scroll by the number of pixels specified as its second argument – or until it reaches the extreme of the content.

There is also a **scrollTo( )** method that accepts two arguments specifying X and Y coordinates that the top-left corner of the window should scroll to when content overflows the window horizontally and vertically. This can be used to shift away from the default X=0, Y=0 coordinates to a specified alternative position. For example, where the browser is displaying data in a tabular spreadsheet format, with the first cell of the first row in the top left corner of the browser window, the **scrollTo( )** method can place a particular cell at the top-left corner of the browser window instead.

The DOM **window** object has a **scrollX** property that stores the number of pixels by which the window is scrolled horizontally. This denotes the position of the "thumb" (scroller box) along the scrollbar at the bottom of the window, relative to its left corner. The **window.scrollX** property is an alias for an older property named **window.pageXOffset** that still exists in the DOM, and can be used instead of **window.scrollX** for backward compatibility.

Similarly, there is a **scrollY** property that stores the number of pixels by which the window is scrolled vertically. This denotes the position of the thumb along the scrollbar at the right of the window, relative to its top corner. The **window.scrollY** property is an alias for an older property named **window.pageYOffset** that still exists in the DOM, and can be used instead of **window.scrollY** for backward compatibility.

Hot tip

Supply negative values to the **scrollBy( )** method to move up and left.

Beware

The effect of the **scrollBy( )** method is only apparent when the content overflows the window – causing scroll bars to appear.

1 Create an HTML document with a wide empty paragraph that is inset from the left of the window

```
<p id="info" style="width:2000px; margin-left:300px;
                    font:1.2em sans-serif"></p>
```

scroll.html

2 Next, in a script element, create a self-invoking function that begins by initializing two variables

```
const info = document.getElementById( 'info' )
let i = 0
```

3 Now, add a loop to write a column of 40 numbers into the paragraph

```
for( i = 1 ; i < 41 ; i++ )
{
  info.innerHTML += ( i + '<br>' )
}
```

4 Then, add a statement to scroll the widow 200 pixels horizontally to the right, and by the height of the paragraph element vertically downward

```
window.scrollBy( 200, info.clientHeight )
```

Hot tip

Notice the use of the element's **clientHeight** property here. Elements also have a useful **clientWidth** property.

5 Finally, add a statement to append a confirmation of the current window's thumb positions

```
info.innerHTML += 'scrollX: ' + window.scrollX +
                  '& scrollY: ' + window.scrollY
```

6 Save the HTML document, then open it in your browser to see the window scroll and thumb positions

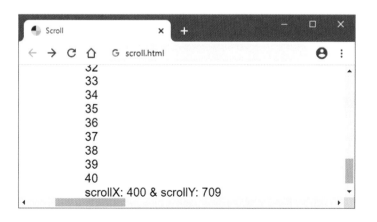

Pop-up Windows

A new browser window can be opened using the **window** object's **open( )** method. This requires three arguments to specify the URL address of the HTML document to be loaded in the new window, a name for the new window, and a comma-separated list of features that the window should include – from the possible features described in the table below:

Feature	Description
directories	Adds the links bar
height	Sets height in pixels of the document area
left	The screen X coordinate of the window
location	Adds the address bar
menubar	Adds the standard menu bar
resizable	Permits the window to be resized
scrollbars	Enables scrollbars when needed
status	Adds the status bar
toolbar	Adds the Forward and Back buttons bar
top	The screen Y coordinate of the window
width	Sets width in pixels of the document area

When successful, the **window.open( )** method returns a new **window** object and opens the new "pop-up" window or if it fails, the method simply returns **null**. The returned result should be assigned to a variable that may be subsequently tested – if the variable is not **null** it must then represent the pop-up window object. That window may then be closed by calling its **close( )** method, or its contents printed by calling its **print( )** method.

Windows can also be positioned by specifying X and Y screen axes coordinates as arguments to a **window.moveTo( )** method. There is also a similar **window.moveBy( )** method that accepts two arguments to specify how many pixels along the X and Y axes the window should be shifted from its current screen position.

Don't forget

Browser makers have added Pop-up Blockers due to the annoying proliferation of pop-up windows – so the use of pop-ups is no longer recommended, but they are demonstrated here for completeness.

...cont'd

1 Create an HTML document containing a heading
`<h1>Pop-up Window</h1>`

2 Create a second HTML document containing a heading
`<h1>Main Window</h1>`

3 Next, within a script element in the second document, add a self-invoking function that creates a window object
`const popWin = window.open( 'popup.html', 'Popup', 'top=150,left=100,width=350,height=100' )`

4 Save both HTML documents, then open the second document to see its pop-up window is blocked

5 Open the browser's Pop-up Blocker dialog and choose to allow pop-ups from this page

6 Now, refresh the browser window to see the pop-up window appear with the specified features

popup.html   opener.html

Do not put any spaces in the features list string as it may cause the **window.open( )** method to fail.

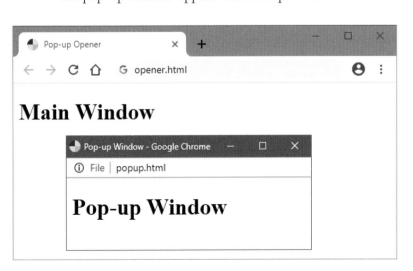

Notice that the pop-up window does not display the specified "favicon" on its title bar.

433

Make Timers

The JavaScript **window** object has an interesting **setTimeout( )** method that can repeatedly evaluate a specified expression after a specified period of time. Where the specified expression calls the function in which the **window.setTimout( )** statement appears, a recursive loop is created – in which the function is repeatedly executed after the specified period of time.

The expression to be evaluated by the **setTimeout( )** method must be specified as its first argument, and the period of time must be a number specified as its second argument. The time is expressed in milliseconds, where 1000 represents one second.

The **setTimeout( )** method returns a numeric value that can be assigned to a variable to uniquely identify the waiting process. This value can be specified as the argument to the window object's **clearTimeout( )** method to terminate the timer loop at some point.

The **window** object also has **setInterval( )** and **clearInterval( )** methods that take the same arguments and work in a similar way. The difference is that the time specified to **setInterval( )** specifies the interval at which point the expression is to be evaluated, irrespective of how long it takes to execute. Conversely, the time specified to the **setTimeout( )** method specifies the period of time between the end of one execution until the start of the next execution. This means that it is possible for **setInterval( )** to attempt overlapping executions where the interval is short and the time taken to execute the expression is lengthy. For this reason it is generally preferable to use the **setTimeout( )** method.

Don't forget

A two-minute task set to an interval of 10 minutes gets started every 10 minutes, but the same task set to a timeout of 10 minutes gets started every 12 minutes (10+2).

HTML

timer.html

Hot tip

For a refresher on closure functions see page 334.

1 Create an HTML document with an empty paragraph
`<p id="info"></p>`

2 Next, in a script element, initialize a variable with a closure function that returns a decreasing integer

```
const count = ( function ( ) {

  let num = 10
  return ( function( ) { return num-- } )

} ) ( )
```

3 Now, add a timer function that begins by initializing three variables

```
function countDown( )
{
  const info = document.getElementById( 'info' )
  let timerId = null
  let num = count( )
  // Statements to be inserted here.
}
```

4 Insert statements to write the decreasing integer into the paragraph at one-second intervals until it reaches zero

```
if ( num > 0 )
{
  info.innerHTML += '<span>'+ num + '</span>'
  timerId = window.setTimeout( countDown , 1000 )
}
else
{
  info.innerHTML += '<span>Lift Off!</span>'
  window.clearTimeout( timerId )
}
```

Hot tip

You could usefully add a **console.log(timerId)** statement to the timer function to see the timer's ID value.

435

5 After the function block, add a statement to call the timer function when the page has loaded

```
countDown( )
```

6 Save the HTML document, then open it in your browser to see the timer count down for 10 seconds

Examine Browsers

In the DOM hierarchy, the top-level **window** object has a number of child objects, which each have their own properties and methods. One of these is the **window.navigator** object that contains information about the web browser. As the top-level **window** object exists in the "global namespace", all its child objects can omit that part of the address, so the **window.alert( )** method can be simply called using **alert( )**, the **window.onload** property can be referenced using **onload**, and the **window.navigator** object can be referenced using **navigator**.

The **navigator** object has an **appName** property that contains the browser name, an **appCodeName** property that contains its code name, and an **appVersion** property that contains its version number. But you may be surprised with the values as Google Chrome, Firefox, Safari, and Opera all give their code name as "Mozilla".

Each browser sends the browser code name and version in a HTTP header named "User-Agent" when making a request to a web server, and this string can also be retrieved from the **navigator.userAgent** property. There is also a **navigator.platform** property that describes the browser's host operating system.

In previous years, much was made of browser detection scripts that attempted to identify the browser using its **navigator** properties so that appropriate code could be supplied to suit that browser's supported features. This is now considered bad practice and it is now recommended that feature detection be used instead.

For example, querying if the browser supports the useful **addEventListener( )** method determines whether that browser supports the modern Document Object Model.

browser.html

1 Create an HTML document with an empty list
```
<ul id="list"></ul>
```

2 Next, in a script element, create a self-invoking function that begins by initializing a variable reference
```
const list = document.getElementById( 'list' )
```

3 Now, add statements to list your browser's names
```
list.innerHTML = '<li>Browser: ' + navigator.appName
list.innerHTML += '<li>Code Name: ' +
                         navigator.appCodeName
```

4 Then, add statements to list the version details of your browser and of your operating system
```
list.innerHTML += '<li>Version: ' + navigator.appVersion
list.innerHTML += '<li>Platform: ' + navigator.platform
```

5 Finally, add a statement to confirm that you have a modern browser
```
if( window.addEventListener )
{
  list.innerHTML += '<li>This is a modern DOM browser'
}
```

6 Save the HTML document, then open it in any browser to see the name and version details

Hot tip

In all modern web browsers, the **window** object has an **addEventListener( )** method – you will discover more about this in Chapter 21, which demonstrates window events.

Hot tip

The reason that Google Chrome and other browsers describe themselves as Netscape, Mozilla emanates from the era of the "Browser Wars" – when browsers had to assume those names so they could be served all the web pages that Netscape Mozilla browsers could load.

Check Status

The DOM **window** object's **navigator** child object has a **javaEnabled( )** method that will return **true** only if Java support is enabled in the web browser.

There is also a **cookieEnabled** property that will be **true** only if cookie support is enabled in the browser.

Additionally, **navigator** has a **plugins** child object and a **mimeTypes** child object. As with other arrays, the **plugins** and **mimeTypes** arrays both have a **length** property containing the numeric total of their elements.

Each **plugin** array element has a **name** and **description** property containing details of one installed plugin feature. These can be referenced using the element index number as usual. For example, **navigator.plugins[0].name** references the **name** property of the first element in the **plugins** array.

Similarly, each **mimeTypes** array element has a **type** and **description** property containing details of one supported MIME feature. These can be referenced using the element index number as usual. For example, **navigator.mimeTypes[0].type** references the **type** property of the first element in the **mimeTypes** array.

The contents of these array elements vary according to which features are supported by each browser.

enabled.html

1 Create an HTML document with an empty paragraph
`<p id="info"></p>`

2 Next, in a script element, create a self-invoking function that begins by initializing two variables
`const info = document.getElementById( 'info' )`
`let status = ''`

3 Now, add statements to write a confirmation in the paragraph only if Java support is enabled
`status = ( navigator.javaEnabled( ) ) ? 'Enabled' : 'Disabled'`
`info.innerHTML += 'Java Support is ' + status + '<hr>'`

4 Then, add statements to write a confirmation in the paragraph only if cookie support is enabled
`status = ( navigator.cookieEnabled ) ? 'Enabled' : 'Disabled'`
`info.innerHTML += 'Cookie Support is ' + status + '<hr>'`

5 Now, add statements to write the length of the plugins array and an example element

```
if ( navigator.plugins.length !== 0 )
{
  info.innerHTML += 'No. of Plugins: ' +
              navigator.plugins.length
  info.innerHTML += '<br>Example: ' +
              navigator.plugins[ 0 ].name
  info.innerHTML += '<br>For: ' +
              navigator.plugins[ 0 ].description + '<hr>'
}
```

Hot tip

You could use loops to write all **plugins** and **mimeTypes** element contents.

6 Finally, add statements to write the length of the MIME types array and an example element

```
if ( navigator.mimeTypes.length !== 0 )
{
  info.innerHTML += 'No. of MIME Types: ' +
              navigator.mimeTypes.length
  info.innerHTML += '<br>Example: ' +
              navigator.mimeTypes[ 1 ].type
  info.innerHTML += '<br>For: ' +
              navigator.mimeTypes[ 1 ].description
}
```

7 Save the HTML document, then open it in any browser to see the status of its enabled features

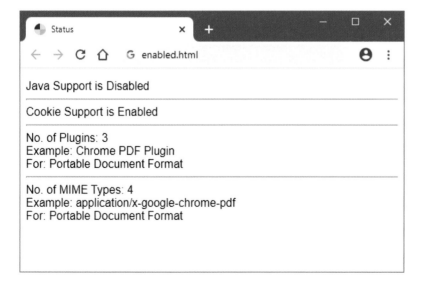

Control Location

The window's **location** object has five properties containing the components of the full URL address of the document currently loaded in the browser window. The complete address, describing the protocol, domain name, file name, and fragment anchor if applicable, is contained in the **location.href** property. Separate components of the complete address are contained in the **location.protocol** (http: or https:), **location.host** (domain name), **location.pathname** (file path), and **location.hash** (fragment anchor). Assigning a new URL to the **location** property will cause the browser to load that page or other resource at that address.

location.html

1 Create an HTML document with a paragraph that contains a hyperlink anchor
```
<p id="info">
<a id="frag">Fragment Anchor</a>
</p>
```

2 Next, in a script element, create a self-invoking function that begins by initializing two variables
```
const info = document.getElementById( 'info' )
let jump = confirm( 'Jump to Fragment?' )
```

3 Now, add a statement to change the window's location if the user has agreed to a request
```
if ( jump )
{
  location = location.href + '#frag'
}
```

Don't forget

A web browser can load a file of any supported MIME type – for example, the MIME type of **image/png for** all PNG image files.

4 Then, add statements to write each component of the current location address in the panel
```
info.innerHTML += '<hr>Href: ' + location.href
info.innerHTML += '<br>Protocol: ' + location.protocol
info.innerHTML += '<br>Host: ' + location.host
info.innerHTML += '<br>Path: ' + location.pathname
info.innerHTML += '<br>Hash: ' + location.hash
```

5 Save the HTML document, then open it in any browser to see a confirm dialog request a change of location

6 Click the Cancel button to deny the request and see the page load at its "root" location, as usual

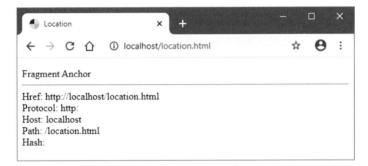

The location shown here is that of the page located on a web server on the local system. If the page was located on your desktop, the protocol would be **file:** and there would be no **host** value.

7 Refresh the browser, then click the OK button to accept the request and see the page load at its fragment location

441

Travel History

The web browser stores a history of the URLs visited in the current session as an array within the **window** object's **history** child object. Like other arrays, this has a **length** property, but also **back( )** and **forward( )** methods to move between elements. Alternatively, the history object's **go( )** method accepts a positive or negative integer argument specifying how many elements to move along the array. For example, **history.go(1)** moves forward one element, and **history.go(-2)** moves back two elements.

page-1.html
page-2.html
page-3.html

1 Create three identical HTML documents that contain an empty paragraph and embed the same external script file

```
<p id="info" > </p>

<script src="history.js" > </script>
```

history.js

2 Next, create the script file with a self-invoking function that begins by initializing a variable reference
const info = document.getElementById('info')

3 Now, in the function block, add statements to write content into the empty paragraphs
```
info.innerHTML +=
  '<a href="page-1.html">Page 1</a> | '
info.innerHTML +=
  '<a href="page-2.html">Page 2</a> | '
info.innerHTML +=
  '<a href="page-3.html">Page 3</a>'
info.innerHTML +=
  '<br>History Length: ' + history.length
info.innerHTML +=
  '<br>Current Location: ' + location.pathname + '<br>'
```

4 Then, add statements to create buttons in the paragraphs
```
info.innerHTML +=
  '<button onclick="history.back( )">Back</button>'
info.innerHTML +=
  '<button onclick="history.forward( )">Forward</button>'
```

Hot tip

To clear the browser history in the Google Chrome browser, click the ⦂ button, then select **More tools**, **Clear browsing data**, and click the **Clear data** button.

5 Save the HTML document and JavaScript script file in the same folder, then clear your browser's history

6 Open the first page to see the initial history length is 1

7 Click a link to load the third page and see the history length increase to 2

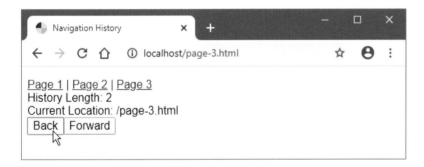

8 Click the Back button to return to the first page but see the history length remain the same as 2

Summary

- The Document Object Model (DOM) is a hierarchical tree representation of all components of a web page.

- The **window** object is the top level in the DOM hierarchy and has properties describing the browser window.

- The **screen** object is a child of the **window** object and has properties describing the screen dimensions and color depth.

- The **window** object has **scrollBy( )** and **scrollTo( )** methods and **scrollX** and **scrollY** properties that specify the scroll position.

- Dialog messages can be displayed using the **window** object's **alert( )**, **confirm( )**, and **prompt( )** methods.

- A pop-up window can be created using the **window** object's **open( )** method, but may be obstructed by a pop-up blocker.

- The **window** object's **setTimeout( )** method creates a timer, which can be canceled later using the **clearTimeout( )** method.

- The **navigator** object is a child of the **window** object and has properties describing the browser and host platform versions.

- The **window** object exists in the global namespace so all its child objects need not include the **window** part of the address.

- Feature detection is used to identify the modern DOM.

- The **navigator.plugins** and **navigator.mimeTypes** properties are arrays that contain details of supported features.

- The **location** object is a child of the **window** object and has properties describing the address of the loaded document.

- The **history** object is a child of the **window** object that contains an array of visited locations in the current session.

- The **history** object has **back( )**, **forward( )**, and **go( )** methods that are used to move through pages in the current session.

21 Interact with the Document

Extract Info

Most interesting of all the DOM **window** object's children is the **document** object, which provides access to the HTML document.

The **document** object has a number of properties describing the document and its location:

- The **document.title** property contains the value specified within the HTML document's title element.

- The location of the HTML document is contained within the **document.URL** property, and is similar to the value contained in the **location.href** property.

- The domain hosting the document is contained in the **document.domain** property, similar to the **location.host** value.

- HTML documents supply the date of their creation or last modification as an HTTP header to the browser so it may decide whether to use a cached copy of the document or seek a new copy. This date can also be retrieved in JavaScript from the DOM's **document.lastModified** property.

- There is a **document.referrer** property that stores the URL of the web page containing the hyperlink that the user followed to load the current HTML document. This is only set if the user followed a hyperlink to load the page, not if they typed in the URL or used some other method to load the page.

info-1.html

1 Create an HTML document that provides a hyperlink to a second (target) HTML document within its body section
```
<p>
<a href="info-2.html" >Link to the Next Page</a>
</p>
```

info-2.html

2 Next, create the target HTML document, which contains an empty unordered list
```
<ul id="list"></ul>
```

3 Now, in a script element, create a self-invoking function that begins by initializing a variable reference
```
const list = document.getElementById( 'list' )
```

...cont'd

4 Then, add statements to list features of the document

```
list.innerHTML = '<li>Linked From: ' + document.referrer
list.innerHTML += '<li>Title: ' + document.title
list.innerHTML += '<li>URL: ' + document.URL
list.innerHTML += '<li>Domain: ' + document.domain
list.innerHTML += '<li>Last Modified: ' +
                                 document.lastModified
```

5 Save the HTML documents in the same folder, then open the document containing the link in your browser

6 Now, click on the hyperlink to load the second HTML document in the browser and see document information

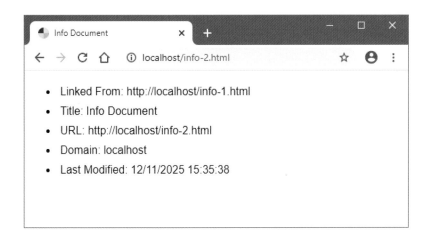

The date contained in **document.lastModified** only relates to the HTML document itself, not to any external style sheets or external script files that the HTML document may import.

The domain shown here is that of the page located on a web server on the local system. If the page was located on your desktop, the **document.referrer** and **document.domain** properties would not be set with any values.

Address Arrays

The DOM **document** object has child objects of **forms, images, links, styleSheets**, and **scripts**. Each of these children is an array in which every array element represents a document component in the same order they appear within the HTML document. For example, the first image in the document body, specified by an HTML **<img>** tag, is represented by **document.images[0]**. This means its URL can be referenced using **document.images[0].src**, which reveals the path assigned to the **src** attribute of the HTML **<img>** tag. Assigning this component a new URL in a script will dynamically replace the old image with a different image.

Notice the "camelCase" capitalization of the **styleSheets** array.

The **links** array represents HTML **<a>** tags within the HTML document; the **styleSheets** array represents HTML **<style>** tags; and the **scripts** array represents HTML **<script>** tags.

The **forms** array represents HTML **<form>** tags but also has its own child **elements** object that is an array of all the form components. For example, the value of the first component of the first form in an HTML document can be referenced using **document.forms[0].elements[0].value**. Assigning this component a new value in a script will dynamically replace the old value.

448

components.html

1 Create an HTML document containing a form and an empty list

```
<form>
<img src="user.png" alt="User" height="64" width="64" >
<input type="text" name="topic" size="30"
                   value="Type Your Question Here" >
<input type="button" value="Ask a Question" > <br>
<a href="formhelp.html" style="margin:5px">Help?</a>
</form>

<ul id="list"></ul>
```

2 Now, add a style sheet to style the font and form

```
< style>
* { font : 1em sans-serif ; }
form { width : 500px ; height : 100px ;
                   background : url(bg.png) ; }
</style>
```

user.png
64px x 64px
(gray areas are
transparent)

bg.png
24px x
100px

3 Next, in a script element, create a self-invoking function that begins by initializing a variable reference

```
const list = document.getElementById( 'list' )
```

4 Now, add statements to list components of the document

```
list.innerHTML = '<li>No. Forms: ' +
                        document.forms.length
list.innerHTML += '<li>No. Links: ' +
                        document.links.length
list.innerHTML += '<li>No. Images: ' +
                        document.images.length
list.innerHTML += '<li>No. Style Sheets: ' +
                        document.styleSheets.length
list.innerHTML += '<li>No. Scripts: ' +
                        document.scripts.length
```

5 Finally, add statements to list two attribute values

```
list.innerHTML += '<li>First Image URL: ' +
                    document.images[ 0 ].src
list.innerHTML += '<li>First Form Element Value: ' +
                    document.forms[ 0 ].elements[ 0 ].value
```

6 Save the HTML document, then open it in your browser to see components of the document listed

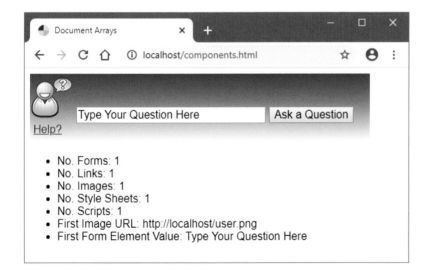

The array elements only represent the relevant HTML tags.

Notice that images incorporated within a document by style rules are not included in the **images** array, only those that are incorporated by HTML **<img>** tags – so here the form background image (**bg.png**) does not appear in the **images** array. Similarly, the style rule assigned inline to the **style** attribute is not included in the **styleSheets** array.

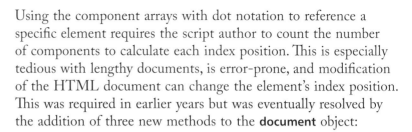

Address Elements

Using the component arrays with dot notation to reference a specific element requires the script author to count the number of components to calculate each index position. This is especially tedious with lengthy documents, is error-prone, and modification of the HTML document can change the element's index position. This was required in earlier years but was eventually resolved by the addition of three new methods to the **document** object:

● The **document.getElementById( )** method, used by previous examples in this book to add content from JavaScript code, allows any component to be referenced by its HTML **id** attribute value. This method simply specifies the target **id** value as its argument and is used to reference a single specific HTML element.

● The **document.getElementsByTagName( )** method returns an array-like **HTMLCollection** object that references all HTML elements of the tag name specified as its argument. A specific HTML element can then be referenced using its element index number, as you would do in an array.

● The **document.getElementsByClassName( )** method returns an array-like **HTMLCollection** object that references all HTML elements containing a **class** attribute that has been assigned the name specified as its argument. A specific HTML element can then be referenced using its element index number, as you would do in an array.

In the name of the two methods that return an **HTMLCollection** it's "Elements" (plural) but in the name of the other method it's "Element" (singular).

collection.html

1 Create an HTML document containing two lists and an empty paragraph

```
<ol>
<li class="fruit">Apple</li>
<li class="nut">Almond</li>
<li class="fruit">Apricot</li>
</ol>

<ol>
<li class="fruit">Blackberry</li>
<li id="country" class="nut">Brazil</li>
<li class="fruit">Banana</li>
</ol>

<p id="info"></p>
```

2 Next, in a script element, create a self-invoking function that begins by initializing five variables

```
const info = document.getElementById( 'info' )
const item = document.getElementById( 'country' )
const lists = document.getElementsByTagName( 'ol' )
const fruits = document.getElementsByClassName( 'fruit' )
let i = 0
```

3 Now, add a statement to describe an element object and the text that element contains

```
info.innerHTML = item + ' Id: ' + item.innerText + '<br>'
```

4 Then, add statements to describe an **HTMLCollection** object and the text its elements contain

```
info.innerHTML += '<br>' + lists + ' Tags:<br>'
for( i = 0; i < lists.length ; i++ ) {
  info.innerHTML += ( i + 1 ) + ' of ' + lists.length
  info.innerHTML += ' : ' + lists[ i ].innerText + '<br>'
}
```

5 Finally, add statements to describe a second **HTMLCollection** object and the text its elements contain

```
info.innerHTML += '<br>' + fruits + ' Class:<br>'
for( i = 0 ; i < fruits.length ; i++ ) {
  info.innerHTML += ( i + 1 ) + ' of ' + fruits.length
  info.innerHTML += ' : ' + fruits[ i ].innerText+ '<br>'
}
```

6 Save the HTML document, then open it in your browser to see the element values retrieved by different methods

The **innerText** property of an element returns only the content between its opening and closing tags, whereas the **innerHTML** property also returns the HTML tags. Change this to **innerHTML** to see the difference.

451

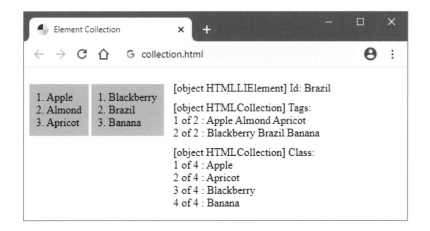

```
Element Collection          ×    +
←  →  C  ⌂   G  collection.html              ⊖  :

1. Apple      1. Blackberry    [object HTMLLIElement] Id: Brazil
2. Almond     2. Brazil
3. Apricot    3. Banana        [object HTMLCollection] Tags:
                               1 of 2 : Apple Almond Apricot
                               2 of 2 : Blackberry Brazil Banana

                               [object HTMLCollection] Class:
                               1 of 4 : Apple
                               2 of 4 : Apricot
                               3 of 4 : Blackberry
                               4 of 4 : Banana
```

Write Content

As witnessed in previous examples, the **innerHTML** and **innerText** properties of the **document** object can be used to write content into existing elements. The **document** object also has a **write( )** method that provides another way to write content, but this automatically calls a **document.open( )** method to start a new document – so the current document is no longer displayed.

More usefully, a **document.createElement( )** method accepts a tag name as its argument and creates an element of that type. Content can then be added to the new element by assignment to its **innerHTML** or **innerText** properties. It can then be inserted into the web page within an existing element by specifying the new element as the argument to a **document.appendChild( )** method.

You can also dynamically write attributes into elements by specifying an attribute name and value as two arguments to an element's **setAttribute( )** method.

write.html

1 Create an HTML document that contains a heading and an ordered list of three items
```
<h1 id="heading">Top 3 Cities</h1>
<ol id="list">
<li>Tokyo, Japan
<li>New York, USA
<li>Rio de Janeiro, Brazil
</ol>
```

2 Save the HTML document, then open it in your browser to see the web page

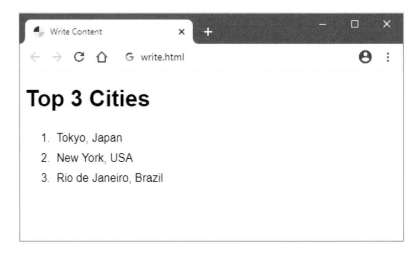

...cont'd

3 Next, in a script element, create a self-invoking function that begins by initializing two variables as new list item elements and one variable reference
```
const itemFour = document.createElement( 'li' )
const itemFive = document.createElement( 'li' )
const heading = document.getElementById( 'heading' )
```

4 Now, assign text content to the two new elements
```
itemFour.innerText = 'London, England'
itemFive.innerText = 'Cape Town, South Africa'
```

5 Then, insert the new element content into the web page as children of the ordered list element
```
document.getElementById( 'list' ).appendChild( itemFour )
document.getElementById( 'list' ).appendChild( itemFive )
```

6 Add an attribute to the existing heading element to change its font color
```
heading.setAttribute( 'style', 'color:Red' )
```

7 Finally, change the heading to better describe the extended list
```
heading.innerText = 'Best Five Cities'
```

8 Save the HTML document once more, then refresh your browser to see the newly written content

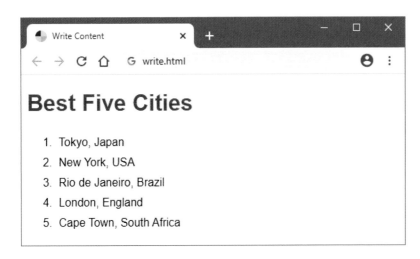

An existing element may be removed from the web page by specifying it as the argument to a **document.removeChild( )** method, or replaced by specifying new and old elements as arguments to a **document.replaceChild( )** method.

You can remove an attribute by specifying the attribute's name as the argument to an element's **removeAttribute( )** method.

453

Manage Cookies

For security reasons JavaScript cannot write regular files on the user's hard drive, but it can write "cookie" files to store a small amount of data. These are limited in size to a maximum of 4KB and in number to 20 per web server. Typically, the data stored in a cookie will identify the user for subsequent visits to a website.

Cookie data is stored in the DOM **document** object's **cookie** property as one or more "key=value" pairs, terminated with a ";" semicolon character. The value may not contain whitespace, commas, or semicolons, unless passed as the argument to the built-in **encodeURI( )** function, which encodes the string in Unicode format – for example, this represents a space as **%20**.

By default, the lifespan of a cookie is limited to the current browser session unless an expiry date is specified when the cookie is created as an "expires=date" pair, in which the date value is a UTC string. Typically, this is achieved using a JavaScript **Date** object converted with its **toUTCString( )** method. Setting an existing cookie's expiry date to a past time will delete that cookie.

Retrieving data from a cookie requires some string manipulation to return Unicode to regular text, using the built-in **decodeURI( )** function so **%20** becomes a space character once more, and to separate the name and value items of data. Within the cookie string multiple pairs can be separated by specifying the ";" semicolon as the argument to the **split( )** method. Similarly, keys and values can be separated by specifying the "=" character as the argument to the **split( )** method. Likewise, where the value is a comma-separated list of items, the "," comma can be specified as the argument to the **split( )** method to separate them as array elements.

It is useful to create an external JavaScript file containing "setter" and "getter" utility functions that can easily be called to store and retrieve cookie data.

454

cookie.js

 Begin a JavaScript file with a setter function that has parameters for key, value, and expiry arguments

```js
function setCookie( key, value, days ) {
    const d = new Date( )
    d.setTime( d.getTime( ) + ( days * 86400000 ) )
    document.cookie = key + '=' + encodeURI( value ) +
                        ';expires=' + d.toUTCString( ) + ';'
}
```

...cont'd

2 Then, add a getter function to accept a key argument
```
function getCookie( key ) {
  if( document.cookie )
  {
    const pairs = decodeURI( document.cookie ).split( ';' )
    let i, name, value
    for( i = 0 ; i < pairs.length ; i++ )
    {
      name = ( pairs[ i ].split( '=' )[ 0 ] ).trim( )
      if( name === key ) { value = pairs[ i ].split( '=' )[ 1 ] }
    }
    return value
  }
}
```

Beware

Notice that the **trim( )** method is used here to remove any whitespace from ends of the name.

3 Next, create an HTML document that contains an empty list and imports the external JavaScript file
```
<ul id="list"></ul> <script src="cookie.js"></script>
```

cookie.html

4 Now, in another script element, create a self-invoking function that sets a cookie, then gets its values
```
setCookie( 'User','Mike McGrath,12345', 7 )

const list = document.getElementById( 'list' )
let i, value = getCookie( 'User' )
if( value.indexOf( ',' ) )
{
  value = value.split( ',' )
}
for( i = 0 ; i < value.length ; i++ )
{
  list.innerHTML += '<li>' + value[ i ]
}
```

Don't forget

A cookie may be deleted by setting its expiry date to a date prior to the current actual date.

5 Save the HTML document and JavaScript file in the same folder on a web server, then open the web page in your browser to see the retrieved cookie values

Cookies — localhost/cookie.html

- Mike McGrath
- 12345

Load Events

The DOM allows JavaScript to react to "events" that occur on a web page by the script author providing functions that will be executed when a particular event happens. These functions are known as "event-handlers", and can react to events such as:

● **load** – fires when the page has loaded into the browser

● **click** – fires when the user clicks a mouse button

● **keydown** – fires when the user presses a keyboard key

● **change** – fires when the user modifies an input field

● **submit** – fires when the user submits an HTML form

To react to a load event, an event-handler function name can be nominated by assignment to the **window** object's **onload** property, using this syntax:

onload=*function-name*

Alternatively, the event name and the event-handler function name can be specified as arguments to the **window** object's **addEventListener( )** method, but the event name must be enclosed within quotes, like this:

addEventListener('load' , *function-name* **)**

An event-handler for the load event might be used to examine the browser's features, and can usefully check for cookie data.

Hot tip

There is also an unload event that fires when the user leaves the page. Its event-handler can be nominated by assignment to the **window.onunload** property, or can be specified to the **addEventListener( )** method.

HTML

load.html

① Create an HTML document that contains a paragraph with a link to the cookies example on pages 454-455, an empty paragraph, and imports the external JavaScript file from the previous example
<p><a href="cookie.html">Link</a></p>
<p id="info"></p>
<script src="cookie.js"></script>

② Next, in a script element, nominate an event-handler function to be executed when the page has loaded
addEventListener('load', welcome)

3   Now, add the event-handler function to greet the user

```
function welcome( ) {
  const info = document.getElementById( 'info' )
  if( getCookie( 'Name' ) )
  {
    info.innerHTML = 'Welcome Back, ' + getCookie( 'Name' )
  }
  else
  {
    let name = prompt( 'Please Enter Your Name', 'User' )
    setCookie( 'Name', name, 7 )
    info.innerHTML = 'Welcome, ' + name
  }
}
```

The second argument to the **prompt( )** method is the default input value.

4   Save the HTML document and open it in your browser, – enter your name, follow the link, then click the back button

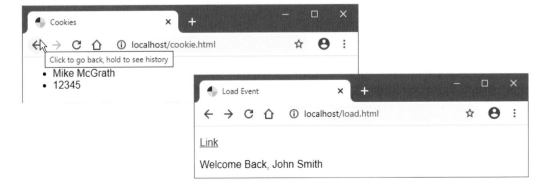

Any visible object in an HTML document can have an event-handler assigned for its **click** event, so that object can act like a button. Most developers prefer to nominate event-handler functions with the **addEventListener( )** method, rather than by assignment to the **onclick** property.

458

Mouse Events

Event-handler functions that execute when the user clicks on a particular object in the HTML document can be nominated by assigning the function name to the object's **onclick** and **ondblclick** properties. These respond to the "click" event that fires when the user clicks the mouse button once, and the "dblclick" event that fires when the mouse button is pressed twice in quick succession.

Additionally, an object's **onmousedown** and **onmouseup** properties can nominate event-handler functions to execute when the mouse button gets pressed down, firing the "mousedown" event, and when it gets released, firing the "mouseup" event.

Similarly, an object's **onmouseover** and **onmouseout** properties can nominate event-handler functions to execute when the mouse is placed over an element, firing the "mouseover" event, and when it moves off the element, firing the "mouseout" event. These are often used to create a rollover effect, such as changing the value of that element's **style.background** property to a different color value.

Alternatively, the event name and the event-handler function name can be specified as arguments to that object's **addEventListener( )** method. This can be used just like the **window** object's **addEventListener( )** method in the previous example to nominate a function by name, or you can write a function definition inline as the second argument.

When an event occurs, an **event** object can be passed to an inline event-handler function. This has a **type** property that identifies the name of that event.

mouse.html

1 Create an HTML document that contains two paragraphs and a button
```
<p id="box">Target</p>
<p id="info">Place Mouse Over Target</p>
<button id="btn">Click Me</button>
```

2 Next, in a script element, create a self-invoking function that begins by initializing two variables
```
( function ( ) {
  const box = document.getElementById( 'box' )
  const btn = document.getElementById( 'btn' )

  // Statements to be inserted here.
} ) ( )
```

3 Now, insert statements to nominate inline event-handlers that will pass arguments to a second function

```
box.addEventListener( 'mouseover',
        function ( event ) { reactTo( event, 'Red' ) } )
box.addEventListener( 'mouseout',
        function ( event ) { reactTo( event, 'Purple' ) } )
box.addEventListener( 'mousedown',
        function ( event ) { reactTo( event, 'Green' ) } )
box.addEventListener( 'mouseup',
        function ( event ) { reactTo( event, 'Blue' ) } )
btn.addEventListener( 'click',
        function ( event ) { reactTo( event, 'Orange' ) } )
```

If removing an object that has event-handlers attached, you should also remove its event-handlers to avoid creating memory leaks.

4 Finally, add a second function to display the event type and change the first paragraph's background color

```
function reactTo( event, color ) {
  document.getElementById( 'box' ).style.background = color
  document.getElementById( 'info' ).innerText = event.type
}
```

5 Save the HTML document and open it in your browser, then use your mouse to see the events and reactions

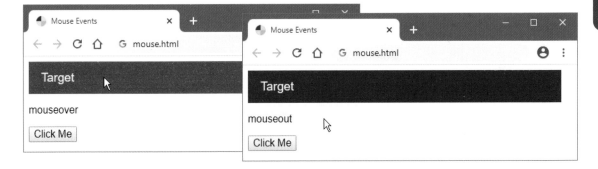

Unicode values for common characters are the same as ASCII code values, where lowercase a-z is 65-90 and A-Z is 97-122.

values.html

Event Values

In addition to the mouse events described in the example on pages 458-459, there is a "mousemove" event. This can pass an **event** object to an event-handler function with **x** and **y** properties that contain the current window coordinates of the mouse pointer.

There is also a "keydown" event that fires when the user first presses a key, a "keypress" event that fires when the key is pressed down, and a "keyup" event that fires when the key is released. These can each pass an **event** object to an event-handler function with a **type** property that identifies the name of that event, and a **keyCode** property that stores the numerical value of the last key pressed.

The numerical value of a key is its Unicode value, which can be specified as the argument to a **String.fromCharCode( )** method to translate it to a character value.

Event-handler functions can be nominated to **onmousemove, onkeydown, onkeypress**, and **onkeyup** properties, or be specified as arguments to an object's **addEventListener( )** method.

1 Create an HTML document that contains an empty paragraph
```
<p id="info"></p>
```

2 Next, in a script element, create a self-invoking function that nominates an event-handler function for three events and passes an event argument to that function
```
( function ( ) {
  document.addEventListener( 'keydown',
            function ( event ){ reactTo( event ) } )
  document.addEventListener( 'keyup',
            function ( event ){ reactTo( event ) } )
  document.addEventListener( 'mousemove',
            function ( event ){ reactTo( event ) } )
} ) ( )
```

3 Now, begin the event-handler function with a statement to initialize a variable
```
function reactTo( event ) {

  const info = document.getElementById( 'info' )

  // Statements to be inserted here.
}
```

...cont'd

4 Then, insert statements to display the current window coordinate values of the mouse pointer

```
if( event.type === 'mousemove' )
{
  info.innerHTML =
  'Mouse pointer is at X:' + event.x + ' Y:' + event.y
}
```

5 Next, add statements to display the Unicode value of a keyboard key when pressed

```
if( event.type === 'keydown' )
{
  info.innerHTML += '<hr>' + event.type
  info.innerHTML += ': ' + event.keyCode
}
```

The **keydown** and **keyup** events work on all keyboard keys, but **keypress** only works on the alphanumeric keys.

6 Finally, add statements to display the character of that keyboard key when released

```
if( event.type === 'keyup' )
{
  info.innerHTML += '<br>' + event.type + ': ' +
        String.fromCharCode( event.keyCode ) + '<hr>'
}
```

461

7 Save the HTML document then open it in your browser and move the mouse pointer over the window to see its displayed coordinate values change as the mouse moves

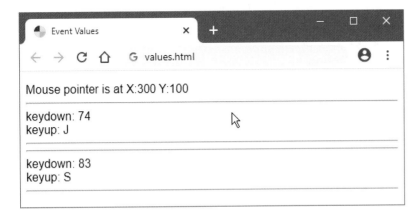

The coordinate values always relate to the window position even if the event-handler is attached to an object other than the **document** object.

8 Press any alphanumeric keyboard key to see that key's Unicode number and character value

Check Boxes

Radio button groups allow the user to select any one button from the group, and the HTML name attributes of all radio button input elements in that group share the same name. In scripting terms, that group name is the name of an array in which each radio button object can be referenced using its array index value.

Unlike radio button groups, checkbox button groups allow the user to select one or more buttons in that group. But as with radio button groups, each name attribute shares the same group name. That group name is also the name of an array in which each checkbox button object can be referenced by its array index value.

Both radio button objects and checkbox button objects have a **checked** Boolean property, which is **true** when the button is selected and **false** otherwise. Looping through a button group array to inspect the **checked** property of each object determines which buttons are selected. A script statement can also assign a **true** value to the **checked** property of a button to select it.

checkbox.html

1 Create an HTML document that contains a form with a group of three checkboxes and a submit button

```
<form id="pizza" action="echo.py" method="POST">
<fieldset>
<legend>Select Pizza Toppings</legend>
<input type="checkbox" name="Top"
                              value="Cheese">Cheese
<input type="checkbox" name="Top"
                              value="Ham">Ham
<input type="checkbox" name="Top"
                              value="Peppers">Peppers
</fieldset>
<input type="submit">
</form>
```

2 Next, in a script element, create a self-invoking function that nominates an event-handler function for the form's "submit" event and checks one checkbox

```
( function ( ) {

  const form = document.getElementById( 'pizza' )
  form.addEventListener( 'submit',
        function ( event ) { reactTo( form, event ) } )
  form.Top[ 0 ].checked = true

} ) ( )
```

Hot tip

When multiple buttons in a checkbox button group have been selected, their values are submitted as a comma-separated list.

3 Now, begin the event-handler function by declaring three variables and a loop to determine which boxes are checked

```
function reactTo( form, event ) {
  let i, ok, summary = ''

  for( i = 0 ; i < form.Top.length ; i++ )
  {
    if( form.Top[ i ].checked )
    {
      summary += form.Top[ i ].value + ' '
    }
  }

  // Statements to be inserted here.
}
```

4 Then, add statements to confirm the choices and submit them to the web server, or cancel the submission

```
ok = confirm( 'Submit These Choices?\n' + summary )
if( !ok ) { event.preventDefault( ) }
```

5 Save the HTML document on a web server then open it in a browser, make your choices, then confirm submission

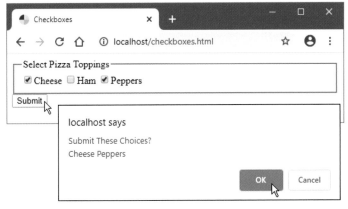

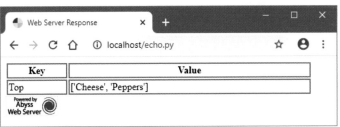

Hot tip

When a form button gets clicked it triggers the form's default **event** action, which is to submit the form data to the web server. Calling the form event's **preventDefault( )** method stops the form data submission.

Don't forget

This example is run on a local web server that supports the Python server-side script that processes the form submission and provides the response to the web browser.

echo.py

Select Options

Options presented in an HTML **<select>** dropdown list object are uniquely represented in the DOM by an **options[ ]** array, in which each array element contains the option specified by an HTML **<option>** tag. Upon submission to the web server, the value assigned to the **name** attribute of the **<select>** tag, and that assigned to the **value** attribute of the currently selected **<option>** tag are sent as a name=value pair.

Importantly, the selection list object has a **selectedIndex** property, which contains the index number of the currently selected **options[ ]** array element, and this can be used to retrieve the value of the current selected option.

When the user changes the selected option in a selection list, a "change" event fires. The list object's **onchange** property can nominate an event-handler function to execute when the selected option changes. Alternatively, the event name and the event-handler function name can be specified as arguments to the list object's **addEventListener( )** method.

options.html

Notice that the HTML **selected** attribute selects the first option element, which is represented in the DOM by **options[0]**

1 Create an HTML document that contains a form selection list and a submit button, plus an empty paragraph

```
<form action="echo.py" method="POST">
<select id="list" name="City">
<option value="Rome" selected>Rome</option>
<option value="London">London</option>
<option value="New York" >New York</option>
</select>
<input type="submit">
</form>

<p id="info"></p>
```

2 Next, in a script element, create a self-invoking function that nominates an event-handler function for the form's "submit" event and for the window's "load" event

```
( function ( ) {

  const list = document.getElementById( 'list' )
  list.addEventListener( 'change' ,
              function ( ) { reactTo( list, event ) } )
  addEventListener( 'load' ,
              function ( ) { reactTo( list, event ) } )

} ) ( )
```

3 Now, add the event-handler function, which will display the event and current list selection in the paragraph

```
function reactTo( list, event ) {

    const info = document.getElementById( 'info' )
    let index = list.options.selectedIndex
    let city = list.options[ index ].value
    info.innerHTML = event.type + '<br>Selected: '
    info.innerHTML += city + '<br>Index: ' + index
}
```

4 Save the HTML document on a web server then open it in a browser, select an option, and submit the form

Hierarchically, this selected option can be referenced using **document.forms[0]. elements[0].options[1]. value** – the deepest level of the DOM.

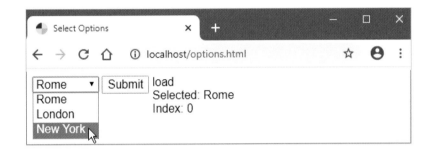

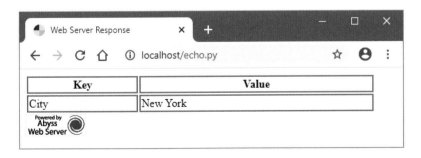

echo.py

Reset Changes

An event-handler can be nominated to the **onfocus** and **onfocusout** properties of form text input objects and textarea objects to recognize the active element. A "focus" event fires when the user selects a text field, and a "focusout" event fires when the user leaves that text field.

Usefully, an event-handler can be nominated to the **onreset** property of a form object to remove content related to form input when the form is returned to its original state by a reset button.

As with other objects, the event name and the event-handler function name can be specified as arguments to the text field and form object's **addEventListener( )** method.

reset.html

Hot tip

Text fields also have an **onselect** property to which an event-handler can be nominated to respond to a "select" event that fires when the user selects some of its text.

1 Create an HTML document that contains a form with a text field and reset button, plus an empty paragraph

```
<form id="code" >
<input id="lang" name="Language" type="text" >
<input type="reset">
<input type="submit">
</form>

<p id="info"></p>
```

2 Next, in a script element, create a self-invoking function that nominates an event-handler function for the text field's "focus" and "focusout" events, the form's "reset" event, and for the window's "load" event

```
( function ( ) {

  const form = document.getElementById( 'code' )
  const lang = document.getElementById( 'lang' )
  const info = document.getElementById( 'info' )

  lang.addEventListener( 'focus' ,
              function ( event ) { reactTo( event, info ) } )
  lang.addEventListener( 'focusout' ,
              function ( event ) { reactTo( event, info ) } )
  form.addEventListener( 'reset',
              function ( ) { defaultMessage( info ) } )
  addEventListener( 'load',
              function ( ) { defaultMessage( info ) } )

} ) ( )
```

3 Now, add the event-handler function for the text field's "focus" and "focusout" events, to display the event type

```
function reactTo( event, info ) {
  info.innerHTML = event.type
}
```

4 Then, add the event-handler function for the window's "load" and the form's "reset" events, to display a message

```
function defaultMessage( info ) {
  info.innerHTML =
         'Please enter your favorite coding language'
}
```

5 Save the HTML document, then open it in your browser, to see the default message appear in the paragraph

6 Select the text field and see the "focus" event fire, then type in the name of your favorite coding language

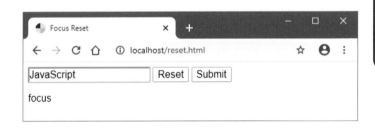

7 Hit the Tab key to move focus onto the Reset button and see the "focusout" event fire

8 Hit the Enter key (to push the Reset button) to clear the text field and see the default message once more

Validate Forms

A form object's **onsubmit** property can nominate an event-handler function to validate user input entered into a form before it is submitted to the web server for processing. Alternatively, the "submit" event name and an event-handler function name can be specified as arguments to the form object's **addEventListener( )** method.

The simplest level of form validation examines a text input where an entry is required to ensure the user has made an entry. When its value remains an empty string, no entry has been made, so the validating function can call the **event.preventDefault( )** method to prevent form submission.

A higher level of form validation can examine the string entered by the user to ensure it meets an expected format. For example, where an email address is expected, the format requires the string to contain an "@" character and at least one "." character. When either of these are absent, the string is not a valid email address, so the validating function can prevent form submission.

A form element can be referenced by quoting its **name** attribute value in the form's **elements[ ]** array brackets.

validate.html

1 Create an HTML document that contains a form with two text fields and a submit button

```
<form id="contact" action="echo.py" method="POST">
<fieldset>
<legend>Please Enter Your Details</legend>
Name: <input type="text" name="Name" value="">
<br><br>
Email: <input type="text" name="Email" value="">
</fieldset>
<input type="submit">
</form>
```

2 Next, in a script element, create a self-invoking function that nominates an event-handler function for the form's "submit" event

```
( function ( ) {

  const form = document.getElementById( 'contact' )

  form.addEventListener( 'submit' ,
        function ( event ) { validate( form, event ) } )
} ) ( )
```

...cont'd

3 Now, add the event-handler function to validate input

```
function validate( form, event ) {
  let value = form.elements[ 'Name' ].value
  if( value === '' ) {
    alert( 'Please Enter Your Name' )
    event.preventDefault( ) ; return }

  value = form.elements[ 'Email' ].value
  if( ( value === '' ) || ( value.indexOf('@') === -1 ) ||
  ( value.indexOf('.') === -1 ) ) {
    alert( 'Please Enter A Valid Email Address' )
    event.preventDefault( ) }
}
```

The **indexOf( )** method returns an integer that is the character position in the string, or -1 if the character is not found. For details see page 418.

4 Save the HTML document on a web server, then open it in a browser, enter your details, and submit the form

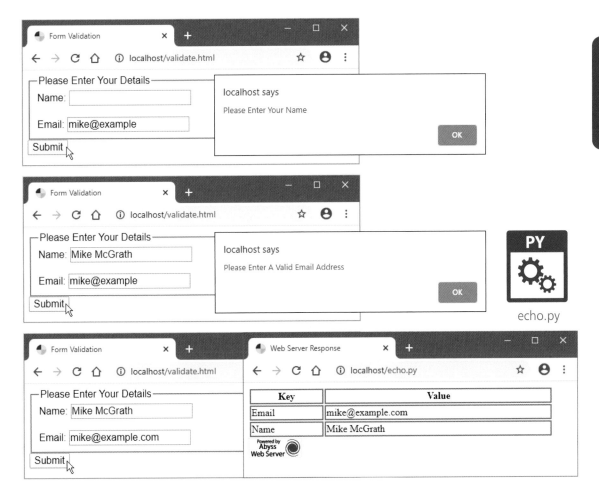

echo.py

Summary

- The **document** object has **title, URL, domain, lastModified,** and **referrer** properties that describe that document.

- The **document** object has **forms, images, links, styleSheets,** and **scripts** child objects that are arrays of document components.

- The **forms** array represents **<form>** tags and has an **elements** child object that is an array of form components.

- The **document** object has **getElementById( )**, **getElementsByTagName( )**, and **getElementsByClassName( )** methods that can be used to reference HTML elements.

- The **innerHTML** and **innerText** properties of the **document** object can be used to write content into existing elements.

- The **document** object has **createElement( )**, **appendChild( )**, and **setAttribute( )** methods that can add content to a document.

- The **document** object's **cookie** property has "key=value" pairs that can store a small amount of data on the user's system.

- The **encodeURI( )**, **decodeURI( )**, **toUTCString( )**, and **split( )** functions are used for string manipulation with cookie data.

- The DOM allows JavaScript to react to events such as **load**, **click, keydown, change,** and **submit** in response to user actions.

- Event-handler functions can be assigned to an object property or specified by the **addEventListener( )** method.

- An **event** object can be passed to an event-handler function and the event can be identified by its **event.type** property.

- The mousemove **event** object has **x** and **y** properties that contain the current window coordinates of the pointer.

- Radio and checkbox button objects have a **checked** boolean property, which is only **true** when the button is selected.

- A selection list object has a **selectedIndex** property, which contains the index number of the currently selected **options[ ]** array element.

- The form submit event has a **preventDefault( )** method that can be called to stop submission of a form to the web server.

Index

E

F

G

H